# Picturing Identity

AF479014

# PICTURING IDENTITY

Contemporary American Autobiography
in Image and Text

**Hertha D. Sweet Wong**

THE UNIVERSITY OF NORTH CAROLINA PRESS
*Chapel Hill*

*The publisher gratefully acknowledges the generous contribution to this book provided by University of California Humanities Research Fellowships, the UC Berkeley Institute of International Studies, the UC Berkeley Townsend Center for the Humanities, the UC Berkeley American Cultures Center, and the Hewlett Foundation.*

© 2018 The University of North Carolina Press

*All rights reserved*

Designed by Jamison Cockerham
Set in Scala, Scala Sans, and Klavika
by Tseng Information Systems, Inc.

*Cover illustrations from stock.adobe.com*

A version of chapter 8 appeared earlier in somewhat different form in Hertha D. Sweet Wong, "Countering Visual Regimes: History, Place, and Subjectivity in the Art of Hachivi Edgar Heap of Birds," in *Ethnic Literatures and Transnationalism: Critical Imaginaries for a Global Age*, ed. Aparajita Nanda (New York: Routledge, 2015), 231–47. Reproduced by permission of Taylor and Francis Group, LLC, a division of Informa plc.

*Manufactured in the United States of America*

The University of North Carolina Press has been a member of the Green Press Initiative since 2003.

LIBRARY OF CONGRESS
CATALOGING-IN-PUBLICATION DATA
Names: Wong, Hertha Dawn, author.
Title: Picturing identity : contemporary American autobiography in image and text / Hertha D. Sweet Wong.
Description: Chapel Hill : The University of North Carolina Press, [2018] | Includes bibliographical references and index.
Identifiers: LCCN 2017054461 |
ISBN 9781469640693 (cloth : alk. paper) |
ISBN 9781469640709 (pbk : alk. paper) |
ISBN 9781469640716 (ebook)
Subjects: LCSH: American literature—History and criticism. | Autobiography. | Autobiography in literature. | Autobiography in art. | Group identity—United States.
Classification: LCC PS169.A95 W66 2018 |
DDC 810.9/35—dc23
LC record available at https://lccn.loc.gov/2017054461

*For my sister, JoyDawn Hinds*

# Contents

# Figures

# Acknowledgments

Throughout the numerous hibernations and emergences of this book and its different iterations, I have benefited from many and varied support systems, relationships, and critiques. I thank the University of California, who supported my research and writing with humanities research fellowships over the years. I am especially grateful for Lewis Watts, my codeveloper and coinstructor of the visual autobiography course in which many of the ideas in this book were explored, and to our teaching assistants and coinstructors—Eileen Callahan and Susannah Hays—who were invaluable partners. Certainly, both undergraduate and graduate students in the visual autobiography courses at the University of California, Berkeley, helped to clarify and refine my approach. I am very grateful to the Hewlett Foundation, which supported us with a generous course development grant. Thanks also to Umeå University in Umeå, Sweden, where, as a visiting professor, I explored some of my ideas in a graduate seminar, and to Raoul Granqvist, who supported this project at its origin.

The staff at several special collections libraries have provided invaluable help. Executive Director Erika Torri and librarian Andi Hawkins at the Atheneum Music and Arts Library in La Jolla, California, gave me unlimited access to their impressive artists' book collection, as well as a warm welcome punctuated with illuminating conversations. Thanks to Janice Braun, special collections curator, and Karma Pippin, librarian and special collections curator, archivist, and director of the Mill Center for the Book, at the Heller Rare Book Room at the F. W. Olin Library at Mills College in Oakland, California, who made possible my numerous visits to examine Julie Chen's collection of artists' books. Thanks also to the staff at the Mandeville Special Collections in the Geisel Library at the University of California, San Diego, where I first encountered the work of Julie Chen.

A special thanks to the participants of my UC Berkeley Institute of International Studies–sponsored Book Manuscript Draft Mini-Conference—Shari Huhndorf, Beth Piatote, Leigh Raiford, and Julia Watson—whose feedback was invaluable in the early stages of the writing. And to Julia Watson for copious feedback and encouragement. Thanks also to Deirdre Golash, an editor-reader extraordinaire. I am grateful also to the Slusser Manuscript Review Conference Grant offered through the UC Berkeley Townsend Center for the Humanities. Thank you to my readers—Elizabeth Abel, Donald McQuade, Genaro Padilla,

Karin Sanders, and Celia Rabinovitch—who convinced me to rethink my original structure. With a nuanced understanding of transdisciplinary work, Celia's reading of my manuscript was a tour de force in itself. I am grateful to the UC Berkeley American Cultures Center for Faculty Summer Seminar Fellowships. Thank you also to Jon Peterson who read a couple of drafts of the manuscript with an academically skeptical eye. Thanks, finally, to my anonymous reviewers for their many insightful questions and suggestions.

There are several people to thank at the University of North Carolina Press. I am immensely grateful for Mark Simpson-Vos's willingness to check out this project and, especially, for the support and assistance of Lucas Church, with whom it was a joy to work. Thanks also to Becki Reibman, who was an early help; to Catherine Hodorowicz, whose kindness, patience, and attention to detail were immeasurable; and to Mary Carley Caviness, who guided this book through the process with graceful expertise. Thanks also to Dino Battista and to the production team, who were so attentive to the design of the book.

Heartfelt gratitude to my writing group—Kathleen McCarthy, Beth Piatote, Linda Rugg, and Susan Schweik—whose incisive questions, acute insights, and sage advice helped me clarify the final shape of the project and whose friendship has sustained me. I thank Edith Ng Welsh, Chansonette Buck, and Ann Hyde for their sustained curiosity about my book. Thanks also to Lauren Stuart Muller for parallel writing sessions and long walks; and to Richard Wong, Jody Parsons, and Judith Wong for their unwavering belief in this project.

I am especially indebted to my graduate research assistants: Brian Gillis, Sharon Hsu, and Jason de Stefano. Brian helped organize the Book Manuscript Mini-Conference and developed the Native American writing group from an informal gathering to a UC Berkeley Townsend Center Reading Group. Sharon Hsu orchestrated a graceful dance through the minefield of permissions requests that Jason de Stefano brought to fruition with polished professionalism.

I am grateful for all the artists/writers I discuss in this book. Thank you especially to Julie Chen for generous conversations in her studio; to Edgar Heap of Birds for his Berkeley lecture, conversations, and e-mail correspondences; to Pete Najarian for inviting me for coffee and tea in his cottage so I could learn more about his writing and art; and to Carrie Mae Weems for our e-mail correspondence and phone conversation to discuss just what this book was about.

Finally, thanks and love to my family, Jon Peterson and our wondrous children—Philip, Crystal, Sita, and Xian—and grandson, Ayden—and especially my dear sister, JoyDawn Hinds, to whom this book is dedicated.

# Picturing Identity

# Introduction

A period of intense social upheaval and technological innovation, the last thirty to forty years of the twentieth century were notable for the vibrant and fractious struggles of ethnic and racial minorities, women, and the underclass overall. The era gave rise to second- and third-wave feminisms, ethnic studies programs, antiwar movements, the multicultural wars, postcolonial voices, and radical transdisciplinary experimentation in literature and art. Historical recovery projects, ethnic and feminist manifestos, and an unapologetic politicized (re)interpretation of inherited modes and media sprung up. Part of the postmodern era, this was a period in which scholars claimed that history was over, at least for Europeans; a diminished present, the only reality; unmediated representation, impossible; and identity, a fiction. Writers and artists contended with the question of how to do creative work if there was no history or agreed upon cultural context, only the shattered remnants of a broken world with no possibility of representation and no self to represent it. A growing body of artistic production by women and ethnic minorities exposed the myth of universality as a Western notion that disregarded non-Western epistemologies and experiences. Individual identity was itself deconstructed: the notion of an autonomous, unchanging, singular self was determined to be a sociohistorical construction. Scholars, artists, and activists redefined identity as relational, fluid, and multiple. But even as certain sectors of the academic world were declaring the death of the subject or making claims about post-identity, publication of autobiographies and memoirs in the United States burgeoned. The self was very much alive and now, more than ever before, clamoring to be seen and heard in previously unfathomable modes.[1] By the 1970s, American culture, previously described as a melting pot, began to be acknowledged as a stew.[2] Rather than an undifferentiated union, then, the United States was seen as a collection of variables in proximity. Relatively unheard voices and unseen images of women and underrepresented minorities proliferated in literature and art, often in hybrid autobiographies composed of image and text.

Although visual and literary studies have historically been considered separate disciplines,[3] over the past fifty years disciplinary borders and medium-specific art practices have become increasingly permeable. Scholars, writers, and artists are more likely than ever to work across disciplines and media. In this book I use approaches from literary and visual studies to examine hybrid forms of autobiography that blur established disciplinary boundaries. Although pictures have been used to communicate since cave paintings and images and texts have been together since at least the sumptuously illustrated *Book of Kells*,[4] this is a new category of autobiographical expression that I call variously visual autobiography (a term British photographer Jo Spence used to refer to her work as early as 1979), "intermedia autobiography," "interart autobiography," "intersectional autobiography," "transmedia autobiography," "hybrid autobiography," or simply "autobiography in image and text." In a 1964 essay, writer-artist-composer-publisher and cofounder of Fluxus (an international experimental art movement of the 1960s and 1970s) Dick Higgins introduced the term "intermedia"—artwork that "seems to fall between media" (*Horizons* 18), a practice-form he praised (rather naively) as arising because "we are approaching the dawn of a classless society, to which separation into rigid categories is absolutely irrelevant" (18). In 1984, Higgins revised his comments. Borrowing the term "intermedia" from the 1812 writings of Samuel Taylor Coleridge, Higgins defined intermedia as "works which fall conceptually between media that are already known" (23). Distinguishing mixed media from intermedia, Higgins explained that mixed media "covers works executed in more than one medium, such as oil color and gouache" (24). Intermedia are works in which "the visual element . . . is fused conceptually with the words" (24). He described the "tendency for intermedia to become media with familiarity" (26). Once an intermedia becomes recognized as its own form, then, it ceases to be intermedia. The illustrated memoir, the graphic memoir, and perhaps now even the artists' book are examples of this historical process of recognition of new artistic forms. Higgins's point, then, is that the condition of intermediality is temporary. The visual autobiographies I discuss in this book are at various stages.

Each of these terms emphasizes a set of relations between the visual and the verbal. I will use them interchangeably throughout. A necessarily capacious category, visual autobiography encompasses a wide range of *self-representations*—glimpses into a moment of a life or self—and *self-narrations*—stories of a life or self developing over time. Like short stories, self-representations emphasize an epiphany or brief insight. Like novels, self-narrations tend to offer or withhold a resolution. These intermedia autobiographies take many forms. They can be conventional books in which images are integral to the whole rather than mere supplementation or illustration. They include also photo-autobiographies and artists' books—individually handmade textual objects that are experienced as both text and sculpture. They can be in the form of story quilts, comics, word paintings, installation art, performances, and other visual forms. Such a proliferation of hybrid autobiographies testifies to a serious search for new verbal-visual modes with which to explore and articulate a complex sense of self, to reexamine received and conventional histories in order to challenge social inequities, and, often, to offer a metacommentary on the process of self-representation itself. This metacommentary, an awareness of the process of autobiographical construction, documents how autobiographers imagine individual and collective histories in response to conventional concepts of selfhood and history. It implies the collagelike nature of a marginalized self that both participates in the dominant culture and stands apart from it, claiming alternative notions of and possibilities for subject formation.

This book focuses on eight American writers and artists from diverse backgrounds who create self-representations and self-narrations in imaginative configurations of image and text, from the 1970s to the present: Peter Najarian's illustrated memoirs, Leslie Marmon Silko's photo-narratives, Art Spiegelman's two-volume autobiographical comics *Maus*, Julie Chen's artists' books, Theresa Hak Kyung Cha's experimental autobiography *Dictée*, Carrie Mae Weems's photo-(auto)biographies, Faith Ringgold's story quilts, and Hachivi Edgar Heap of Birds's site-specific installations, word paintings, and abstract landscape paintings.[5] Although the writers-artists I discuss participate in the age-old act of telling personal and cultural stories, they find it too restrictive to articulate themselves in linear texts or conventional self-portraits.[6] They search, instead, for alternative forms in which to represent themselves and convey their stories as part of our diverse, "multicentered" society (Lippard, *Lure of the Local* 7). They seek also to correct or refine historical narratives that distort or omit them. Through close reading of their works, I focus on questions about the possibilities of self-formulation and self-representation in the past fifty years. What are the relations between life writing and self-portraiture, between past and present, and between image and text in these autobiographies? Often, these writers and artists link their personal experiences to larger historical events and to contemporary social structures. Some envision their identities as shaped by the history they share with a community. Others, especially a post-generation of survivors of genocide, slavery, or colonization, define themselves through an inherited history of loss, using their life narratives to "untrammel the subject from discursive helplessness" (Egan 4) or to seek "safe ground and ultimately survival" (Fuchs 4).[7] Some share details of their extended personal histories; others depict their personal narratives in general terms; still others don't share any personal details at all, but instead represent their subjectivity as a structure of consciousness or a unique epistemology. Each artist and writer engages in an act of word-image self-articulation, representing individual subjectivity as an expression of a network of times, places, and people.[8] These artists transform inherited literary and artistic norms through experimenting with visual-verbal modes in autobiography, insisting that their audience sees through new eyes to arrive at a new awareness. This creative intervention performs a shift from the margins to the center and then deconstructs that binary opposition itself. It makes visible the invisible nature of underrepresented peoples' experiences in fresh autobiographical forms.

My interest in visual autobiography arises out of my first book, *Sending My Heart Back across the Years: Tradition and Innovation in Native American Autobiography* (1992). In it I challenged the western European limits of autobiography studies by considering non-Western concepts of self and indigenous forms of unwritten personal narrative. As part of a project of mapping Native American modes of self-narration from pre-European contact to the present, I examined preliterate self-narration in oral and picture-writing forms. Nineteenth-century Plains Indian male personal narratives often took the form of pictography: picture writing on animal hides and tipis and, later, in ledger books. This special focus also encompassed N. Scott Momaday's genre-bending autobiography, *The Way to Rainy Mountain* (1969), which referenced and updated nineteenth-century pictographic narratives. I soon realized that numerous Native and non-Native writers were self-consciously experimenting with autobiographical forms. They eschewed linear chronology, for instance, or blended personal, ethnographic, and mythic modes, or incorporated images as an integral part of the text, not as a mere supplement. My interest in visuality and autobiography coincided with "the pictorial turn" (Mitchell 11)—a move not only toward the dominance of the image rather than text but also toward considering the visual as a "place where meanings are created and contested" (Mirzoeff, *What Is Visual Culture?* 6) as well as a site of memory itself. This book, then, brings together the distinct, but interrelated, fields of autobiography studies, ethnic American literary and cultural studies, and visual studies.

## Autobiography Studies

In the 1980s, just as it was emerging as a literary field at universities, autobiography studies (later to become life writing) deconstructed the Western Enlightenment notion of a singular, autonomous, individual, unchanging, normatively male self into multiple, relational, sometimes collective, fluid, and gendered subjectivities. Feminist, ethnic, and cultural studies projects contributed substantially to this process of reconsidering what constitutes identity or subjectivity. The classic idea of a coherent self sustained over a lifetime continues to flourish outside of academia but is challenged by at least three key subject-formation models that circulate in autobiography studies: subjectivity as performative; subjectivity as situational; and subjectivity as dialogic and narrative-based.

The self as performance is best defined by Judith Butler's formulation of "gender performativity." Butler reveals that the "appearance of an abiding substance or gendered self" is socially "produced by the regulation of attributes along culturally established lines of coherence" (*Gender Trouble* 33). She suggests that gender is not biologically but socially constructed and enforced by society. Artists such as Cindy Sherman and Nikki S. Lee expand Butler's conception of gender as discursively constructed and socially regulated to explain not only gender identity but also racial, ethnic, and cultural subjectivity. All are socially constructed and performed according to sociohistorical scripts that too often remain uninterrogated. But unlike Butler, who insists that "performativity must be understood not as a singular or deliberate 'act,' but, rather, as the reiterative and citational practice by which discourse produces the effects that it names" (*Bodies* 2), Sherman and Lee present exaggerated satiric performances of identity, compelling viewers to ask: What if we simply move in and out of performances? What if there is no core identity but only changing surfaces (for example, clothing, makeup, and learned postures and gestures) and contexts (such as culture, society, and community)?

Similar to performative identity, the notion of situational identity underscores how identity shifts according to its context and community. It highlights how each of us, in a mobile, global world, is interpreted, read, and seen (or not) by the various communities that we traverse. Individuals have multiple identities simultaneously; these identities continuously shift and are reprioritized from moment to moment (Hall, "Subject in History" 291). None of us have a singular identity, then, but we all have a proliferation of multiple selves according to ever-shifting contexts. Individuals reshape themselves and are reshaped in relation to the many disparate communities with which they interact.

A third notion of subject formation is "the dialogic and narrative model of identity constitution" within contemporary global cultures in which both identity and culture are generated from "contested and contestable narratives" (Benhabib 16). Individuality is "the unique and fragile achievement of selves in weaving together conflicting narratives and allegiances into a unique life history" (16). Restoring agency and choice to overly limited social constructionist theories of identity, a narrative model of identity emphasizes that each person is born into a set of cultural narratives and that the project of becoming a self is to claim the act of self-narration in a discursive web of signification and questioning. This narrativity of subjectivity is discussed by many scholars of autobiography, most notably Paul John Eakin, who concludes that "there are many stories of self to tell and more than one self to tell them" (*Fictions in Autobiography* xi).[9]

Unlike some social constructionists who emphasize the freedom to choose or invent identity, many of the artists I focus on hold onto a notion of self that has been shaped by communities and cultures over long periods of time. This temporalized self allows for far-sighted interventions into sociopolitical inequities. Unlike those who abstract themselves from time and whose fluid identities are exaggeratedly, repeatedly, and variously constructed and reconstructed, most of the artists-writers in this book insist on history, on a set of shared experiences that shape subjectivity and community over time. At the same time, they engage actively in individual creative processes of self-construction and narration.

## Visual Studies

Visual studies was first conceived of as an antidote to the perceived elitism of art history, which focused on a few Western, usually male, artists and their rarefied productions collected and exhibited in art museums and galleries. In the early 1970s, the English art critic John Berger famously challenged the "privileged minority" of art scholars (11). Rather than perpetuate an outmoded "esoteric approach of a few specialized experts who are the clerks of the nostalgia of a ruling class in decline," Berger proposed a "total approach to art" that relates it to all aspects of human experience (32). In contrast to the traditional focus of art history on fine art of the past, then, visual studies examines the role of the visual in everyday contemporary life.[10] W. J. T. Mitchell claimed that by the 1990s we were undergoing "the pictorial turn"—a focus on image—because we entered an era of video and cyber technology (15) and "we live in a culture of images, a society of the spectacle, a world of semblances and simulacra" (5). The pictorial turn, Mitchell insists, is not "mimesis," simplistic "theories of representation," or a mystifying belief in "pictorial 'presence'" (16), but "rather a postlinguistic, postsemiotic rediscovery of the picture as a complex interplay between visuality, apparatus, institutions, discourse, bodies, and figurality. It is the realization that *spectatorship* (the look, the gaze, the glance, the practices of observation, surveillance, and visual pleasure) may be as deep a problem as various forms of *reading* (decipherment, decoding, interpretation, etc.) and that visual experience or 'visual literacy' may not be fully explicable on the model of textuality" (16). Mitchell urges precise attention to various modes of looking. The danger, however, is conceiving of image and text as a binary opposition or of oversimplifying the distinctions between them. It is important to remember that there are no "purely visual or verbal arts" because "all media are mixed media, and all representations are heterogeneous" (5).

A related set of concerns about visual experience in visual studies arises from the ubiquity of visual media in contemporary life. These concerns are best explained by Nicholas Mirzoeff, who provides an overview of the ways that "modern life takes place onscreen" (Introduction 1) and the ways people are not only looked at (for example, via video surveillance or satellite tracking) but look back (for example, via camcorders and cameras). In addition, both work and leisure are often focused on visual media (including computers, digital games, YouTube, and social media). "Human experience," Mirzoeff claims, "is now more visual and visualized than ever before" (1). From satellites to magnetic resonance imaging, what Paul Virilio calls the "automation of perception" (59)—seeing what could not have been seen without technological enhancement—has transformed our visual possibilities. In short, just as the invention of perspective in painting changed human perception, so, too, did the microscope, the telescope, and photography (with its emphasis on focus and framing). Not only can we see smaller and larger magnitudes, we can imagine seeing objects and forms undetectable to the unaided human eye. Finally, there is a preponderance of interactive visual media (such as the Internet, virtual reality, and digital games). This point was made much earlier by Marshall McLuhan, who warned that "all media transform humans" (26). No one is left unaltered. "In this swirl of imagery, seeing is much more than believing," Mirzoeff claims. "It is not just a part of everyday life, it is everyday life" (1).

Insisting on the dominance of images in our everyday life, Mirzoeff, like Berger before him, emphasizes that this focus on the visual is embedded in a capitalist economy—"visual events sought by the consumer in an interface with visual technology" (3). Examining the transcultural and global visuality of everyday life offers the possibility of critiquing "postmodern everyday life from the point of view of the consumer, rather than the producer" (3). Visual studies in this vein, then, focuses on "the centrality of visual experience in everyday life" as opposed to formal modes of looking such as those experienced at a cinema or art gallery (7) and on "the visual as a place where meanings are created and contested" (6). Furthermore, Mirzoeff undertakes "a strategic reinterpretation of the history of modern visual media understood collectively, rather than fragmented into disciplinary units" (13). Visual culture is "not defined by medium" but rather is denoted "by the interaction between viewer and viewed" (13).

Visual studies, then, is multidirectional, including a focus on "contemporary transnational mass media," "the philosophic interrogation of vision and visuality," and "a social critique of current image-making practices" (Elkins, *Visual Studies* 17). In addition, visual studies may focus on alternative modes of looking, practices of resistant looking, and possibilities of looking back. Discussions of who is entitled to look or not are fraught with complications of race, class, and gender. The male gaze, introduced by Laura Mulvey and well known in film studies and feminist studies, subsumes all viewers into a heterosexual male consumptive viewing, relegating females to the status of objects. In the American South, "white slaveholders punished enslaved black people for looking" (hooks 115), especially for daring to look back. Looking back was tantamount to talking back. In fact, bell hooks explains that "from slavery on, white supremacists have recognized that control over images is central to the maintenance of any system of racial domination" (2). The challenge, then, is not merely to critique racist and sexist images but to change the images, create alternatives, and transform paradigms, perspectives, and "ways of looking" (4). In his most recent book, Mirzoeff begins the ambitious task of documenting a history of the role of the visual in global slavery, imperialism, and militarism and the consequent response from oppressed subjects who countered dominant visual regimes and asserted the right to look. The right to look, explains Mirzoeff, is "the claim to a subjectivity that has the autonomy to arrange the relations of the visible and sayable" (*Right to Look* 1). Scholars also seek possibilities of "the reciprocal look" to counter a colonizing, cannibalizing gaze.[11]

### Image-Text Relations in Autobiography

With the exception of three books on autobiography and photography, several books on autobiography and comics, a book on autobiography and art cinema, and a single collection of essays on the visual-verbal in autobiographical performances, there is no substantive consideration of what I focus on in this book.[12] Sidonie Smith and Julia Watson's collection of essays, *Interfaces: Women, Autobiography, Image, Performance*, is the only book to address the topic of my book explicitly. Claiming that visual-verbal autobiography "expands the modes of self-representation at a shifting matrix of visuality and textuality" (3), they illustrate an array of visual autobiographies and begin to articulate a vocabulary with which to discuss them. Whereas their focus is on how women autobiographers find the visual-verbal interface to be a fruitful site for exploration of gendered identities as an alternative and an amplification, my analysis examines the visual-textual matrix as a place of intense personal and political engagement in which both men and women reenvision subjectivity, reclaim history, and challenge the status quo. This task of self-formulation as a process of cultural and historical critique is not limited to women or ethnic Americans. Nor is it a job that can ever be completed. The clash of competing representations and narratives—both personal and historical—is ongoing.

Focusing on the formal relations between image and text, W. J. T. Mitchell, Sidonie Smith, and Julia Watson offer useful categories. Mitchell identifies three types of visual-verbal interaction: *image-text* denotes a relation between image and text; *image/text* emphasizes a juxtaposition of image and text; and *imagetext* synthesizes image and text (89n9). Extending Mitchell's image-text categories, Smith and Watson outline four basic ways in which artists "texture the interface to mobilize visual and textual regimes" (21): relationally, contextually, spatially, and temporally. A *relational* interface is one in which "visual and textual are set side by side, with neither subordinated to the other" (21). In the relational interface, image and text are in dialogue; they either parallel or interrogate each other. A *contextual* interface explicitly cites "sociohistorical sources" that provide a cultural context for the autobiographical persona (25). A contextual interface can be either documentary or ethnographic. A *spatial* interface is one that can be "infiltrated either from outside in as a *paratext* or inside out as a *palimpsest*" (28, emphasis in original). The supposed "surface is redefined by its surround; or, alternately, shown as making a history of previous iterations" (28). Finally, a *temporal* interface involves a contraction or expansion of action over time. This mode may collapse distinctions between image and text (31), or it may consist of serial self-presentations that emphasize "subjectivity as processual" (34). These categories are still being explored and refined.[13] Certainly, they are not all-inclusive. For instance, because virtually all visual-verbal interfaces are relational, Smith and Watson's relational interface and Mitchell's image-text function primarily as a single catch-all category. Also, it is important to note that different types of interfaces are not mutually exclusive. Often writers-artists experiment with several types of visual-verbal interfaces simultaneously in a single project, creating complex and layered sets of image-text relations. In place of a single interface, it is more accurate to envision multiple, simultaneous sets of image-text relations as a matrix or a network or a crystal, with many surfaces and axes of interaction.

In addition to refining the Smith-Watson structural analysis, I consider where a particular image-text falls on the spectrum of text to image (and it is a spectrum, not a binary opposition), how writers-artists often confound the supposed image-text divide, and most important, the interaction between viewer-reader and what is viewed and read. Visual autobiographies, in their multifarious forms, demand an intense engagement to *read* creatively and *look* mindfully. How does this dual process affect the reader? Although visual-verbal forms may include conventional *text*, they often require readers to learn new ways of traversing the image-word by including experiments with pagination and textual flow, unconventional line breaks, reconceptualizations of the page—as is often the case in artists' books—presentation of words as images (for example, word paintings), and by reading image and text simultaneously, as in comics. The *visual elements* claim our immediate attention, setting a mood and eliciting emotions such as shock, confusion, or curiosity that pull us into attentive relationship with what is viewed. Visual elements may be translated into a standard page, such as in Cha's cinematic techniques, or require that the text be reconfigured as a visual feature in an image, such as in Ringgold's use of text as a frame or a quilt square as a page. Writers like Henry David Thoreau and Walt Whitman emphasized how reading books demands intense focus and active engagement, comparing reading to the toil of writing or to the exertion of a "gymnast's struggle." Generally, visual autobiography demands from readers-viewers more intensely active participation because moving between image and text relies on defamiliarization that requires us to become more self-aware about the process of decoding and interpreting image and text at the same time. Reading and looking demand constant comparison, shifting the frame of reference, just as modernist poetry does with verbal images.[14] The difference between image and text generates perceptive dissonance leading to new cognitive resolutions. By examining the varied experiments in a network of visual-verbal interfaces, we learn why it matters how words and images are linked, juxtaposed, fused, or separated in the service of autobiography.

In focusing on a select group of writers-artists rather than attempting comprehensive coverage, my purpose is to explore a spectrum of visual-verbal structures or image-text relations that provide a common frame of reference for visual autobiography. There are works that arise from (textual) book form and those that are produced as visual art. This is not a developmental model; one intermedia autobiographical form does not inspire, or even necessarily inform, the next. Rather, writers and artists have produced a variety of hybrid autobiographies simultaneously, sometimes in isolation, sometimes in dialogue with each other. These structures appear as overarching gestalts in each work under consideration. Collectively, they suggest a range of interart autobiography forms and create a matrix of American identity in all its plurality, creativity, and messiness. Each of these artists-writers innovates with image and text to represent subjectivity, reexamine history, and intervene in the tangled network of power relations by self-reflexively critiquing verbal and visual regimes. In the process, each addresses many of the concerns central to autobiography studies—subjectivity, representation, and narration—and visual studies—visual experience, visual regimes, and modes of looking.

## Content and Organization

I have organized the book by visual-verbal forms, moving from the most familiar relations between autobiographical image and text in book form to the least recognizable, from the most traditional to the most experimental. The book is divided into three sections. Part I includes discussions of illustrated memoirs, photo-text self-narrations, and graphic memoirs (or comics). Part II is devoted to hinge word-and-image forms: artists' books and the experimental book *Dictée*, which references visual arts, cinema, and performance art. Part III examines photo-autobiography, installations, story quilts, word paintings, abstract landform paintings, and site-specific installations. The organization, then, highlights a spectrum of intermedia forms. Rather than film, performance art, or social media, I focus on experiments in literary and visual arts.[15] In this book, I consider writers-artists who came of age in the 1960s or shortly thereafter: individuals who question authority, received wisdom, and narrowly defined disciplines and who seek actively for new forms of self-expression or new relations of old forms (for example, writing, drawing, painting, and photography). This is a generally pre-Internet generation that straddles the late twentieth and early twenty-first centuries. After decades of development by the U.S. government, the Internet (as we know it) was created in the 1970s just as many of these artists were beginning their careers. Writers and artists born in the 1970s, certainly those born in the 1990s and after, use the newest technology more readily, designing and experimenting with digital forms and social media. Today people of all kinds use social media in the practice of everyday autobiography. With few exceptions, the writers-artists of the generation I examine are makers of words and images using mostly nondigital forms in new ways. This historical moment, largely pre-Internet, deserves serious scholarly attention. It is important that it is not left behind in a rush to focus on the latest technological interventions.

All eight writers-artists insist that readers-viewers negotiate between reading and looking at the page, the canvas, the installation, the photograph, the panel or frame, the image-text, or a particular point of view. In chapter 1, I discuss the little-known illustrated memoirs of Armenian American writer and artist Peter Najarian. In traditional book form, Najarian's hybrid memoirs present a lively interplay between image and text. Unlabeled, the images float throughout the text like bits of memory, evoking a sense of Najarian's process. Incorporating first drawings, then drawings and paintings, and then drawings, paintings, and photographs into his sequence of personal narratives, Najarian increasingly performs the interrelatedness of art and writing. In all his work, Najarian narrates the story of his family lost during the Armenian Genocide, his mother immigrating to the United States, his own alienation and complex relation to an imagined Armenian homeland, and his obsession with capturing transcendental beauty through art.

Laguna Pueblo writer Leslie Marmon Silko's photo-text narratives are the focus of chapter 2. In *Storyteller* and the handmade *Sacred Water*, Silko uses photographs to illustrate her personal narratives in original ways. As it is for Najarian, the writing is central, but set in creative dialogue with and juxtaposition to images. In *Sacred Water*, rather than including photographs to supplement her writing, Silko is interested in "photographs that obscure rather than reveal," photographs that both participate in a dialogue with the text and serve as a visual field within which the text is read ("As a Child" 169).[16] She highlights an indigenous geocentric sense of time, focused on natural cycles of the earth—seasons, meteorological patterns, and geological processes—even as she emphasizes the importance of the present. She renders time spatially, insisting on an embodied Laguna Pueblo, contemporary female subjectivity that is grounded in place, specifically New Mexico and Arizona. Time and place, then, are interpenetrating.

Chapter 3 focuses on comics artist and writer Art Spiegelman's two-volume graphic memoir *Maus*. In the comics form, word and image are coequal; we look and read simultaneously. Spiegelman's drawings are "a kind of commemorating, witnessing, and recording of information" and "a way of forcing [himself] and others to look" (Spiegelman and Chute, *MetaMaus* 49, 50). Spiegelman (re)tells the stories of his father, Vladek, who survived Auschwitz; his process of recording, translating, and shaping his father's story; and his troubled relationship with his father, complicated by his own anxiety about being the son of survivors. A fourth story, the absent narrative haunting both volumes, is the story of Anja, Spiegelman's mother, whose diaries were destroyed after her suicide. Of course, Spiegelman addresses the theme of transgenerational trauma, returning again and again (before, during, and after *Maus*) to the site and moment of the wounding and its seemingly endless metamorphosing consequences. The comics form, with its capacity to depict past and present simultaneously, is an especially appropriate mode for autobiography.

I examine the artists' books of Chinese-Japanese American book artist Julie Chen in chapter 4. In artists' books, writing and image making meet sculpture. Book artists allude to the long history of book structures—Western codex, folding books, fan books, accordion books, concertina-bound books, slat books, tunnel books, boxed books, and more—creating forms that themselves reflect the meaning of the text and images within them. They are both texts and art objects simultaneously. Chen creates a disembodied, deracialized, dehistoricized, almost ungendered autobiographical persona that ranges free of material referents but renders spatially a Western linear sense of time. The elaborate design of Chen's unique book forms demand that reader-viewers have a temporal-spatial experience of her cognitive processes. She creates what I call architectures of cognition through which readers navigate.

Chapter 5 considers Korean American artist Theresa Hak Kyung Cha's experimental autobiography, *Dictée*, in relation to her performance art, experimental video, handmade books, mail art, and mixed media installations. Like Art Spiegelman and Peter Najarian, Cha uses both image and text to address themes of historical violence, displacement, postmemory, transgenerational trauma, and the difficulty of articulating a complicated legacy of loss, in her case initiated by the Japanese colonization of Korea in the years 1910 to 1945. She relies on what I call a cinematic style: in some sections she creates detailed storyboard narration in which each camera angle is determined; conceives of the page both as a "unit of space and time," as Spiegelman describes it (*MetaMaus* 168), and as a screen; and juxtaposes diagrams, letters, documents, archival photographs, and film stills with textual narrative.

In chapter 6, I examine the unapologetically political photo-(auto) biographies of African American photographer and folklorist Carrie Mae Weems. Envisioning the artist as the narrator of history, Weems shows and (re)tells the historical legacy of violence, both for African Americans and for Native Americans. As well as critiquing racialized and racist representations, Weems's work examines the nature of memory and history, both individual and collective. Weems moves from telling a story through a sequence of photographs and texts on the wall to designing a multisensory architecture of image and text copied onto large banners hanging from the ceiling, accompanied by an oral narrative. Viewers literally walk through the pages of her narrative, experiencing a palimpsest of images and texts.

I discuss the work of African American artist Faith Ringgold, particularly her story quilts, in chapter 7. Ringgold's story quilts, like artists' books, are in dialogue with ideas of the book and the page as well as with concepts of piecing and framing. Like Carrie Mae Weems, Ringgold consciously challenges racist and sexist stereotypes, retells history from an African American woman artist's perspective, and imagines a creative multiplicity of identities for African American women. Ringgold not only revises the history of Western art, correcting its exclusion of people of color and women, but rethinks the basic materials of the artist by working with fabric and the quilt form. In addition, she engages playfully with the concept of framing, using text as frame, often reframing familiar images, sometimes unframing others. She also puts her quilts in direct dialogue with books, positioning her quilt squares as pages and providing cues about how to read the pages and, at the same time, look at the quilt.

In chapter 8, I explore the site-specific installations, word paintings, and abstract landform paintings of Cheyenne-Arapaho conceptual artist Hachivi Edgar Heap of Birds. Resisting being pigeonholed as an Indian artist, Heap of Birds addresses the past and present, local and global, individual and collective, and insists on a contemporary, not museumized, indigenous identity. His word paintings remind us that words are images, too; and his abstract landscape paintings create a private language of place linked to identity, community, and history. Considered together, his artwork evokes the haunting specter of indigenous loss yet affirms native presence in the here and now. Like so many others—Najarian, Silko, Spiegelman, Cha, Weems, and Ringgold—Heap of Birds situates himself in relation to history (time) and place (space and memory). Like Silko and Weems, he calls attention to the historical palimpsest of indigenous presence, and like everyone considered in this volume, he revisualizes himself in modes that require new ways of seeing and reading at the visual-verbal interface.

Each of these visual autobiographies is, in some way, in dialogue with historical trauma and its consequences. Najarian and Spiegelman give voice to genocide, Cha, Weems, and Heap of Birds to colonization, and Weems and Ringgold to slavery and racism. Through not as explicitly as the others, Silko and Chen refer implicitly to violence. The ongoing aftermath of colonization haunts the land and Silko's daily experience. Chen grapples not with military, political, or social violence but with the natural oppression of being bound to time and its ever-eroding passage. These artists and writers are linked, then, not only through their formal experimentation with image and text but also through their variable experiences of loss.

Throughout I offer triangulated readings that weave together discussions of *genre* (autobiography), *media* (book, drawing, painting, photography, sculpture), and *theme* (race, ethnicity, gender, indigeneity, immigration, diaspora, trauma), all informed by historical and political contexts. *As well as offering close readings of a wide range of formal innovations and image-text relations, I discuss recurrent themes*—the necessity to retell history from subaltern perspectives; transgenerational trauma; untangling history, family, and community; loss and survival; and time and place—as they are illuminated by visual autobiographers working with different materials and forms. *Although I focus on one writer-artist per chapter, my readings cross-reference thematic and formal relations. For in-*

    Introduction

stance, I discuss the cinematic techniques of both Spiegelman's comics books and Cha's experimental autobiography; examine the innovative uses of framing in Chen's artists' books, Ringgold's story quilts, Weems's photo-autobiographies, and Spiegelman's comics; and consider formulations of spatialized time in Chen's artists' books and Silko's photo-text narratives. This practice of reading across differences allows for some strikingly new sets of associations as I read seemingly disparate visual-verbal forms in relation to one another. *Using a variety of critical lenses, my method is close reading of image and text across a spectrum of visual-verbal forms. My argument is cumulative and prismatic.*

Similarly, rather than isolating writers-artists into ethnic or racial categories (Native American, African American, Asian American, and so on) and seeking to locate cultural affinities or historical trajectories in their work, I discuss a diverse range of American autobiographers, who use very different media, in relation to one another.[17] This, I believe, is closer to how artists-writers work because they are influenced not merely by an often imposed identity group but by a full spectrum of local and global creative forces. Despite the dramatic formal differences in their visual narratives, these writers and artists focus on a set of crucial questions about American identity. How does race or gender or geography or history define us? Who are we when we are most authentic? How can we renarrate the legacies we inherit? In addition, they share an autobiographical storytelling impulse and a passionate belief in the power of creative interventions that provoke dialogue about American identity and history.

Experimenting with image-text relations, these writers-artists link the personal and the political. They participate consciously in a process of creative rewriting and reimaging of "haunting legacies" (Schwab)— genocide, colonization, and slavery as well as ongoing forms of discursive violence—in order to break free of inherited verbal-visual regimes and to revise painful histories. Each wrestles with histories of contested self-representations and webs of intersubjectivity as he or she envisions liberatory possibilities of selfhood and fresh modes of self-narration in image and text.

# Literature-Based Image-and-Text Forms

# Peter Najarian's Illustrated Memoirs

## "'The Terror of Our History' and a Love That May Redeem It"

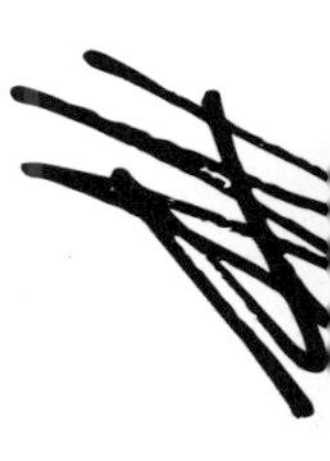
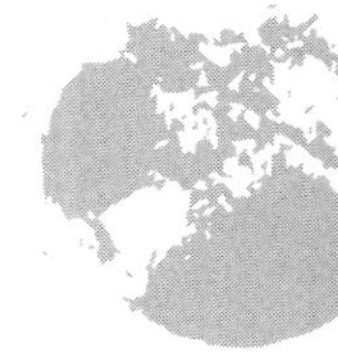

Peter Najarian creates illustrated memoirs—autobiographical narratives in book format that incorporate drawings, paintings, and photographs. Words and images are arranged as an assemblage, with images serving to evoke memories, visualize musings, generate moods, or reference art history.

"The past," William Faulkner claimed famously, "is never dead. It's not even past." Personal and collective experiences, especially the trauma of genocide, haunt the present moment. In the form of memories, the past may erupt into the present, insinuate itself into consciousness, and destabilize seemingly constant subjectivities. Although artists and writers of all eras grapple with the inescapable burden of inheriting a violent past, those from the late twentieth century seek it out—as if facing it, outing it, naming it, representing it can redeem the painful legacy of their fathers and mothers. Peter Najarian examines in image and text the nature of memory and history and insists on an intense engagement with the wrongs of the past as part of a process of self-formulation. Like most of the other writers and artists discussed in this book, Najarian thematizes the collision of personal history with world history. Through the process of showing and telling in a variety of visual-verbal modes, he represents his family's legacy of violence in an effort to testify to it and redeem it.

Najarian's illustrated memoirs are the least experimental hybrid autobiography discussed here, but unlike conventional autobiographies, in which images, if included at all, are designed to illustrate or support the text, in Najarian's memoirs the drawings, paintings, and photographs are in a complex dialogic relation with the text. Sometimes the images serve as commentary on, sometimes as counterpoint to, the text and its imagery; and sometimes the images function as part of a visual-verbal field, generating a mood more than a specific point. Overall, Najarian's image-texts create a resonant network of memory, experience, and imagination.

With his unique interartistic sensibility, Najarian filters the story of his Armenian American family and community through Western art and literature. Engaging a long history of literary and artistic aesthetics, Najarian thematizes his process of looking. At times, Najarian's looking is acquisitive or penetrating—a version of the classic male gaze that consumes, rapes, or dominates that which is observed. At other times, Najarian becomes the expansive Whitmanesque eye/I that absorbs everything he sees into a transcendental unity. In constituting his personal and collective history, Najarian relies on a process of refiguration and assemblage; he reimagines the people in his life filtered through canonical Western art, and he brings together heterogeneous connections between his text and images.

Peter Najarian was first a writer and later became a visual artist. As both a textual and a visual storyteller, he interrelates image and text to tell his story. In all his writing and artwork, Najarian tells and retells one complex, multilayered tale: the tragic loss of his family during the Armenian Genocide, his mother's incredible escape and new life as an immigrant in the United States, his profound sense of alienation and deep longing to return to an Armenian homeland that no longer exists, and his all-consuming desire to capture the fleeting moments of life and the elusive essence of beauty, often symbolized for him as Woman or Art. A tragic futility permeates these interrelated narratives: the perfect woman is never found; the past is never clear; the line or color or shape in art or language is never adequately sublime; and the return home is never possible. Everything is fleeting; only death is inevitable. Even so, Najarian returns, again and again, to his search for woman, beauty, art, and home, looking to art and literature for models and documenting his journey in text and image. Najarian's obsession with this hero's journey meshes perfectly with what James Olney described as "the very emblem of our time": "an agonized search for self, through the mutually reflexive acts of memory and narrative, accompanied by the haunting fear that it is impossible from the beginning but also impossible to give over" (xiv–xv).

Furthermore, inspired, in part, by Armenian American painter Arshile Gorky (1904–48), Najarian suggests that it is only through literature and art that he can maintain a link, however tenuous, to Armenia. For some time, Gorky's letters were believed to be filled with poetic links between his art and his lost homeland. In one letter, Gorky is said to have written: "I dream of it always and it is as if some ancient Armenian spirit within me moves my hand to create so far from our homeland the shapes of nature we loved in the gardens, wheatfields and orchards of our Adoian family in Khorkom. Our beautiful Armenia which we lost and which I will repossess in my art" (Mooradian 32). It turns out, however, that Gorky's nephew Karlen Mooradian, who claimed to have found his uncle's letters, was, in fact, their author.[1] It is unclear how Gorky

    Literature-Based Image-and-Text Forms

might have articulated the connection between his art and Armenia. As another second-generation survivor, Lorne Shirinian, explains: "Those of us of the second generation after the Genocide can have no spontaneous memory of the terrible events, but we do create sites of memory, books, films, art, archives, and museums . . . to keep these remnants and new diaspora creations alive in the hope that someone will be able to offer a significant interpretation of them and provide a context for our post-genocide and diasporan lives" (*Landscape of Memory* 35). Fittingly, Najarian describes his art as arising from a "formless longing" (*Great American Loneliness* xii) that motivates if not fulfills him. His illustrated memoirs function as visual-verbal "sites of memory."

Unlike Carrie Mae Weems and Faith Ringgold, who inherited a full canvas of racist representations of African Americans that they must deconstruct before conveying their own self-representations, Najarian begins with a relatively empty slate. How many of his readers know anything about Armenians, immigrant or otherwise? Rather than correct misrepresentations of Armenians, Najarian must testify to their very existence. The defining experience for diasporic Armenians was the Armenian Genocide, known by Armenians as Meds Yeghern, the Great Crime. The atrocities occurred in 1915–18 and 1920–23, during and shortly after World War I, when Turkish soldiers massacred 1 to 1.5 million Armenians, sending those remaining on forced marches through the Syrian desert.[2] As early as 1915, "the Armenian Genocide was condemned by the international community as a crime against humanity."[3] The continuing effect of Armenian history on Armenian-American writing has been threefold: "a pervasive numbness," "bitterness" and "paranoia," and a "corroded spirit" (Bedrosian 19). "The saving grace for the survivors," Margaret Bedrosian concludes, "was the shared will to cherish the fragments; they were bound to one another by a scarring so profound that it knit them into singular new wholes" (19).

Second-generation survivor Peter Najarian grew up listening to massacre stories told by his mother and other Armenian survivors in the tight-knit immigrant communities of New Jersey and Fresno, California. The story he wants to tell, however, is "not about the massacre but about the wake of the enormous upheaval. . . . We, all of us, Armenians or [American] Indians or whoever," he says, "are in some way the children of rape and plunder" (Preface, *Voyages* n.p.). Just as Art Spiegelman and Theresa Hak Kyung Cha experience the reverberations of their parents' trauma a generation later, so too does Najarian. Najarian's autobiographical persona is a "second-generation Armenian-American who is unable to reconcile himself to his past, his family, and the country in which he was born" (Shirinian, 17). "He exists between the atrocities of history and the haven of art" (Hadas n.p.). The United States, the country that was a place of refuge and new beginnings for his mother, is for Najarian a place of exile, exacerbating a lost family and history. Art—both literary and visual—is his only hope for identifying and claiming the remnants of a tortured past and refashioning them into a new diasporic subjectivity.

Najarian's mother figures prominently in his story. This is not surprising, given the challenges for the Armenian diaspora of keeping cultural memory alive, of anguishing over the question of "how to populate our consciousness with the ghosts while lighting our way to a future full of vigor and imagination. In this struggle there is no more monumental a figure than the Armenian mother. She represents all that is lost, all that has come of that loss, and what it takes to move beyond it" (Janigian n.p.). The figure of the Armenian mother, then, is a multivalent representation of loss, survival, and the ongoing work of forging a new identity.

In one of Najarian's versions of his personal narrative, his mother is "little Zaroohe, the sole survivor" (*Great American Loneliness* 110) of her family, who was forced to flee through the Syrian desert. As an adult, Zaroohe tells stories about her mother, though she cannot remember her mother's face. She describes how, after the deaths of her father, her older brother, and a new baby, her mother told her to go with a soldier who put her on a train with other confiscated children. All the while, she cried, "Dudi! Dudi!"—"Mama!" in Turkish. She tells of learning to speak Armenian after she was liberated from the Turks by the invading English soldiers who brought Armenian teachers for the Turkish-speaking orphans. She narrates how a Christian Armenian family claimed to want to adopt her but forced her to work as a servant once she got to their home. She describes her rescue and immigration to the United States, where an arranged marriage to a man almost twice her age awaited her.[4] She was sixteen years old. His father long dead, the narrator's mother is his only link to his family history. As the son became an adolescent, he found his mother embarrassing: an overweight, illiterate immigrant woman with hair sprouting from her upper lip. At the same time, however, his mother is always, always the Earth Mother who nurtures her son with food, unconditional love, and lots of story fragments.

Najarian has published five books, three of which incorporate his drawings and paintings, as well as many essays and stories included in other volumes. Although his work is the least experimental of any discussed in this book, his illustrated memoirs use a temporal interface presenting a sequence of events; a relational interface in which image and text are in dialogue, most often complementing but occasionally interrogating or challenging each other; a contextual interface depicting cultural and historical contexts; and an evocatively allusive style in which he refers to images of Western art and literature in innovative contexts. With each publication, his use of images expands, from drawings in *Daughters of Memory* (1986), to drawings and paintings in *The Great American Loneliness* (1999), to drawings, paintings, and photographs in *The Artist and His Mother* (2010).[5] Some of his images are straightforward illustrations depicting what is being described in the text; others allude to well-known paintings that evoke grand Western themes of beauty, art, nature, women, and humanity. Some images are juxtaposed to, rather than illustrative of, the text; some create a mood, while others are more like disparate memories or "graphic meditations floating" (Janigian n.p.) in and out of the multitemporal narrative. Although Najarian calls *Daughters of Memory* a novel and insists on the fictionality of his characters, his work is unquestionably autobiographical. And given the general consensus since at least the 1980s that all autobiography is fiction,[6] that the very concept of the self is a socio-historical-cultural and literary construction and the self-narration one cobbles together is full of strategic selections and omissions, Najarian's illustrated books are clearly self-portraiture and family saga in image and text. Najarian himself explains that for quite some time he believed that he needed to name what he wrote fiction because publishers and booksellers had no clear category for his hybrid image-texts and fiction sold better than autobiography.[7] I focus here on his three published illustrated memoirs.

### *Daughters of Memory*

Acknowledging Najarian's lyricism, what Najarian refers to as "narrative in the realm of poesy" (e-mail March 23, 2014), some scholars point out that his language is what elevates *Daughters of Memory* (1986) "above the level of memoir, journal, or scrapbook—all genres [he] embraces, but transcends" (Hadas n.p.). Najarian dedicates *Daughters of Memory* to his grandmother, "who probably starved to death somewhere in the Syrian Desert," to "her young son who would have become an artist had he not died beside her," to "the love of art and for all the kindred souls who share the terror of our history and a love that may redeem it," and to his cousin, Archie Ashod Pinajian, who "nurtured in [Najarian's] heart the dream" of making art. Although these are highly personal dedications, Najarian links his family history to art and literary history, noting that his grandmother "was born around the same time as Picasso and Joyce" and died "when Degas died in Paris" (n.p.). Throughout *Daughters of Memory* and increasingly in later work, Najarian filters descriptions of family members through references to Western art. Imagining his grandmother, for instance, he describes her "with her son in her arms like the Rondanini Pietà"; "with her arms out like Piero's giant Madonna"; like the women in Johannes Vermeer's painting of a girl with a turban, Paul Gauguin's paintings of Tahitian beauties, Rembrandt van Rijn's painting of his mistress Hendrickje, and "all of Degas" (76).[8] The painted women to whom he compares his grandmother are voluptuous, mysterious, often tragic, and bordering on the mythic. Not coincidentally, the real-life women in Najarian's memoir are always filtered through his art-inspired ideal Woman.

In the early eighteenth century, Italian philosopher Giambattista Vico articulated "three different aspects" of memory: "memory when it remembers things, imagination when it alters or imitates them, and invention when it gives them a new turn or puts them into proper arrangement and relationship. For these reasons," he says, "the theological poets call Memory the mother of the Muses" (*New Science* para. 819). The offspring of Mnemosyne (Memory), goddess of memory and language, and almighty Zeus, the Muses create (and later inspire) art, literature, music, and dance. Daughters of memory, of course, refer to the muses that Najarian enlists to inspire and (sometimes) tell this story. Najarian's muses, however, are a chorus of old Armenian women who whisper their memories of Armenia and the fearsome massacre that inspire Najarian's interart storytelling.

For Najarian, memory centers his autobiographical work not only in his title but in epigraphs to the book. He quotes William Blake: "In the New Age the Daughters of Memory shall become the Daughters of Inspiration." While Blake highlights the relation between memory and inspiration, the passage from *I Am That*, conversations with Indian spiritual teacher and philosopher of Advaita (or nondualism) Nisargadatta Maharaj (1897–1981), claims that memory itself is the defining feature of human subjectivity. Nisargadatta explains that while a human being is "all-pervading, eternal and infinitely creative awareness, . . . [a] person is but the sum total of memories" (*Daughters of Memory*, n.p.). Najarian emphasizes the claim that individual identity may be merely an accumulation of one's memories. As Kiowa writer and artist N. Scott Momaday suggests, "If I were to remember other things, I should be someone else" (*Names* 63). Our memories, however, are never completely our own. We share our memories, re-membered and linked, with others. If humans are the sum total of their memories, what happens when memory fades or is lost? What happens when, as in the case of Najarian's autobiographical persona, memories are not only lost but also are always already mediated? Najarian's mother transmits stories, histories, and genealogies, but her memory has enormous blank spots. Throughout the book, Najarian reminds readers that his mother remembers isolated images—riding a donkey across the bridge, viewing her mother's freckles, being warned not to approach her dead baby brother lying under a tree. Poignantly, she cannot remember her mother's face. Throughout his books, then, Najarian re-mediates his mother's already mediated memories, assembling the fragments into a story told in text and image.

In the past half-century, the study of memory has reshaped how we understand it as a phenomenon and as a faculty of mind. The various popular metaphors of memory—as the *memory bank* into which memories are deposited and from which they can be reclaimed or the *file cabinet* into which memories are placed, ordered, and from which they can be extracted—are simply false. Neither stable nor locatable, memory is not a static repository but an active process. Memories are created as much as remembered. Najarian expresses the dynamic complexity of memory when he interweaves all three aspects of Vico's process of memory: memory (remembering), imagination (imitating and altering), and invention (reinterpreting and rearranging) throughout his story.

The italicized first page, "The Old Grapevine," serves as a portal through which the reader enters the text. Najarian announces that *Daughters of Memory* has a simple plot: "an old hairy-nosed and horny artist is reviewing his life's work and he confronts the spirit of history, of our species who kill each other and of his grandmother who was slaughtered in the desert" (3). The autobiographical persona's name in this rendering of the story is Zeke.

Najarian's first lines reference Nisargadatta's mandate to expand the limited referents of individuality to include the larger context of "the vast universe": "As long as you are enmeshed in a particular personality you can see nothing beyond it. But as a tiny point of a pencil can draw innumerable pictures so does the dimensionless point of awareness draw the contents of the vast universe" (n.p.). Najarian begins the first sentence: "Lines upon lines, they flow like food for the tail-eating snake. They love the void and they grow in death, they rise and become part of it like murals on a cracking wall that become the cracks themselves" (3). From his opening lines, Najarian suggests the relations among art, death, desire, and time—the lines on the mural become the cracks of dissolution, transforming death into art and art into a monument to time—and the eternally deferred arrival or completion. The lines proliferate one from another "like food" for the Ouroboros, or tail-eating snake. Art, then, is associated with the cyclical continuity of life and death, with what is lost and what persists. It is by translating his family history into art that Najarian makes meaning of their suffering. In his image-texts his family and Armenian identity endure.

Najarian summarizes briefly his family's history. His mother was a child in Turkey when the Armenian massacre began. Her mother, father, and two brothers were killed; she was the lone survivor. After staying in an orphanage in Lebanon and working as a family servant out-

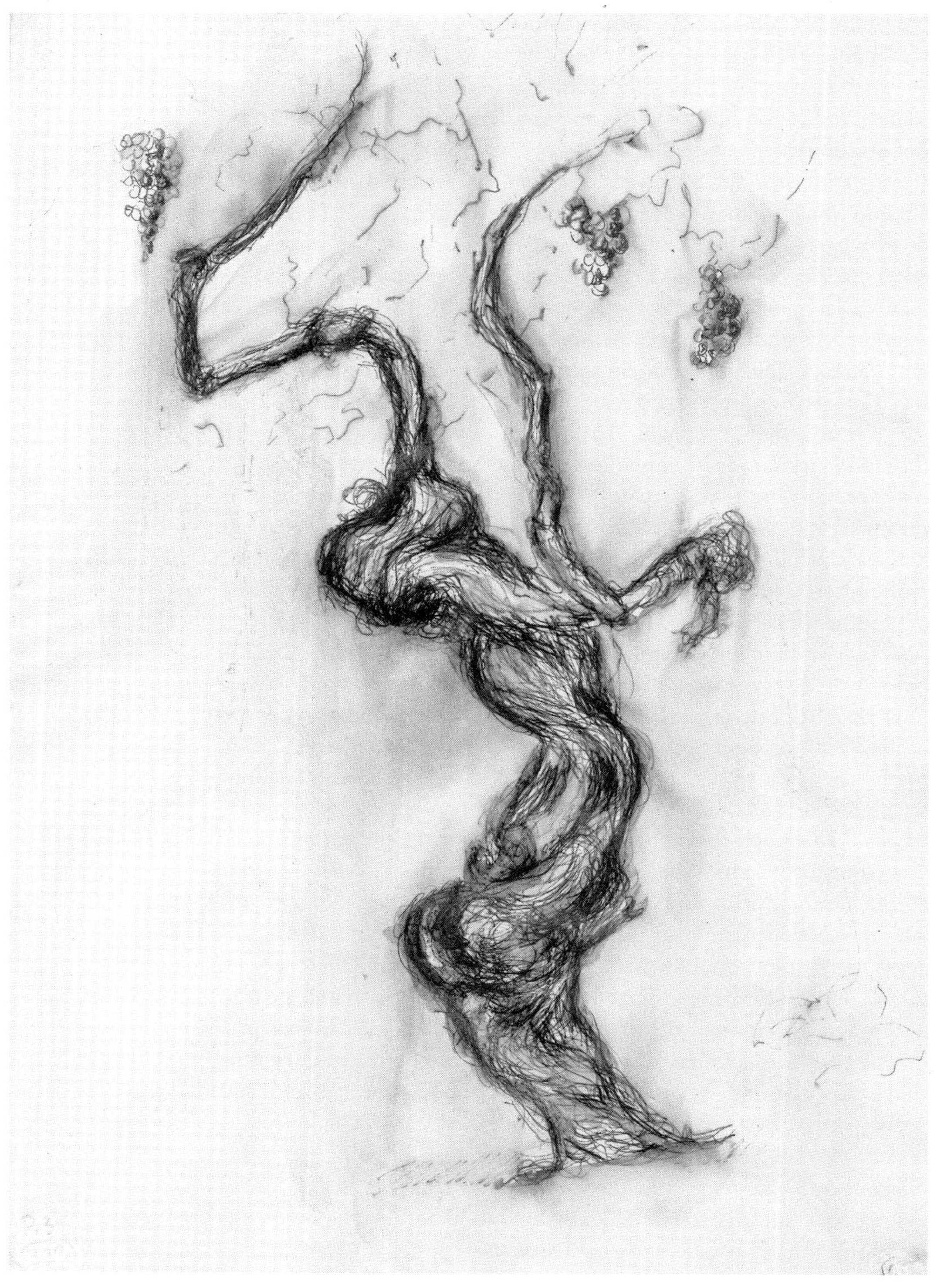

side the orphanage, she was rescued. She and others came to the United States and settled in New Jersey, where they worked and raised families. She retired in Fresno, California, where "the grapevines are like those [she] once knew in Turkey" and where she gathers with other Armenian women to "shoot the bull." The narrator's mother "tells him of her own mother whose face she can't remember." And "he struggles to imagine that face as if it were the image of a home they both lost in their different ways" (3).

He concludes this prefatory page by returning to the lines that "twist and curve like an old grapevine at the end of harvest, the shredded bark and tortured trunk like an old ego on a cross, its arms out as if praying for death" (3). His uncaptioned drawing of the "old grapevine" (fig. 1.1) looks also like a tortured and contorted human form, reminiscent of Christ's crucifixion pose: head slumped forward, hands outstretched toward the heavens as if in supplication or utter surrender. The heavily shaded, dying grapevine may refer to Armenia generally or to Najarian's family history that will die with the narrator, who remains alone and childless. Despite the intense aura of age and suffering, however, the old grapevine still bears a few clusters of grapes, notable on the top branches. This drawing is unique for this book, which includes almost exclusively human figures, primarily female nudes, interspersed with drawings of family members.[9] Also, the depiction of the aged grapevine links Armenian survivors with the land and embodies Najarian's themes of loss and aging. It is difficult not to envision the "old ego on a cross" as the narrator himself, who "sacrifices all for art" that may redeem terrible suffering by transfiguring it into beauty.

## Women

Najarian is obsessed with women in many roles: mother, grandmother, lovers, prostitutes, objects of desire, visual delights to draw or paint, to "fuck" with his eyes. His voracious vision is the embodiment of the male gaze, which sexualizes and consumes the female object of desire, cannibalizing what he sees. The women he depicts are sometimes mythologized, sometimes humanized. Always his images, like his "carnal language" (Hadas n.p.), are physical and earthy; any abstractions about love or art are generated from a glimpse of a full breast or the angle of a voluptuous hip (fig. 1.2). His twenty-one drawings of female nudes punctuate the work, emphasizing his perpetually unfulfilled longing for women, who represent his longing for connection as well as for beauty and art. Here the Rubenesque woman, with full thighs and breasts, poses in a graceful and seductive stance. Her face is deeply shaded, obscuring

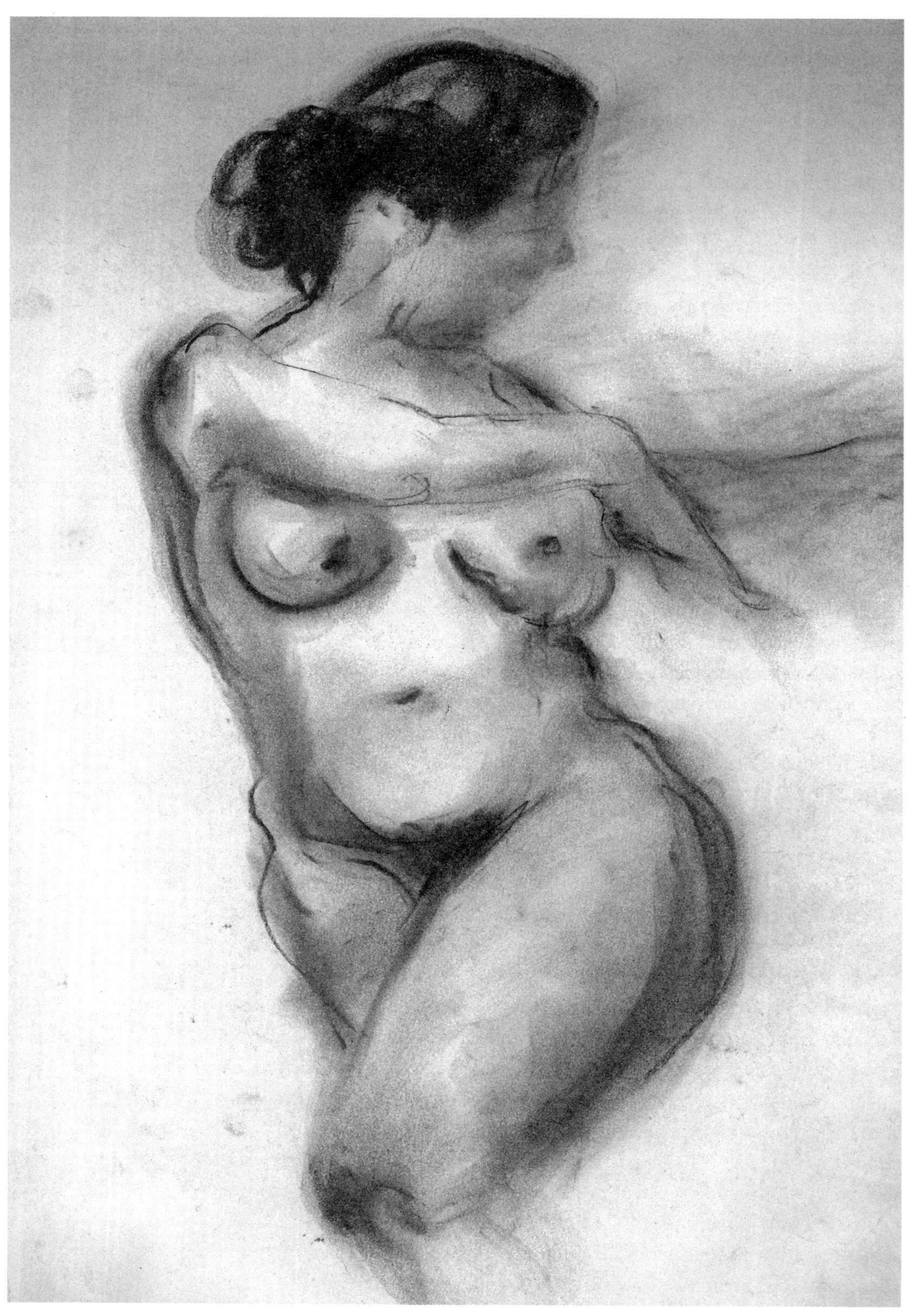

her individuality and enhancing her status as Woman. The shading all around the body suggests movement as well as ethereality.

## Grandmother

Although his mother, the one he struggles to leave and to whom he returns, is the beginning and ending point for his consideration of all women, his grandmother, his mother's mother, who died alone in the Syrian desert after her husband and sons were killed and her daughter taken from her by a Turkish soldier, is the origin. Najarian's grandmother was named "Vartanoush, Sweet Rose in sfumato" (23). Najarian describes the grandmother as if she were painted "in sfumato." From Italian *fumo*, "smoke," sfumato is, according to the online *Art Encyclopedia*, "the technique of oil painting [in] which colors or tones are blended in such a subtle manner that they melt into one another without perceptible transitions, lines or edges." The subtle shading creates a sense of mystery and mood. His grandmother's image is created from his mother's vague memories enhanced by the son's imagination, an imagination that is fired by images of beautiful and tragic women depicted throughout the long history of Western art. "She lies buried," writes Najarian, "like an ancient figure in a peeling wall, the void of her face filled with all the women loved and slaughtered in their turn, a Madonna with a son" (23). Through imagination and sheer will Najarian seeks to envision his grandmother's face where his mother's memory has failed to produce it. His grandmother is "the lost one, the earth her grandson longs to embrace, the young peasant woman who would bring him home again. She is the generous water and friendly light he struggles to touch with all his lines" (24). In his elegiac tone, Najarian depicts the grandmother as a sustaining symbol of loss, of a home never accessible, of a face never apprehensible, of a past deteriorating like a mural on a decaying wall.

In addition, because of his mother's memories of peasant life, Najarian associates the grandmother with the earth. His mother describes how her mother "stomped the grapes in burlap and then boiled them into syrup" (24). Her son muses: "She is the simple life of strong hands and many cousins, all the peasants sketched and studied across the continents." (25). But this idealized pastoral scene is interrupted: "What disease or beast will grind her into the garden she nurtures? The sky now darkens from red to black and the pastoral becomes a nightmare" (25). Just as the family's *aki* (vineyard) has been lost, so have his grandmother, grandfather, and uncles vanished. In the Armenian massacre, Grandmother was ground into the earth she tended, leaving her grandson on the other side of the world to a Whitmanesque musing in which

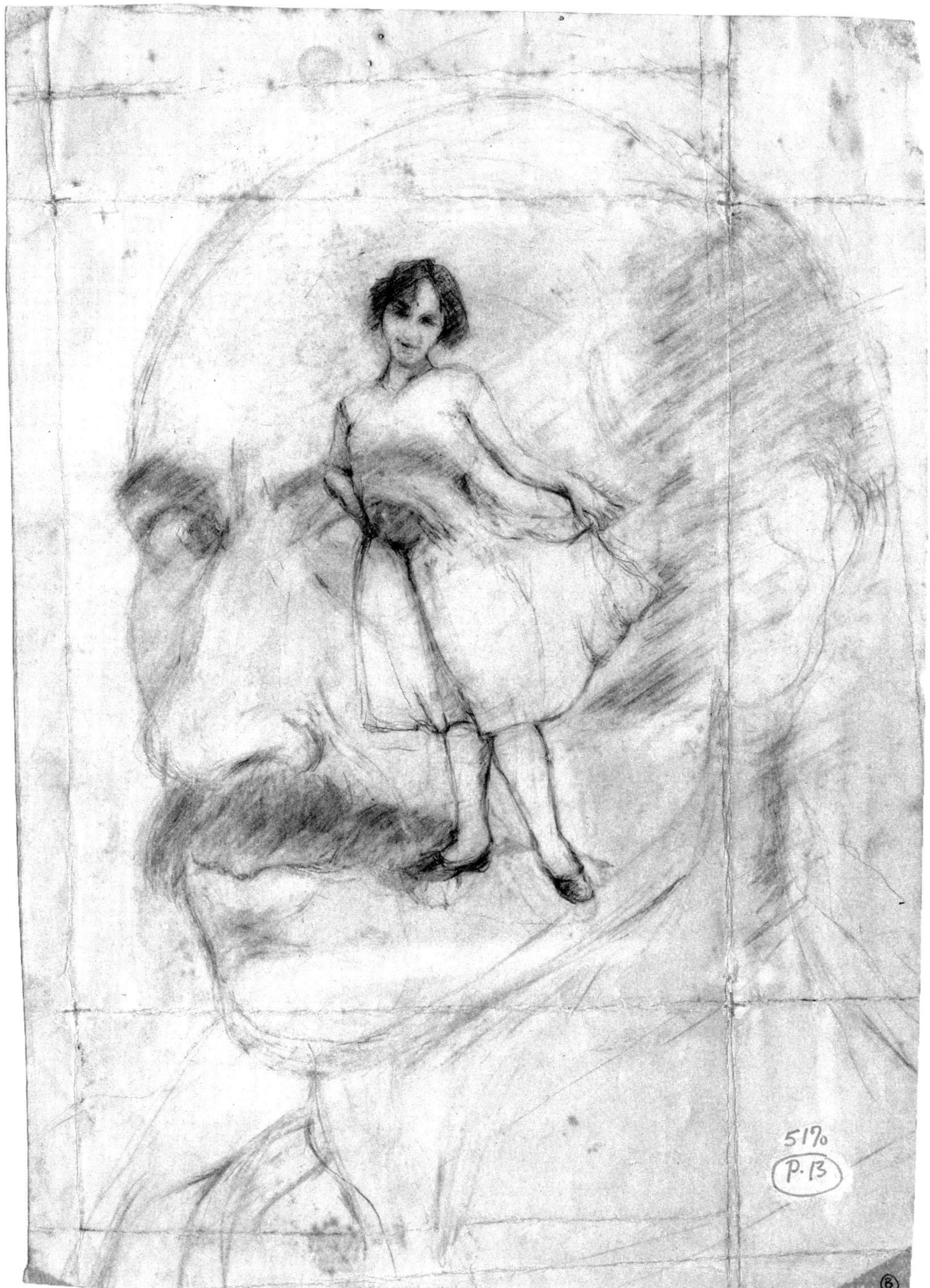

he merges his grandmother's fate with the poverty and suffering of the global poor: "Who is she, what is the face that always fades into history, her portrait always glazed with the women of memory, the young woman on the steps of a bank in Calcutta with her little daughter picking lice from her matted hair, the young Mexican with rotten teeth and tabid lungs, the sad Arab in a whorehouse in Casablanca" (25).

The indeterminate picture of the grandmother, "the one too deep to be recalled" (22), is broken into vivid images of poor women around the world—the mother in Calcutta, the "young Mexican" woman, "the sad Arab prostitute"—and refracted back, linking the grandmother to a timeless history of female oppression and suffering.

## Mother

In her old age, Zeke's mother "moves with the grace of an elephant. She sways her giant buttocks from her kitchen to her garden and back again, a mini Demeter wearing old man slippers and a loud mu-mu" (13). Again, Najarian mythologizes his family, comparing his mother to Demeter, goddess of the harvest, also known as Earth Mother. She is the family provider: the one who works long hours at the sewing factory in New Jersey to support her son; the one who does laundry and cleans incessantly and does not complain when her young son draws on the walls of his bedroom, but wipes them clean each week to provide a new canvas; the one who gardens and cooks and envelops her son in an adoring mother's embrace. "She is her kitchen, the source of *zahd*, the warm meal. She is the Ma of stuffed eggplant and zucchini, of stuffed cabbage and grapeleaves and even lettuce and cucumber and gutskin and tripe" (40). "She holds the fort" (42) and "her voice becomes the song of survival, the music of food and warmth" (40).

The drawing of Zeke's mother on this page contrasts with, if not contradicts, his written description of her as "massive like the flank of a beautiful animal" (13), a technique described as "an undercutting of the visual by the verbal" (Adams 90), part of an interrogatory interface between the image and the text. Although he has just described his mother as "elephantine," Najarian's drawing of his mother is based on "an old brown photograph of her youth" in which "she poses like a princess" (13). Making a drawing of the photograph highlights a long process of mediated images—the photograph a representation of a posed and frozen moment, his drawing an interpretive copy and re-representation. He draws his mother as a young girl striking a feminine pose, with one hand on her hip and the other spreading her skirt as if she is about to curtsy (fig. 1.3). The dialogue between image and text and the palimpsestic drawing itself emphasize the interpenetration of past and present. Her image is superimposed upon the self-portrait of her son, who looks out from the page, directly at the viewer, and whose youthful mother appears to be a projection of his mind. Eerily, the shading of the drawing focalizes the son's eye to his mother's vagina, underscoring her as the source of his existence, the object of his lifelong devotion, and her larger-than-life role as a feminized landscape. Like her mother before her, the narrator's mother is "one of them, a model for the figure who never comes clear" (13). She is the one he leaves to travel around the world in pursuit of the elusive glow of art and love. She is the one to whom he returns, even if, at first, begrudgingly.

### Sexual Partners

Najarian's earthy descriptions of his grandmother and mother are sensual, but when he talks about Zeke's lovers and the prostitutes he has frequented his descriptions become explicitly sexualized. Waxing eloquent about Nelly, one of his lost loves, the narrator queries: "What are the lines for the taste of her nipples, what are the colors for the smell of her neck . . . ?" (27). How is it possible to translate smell, touch, and taste into the visual realm?[10]

More than any other woman, however, Dolores is his central, recurrent love. Not surprisingly, her name is derived from the Spanish *dolor*, meaning pain, grief, or sorrow. Significantly, Dolores is not just a beautiful woman but also the embodiment of mother, wife, friend, and sexual partner—a composite object of desire. She is the wife of his good friend, a mother, and a friend of his. Like his mother, who sustains her home with food and warmth, Dolores is always there to listen and to feed them when he and his inner circle of friends—all young aspiring artists and writers—gather to share their heroic dreams of making great and enduring Art. After years, Dolores was filled with her own unfulfilled longing, and Zeke's ever-present yearning fixed on Dolores. Betraying his close friend and her husband, they had an affair. Zeke was deeply in love, but she "panicked." It was too late. Hearts were broken all around. Of all women, only Dolores was "the one inside the pulse of the glow" (72), but she, too, was ultimately unattainable.

Unlike his more sustained relationships with lovers, Zeke's encounters with prostitutes punctuate the narrative and highlight his restless desire. Early in *Daughters of Memory*, Zeke describes his eyes and "their unending hunger" (7). His vision is profoundly consumptive, absorbing and digesting what he sees. After being sexually aroused as he draws a nude female model, the protagonist visits a prostitute. Cynthia works to support her two children. Zeke's liaison with Cynthia is simply a friendly business transaction. As he departs, Zeke encounters an old tomcat who "keeps wandering the neighborhoods and spraying his needs like frescoes to a god" (10). Comparing semen to paint and sexual release to painting, the wandering hero sees his animal counterpart, who participates in the "caterwaul of the ages, the search for the one inside" (10). In this instance, Najarian sexualizes William Wordsworth's romanticism: poetry (art) is "the spontaneous overflow of powerful feeling"—and bodily fluids. Again, Najarian's corporeal and spiritual search can be fulfilled only fleetingly, never sustained.

Near the end of the book, he looks for a prostitute in Ankara, Turkey, where he has traveled to see his mother's childhood home. "Here now was the money for the woman of the underworld, his emigrant money coming back to the land of bones. He could finally pay for her who disappeared so long ago" (147). Sexualizing his return, he seeks a union with a lost and now degraded past, place, and self. He selects a prostitute who reminds him of a former innocent lover, but this woman has "needlemarks" and a "childhood in a gutter" (152). As he enters the young prostitute, the narrative shifts into a long memory. He remembers his boyhood terror of descending into the darkness of the basement, where "serpents or monsters or whatever" lay in wait. He would always race out of there as quickly as possible. One time, however, the landlord's granddaughter invited him to play doctor and patient in the dark and monster-ridden basement. "She was the first one, the brazen little girl of the shadows" (154). As he returns from his memories to the present moment of his lovemaking, he realizes that he "didn't want to come," he "wanted to stay inside her" (154). His desire is insatiable, not only for his sexual fulfillment, but for his history, his family, his compulsive need to make art, his search to access the ever-receding glow within women-art.

All of these women—the grandmother, the mother, the lovers, and the prostitutes—are overshadowed by Najarian's idea of Woman, an abstract concept linking women to beauty, desire, nature, and art. With deep roots in Western epistemology that associates women with nature (and intuition) and men with civilization (and reason), reanimated in some second-wave feminist conflations of Women and Nature, Najarian's abstract Woman is an essentialist fiction. As unrealistic as she may be, Najarian's Woman-Nature is a powerful seductress. "Whoever she is she goes all the way back in all the dreams of water and flying" (11–12), explains Zeke. "She was in the vision on the way home from kindergarten . . . ; She appeared again in the blaze of adolescence" (12). "She appeared as if through a veil in that first wet dream, a pubescent girl whose glow brightened as she approached" (28). "Where did she go? Who was she . . . ?" (28). When his mother came to make the bed and saw the wet spot, without a word she placed "a square of old flannel" on the mattress and covered it with a clean sheet. As he grows older, the stains overlap. He traveled to find her in Mexico. "But she was not there. Nor in England or India and the years passed like pages of an atlas" (12). The enduring woman of flesh, however, is: "Ma. Always Ma. Who looms over the question with hands like a butcher's and the legs of a fullback, her grip relentless with mounds of dough, her arms full of laundry" (12).

At this point in the narrator's meditation on his personal history of desire, he makes a Whitmanesque turn to expand his love for women to an indiscriminate, all-inclusive love for everything:

> And not only of women but of the algae on an old tugboat or the gulls by the dock, of the palisades rising like gods by the waterfront or the clouds rolling above the city, of the grass one afternoon in football practice . . . the sky suddenly opening and the autumn clouds glowing in the aftermath of rain . . . in the soft rainbow colors of a waning light, a deep silence suddenly throbbing with the rich colors of the turf and the sweat from the helmet, a mysterious love rising with tears and mixing in a boy's heart with a grief he couldn't fathom. (29)

This painterly description, a kind of textual painting, with its emphasis on the glow, light, and color of specific objects, depicts a scene of the boy's expanding consciousness. The sheer beauty of the everyday gives rise to a "mysterious love" mingled with "grief." Unsure for whom he grieved—"who was she who always disappeared?"—the young man vows to be an artist to "paint that glow and find her whoever she is who lives inside it" (29). Najarian concludes this section with a poetic lamentation to the idealized Woman, the "glow" that invites and entices but remains forever unattainable.


### Elderly Armenian Women

In contrast to the depressed artist's musings, the elderly Armenian women serve as an almost cheerful chorus throughout. They are the collective voices of a maternal history of loss and survival, commenting on everything from the price of raisins, relations between Muslims and Christians, husbands who drink too much *arak* (a raisin-based alcohol), and memories of eating almonds in their home villages to a sale on tombstones. Interwoven into the mundane everyday gossip about children, grandchildren, and television soap operas are matter-of-fact statements about rape, slavery, and slaughter during the massacre. In addition, the women offer an unwittingly ironic commentary on the twentieth-century United States:

My grandson's girlfriend came the other day to write recipes. She
    wants to cook for him, but she's an *odar*.[11] . . .

What kind of *odar* is she?

I don't know, she says she's American.

They all say that.

I asked her what kind of American and she said a little of this and
    a little of that as if she were a recipe.

There are no Americans. They just say that to make themselves
    feel like they're somebody.

They're [*sic*] won't be anymore of us either.

Not if we marry a part of this and a part of that.

We will be gone when we lose the language.

Why should anyone want to keep the language.

The language is everything.

It gives us history.

I don't like history.

Let us be part of this and part of that.

It's safer.

What are you saying? Did my father die for nothing?

I don't know why your father died.

He died because he would not become a Moslem.

So they ripped his nails out and slit him open with a butcher
    knife, that's better than being a Moslem?

.   .   .   .   .   .   .   .   .   .   .   .   .   .   .   .   .   .   .

They ripped my baby daughter from my arms and threw her in
    the river.

Do you think I could ever be a Moslem after that?

They did something else to me.

Christians do those things too.

I'm not Moslem and I'm not Christian.

What are you then?

I'm a grandmother, that's what I am. (55–56)

The women gossip, reminisce, and share stories that construct an Armenian American identity. Their conversations highlight everyday pragmatism—the hard work of supporting families, the tough resilience that helped them survive. Just as importantly, they offer a bit of humor, some ironic perspective on the problems of the next generations. Is it "safer" to assimilate into the United States, to be "a little of this and a little of that" so that it's impossible to become a clear target of otherness? If losing the language and marrying out continue, though, what will happen to their Armenian identity and history? As Lorne Shirinian explains, the "central problematic for diasporic Armenians in North America has become how to move forward as a community without losing a sense of their Armenian identity as they have traditionally understood it" (1). Both the elder Armenian women and Zeke, survivors and children of survivors, then, grapple with this. But unlike Zeke, the lonely artist narrator, the women are not brooding about the past; they are neither elegiac nor poetic. They are pragmatic survivors in the here and now.

Unlike some of the other artists-writers in this book, who choose to highlight the explicit politics of their art, Najarian takes the highly political topic at the heart of his story—the Armenian Genocide—and tells both a personal tale and a universal one. Mirroring the process of memory in which memories return in bits and pieces, he weaves small snippets of his mother's memories throughout. The family story unfolds for the reader in small fragments, much as it must have unfolded for Najarian. Rather than raging against Muslims or Turks, rather than trying to correct the historical record, especially to counter the few who claim that the Armenian Genocide never happened, Najarian links this tragic violence to a long history and contemporary practice of the unspeakable violence humans do to each other.[12] In one section, the narrator describes his mother as "the international lady of the garment" (92), one of many immigrant women who toil in sweatshops to sew the latest fashions for those who can afford them, "her genes knotted to who knows where in the web of rape and plunder" (92).

When, as a young man, Zeke sets out on his rite-of-passage road trip from New Jersey to California, he is excited to see America. Soon, however, like many of his generation, he decides that "there was no America, there was nowhere that could be named and the road pushed through a history of massacres and a cemetery of another culture" (87). Acknowledging the genocide upon which the United States was built, Najarian insists on looking at the long histories of dominance and oppression, not



Literature-Based Image-and-Text Forms

as local exceptions, but as global patterns. Even the chorus of old women concludes: "We all come from killing and sex" (79).

As Zeke examines a map to try to determine how far his mother walked as she fled the Turkish soldiers, the notations of the land become markers of death, a gravesite memorial. "The line squirms between the cities like a caravan of death through the womb of history," writes Najarian, "the exotic names stippled in the cradle of civilization, each syllable a ditch, each letter a mound of skeletons, each city a prayer bead" (74). Here names, syllables, even letters become images. Like recitations of the dead, Najarian catalogs the atrocities inflicted on individual Armenian women:

Ninevah whose breasts were sliced when she tried to rebel.

Palmyra who leapt in the river to escape but she could not swim.

Haran who leapt in the river because she could not swim.

Carchemish whose baby was ripped from her arms and flung
    into the river.

Gurgum whose baby's skull was crushed with a rock.

Tyre who dropped her baby into a well.

Tirqa who jumped into the well herself.

Damascus who came back from the well because it was full and
    hanged herself instead.

Antioch who was clubbed to death.

Ugarit who was ripped to death.

Sidon who starved to death.

Mari who smeared her hair with shit but he raped and killed her
    just the same.

Asshur who when her last child was slaughtered and someone
    tried to offer her comfort turned and said, *"Don't you see,
    don't you understand, God has gone mad, He wants to drink our
    blood"* (74).

Here, like Weems in *The Hampton Project* (see chapter 6), Najarian offers his version of a sorrow song, a song of lamentation and remembrance. All of the women's bodies are "naked but they are not nudes" (74). Their contorted limbs testify to atrocity, not beauty. Even art cannot elevate their degradation. Similarly, the land itself is no longer a landscape but a memorial of death, "each wrinkle in the map a valley of screams" (74).

**Return**

Zeke's lifelong longing; his desire for beauty, women, and art; his desire to gain wholeness through physical and psychic union; and his desire to know his past lead him to return to his mother's homeland. When he arrives in Turkey, the people are welcoming and stare back at him "like innocent models" (130). An awareness of history, particularly knowledge of the Armenian massacre, is absent. "They heard of the past but it was not theirs, it was erased from their history books" (130). He visits Boghos and Boghos's Muslim neighbor, Gambar, both born during the genocide and now living together in peace, quite unaware of their own local history. Pondering similarities between Boghos and Gambar, Zeke muses: "Another story, another knot in the tapestry of everyone killed or gone to Fresno or Shanghai, the great scythe scattering big noses across the continents" (135). Not surprisingly, when he finally discovers his mother's *aki*, "the acre was now a suburb of tickytacks and the little shack a gasoline pump, the grapes a *Coca-Cola* sign and the donkey making way for U.S. Army trucks" (141). In the former Armenian quarter of the ancient city of Diyarbakir, where his grandfather was born, he ponders how he can paint "the never-ending saga of mythical kin," each place a site of loss of those beheaded, gutted, starved, or raped, "the terror of history impossible to draw, all drawing a transformation and every suffering doomed to become art" (140).

As the narrator reflects on the pointlessness of return to his mother's land now that it has been transformed into contemporary commercial squalor, he decides that there was "no point in anything, every point became a line and every line led to another. There was nothing and yet it moved, a line reaching into the void like a boy fishing on a bridge" (141). He imagines himself the boy and his pencil "now a fishing pole" seeking within the depth and waiting. "He would lose his fish in the river and he would keep casting his line to catch it again" (142). Would the process of drawing, writing, fishing, and (given the fact that he often links his pencil or paintbrush to his penis) having sex "make him whole, would each line help him?" (142) is the question he leaves with the reader.

Given the all-encompassing tone of loss and nostalgia throughout, it is somewhat surprising that Najarian concludes on an ironic and humorous note. Fittingly, the chorus of elderly Armenian women has the final word:

I'll talk with you in the morning

If I'm still alive.

If you're not alive you can tell me in my dreams.

Listen to these two.

They think they're funny.

We are funny.

Death is not funny.

I can make it funny if I want to make it funny.

I don't care what it is.

I still got some life left. My passport made me three years older
than I really am.

When your time comes you can say your passport is wrong.

. . . . . . . . . . . . . . . . . . .

Do you have any yoghurt starter? My yoghurt is all worn out.

I have fresh yoghurt at home. I'll tell my granddaughter to bring
you some.

. . . . . . . . . . . . . . . . . . .

Is she back in school?

Yes, she decided to go back.

What is she studying?

Life, she says she's studying life.

What do you mean she's studying life?

That's what she told me, she said she was studying life sciences.

Is there any money in that kind of subject?

There's money in everything.

Not in raisins. There's no money in raisins anymore.

You wait, in a few years there'll be money in raisins again too.
(157)

And below the lively bantering of the old women is a final drawing
(fig. 1.4). Najarian's (almost) final image—the final drawing in the story
itself—serves as a playfully ironic coda. The titles of the three books
identify shaping influences for the writer-artist as well as key themes.
*The Burro* by Frank Brookshier, a book that Najarian checked out of the
library and used to draw the illustrations on pages 30, 59, and 156 of
*Daughters of Memory*, offers a substantial history of the donkey through-

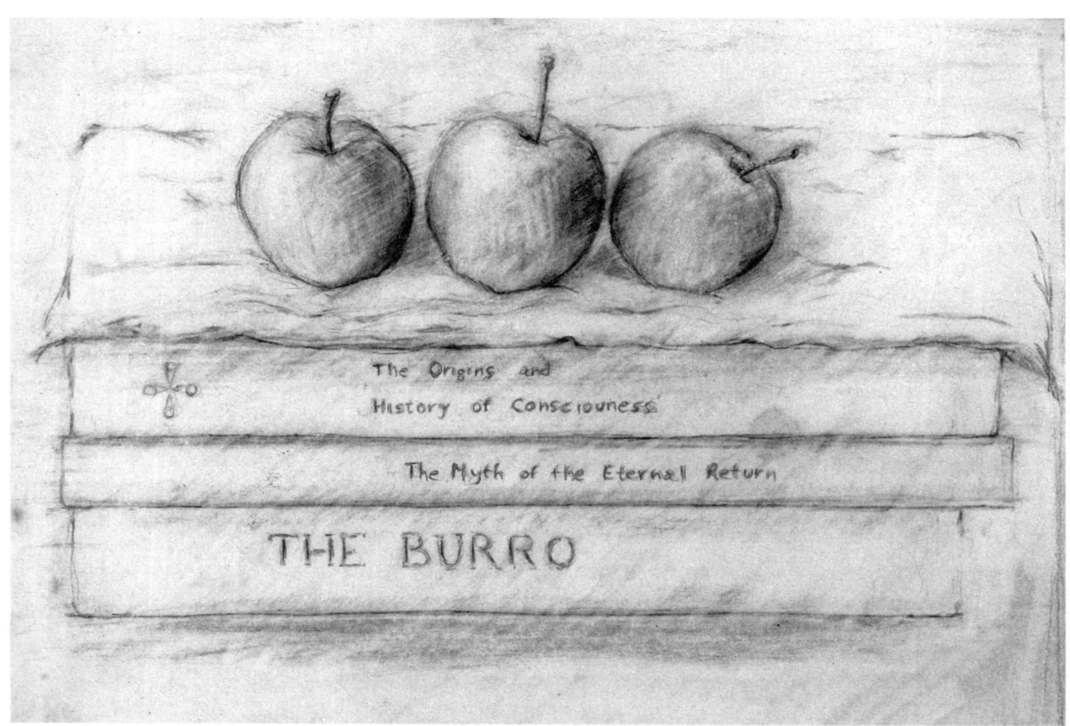



FIGURE 1.4.
Peter Najarian.
*Books and Apples*
(*Daughters of
Memory*, 1986, 157).
(Courtesy of
Peter Najarian.)

out the ages. More importantly, the burro is a recurring image of his mother's pre-American life. Najarian's mother's childhood donkey was important for her throughout her life, a mnemonic device for triggering memories of her family and homeland. For Najarian the burro is crucial because of its significance to his mother and his family history but also for its association with *The Metamorphoses of Apuleius*, an ancient Roman novel that Saint Augustine called *The Golden Ass*. In this collection of picaresque stories, the protagonist, Lucius, is transformed into an ass and has many educational adventures before he returns to human form. But it is German Jungian psychologist Erich Neumann's analysis of the psychology of the feminine in the story of Amor and Psyche (found in books 4–6 of *The Golden Ass*) that was particularly influential for Najarian. This sense of the feminine linked to an ideal form appears in Najarian's depictions of his mother, the women in his life, and a feminized art.

On *The Burro* sit two other influential books: *The Myth of Eternal Return* and *The Origins and History of Consciousness*, both clearly related to Zeke's search for a self, a history, and a home. These references reveal some of the source material for Najarian's illustrated memoir. In *The Myth of Eternal Return: Or, Cosmos and History*, published in 1954, historian of religion Mircea Eliade argues for the importance of a return to the mythic, a return to origins where, he says, the power of a thing exists. He develops the concept of sacred and profane space and time. The mythical

     Literature-Based Image-and-Text Forms

age is associated with the sacred that gives meaning to everyday life; the sacred can intersect with mundane life, allowing humans access to it. Erich Neumann's *Origins and History of Consciousness* (1949) was translated into English in 1954. Studying ancient cultures throughout the world as well as patients from his own practice, Neumann formulates the idea that the individual ego emerges from undifferentiated unconsciousness, often symbolized as the Ouroboros, the tail-eating snake. As the ego emerges, it experiences primordial (un)consciousness in two opposing ways: as a life-giving origin and as a threat to its emerging autonomy. This conflicted experience appears in the form of the Great Mother, who contains both life and death. For genuine freedom and independence, Neumann concludes, the individual ego must wrest itself free of the Great Mother's control. There are two stages to this process: (1) separation into male and female opposites, and (2) the ego associating itself with the masculine and going on a hero's journey to free itself from the mother's domination.

Throughout *Daughters of Memory* and in his other books, Najarian invokes the myth of the eternal return in his desire to return to origins (particularly Armenia and his murdered ancestors), origins that he perceives as powerfully self-defining. One way he attempts this return is through experience of the ideal forms of this world, forms that for him include art and women. Just as important are the mythic and Jungian references to the Ouroboros — an image Najarian invokes in the prefatory materials — and the Great Mother, who permeates his story literally in the fleshy form of his mother and mythically in his mother's connection to a near mythic past. Najarian, the "mama's boy," figures himself as Attis, the son and lover of Cybele, the Great Mother. Just as Attis is about to wed the king's daughter, Cybele appears in her breathtaking splendor, and Attis castrates himself to become a priest of the Universal Mother. Zeke's identification as a male hero ready to go on a self-fashioning quest, always seeking to escape his mother's suffocating embrace, yet desiring it at the same time, is derived directly from Neumann.[13] Atop the three books are three apples, associated with the biblical fall from Eden — the fall and the consequent exile the price of knowledge. Zeke longs to end his exile and return to an Edenic state that is linked in his imagination to the Armenia of his mother's past and his own ancestral origins.


### The Great American Loneliness

Najarian dedicates his fourth book, *The Great American Loneliness* (1999), to his friends. It is a more conventional and explicitly autobiographical narrative in which he focuses on his own experiences, particularly noting his travels and literary influences. The cover advertises the book as an "autobiography in the form of short narratives written between the Seventies and the Nineties, its central theme the journey of an artist in the middle of his life where the way is sometimes lost."

Another collection of vignettes, this time in dialogue with drawings and paintings, *The Great American Loneliness* can be divided into three sections. The first four chapters-stories and the last four chapters serve as a frame for the center of the book: three stories, entitled "The Girl I," "The Girl II," and "The Girl III," ostensibly about encounters with women, and my focus here.[14] In "The Girl I," Najarian links the act of lovemaking with the act of looking at art. He begins by contrasting his experience with two prostitutes in Holland. The first is the sensuous Tanya, "a gentle nurse in a sea world" (67), with whom he shares tender lovemaking and a connection that goes beyond the context of sex for hire. The second is a nameless "business woman who would use her body like a tool she would polish and sharpen" (67). When he leaves Tanya, he is well aware that he could not "reconcile her misery with his peace" (57). When he returns to find her again, Tanya has disappeared; and he settles for a nameless and soulless prostitute whose perfect body is trained for mechanical pleasure. Unlike his experience with Tanya, this unfulfilling encounter does not satiate his longing to be held and touched but instead leaves him meditating on death.

More than lust for women, his real desire is for art. Since for Najarian, art is female, he often sexualizes the act of looking at art. In the time between his two sexual encounters, he visits an art museum that he enters as if it were a holy temple or a beautiful woman. As he ascended the stairs, "he climbed into his life of art and all the years he was her monk who wanted to see her naked" (62). He lingers over Vermeer's *Girl with the Pearl Earring.* "Here she was," he writes, "the girl of his dream who embraced him into radiance and disappeared when he woke, his day becoming night" (63). *"Let me in . . . you in the radiance behind the window I can never penetrate. . . .* She would answer, *I am the girl in the distance you can never approach, I am the pearl beyond reach"* (63). He wishes not only to "penetrate" Vermeer's girl with the pearl earring but to enter the painting itself: "Millimeter by millimeter he crawled through the cracked pigment as if he were Vermeer himself. . . . Century by century he crawled across her figure" (64), noting each stroke, influence, and pigment as well as the labor behind them. Just as his sexual pleasure with prostitutes or lovers can never be sustained, his fulfillment from art can never be complete. There is always another line or shade or color or texture to apprehend, to penetrate with his gaze. In fact, that is the continual draw—the pull, again and again, to try to locate and hold onto the source of the beautiful female mystery of art that will outlive him.

     Literature-Based Image-and-Text Forms

In "The Girl II," Najarian's autobiographical persona travels to Soviet Armenia on a Fulbright fellowship. There he takes up with a prostitute named Sirpuhi, meaning Saint or Holy in Armenian. He divides his time between the art institute and Sirpuhi—between art and woman (fig. 1.5). A survivor, Sirpuhi comes across as independent and honest. She asks the persona to marry her and take her to America. He refuses because he knows that she will leave him—a fact that she does not deny. Like his other female nudes, Sirpuhi is lovely and full-bodied.[15] Unlike many of his female nudes, however, Sirpuhi has a face, a face that resists abstraction. She sits, a reflective look on her countenance, as if pondering the limited possibilities of her world.

When an earthquake hits nearby Leninakan, the persona joins artist friends traveling into the mountains to take supplies and offer assistance to the victims. After days of digging and sifting, they locate a body: "They dug through the dust and hauled away the scraps of plaster and lathing and linoleum, then the one who had been searching for someone all his life was on his knees stretching into a jagged hole like into a secret and the hem of dress suddenly appears and an instant later a knee and a bicep. . . . She must have been about eleven or twelve, her leg emerging from the dust with an intimacy only the dead can offer" (82). Like his fleeting and fragmented moments of intimacy and memory, the girl's body comes into view in bits and pieces—"a knee," "a bicep." He feels a strong desire to touch her and to see her face, but his friend pulls him away when it is clear that it will take hours to lift the heavy beam that has crushed her torso. *"But I needed to see her face,"* he keeps repeating. That night, in his apartment, "the girl returned like a girl in a dream, her leg emerging from the dust and her arm beneath a broken stud" (84). But, like his grandmother's, the dead girl's face is never visible. Later, he returns to help the international teams who had arrived to dig out more dead bodies, feeling the communion of shared labor and of an enhanced awareness of the precious vulnerability of life.

While "The Girl I" and "The Girl II" are about real women and art, "The Girl III" is about a feminized landscape: land and home. Spring has arrived and Najarian's cousin Migurdich leads him on hikes into beautiful Armenian landscapes. When Migurdich asks him to stay, the narrator declines the invitation, explaining: "'I'm not at home wherever I go'" (93). Later, back in Yerevan, the autobiographical persona witnesses the annual remembrance of the Armenian Genocide. In April, "the anniversary of the genocide" (94), a father slaughters a lamb and with the lamb's blood paints a cross on his son's forehead. To commemorate the genocide, people walk to the river and then to "the fire on the hill, but he, whose father's brothers had their necks sliced like a lamb's, waited until sundown after the crowd was gone" (95). Once again, the persona

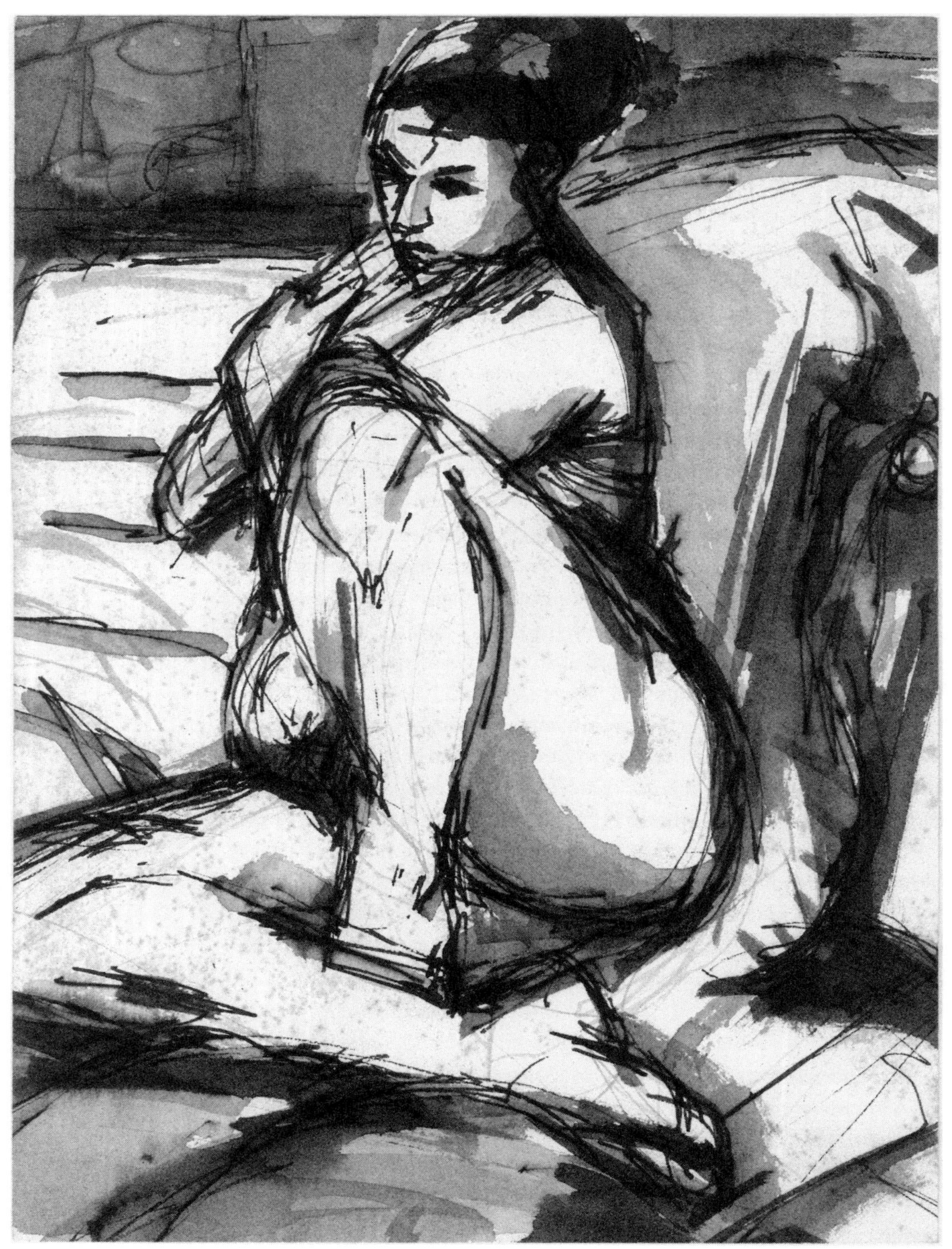

expands his personal (Armenian American) experience to link to others: "It was a walk like those in Belle Isle by the Detroit River and by the Thames and the Tiber and the Tigris and the Ganges, his voice speaking to a void as if it were a girl in a vision whose face was always hidden. Now at least he had touched her leg" (95).

At this point, Najarian's journey becomes increasingly psychological. As he walks over the bridge into the woods, it is as if the trees "were the nightmares of a Nazi and a Turk each hungry for blood" (95). This is the first time that Najarian links explicitly the Armenian Genocide and the Jewish Holocaust. Surprisingly, he imagines an empathetic identification with the oppressors: "He was Nazi and Turk who climbed into the knots of his own hatred, his eyes tight with vengeance and his throat locked by a scream he could not let go . . . until each knot was untied and the scream exploded like the mushrocm of a holocaust" (96). Like Dante's poetic persona in *The Divine Comedy* finding himself in "a dark wood where the straight way is lost" (*Inferno*, canto 1), Najarian descends into a terrifying underworld or wild wood where he must face his demons. He enters the "knots of his own hatred," an animosity no less than that of murderous Nazis and Turks. He must untie his own knots, must face not merely his own pain but that passed on from all his slaughtered ancestors. Finally, he arrives at the site of the deepest wound that holds "grief and more grief" (96). There the "fury" and the very self disappear, and all that remains is "just the breeze and his muscles stretching to embrace the nearest tree" (96). As he hugs the tree—the tree associated with murderous Nazis and Turks, he experiences a Whitman-esque union with nature: he "cried the crying of the ages," "hugging the tree until the crying left him limp upon a shore by the shipwreck of his life" (97). Just as his sexual unions with women result in release and momentary peace, his intense union with nature leaves him spent, "limp," purified, at least momentarily, of his loneliness and grief. When he awakens, "everywhere was fresh and clear as if he were a child again" (97). Finally, he walks to the monument where there is "the fire of those who died in 'The Great Hatred'" (97), ready to face the ghosts of his traumatized ancestors and the human capacity for evil.

Throughout the three "Girl" vignettes, Najarian's women are physical women with whom he has sex; idealized women whom he desires; art, which for him is feminine, that inspires eternal longing; and a feminized landscape that evokes nostalgia for his mother's lost and destroyed homeland. Surprisingly, woman as mother is not emphasized in this section, though she is the one who motivates the son to leave home, to seek an intimate union, to long for what has been lost.

Najarian begins the final section of the book with a reminiscence about his return to Adana, his mother's city, in Turkey. He stays only two days. Because his foot has been injured and because there are "high-rises and traffic," he never crosses the bridge over the Seyhan River into Adana. Similar to Theresa Cha's depiction in *Dictée* of the young girl who, never able to return home, waits on the threshold of home (see chapter 5) and consistent with Najarian's wounded autobiographical persona, who is unable to find happiness or a home and who cannot directly access his mother's experience, the persona is unable to do anything but bear witness from a distance. Instead of visiting the old homesite, like Cha, he visualizes cinematically; he imagines "a movie of the lost *aki* with [his] longing like a zoom":

> Here in my movie, are my mother's family and their donkey crossing the bridge, their figures silhouetted in the morning sun like a Daumier. She can't remember their faces, but she remembers her mother had red and freckled checks, and her father was a gentle man whose heels were cracked like hers are now. They were peasants like those of Daumier and Millet and Van Gogh and their clothes in earth tones and patches of primal color, the little Zaroohe and her younger brother in a donkey cart and the donkey's hooves clicking on the cobbles, the wheels creaking in counterpoint.[16] (100)

"But there was no cart" (100), corrects his mother. After this riff of imagination and his mother's rebuttal, the autobiographical persona realizes that he does not know how to paint a picture of his mother's childhood home. What kinds of wildflowers were there? Was there a church there yet or not? Repeatedly, his mother counters his imaginative vision. Like Art Spiegelman (see chapter 3), Najarian grasps for reliable information from his parent and encounters enormous lacunae that he attempts to fill. He imagines a tidy cabin where his mother's family lived; she explains that it was just a shack to store their few belongings. And what do the roads look like? And what kind of bedrolls? Wool or cotton? "You ask too many questions," his mother complains, "be glad I can remember this much" (102).

Now that his mother is ninety years old, the autobiographical persona visits her once every three weeks, taking his laundry with him. "'That's disgusting,' a friend tells him, "'a man your age taking laundry to his ninety year old mother'" (155). But he has made his peace with his mother, her love for him, and his love for her. And when he arrives, as he did as a child—"the archetypal momma's boy" (Janigian n.p.), Attis devoted to Cybele—he sits, paying rapt attention to "her tales that go back as far as she can remember" (160). At this point, he presents two drawings of his mother (fig. 1.6). Placement of the elderly mother on the

Nevertheless she feels a little guilty now and tries to correct herself. "So tell me," she will say, "how are things with you?" "Well," I start to say, "I. . . ." But before I can finish she says like a child, "I had a wonderful week, did you see my fava beans, how they sprouted so well?" I let her continue. She's alone even more than I and has so much she wants to tell me. As I've done since I was a baby I sit like an audience for her tales that go back as far as she can remember.

Alas, it is not far enough and she can't remember her own mother's face before the death march. She can remember her mother working hard like herself, but the face remains a blur, and it is this blur that feels like the word *mother* itself.

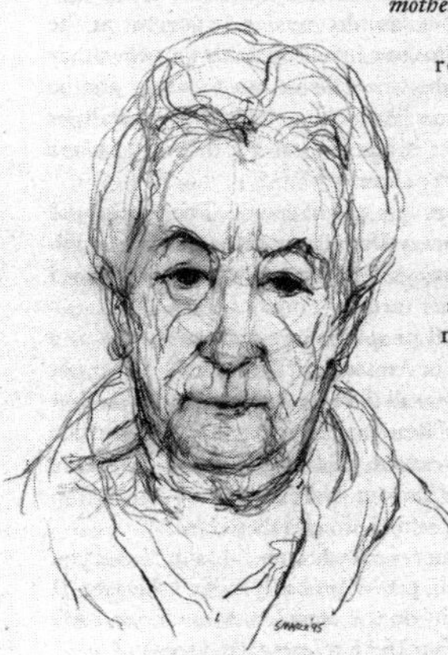

*Mother*: what does it really mean? How revolted I would feel when women used it with pride and selfhood. Like an old male who lost the rut to win a mate and must wander alone, I recoiled at so many females carrying bellies like an insect queen and then squirting into this fallen realm more I's for an

endless longing. Nor was my own mother pardoned from this horror where she was just another uterus for misery and death.

Yet the more my love deepens the less she is *mother* than simply Z, and with her I might learn what the word really means. She, however, knows herself only as a mother. As I became an artist, so too she must have become a mother when she was just a barefoot orphan on her own path through life, as if in needing a mother she had to become one herself. It was her way of joining life and it seems to have worked well regarding my brother who had a family of his own, but with me it feels different.

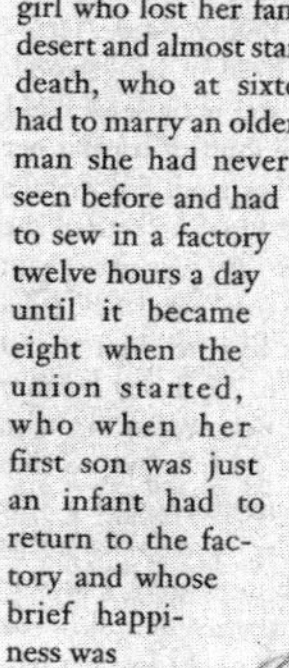
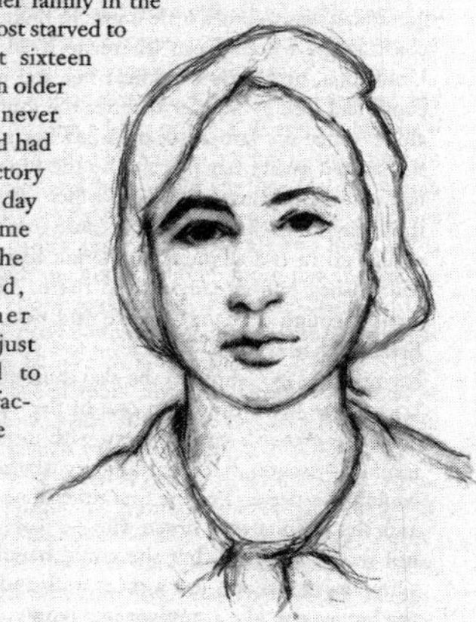

I used to think how much better off I was than the poor girl who lost her family in the desert and almost starved to death, who at sixteen had to marry an older man she had never seen before and had to sew in a factory twelve hours a day until it became eight when the union started, who when her first son was just an infant had to return to the factory and whose brief happiness was



left-hand page and the young fifteen-year-old Zaroohe, sketched from her passport photo as she is about to immigrate, on the right-hand page demands a comparison of now and then. Both women wear a thoughtful, even sad, expression. The text-history comes between them, partially framing them both. The text, then, is both obstacle — the long and tragic history that both links and separates the young and old Zaroohe — and the unifying frame for the images that brings both temporal versions of the woman into relation. The image-text telescopes time and place to offer a glimpse of Zaroohe's historically situated subjectivity. In the text, her amanuensis son reflects on the meaning of "Mother." Her son remembers her stories, the power of her life and strength imbued in him, despite his father's stroke, which left him unable to move or talk:

> I went down the cliffs to the barges on the river like a little
> Wordsworth encountering the deep as if it were alive, always self-
> indulgent and fearless because come dinnertime I could always
> go home and the food would be warm on the table and the sheets
> would be clean, I could go anywhere I wanted and do whatever

FIGURE 1.6. Peter Najarian. *Ma, Old and Young* (*The Great American Loneliness*, 1999, 160–61). (Courtesy of Peter Najarian.)

> I wanted because I had a strong mother who never said no. . . .
> And I stayed that way for the rest of my life, always wandering
> and searching and longing, yet what was I longing for but the
> very warmth back there by her side? (167)

It is tempting to read the power of the autobiographical persona's mother over him psychoanalytically: she was an abandoning mother who had to work long hours, leaving her son to fend for himself; she was a needy mother who, after her husband's early death, clings to her son; or she was a suffocating mother who spoiled her son by anticipating his every need—each of these resulting in his insecurity, dependence, and unhappiness. While any of these (or some combination of them) may be true, it is more important to note that, in Armenian diasporic literature, the mother is often associated with Armenia—a lost motherland to which one longs to return, as a child longs to hold onto a mother from whom he has not fully individuated. The son's lifelong inability to detach from his mother suggests his unwillingness to let go of an Armenian country, language, and identity.[17]

Later, as his mother is dying, Najarian expands the concept of "Mother":

> "Ma!" I cried as a little girl once cried in a desert, 'Ma! Ma,'
> as in the *mah* that meant death in Armenian and Ma as in
> Michelangelo's last Pieta where a crippled Christ returned to
> stone, Ma that was beyond any breasts or vulva and or a feminist
> selfhood about nature and the earth, Ma that had no gender or
> form but was the void that would be plenitude by letting go. Let
> go, let go, it said, don't be afraid, there will be light at the end of
> the darkness like a warm dinner for a boy back from adventuring.
> (169)

Linking his fear of losing his mother to his mother's loss of her mother in the Syrian desert—where she cried "Ma!" (Mother!) as the Turkish soldier was taking her away—Najarian repeats the cry for Ma/Mother but links "Ma" to the Armenian homophone *Mah* (Death). The autobiographical persona describes his mother as death, transcendent—"beyond any breasts or vulva," beyond any feminist concepts linking woman to earth, beyond sex—"no gender or form." As a second-generation survivor of the Armenian Genocide, Najarian has always associated his mother with death and also with homeland. By the end of this passage, Mother becomes "the void," Nisargadatta's vast expanse from which all arise and to which all return. So the autobiographical persona returns to the warmth of his mother's body—a final (imaginative) merging with woman, womb, death, nature, and Armenia—come to fruition in art.

     Literature-Based Image-and-Text Forms

## The Artist and His Mother

In *The Artist and His Mother* (2010), Najarian gives up the pretext of writing fiction and writes full-blown autobiography, which he prefers to describe as "creative non-fiction in the form of a novel."[18] Both the title and the painting process are taken from the Armenian American painter Arshile Gorky's painting *The Artist and His Mother* (1926).[19] In this painting, which Gorky created referring to an old photograph of his mother and himself, the son stands behind and to the left of his stately, seated mother. This is the inspiration for Najarian's choice to make a painting based on an old photograph of his mother and himself and to use both the title and the painting on the cover of his book. In Najarian's painting, his child persona sits on the floor at the feet of his larger-than-life mother seated on a chair behind him.

A full-page photograph preceding the title page shows Najarian's family—mother, father, older brother, and baby Peter (fig. 1.7). The working-class family stands in front of laundry hanging on a clothesline that appears to be on top of an apartment building. Father holds baby Peter in his right arm and rests his left hand protectively on Tom's shoulder. Mother holds her hands in front of her at her waist. Mother and Tom smile broadly at the photographer. Father looks into the camera. Only baby Peter looks down, frowning, perhaps contemplating big thoughts, prefiguring a lifetime of seeking.

Just as important as the figures in the photograph are those not shown. Vahan, Tom's father and Zaroohe's first husband, is absent. Two years from now Peter's father, Armenag, will have suffered a stroke that leaves him unable to move or speak for the last seven years of his life. Of course, like the Holocaust photographs described by Marianne Hirsch that document indirectly who is missing from the family photograph, the mass carnage of their relatives killed during the Armenian Genocide can be filled in only by memory.[20]

Like *Daughters of Memory* and *The Great American Loneliness*, *The Artist and His Mother* is a collection of vignettes. Whereas the assemblage of scenes seems somewhat haphazard in *The Great American Loneliness*, in *The Artist and His Mother* the memories and scenes cohere more organically. Dedicated to his "Uncle Boghos, who disappeared on the death march," *The Artist and His Mother*, for the most part, highlights Najarian's relationship with his mother, particularly documenting her lengthy illness and death. Throughout he provides more genealogy and less fiction. Part One consists of three chapters—"The Artist's Mother," "The Ayki," and "America"—reprinted from *The Great American Loneliness*, although now they provide an introduction to and overview of family history and a counterpoint to an entirely new set of images, including

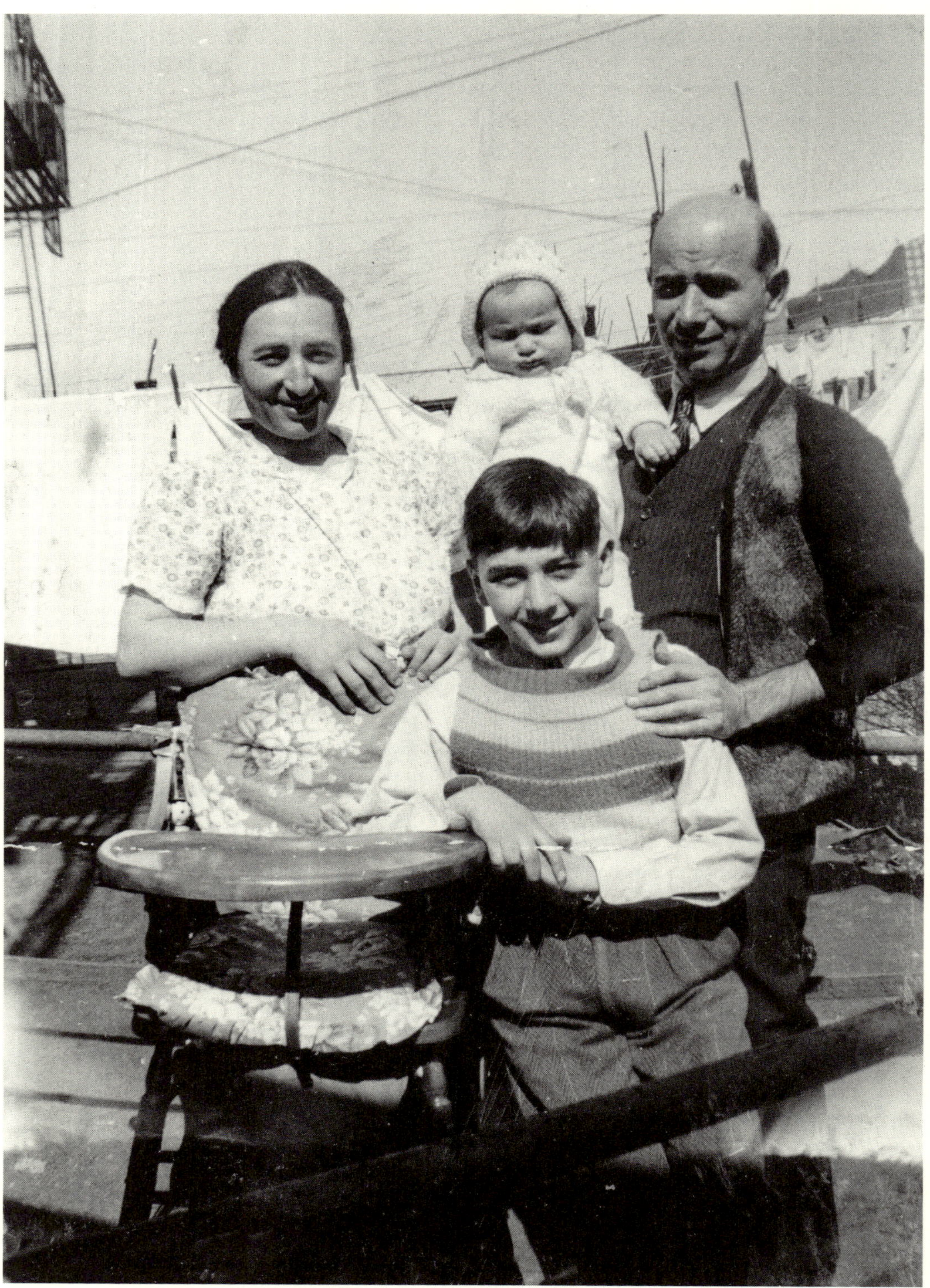

drawings, paintings, and family photographs. The paintings are Berkeley landscapes and self-portraits, but some are inspired by family photographs. As is well documented, photography extends the life of people or objects frozen in discrete moments, but it is also shaped by, even as it shapes, reality.[21] Najarian simultaneously represents and constructs his reality through his drawings, paintings, and photographs. Najarian features one painting of his father (fig. 1.8), who was for him a shadowy, almost absent, presence after his stroke. Entitled *The Artist's Father* but subsumed into a work focused on his mother, Najarian depicts his pre-stroke father holding him in his lap. Echoing Gorky's painting, this painting is inspired by a photograph taken by Najarian's then twelve-year-old brother. The light coming in through the window on the left illuminates two-thirds of his father's face and half of the face of young Peter sitting on his lap. His father's large hands hold the toddler gently. While his father smiles into the camera, Peter's face is half lost in shadows. Just as he interviews his mother and other survivors to research the past, Najarian examines old photographs, looking for a trace of who his father had been. He takes the purported visual evidence of the photograph and reimagines it with paint on a canvas, translating a supposedly mechanical representation into art.

Throughout Part Two, Najarian weaves the distant past into the present. He juxtaposes his memories of his mother's memories—fleeing the Armenian Genocide, going hungry in the orphanage, immigrating to the United States, working in the sewing factory, marrying and divorcing her first husband (the older brother's, Tom's, father), marrying a second time for love (Najarian's father)—with his own memories: growing up in New Jersey; trying to relate to his older brother, who, though also artistic, settled for a union job, a family, and a house in the suburbs; traveling to Turkey; driving from Berkeley to Fresno to visit his ailing mother in the nursing home. Weaving together the past and present underscores the vitality of his mother's stories and how they center the family. In addition, Najarian models the processes of gathering and sorting memories and composing autobiographical narrative.

Najarian's most consistent linear story concerns his mother's slow diminishment and death. The vivacious, talkative, robust mother—who tells stories, gardens, cooks, and cleans—experiences a series of illnesses and accidents that, bit by bit, weaken her. Five years before she died, she was "beyond memory," the result of a series of small strokes, though she remained lucid enough to recognize her sons. Throughout his autobiographical narrative, Najarian's drawings document her demise. "I follow her lines and wrinkles as if they are the map of her life," he reports. "More than ever she is part of the world I longed to embrace and I draw as if it is not only her face but a landscape in *plein air*" (62).

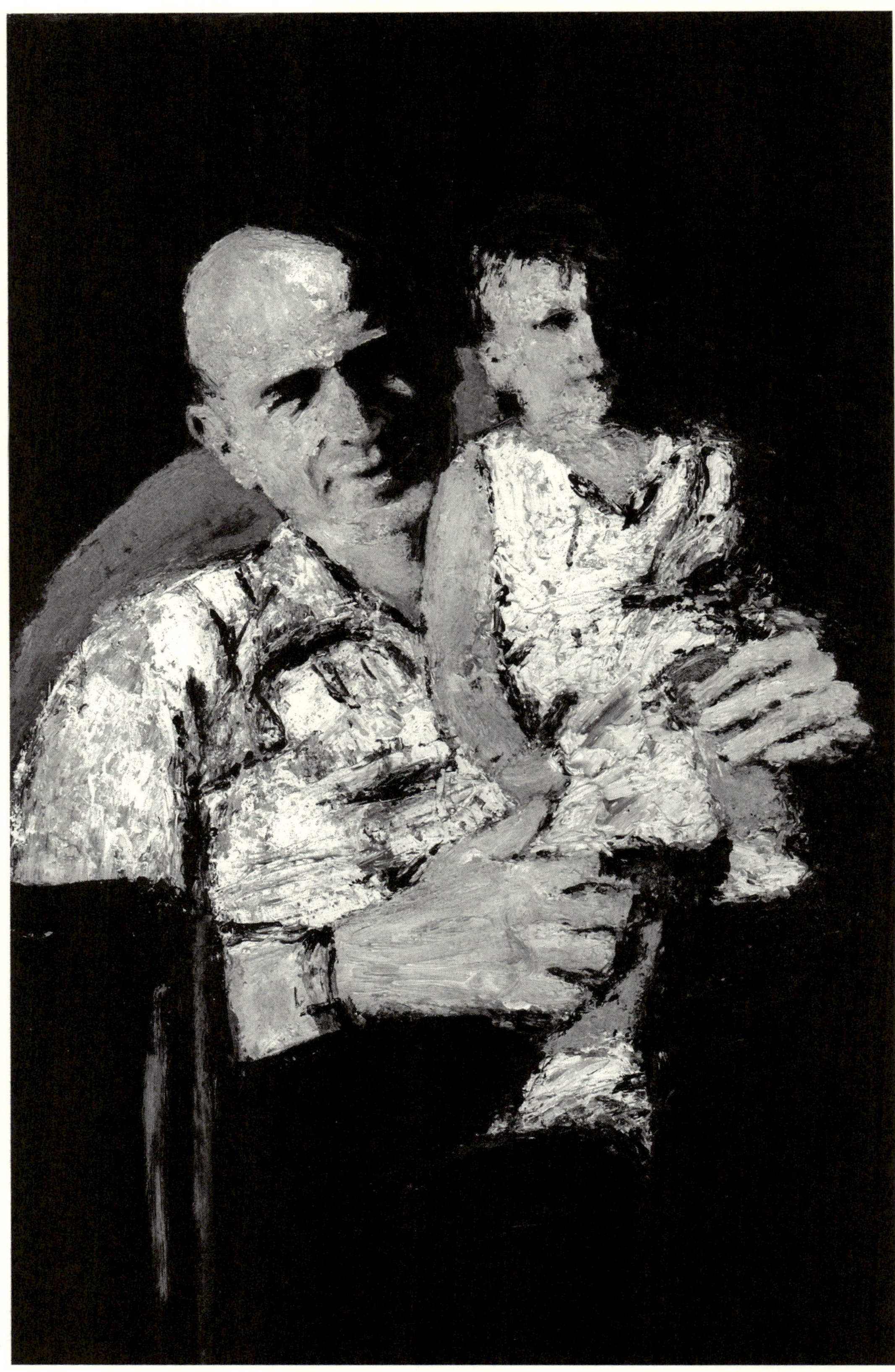

Once again, Najarian associates his mother's body with a physical landscape—Armenia, New Jersey, California—and a historical landscape of suffering and loss.

Every time he visits his mother in the nursing home, he draws her in almost the same pose. In each dated drawing, she looks at him from her bed. Although his drawings are not organized chronologically, they convey an overall sense of slow deterioration. The sketch that introduces Part Two is the template for all the others (fig. 1.9). In this drawing, dated September 3, 2005, Saturday, 2:00 p.m., Najarian's mother's head lies on a pillow; her right hand rests on her chest; and she looks out at him from her bed. Without her dentures, her lips are sunken. Wrinkles abound. Her expression is sad and her dark eyes stare through her son, or perhaps into the past or the void.

In another drawing, dated January 8, 2005, Monday, 8:00 a.m., Najarian provides a close-up (fig. 1.10). The pillow and bed disappear, but his mother's head and arm are in the same position as they are the preceding illustration. The strong lines and the deep shading on the lower two-thirds of her face, which is shaped like a heart, suggest dissolution and decay. The lines are also more broken, as if conveying her continued disintegration.

The "last drawing" Najarian made of his mother was on March 3, 2006, on Saturday, 3:00 p.m. (fig. 1.11). Here Najarian tilts the angle to the right slightly so that although his mother is in bed, a pillow and blanket suggested by a few lines, she seems to be sitting up. The lines, though dark, are thin and often short, degenerating into tiny scribbles, dashes, and dots. It is as if Najarian is trying to capture the process of his mother's deterioration at the level of the line.[22] The ink recedes into the paper, just as his mother's remains will break down and be absorbed into the earth. Najarian compares his mother to "an old plant with only a leaf still alive while the rest of her rotted and returned to the earth" (154). As he drives through the hills between Berkeley and Fresno, he muses that "the valley and her body grew more and more alike, the lines of my pencil probing her wrinkles as if they were the hills and fields I longed to embrace" (154).

As he struggles to produce the lines to capture his mother (and by association—beauty, love, death) in both drawings and sentences, Najarian comments on how his mother's sewing was her creativity with lines. When he hears news of his mother's death, the tears flow, "especially now," he says, "as I try to sew these sentences like you once sat at your machine with your fingers fluttering line by line" (181).

Although she lacked a formal education, Zaroohe was wise about life and about life writing. *"If you write a book about me,"* his mother "once said before her fall, *'you won't be able to end it'"* (136, emphasis in

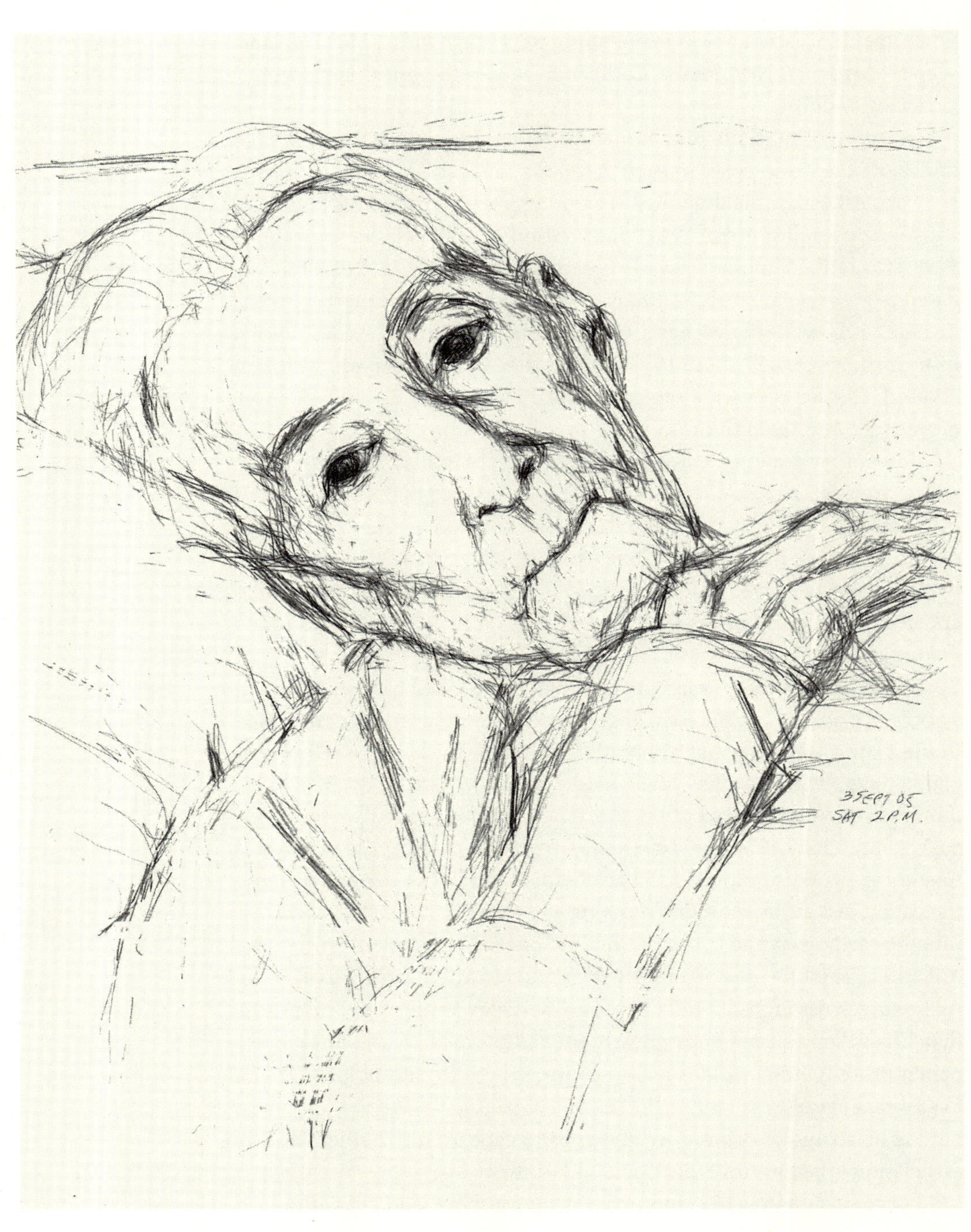
3 SEPT 05
SAT 2 P.M.

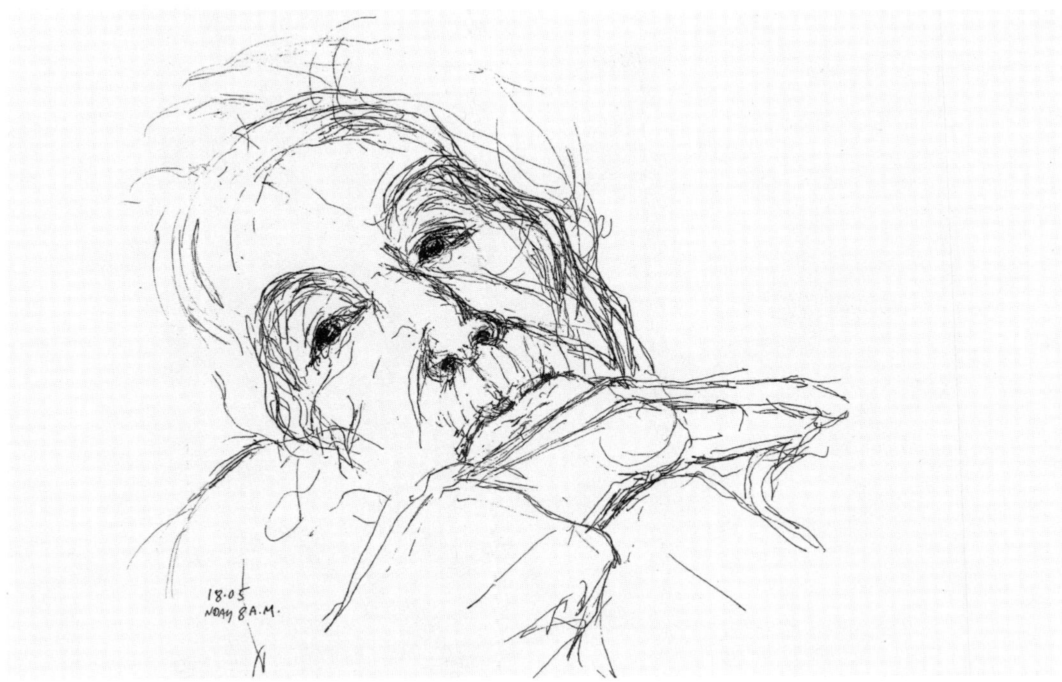

original). Where does one's story end? With death. But we live in each other's stories as much as in our own. Her son now carries her stories; for him her story lives on. And as was true when she lived, the son still cannot let go. Although logically the book would end with his mother's death, the narrator forestalls the news by inserting a long chapter, "The Artist and His Dog," in which he describes the heartbreaking process of euthanizing his beloved dog Keiko. At first, the inclusion of this chapter seems inappropriate, deflecting the narrative from its conclusion and redirecting attention from his mother's slow and tortuous death to Keiko's peaceful one. Najarian uses it as an opportunity to contrast the repellent "American way of death"—prolonging life even though the result is a kind of living death or, worse yet, suffering. Although he provided a dignified conclusion to Keiko's life, he could not offer his mother the same departure.

As we will see throughout this book, most of these autobiographers struggle to bring their life stories to closure. After narrating Keiko's death, Najarian presents a serial nonconclusion to his mother's story. In a sequence of six letters, he reports rather than narrates. The first letter, addressed to "Mah" (Death), is embellished with lush descriptions of nature that soften his awareness of his mother's imminent death. This time her departure would be final. He and his brother discuss funeral arrangements. The next five letters are addressed to "Ma" (Mother). In the first, Tom calls to inform him that their mother has died. The persona

(OPPOSITE)
FIGURE 1.9.
Peter Najarian.
*Najarian's Mother,
September 3, 2005*
(*The Artist and His
Mother,* 2010, 42).
(Courtesy of
Peter Najarian.)

(ABOVE)
FIGURE 1.10.
Peter Najarian.
*Najarian's Mother,
January 8, 2005*
(*The Artist and His
Mother,* 2010, 52).
(Courtesy of
Peter Najarian.)

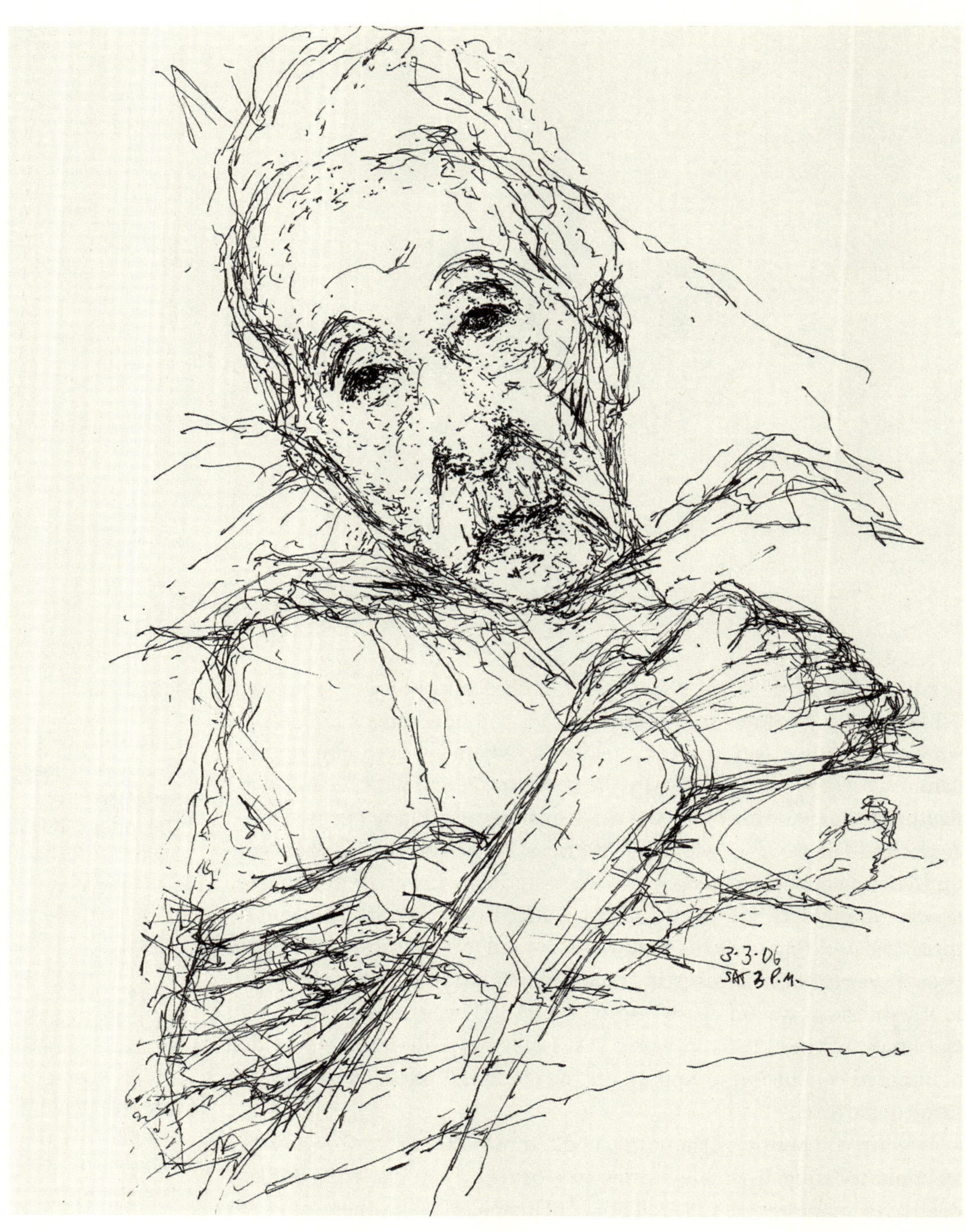

3.3.06
SAT 3 P.M.

ponders his last memory of her and his disappointment that he was not with her at her death. In the next two letters, he rails against the American death industry, ponders his mother's religious beliefs, describes the funeral and the family's *"hokee-jash*, the soul meal," that follows, and muses about future generations of Najarians—his brother's children.

An afterword contains two final letters. Two years after his mother's burial, he is still writing to her. He tells her all about this book he has written. He asks for her guidance because the "memories endure like radio waves that float through the galaxies, but my little talent is not enough to gather from the air a line that can hold them" (195). Najarian's lines, of course, are in both writing and drawing. "Dear Ma," he writes, "You are death now as you had once been life and the lessons they are the same" (196). "Death," he concludes, "is the mother of all writing . . . we write and paint to a page and canvas as if they are a void we seek to fill with plenitude" (197). As he drives from Fresno to Berkeley, he makes his usual stop at an almond orchard to urinate. He finds that "now it was an empty field like the cemetery of [his mother's] grave" (196). Mother, death, and nature are all one—the tailing-eating snake that signifies the cycles of life—and each is a source of art.

The story is not over. Even though he sees how "a clan falls apart in the waves of massacre and the dissolution that follows in its wake" (193), even though the "massacre is almost as old as [his mother]" and still "its karma has yet to be cleaned" (190), Najarian concludes on a hopeful note. On his last trip from Fresno, when he "stopped for a leak at the old almond orchard, it was filled with new seedlings" (200). The drawing on the right-hand page shows his elderly, yet robust mother looking back into the pages of the book as if into her past. Only at the very end, after readers think that the story is over, does Najarian reveal himself in the form of a self-portrait. Finally, we see the man: the author, the son, the lover, the artist, the seeker.

Although Najarian's illustrated memoirs, "narrative in the realm of poesy," retain the conventional book form, they demand that readers-viewers both look and read in new ways. Najarian requires us to navigate the pages, moving from image to text, from text to image, from image to image, from textual images to drawn, painted, or photographic images. None of the images are labeled, a technique we will see again in the next chapter. The images are not merely illustrative or supportive of the narrative. Rather, they stand on their own, in a dialogic relation to the text. In his assemblage of text and images, Najarian grapples with the complex issues of representation, memory, history, and subjectivity. He examines historical and visual archives, making visible Armenian history, struggle, and survival, figuring personal narrative and refigur-




(OPPOSITE)
FIGURE 1.11.
Peter Najarian.
*Najarian's Mother,
Last Drawing* (*The
Artist and His
Mother*, 2010, 180).
(Courtesy of
Peter Najarian.)

ing historical narrative to nudge his readers-viewers into awareness and to illustrate how artistic processes and products might redeem "the web of rape and plunder." He returns to "the terror of [his] history" in order to attempt to get the facts right, to assess the continued influence of past atrocity on the present, and to seek at least temporary redemption through art.

# Leslie Marmon Silko's Photo-Narratives

## "A Story Connected with Every Place,<br>Every Object in the Landscape"

Leslie Marmon Silko creates autobiographical photo-texts—
narratives in book form in which words and photographs inform,
parallel, or contradict each other. The uncaptioned photographic
images float like memories and create "a part of the field of vision
for the reading of the text." Rather than overwhelm the image,
the words "depend upon the pictures for a subtle resonance."
("As a Child," *Yellow Woman and a Beauty of the Spirit* 169)

Like Peter Najarian, Laguna Pueblo writer-artist Leslie Marmon Silko
interweaves text and photographs in the service of self-narration. Rather
than focus on historical trauma, however, Silko emphasizes the interpenetration of past and present. In her photo-text autobiographies, Silko
moves back and forth between Western linear time and Pueblo cyclical
time and emphasizes the coexistence of past and future in the present
moment. Educated in the United States and raised at Laguna Pueblo,
about forty miles west of Albuquerque, New Mexico, Silko is schooled
not only in two distinct conceptions of time but in the process of negotiating between them. Silko's Pueblo sense of time is geocentric, focused
on natural cycles of the earth—seasons, meteorological patterns, and
geological processes. Silko's autobiographical persona is grounded in
specific places, and those places are temporalized. Time and place, then,
are interpenetrating.

"My interest in time," Silko explains, "comes from my childhood
with the old-time people" for whom "time was not a series of ticks of
a clock" but rather "round" with "specific moments and specific locations" ("Notes" 136). Silko elaborates on the traditional Pueblo notion of
time: "All times go on existing side by side for all eternity. No moment is
lost or destroyed. . . . The past and the future are the same because they
exist only in the present of our imaginations" (136–37). For the old-time
Pueblo people, time passes, one day succeeds another, one week follows another, but the "succession is cyclic" (137). In *The Turquoise Ledge*,
Silko's autobiographical account of family, indigenous, and geological
history, she explains: "I learned the world of the clock and calendar when

I started school, but I've never lost my sense of being alive without reference to clocks or calendars" (47). For Silko "nothing is lost, left behind, or destroyed. It is only changed" ("Notes" 137). This is the continuum, noted by historian of Maori art Ngarino Ellis, a nonlinear evocation of time notable in indigenous life writing, that "moves back and forth into and from the past and present" (440).

As well as embracing Pueblo cyclical time, Silko has come to believe in an ancient Mayan notion of time as "a living being" with "a personality, a sort of identity. Time was alive," she explains, "and might pass, but time did not die; moreover, the days and weeks eventually would return" ("Notes" 136). Of course, Silko does not naively deny the ravages of colonialism. Rather, she emphasizes a Pueblo epistemology that considers cycles of time on a grand geological scale. Throughout her work, Silko displays an acute awareness that despite the massive losses of the more than five hundred years since Europeans arrived, the Pueblo past is very much alive in the present. The ancestors "didn't go anywhere; they are still here, right now" (*Turquoise* 274)—most often in the form of stories embedded in specific places. The Pueblo people in the Southwest are "the descendants of the original natives of North America's vast southwest region" (Sando 1). Scholars estimate that Pueblo people have lived in the area continuously since "about ten thousand years before Christ" (Sando 1). Indigenous writers, artists, and scholars often need to explain how such a long history in a specific place results in a deep connection between time and place: "Here Indian people remain in their traditional homelands, and much that is vital in life remains as it was, timeless. Here is the oldest continuous record of human habitation on the continent outside of Mesoamerica, a habitation that has fashioned this region into a humanized landscape suffused with meanings, myths, and mysteries" (Ortiz 1). Storied places animate the past. Tribal elders, Silko concludes, appreciate "time as space, infinite generous space on the plane of being" (Bennett n.p.).

Cultural geographers, architects, anthropologists, philosophers, and feminists have written about conceptions of space. Often space and place, two related but distinct concepts, are conflated. Marxist geographers such as David Harvey and Edward Soja claim that "space is socially produced, but that space is also a condition of social production" (Rendell 101). That is, space shapes, and is shaped by, society. Similarly, Marxist philosopher and sociologist Henri Lefebvre seeks to dispel the "illusion of a transparent, 'pure' and neutral space" (292); he critiques "abstract space" as a "tool of domination" and favors the idea of "social space" that is constantly being redefined (370). Cultural geographer Yi-Fu Tuan, emphasizing the *embodied experience* of space—that is, how our human physical bodies are oriented to the world (upright, face forward,



Literature-Based Image-and-Text Forms

and so on)—distinguishes between space and place: "'Space' is more abstract than 'place.' What begins as undifferentiated space becomes place as we get to know it better and endow it with value" (6). Place, then, is space experienced and personalized.

"Landscape" is "place seen from a distance" and "place" is a "lived-in landscape" (Lippard, *Lure of the Local* 9). "Space," then, "defines landscape, where space combined with memory defines place" (Lippard 9). Silko herself has critiqued the term "landscape" because the word assumes that the viewer of the land is outside, distant from, rather than part of, the land. She and others, such as Alfonso Ortiz and Paula Gunn Allen, have explained how indigenous lands are mapped by stories—stories of personal and community experiences on the land (for instance, "That's the arroyo where Uncle Joe's car was swept away by a flashflood"); and myths—the foundational stories of a culture based on a history of interaction in a particular place (for example, "This is where Spider Woman encountered the Twins"). These temporally overlapping stories link Native people to the long ago and the here and now simultaneously.

In colonial discourse, Western concepts of abstract space have provided a rationale to fill and control so-called empty space (actually, often, the home places of indigenous people) with colonizers and settlers. Accompanying this, the idea of individual land ownership has been presented as a noble aspiration to be achieved by hard work, whereas indigenous notions of communality and connection to land have been denigrated as lazy, nonentrepreneurial, and communist. In addition, the history of European conquest and land confiscation in what is now the United States is based on the assumption of human, particularly male, dominance over the land and its resources. This idea, of course, is gendered in a patriarchal context, as feminist critic Annette Kolodny and others demonstrated in the 1970s.[1] Land is associated with the female; both land and woman are to be penetrated, subdued, and controlled.[2] In addition to its Western historical association with women, land is linked also to Native peoples. In colonial propaganda, all three—land, women, and indigenous people—are rendered passively desirable, available to be taken through seduction or force.[3]

Like many postcolonial, neocolonial, and marginalized peoples, Native writers and artists insist on the need to reconsider time and its fundamental connection to space-place on many levels: to retell history from Native perspectives, to make visible an indigenous presence in a contemporary global world, and to articulate a place-based subjectivity (in opposition to a colonizer-settler identity) that is grounded firmly in the present but has deep roots in the past and a stake in the future. As N. Scott Momaday says, the "events of one's life, take place, take *place*"

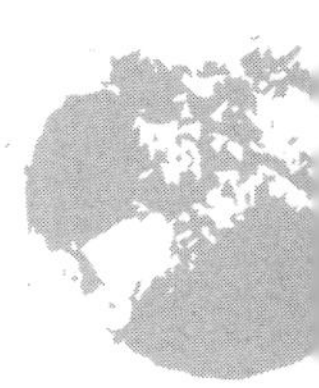

(*Names* 142, emphasis in original). For the Western Apaches, "wisdom sits in places"—all these places have stories and the places and stories together shape a Western Apache person's identity.[4] The stories are a kind of geohistorical and cultural map of self. Here I wish not to conflate distinct cultures and geographies but to reiterate that there is a link between place and subjectivity in many indigenous cultures. "Our stories cannot be separated from their geographical locations, from actual physical places on the land," insists Silko, "there is a story connected with every place, every object in the landscape" ("Language and Literature" 58). And those places trump any linear sense of time; the stories associated with specific places make visible and audible those who have gone before, bringing the departed ones into the consciousness of those in the present, resulting in a multitemporal matrix in which past and present intermingle.

Silko engages seriously with time and place in all of her writing. Her first novel, *Ceremony* (1976), blends the ancient past, the historical past, and the present as it enacts the central character Tayo's contemporary healing in ceremonial time. In *Almanac of the Dead* (1991), Silko remaps the past five hundred years of time and place, illustrating the horrific consequences of a world controlled by Destroyers—those who see the world as a dead thing—and amassing a haphazard army of the dispossessed at the southern border of the United States by the novel's conclusion. *Gardens in the Dunes* (1999) is a historical novel that animates the nineteenth-century experience of Indigo, a woman who struggles to reconcile how to live with both Native and white ways simultaneously. In *The Turquoise Ledge: A Memoir* (2010), Silko illustrates the relations among time, place, subjectivity, and story. She takes "readers along on her daily walks through the arroyos and ledges of the Sonoran Desert in Arizona" (*Turquoise* inside cover flap). Combining personal, family, and indigenous history, Silko animates stories of place by sharing word pictures of her experiences with the desert weather (cloud formations, storms, flash floods), the plant life (chaparral, saguaro, cholla, mesquite, jojoba, night-blooming cactus), the animal life (rattlesnakes, hummingbirds, bees, lizards, grasshoppers, macaws, javelinas), and the rocks and minerals (carnotite, quartzite, malachite, chrysocolla, and especially turquoise).[5] Silko's poetry and short fiction often allude to or retell ancient Pueblo stories in numerous, often contradictory iterations—just like the many tellings of the oral tradition in which a story changes from one generation to the next, one storyteller to the next, one audience to the next. My focus here is Silko's self-narration in image and text in two of her photo-text narratives: *Storyteller* and *Sacred Water*.

## *Storyteller*

In her hybrid autobiography, *Storyteller* (1981), Silko juxtaposes short stories, narrative poems, anecdotes, retellings of Laguna Pueblo myths, personal narratives, letters, and photographs. "Silko rejects European literary paradigms in favor of non-linear text and a blend of photo, sketch, verse, prayer, and anecdote with traditional chronicle" (Snodgrass 4). Like Najarian, whom we saw in chapter 1, Silko plays with the conventional relation between narrative and illustration. Both writers incorporate captionless photographs that float freely, sometimes informing or challenging the text, sometimes suggesting the process of gathering free-ranging memories. Like Julie Chen (see chapter 4), Silko experiments with what a book should be as well as with relations between image and text that require readers to learn new ways of reading. Like Chen, she spatializes time. Silko does not share explicit details of her life in *Storyteller*. Rather, she emphasizes the community, the land (which is inclusive of all time), and the stories as central aspects of individual subject formation, illustrating that individual identity is actually always collective identity.

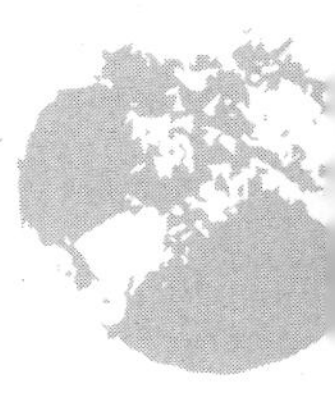

After the dedication and acknowledgments, Silko begins *Storyteller* by describing "a tall Hopi basket" that "holds hundreds of photographs taken since the 1890's around Laguna" (1). She includes the photographs "because they are part of many of the stories / and because many of the stories can be traced in the photographs" (1). From the very first page, then, Silko announces the reciprocity between image and story. In fact, the structure of *Storyteller* may be likened to reaching into the basket, pulling out a photograph, and narrating its story as well as the network of stories (and images) to which it is connected—a pre-family-photo-album collection of photographs that is nonlinear. Collagelike, time moves in multiple directions according to the photograph selected.

Silko is familiar with the history of ethnographic and photographic documentation—domination that has served as a powerful tool of colonization. She is well aware of the problems of objectification, commodification, detachment, and the "cannibalistic" nature of some photographic practices (Lippard, Introduction, *Partial Recall* 37)—for example, a photographic image in which the (often voyeuristic) photographer consumes his or her subject. Many photography theorists are seeking how to develop a reciprocal gaze or "how we might replace the regime of the gaze with the field of the look" (Hirsch, *Family Frames* 15). Silko envisions Native photography as countering predatory photography. In her essay "The Indian with a Camera," she reverses the view: "the Indian" is no longer the object of the white (male) gaze but is now an acting subject who produces her own images.[6] Silko interprets this as "an omen of a time in the future when the indigenous people of the Americas will re-take their land" ("Indian with a Camera" 178)—just as they are reclaim-ing the power of self-representation.

Significantly, Silko's family has a long history of familiarity and ex-pertise with the camera.[7] Her grandfather Henry (Hank) Marmon took photographs beginning in the 1920s, and her father, the esteemed pho-tographer Lee Marmon, has taken photographs since the 1950s. While being the photographer and not the photographic object of another may be empowering, Silko emphasizes that although the photographer con-structs the shot, he or she can never locate an essential object-subject, only a consciousness-influenced posture. That is, she insists that al-though there can be interrelationality between photographer and photo-graphed, what Lippard describes as a "reciprocal moment" (introduc-tion, *Partial Recall* 37), the photographer always shapes the photographic subject—not necessarily through overt staging or conscious intent, but through the filter of a culturally and historically situated consciousness. Silko claims, for instance, that when a Japanese photographer took her picture, influenced by the photographer's cultural and historical gaze, she looked "Japanese" in the photograph ("On Photography" 180–81). Something of the consciousness of the photographer is translated into the photographic image, Silko suggests, or, less metaphysically, "There is no such thing as 'objectivity' or neutrality in portrait photography" (Lippard, introduction, *Partial Recall* 39).

In her almost eight-hundred-page apocalyptic novel *Almanac of the Dead*, Silko provides an indigenous Marxist critique of Western episte-mology as "vampire capitalism," a system in which the few suck the life-blood of the many and all the resources of the earth. Part of the capitalist project is the commodification of everything, and Silko offers a scath-ing denunciation of the production and consumption of photographic art images. After the character Eric commits a bloody suicide, leaving a "three-page suicide note" for David, his photographer lover, there is evi-dence that David not only encouraged the suicide but also exploited it for profit. When looking at David's eight-by-ten-inch color prints, David's female lover, Seese, discovers that in the midst of the riotous and beauti-ful colors that resembled flowers is "a human figure" (106). As the colors and shapes resolve into meaning, she realizes that she is looking at Eric's bloody body. It becomes clear to Seese that David had spent hours set-ting up the scene with reflectors and photographing "Eric's corpse Police Gazette style" (106) before he called the police. Once the photographs are installed at the art gallery, against the protests of Eric's family and amid public outrage that only helps to ensure David's fame, the critics rave about "the richness and intensity of the color" and the artist's "style of clinical detachment and relentless exposure of what lies hidden in



Literature-Based Image-and-Text Forms

flesh" (108). In this gruesome scene, Silko underscores the cannibalizing potential of photography and the crass marketing of human tragedy in an elite art world.[8]

In contrast to the profit-driven and aestheticized violence of David's art photographs, the photographs in *Storyteller* are pictures of family, community, and land. Most are taken by family and friends, and they circulate within the family and within the book, not merely within a commercial literary market. The photographs serve both as mnemonic devices and as stories themselves. Early in *Storyteller*, Silko announces that memory (of time and place) and articulation of those stories is what is necessary to save Laguna Pueblo traditions:

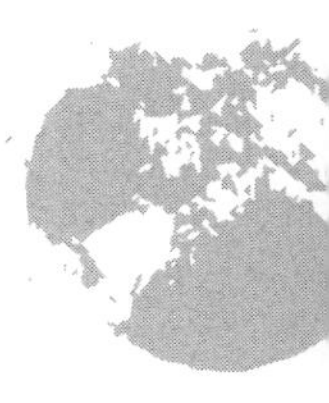

> As with any generation
> the oral tradition depends upon each person
> listening and remembering a portion
> and it is together—
> all of us remembering what we have heard together—
> that creates the whole story
> the long story of the people. (6–7)

Each individual must remember and share the stories. In *Storyteller*, Silko assembles a variety of individual voices and images to construct a polyphonous image-text whose photographs and narratives collide, juxtapose, parallel, inform, and contradict one another. Her image-text interfaces are relational, contextual, and temporal. But, "for all the polyvocal openness of Silko's work, there is always the unabashed commitment to Pueblo ways as a reference point" (Krupat, "Dialogics" 65).

While acknowledging that reading *Storyteller* requires a dynamic "synthesizing" process (11), Helen Jaskoski argues that the story of "Skeleton Fixer" is a key to reading the volume overall. In the story, Old Man Badger comes across "words like bones / scattered all over the place" (*Storyteller* 242); he takes "great care" (243) to reassemble the bones until "Old Coyote Woman jumped up / and took off running" (246). This story, then, "recapitulates the process of fragmentation and reconstitution required of the *Storyteller* reader, who must negotiate the apparently scattered, unrelated, and fragmentary texts and illustrations dispersed throughout the book" (Jaskoski 8).[9] This kind of theoretical-critical voice articulated in the form of a narrative is a central feature of Native American writing by women, "who are often astute theorists of story" in the process of their storytelling (Wong, Muller, and Magdaleno xx).[10] In fact, "*Storyteller* epitomizes a metacritical text; every piece can be read for the story it tells and for its story about storytelling and the role of stories" (Krumholz 64). Silko's self-reflexive commentary about the processes of storytelling is a key feature of *Storyteller*.

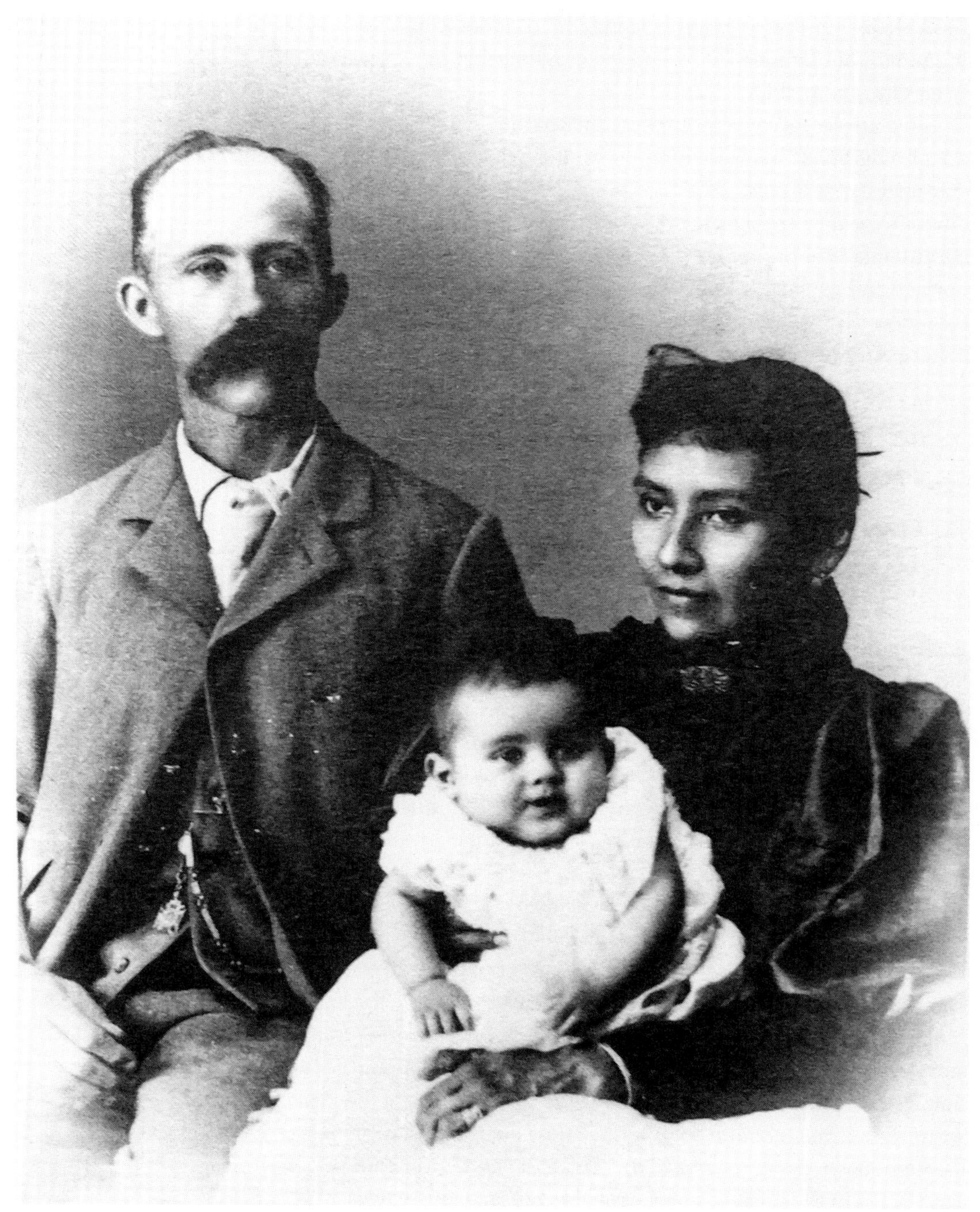

Throughout *Storyteller*, Silko highlights her interest in the relation between image and word. She does not provide captions for the photographs because that might hold the text captive to the photographs or keep the images reliant on the text. Instead, she places brief descriptions and narratives associated with photographs at the end of the volume. By doing so, she attempts to equalize the relation between word and image and to allow (or force) readers to make connections just as Julie Chen, Theresa Hak Kyung Cha, and Hachivi Edgar Heap of Birds (see chapters 4, 5, and 8, respectively) insist that viewers do the work to make sense of textual fragments. Out of the twenty-six photographs in *Storyteller*, twelve are of relatives, seven are of the land, five focus on community members, and two are of Silko herself. Seventeen of the photographs were taken by Silko's father, Lee Marmon, and three by her grandfather Henry (Hank) Marmon.[11] Both the photographic subjects (relatives, community, and land) and the photographers (primarily her father and grandfather) underscore the centrality of relationships in *Storyteller*.

Silko begins the book with a formal studio portrait of her great-grandparents and grandfather and concludes with an outdoor photograph of three generations of her family: her great-grandfather, her grandfather's siblings, and her father and uncle as young boys. These two photographs frame the stories and images within, suggesting the temporal expanse of Silko's family history. This is perhaps why the photographs in *Storyteller* are described as having a "circular design" (B. Hirsch 2). In the first photograph (fig. 2.1), Silko's great grandfather, Robert G. Marmon, a white man who married a Laguna woman and never left, and her great-grandmother, Marie Anaya Marmon, stare out of the photograph and beyond the camera in opposite directions, as if each is lost in an individual reverie. There is no sense of interaction with the photographer or with each other. It is unclear whether Robert towers over Marie because the photographer elevated him—as many studio photographers staged patriarchal gender relations, positioning men to stand with a hand proprietarily on the wife or child—or whether he is simply a tall man. Wearing a sad or perhaps tired or resigned look on her face, Marie holds their baby on her lap. The pretty, full-faced baby also stares off into space, but with a delicately sweet expression. All three are dressed in what must have been their finest clothes: Robert wears a suit and tie adorned with a pocket watch; Marie wears a velvet jacket; and baby Henry (Hank) wears a long frilly white gown.

In the final photograph (fig. 2.2) the wide expanse of the Southwest replaces the studio; the informality of a family snapshot replaces the formal staging of a professional portrait. Silko's relatives include, from left to right, Kenneth (Grandpa Hank's brother), great-grandfather

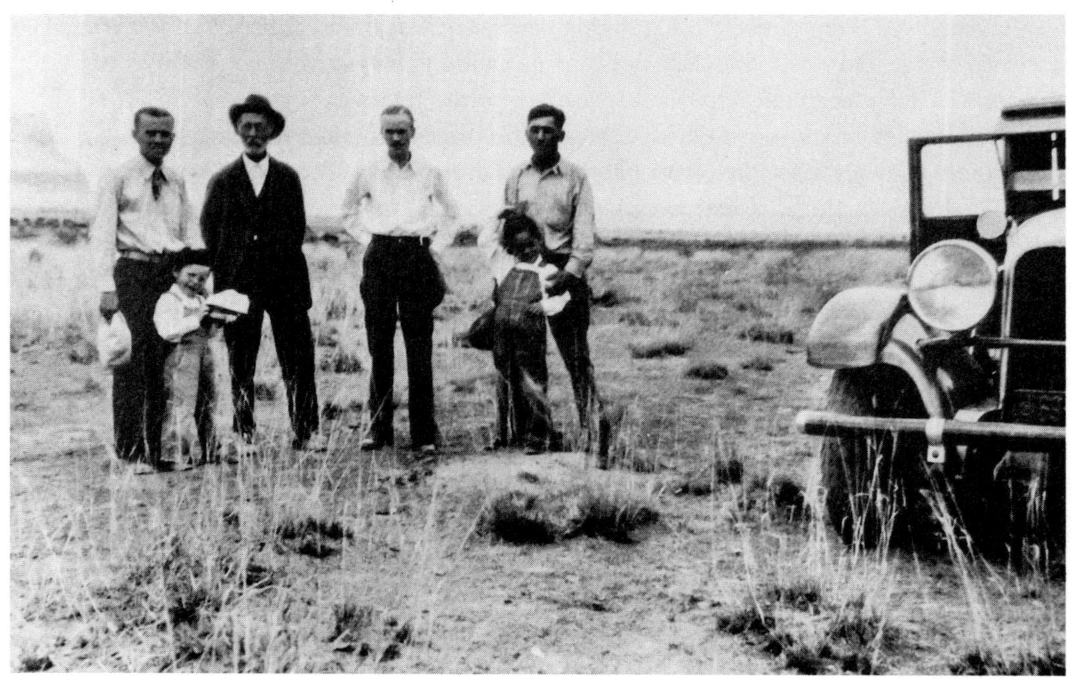



Robert G. Marmon, Charlie (Grandpa Hank's sister's husband), and Walter (Grandpa Hank's brother) (274). The two young boys are Silko's father, Lee Marmon, and his brother, Richard H. Marmon. The faces of the four men and two young boys are not clearly visible as they stand looking directly into the camera. The men are framed by a faint and distant mesa on the left and, nearby, a shiny, new automobile (which looks like Silko's Grandpa Hank's 1933 Auburn speedster) on the right, apt symbols for the ancient and enduring Pueblo connection to the land coexisting with the new technological transformations of the modern world. Or perhaps the automobile, only partially visible, intrudes into the desert, dominating the right quarter of the photograph, not yet fully contained within the frame. Three generations of Marmons are in between, feet planted firmly on the land. In the caption, Silko names the mesa as if it were one of her relatives: "With Pa'toe'ch Mesa . . . are Uncle . . ." (274).

A photograph of Silko's great-grandmother Marie Anaya Marmon with Silko's two sisters (fig. 2.3) links time, place, and the generational transmission of knowledge through storytelling, orally and in books. Silko explains that she did not understand for a long time that her grandma's name was not A'mooh—"the Laguna expression of endearment" that, as a child, Silko heard so often from the woman. A'mooh— the source of unbounded maternal love—was also the one to transmit old Pueblo knowledge, derived from the earth, to Silko: how to wash hair



Literature-Based Image-and-Text Forms

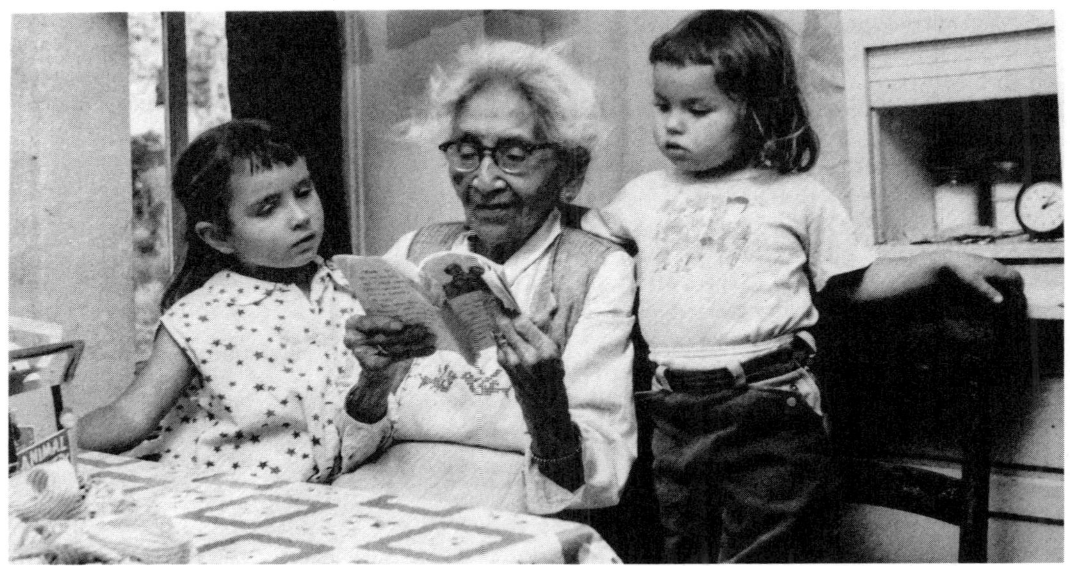

with yucca roots, "how to make red chili on the grinding stone," how it was in the past—using juniper ash for toothpaste or eating crushed *maaht'zini*, instead of cornflakes, with milk (34–35). In the photograph, Marie and two of her granddaughters are gathered around her kitchen table, site of domestic sustenance. The two little girls snuggle close to their grandma, looking intently at the well-worn book that she holds. Marie reads what Silko describes almost sixty pages later as "a worn-out little book that had lost its cover" (93). It was a story about "Brownie the Bear" that Marie read to Silko and her sisters and, before that, to Silko's father and uncles. Great grandma, then, links elders to younger generations as well as storytellers to readers.[12] A'mooh, Aunt Susie, and Aunt Alice, explains Silko, were "women of the book as well as women of the spoken word" (*Turquoise* 28). The entire family remembers "Brownie the Bear" so fondly because Great Grandma Marie "always read the story with such animation and expression / changing her tone of voice and inflection / each time one of the bears spoke— / the way a storyteller would have told it" (93). Along with other everyday kitchen items, a small clock sits prominently on the cupboard on the right, a reminder of the linear time that increasingly encroaches on Pueblo story time.

Although Silko's father is the primary producer of images, the Native male gaze behind the camera, it is Silko who arranges all these photographs into her own design. As well as photographs of family, Silko includes many of the land. Silko's autobiographical persona is site-specific, generated from the Pueblo Southwest, a repository of histories and stories. A photograph of the famous Enchanted Mesa, Kat'sima (fig. 2.4), taken by Lee Marmon, links the present moment to the mythic past

FIGURE 2.3. Leslie Marmon Silko. *Grandma Marie Reading to Silko's Sisters* (*Storyteller*, 1981, 33). (Photograph: Lee Marmon. Image from *Storyteller* by Leslie Marmon Silko. Copyright © 1981 by Leslie Marmon Silko, used by permission of The Wylie Agency LLC.)

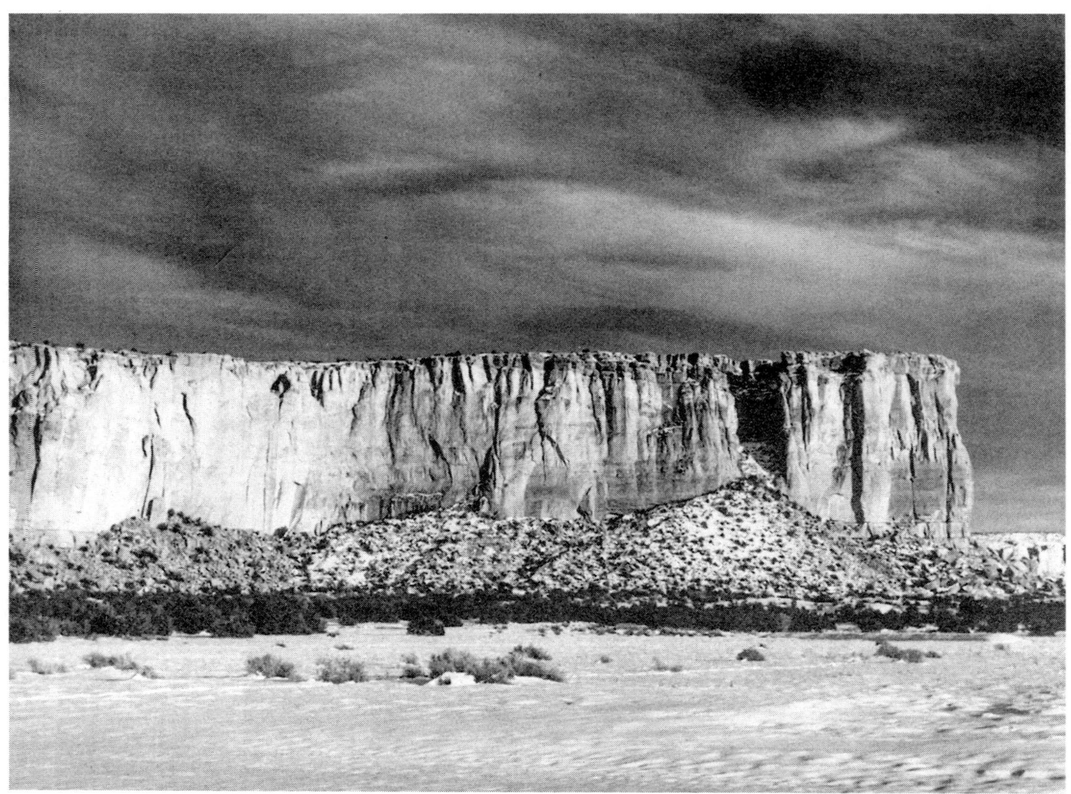



and reverses the Western assumption of human mastery over nature. Enchanted Mesa is a dominant geographical feature of the area, visible from a long distance. In this photograph, Marmon's point of view is from far below and quite a distance away, looking over the land and up at a long expanse of Enchanted Mesa. The sky meets the mesa top at about the halfway point of the photograph as if earth and sky are in balance. And human beings are small—in relation to earth and sky—as the camera angle widens across the desert and moves up the mesa and, beyond that, to the sky. This photograph reminds viewers that humans are tiny participant-observers in the vast scheme of the natural world and geological time. In addition, it reminds viewers of stories that conflate time and space into presence in particular places.

Enchanted Mesa is a storied site, but it is not until forty-three pages after the photograph of Enchanted Mesa that Silko shares the stories about Kat'sima. It is associated with numerous very old cultural stories as well as more recent family narratives. Silko remembers a story her Grandpa Hank told her about Enchanted Mesa: "In 1908 when the Smithsonian Institution / excavated the top of Kat'sima, Enchanted Mesa / Grandpa drove some of the archaeologists / out there in his buggy" (198). Silko asks her grandfather, "'Did they find the bones of that old blind lady / and

    Literature-Based Image-and-Text Forms

that baby? You know, the one they tell about in that old story?'" Before conveying her grandfather's answer to the question, Silko inserts an explanation for the reader: *"There is an old story about a blind woman / being stranded on top of enchanted mesa with a tiny baby / the time the sandstone trail to the top collapsed"* (198, emphasis in original). Silko's emphasis serves as an informative aside to the reader. Grandpa explains that he did not see any bones, "but those Smithsonian people were putting everything / into wooden boxes as fast as they could. They took everything with them . . . back to Washington, D.C." (198). Here Silko illustrates how stories of place include old-time stories as well as family stories. She illustrates the way stories are connected to the land that holds the past, present, and future of the people. She demonstrates how networks of narratives interlink—Grandpa's story of the Smithsonian archaeologists is connected to "that old story" of the lost woman and baby. In fact, the woman and baby lost at the top of Enchanted Mesa bear resemblance to the items "lost" at the top of the mesa when they were confiscated by the archaeologists. Like the woman and baby who never came down, whatever was taken has never been returned. Finally, Silko uses the stories as a way to critique white archaeologists who have boxed up Indian bones in the name of scientific research and stolen Native belongings and histories. "'You know,' concludes Grandpa Hank, 'probably all those boxes of things / they took from Enchanted Mesa / are still just sitting somewhere / in the basement of some museum'" (198–99).

Denny Carr's photograph of Wasson Peak works similarly to Marmon's Enchanted Mesa photograph in the way it positions the viewer as if nestled into the land, looking slightly up and beyond, across the saguaro and prickly pear cacti that frame the scene, across the shrubbery, rocks, and hills, across the mist, and into the Tucson mountains beyond. Far from being the "master of all I survey," the viewer feels part of the land, not separate from it. Although it is a decidedly beautiful composition, it does not feel staged but appears more like someone sharing an intimate experience of natural beauty.

Another photograph, which Silko implies is of her father, comments not only on the human relationship to land but also on its representation (fig. 2.5).[13] On his knees behind a camera on a tripod, the photographer—although front and center—is only a minuscule part of the vast expanse of desert. A faint mesa rises on the distant horizon where earth meets sky. The man in the photograph appears to be setting up a photographic shot. With his back to the desert that looms around him, he seems to focus on the rocks. Using this photograph of her photographer father, whose images are central to the book, Silko self-reflexively reveals the photographer in the process of creating images—just as she comments metacritically on the process of telling stories. A few pages later,



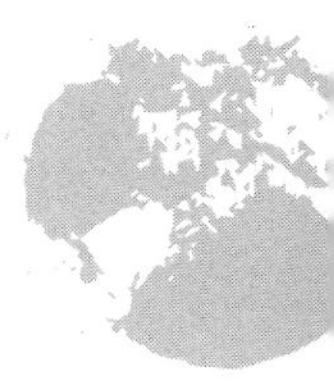

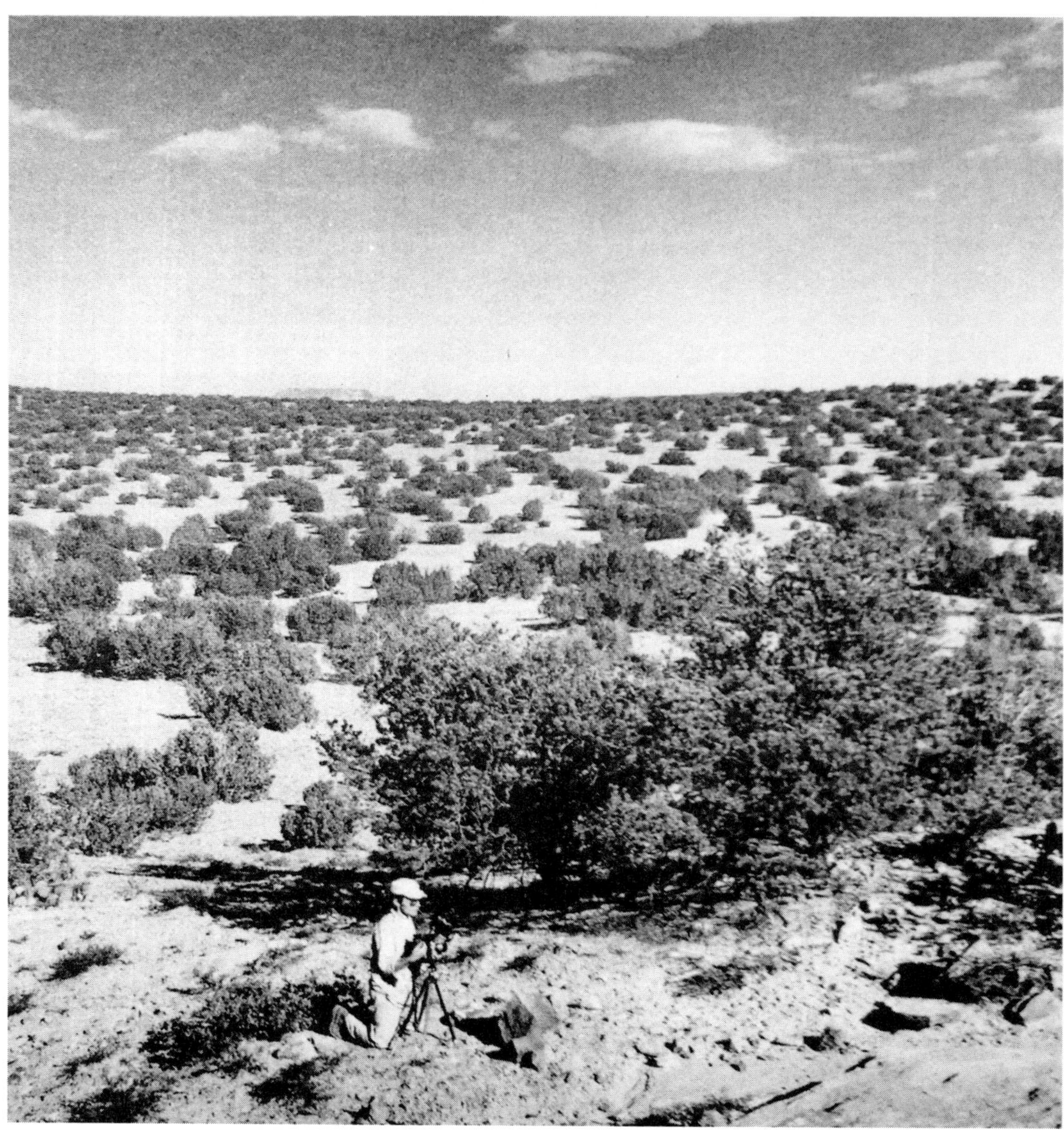

Silko's text elaborates on this photograph: "The hills and mesas around Laguna / were a second home for my father / when he was growing up. . . . He used to wait for the cumulus clouds to come give him the sky / he needed for his photographs" (160). As we will see, photographing the clouds becomes crucial to Silko's photo-narrative *Sacred Water*.

In *Storyteller*, Silko narrates the long history of her Laguna Pueblo family and community through an interactive collage of diverse texts and photographs. Out of the old-time stories, the contemporary written stories, the gossip, the poems, the letters, the memories, the contested tellings and retellings of stories, and the photographs—all of which arise

     Literature-Based Image-and-Text Forms

out of Pueblo land and the time it holds and animates, Silko assembles a sense of her own subjectivity as a storyteller, artist, Laguna Pueblo woman, and human being and leaves a legacy for future generations.

## *Sacred Water*

It is not surprising that after spending so many years writing her colossally long and violent novel *Almanac of the Dead*, in which the Destroyers are unleashed on the world, Silko would return to meditating on the land. More than ten years after *Storyteller*, Silko continues the photo-text narrative in a new form. In *Sacred Water: Narratives and Pictures* (1993), she experiments more boldly with image and text, challenging readers' expectations about the function of a photograph in a written work. *Sacred Water* might be considered as an experiment arising from ideas Silko articulated in earlier published essays, later collected in *Yellow Woman and a Beauty of Spirit* (1996). These essays and *Sacred Water* focus on the relations between humans and the natural world. She asks: "As our modern world spirals downward on intensifying cycles of greed and violence, can we find a better way to live"? (White 136). This question, in fact, is at the heart of all of Silko's work, in part because Laguna Pueblo epistemology is geocentric, and in part because earth is at the center of indigenous-colonizer conflicts about land and culture and identity itself. And because of the desecration of land (and some of its people), the issue is also environmental. How is it possible to live a balanced life in which humans and the natural world are in harmony? To answer this question, Silko focuses on the daily minutiae of her relationship with the natural world.

Again, in *Sacred Water*, Silko uses photographs and text. Again the land is central, but instead of focusing only on Laguna Pueblo, she features the Sonoran desert in Tucson, Arizona. In this hand-made photo-narrative, Silko tells visually and verbally about her life on her ranch outside of Tucson. Although we learn a bit about her daily activities, the real focus is on time and place: her relationships with the long history of human, animal, plant, and geological life in the desert, a kind of photo-book eco-autobiography. This is emphasized in one of Silko's descriptions of her process, a process that is akin to that of autobiographical construction: "I have a dozen or more sketchbooks and notebooks only partially filled," she explains, "then abandoned for years only to have me find them and start using them again for drawing and painting and writing as well. The linear time line is thus tangled and confused as it deserves to be" (*Turquoise* 223). The sketchbooks and notebooks, like recorded memories, are abandoned, rediscovered, and finally reanimated into self-narration. Through photographic images and prose, Silko depicts a self-reflexive sense of memories of childhood at Laguna Pueblo, reflections on various native kinship systems and beliefs, daily observations of the Arizona land and weather—all linked by the central motif of water, a scarce, life-generating resource and the focus of most of the rituals among indigenous peoples of the arid Southwest.

In *Sacred Water*, Silko pushes her experimentation with image and text beyond what she did in *Storyteller*. She continues her interest in telling a story through photographs and written narrative but emphasizes more dramatically the tension between word and image, an exploration of what she describes as "the effect that a photograph or other visual image has on our reading of a text" ("As a Child," *Yellow Woman* 168–69). Describing *Sacred Water* as her "experiment," Silko explains: "I am interested in photographs that obscure rather than reveal; I am intrigued with photographs that don't tell you what you are supposed to notice, that don't illustrate the text, that don't serve the text, but form a part of the field of vision for the reading of the text and thereby become part of the reader's experience of the text" (168–69). "The text of *Sacred Water*," she continues, "was composed so that words do not overpower the odd minimalism of the pictures but instead depend upon the pictures for a subtle resonance" (169).[14] Silko describes her photographic process as printing photographs on a laser copy machine in photo mode to produce an image "more stark and abstract than a traditional photographic print" so that it does not "dominate the page" (169). The thirty-nine photocopied black-and-white photographs in *Sacred Water* eschew the highly professional, glossy color photographs so often found in photographic books and art galleries, just as the handmade edition of *Sacred Water* that I examine here resists professional publication standards with its folded pages that are photocopied and held together by two staples in the middle.[15] By making (and publishing) her own book, Silko removes the hand-made book from the commercial realm, keeping it "outside the networks of capitalist production" (Huhndorf 14).

The hand-made editions of *Sacred Water* are reminiscent of the "democratic multiple" artists' books, produced inexpensively and distributed widely, so popular in the 1970s.[16] Although Silko does not discuss *Sacred Water* in the context of artists' books, she does mention how "the ancient folding books of the Maya, Aztec, and other indigenous American cultures"—often referred to by book artists as early book forms—inspired her "to think more about the written word as a picture of the spoken word" (introduction, *Yellow Woman* 14–15). Also, like book artists, Silko underscores the fact that the written word is itself visual. Finally, in the various handmade editions of *Sacred Water*, "Silko elaborates her narration with every version . . . just like the *storyteller* in the oral tradition" (Coltelli 25, emphasis in original). By operating outside of the dominant modes of production and distribution and resisting the professional aesthetics of book publishing norms, Silko claims both artistic autonomy and flexibility.

With independent control of the production of her book, Silko is attentive to every detail. The very materials of the handmade editions of *Sacred Water* emphasize place—the focal point of the entire book—but place transported elsewhere. In her essay "As a Child I Loved to Draw and Cut Paper," Silko reports that the blue cover of the handmade *Sacred Water* is made of Stephen Watson's Blue Corn paper (made in Albuquerque) and contains "bits of blue corn" (*Yellow Woman* 205n1). This is the edition about which I write here. Another limited edition was covered in Watson's white Volcanic Ash paper, containing "small amounts of fine ash obtained from the volcanoes just west of Albuquerque" (205n1).[17] Silko's *Sacred Water* announces its handmade production out of regional materials. Silko's hands have folded, glued, stapled, or sewn the slim book readers hold in their hands, inviting a gender-revised Whitmanian exclamation: "Who touches this book touches a woman!" And not only that, they hold in their hands the very earth about which they are reading.

In the drawing on the front cover of *Sacred Water* (fig. 2.6), Silko arranges an assortment of traditional Pueblo and invented images into her own unique vision. Her decorative composite glyph includes flowers, mesas, rain clouds, lightning, corn, a parrot, mountains, and insects (perhaps a caterpillar and a water bug), as well as a lively collection of geometric and fluid shapes. Collectively, these images emphasize meteorological patterns, cloud formation, rain, and the abundant life that water enables. Similarly, Silko's prose narratives throughout *Sacred Water* highlight the set of complex interrelations within the desert environment: human relationships with land, animals, plants, and other humans as well as with departed ancestors. This set of relations links past, present, and future into a web of interdependence and emphasizes Silko's ecocentric, rather than homocentric, subjectivity.

Silko's startling dedication, "In memory of the nine Thailand Buddhists assassinated in their temple near Phoenix, Arizona on August 10, 1991," appeared in later versions of the handmade book. In August 1991, "nine people were found dead at Wat Promkunaram, a Thai Buddhist temple. . . . They had been arranged in a circle and shot in the head execution-style."[18] A shocking crime, this seems an odd dedication for a book that focuses on a reverence for life.[19] Revering life, of course, does not blind Silko to destructive forces within the natural world, including the damage that can be inflicted by rain clouds and human beings. The dedication, however, foreshadows the senseless human violence against nature that she documents in both *Sacred Water* and *The Turquoise Ledge*.

Throughout most of the book, there is one page of text accompanied by a page with a photocopied photograph, not in any predictable order.

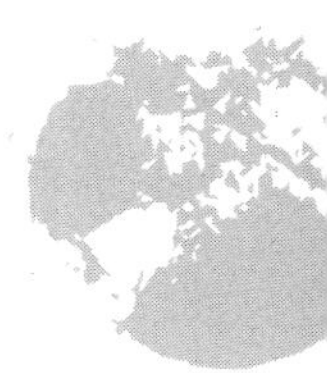

# SACRED WATER

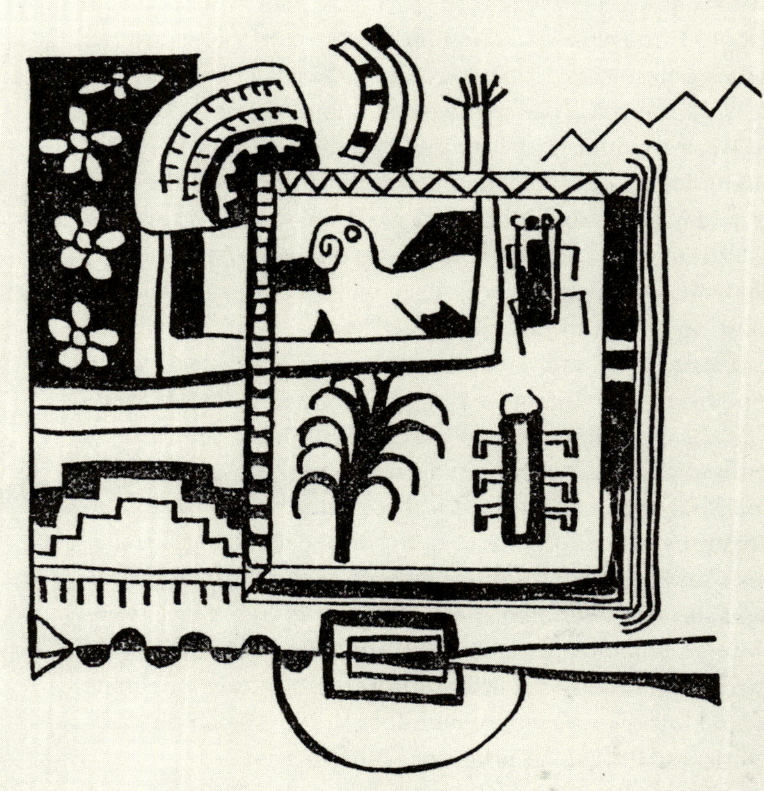

# LESLIE MARMON SILKO

Pages 16–17 and 34–35 contain text on all four pages, while pages 44–45 contain a double-spread photograph and text on both pages. By Silko's design, the text and image are not always explicitly related. There are photographs of clouds, sky, rocks, water, and plants. Whereas the cloud photographs tend to present an expansive vista, most of the other photographs are close-ups, the photographer zooming in so that the reader focuses intently on a small scene: a flower, a few rocks, a small part of a pond, and so on. This resistance to capturing the landscape with a masterful and encompassing long shot and the resulting lack of perspective—that places the viewer as master of the scene—leads Shari Huhndorf to argue cogently that in *Sacred Water*, Silko "reworks the *visual conventions* of landscape," defying "the illusion of mastery and possession central to conventional landscapes" (14, emphasis in original) in order to reveal a Pueblo sense of interrelationality.[20] Both the scale and the focus of the photographs draw readers-viewers into Silko's beautiful desert.

Grainy photocopied photographs of cumulus clouds, cirrus clouds, storm clouds, and "dark rain clouds" (5)—the source of sacred water—meeting the land at the horizon, abound (fig. 2.7.) Generally, in the photographs of clouds, the sky is vast and the land below is a vague dark outline. The photograph seems to dramatize a sense of the clouds' movement across the land. Collectively, the photographs serve as background—as if Silko is mirroring the ubiquity of the land and sky within the book. At times, Silko's prose provides a textual description of the photograph and reports details on the ground. In this example, she invokes the senses of vision, hearing, touch, and smell: "Spring rain clouds follow early / morning gusts of wind, and sudden drops / in temperature. / By dawn, the smell of rain is heavy / in the air. The sun is masked in cumulus / layers of pearl blue" (3).

Throughout *Sacred Water*, Silko provides photographs and word pictures of anything and everything related to moisture. She remembers that as children they "were never permitted to frolic with or waste fresh water." Bothering toads or frogs was forbidden "because the frogs and toads are the beloved children of the rain clouds" (3). She remembers learning "to watch for the fat dark rain clouds" (5), but the accompanying photograph (fig. 2.8) is of water lilies in a small body of water. Rather than one of her numerous photographs of "fat dark rain clouds," Silko's image shows one of the consequences of abundant rain—a clear body of water with healthy water plants. Thus she emphasizes the cycle of water in the desert and refers us to the entire ecosystem she delineates throughout the book.

Silko shares vivid images of water in textual, as well as photographic, form: "hundreds of little toads . . . popping out of the sand everywhere"

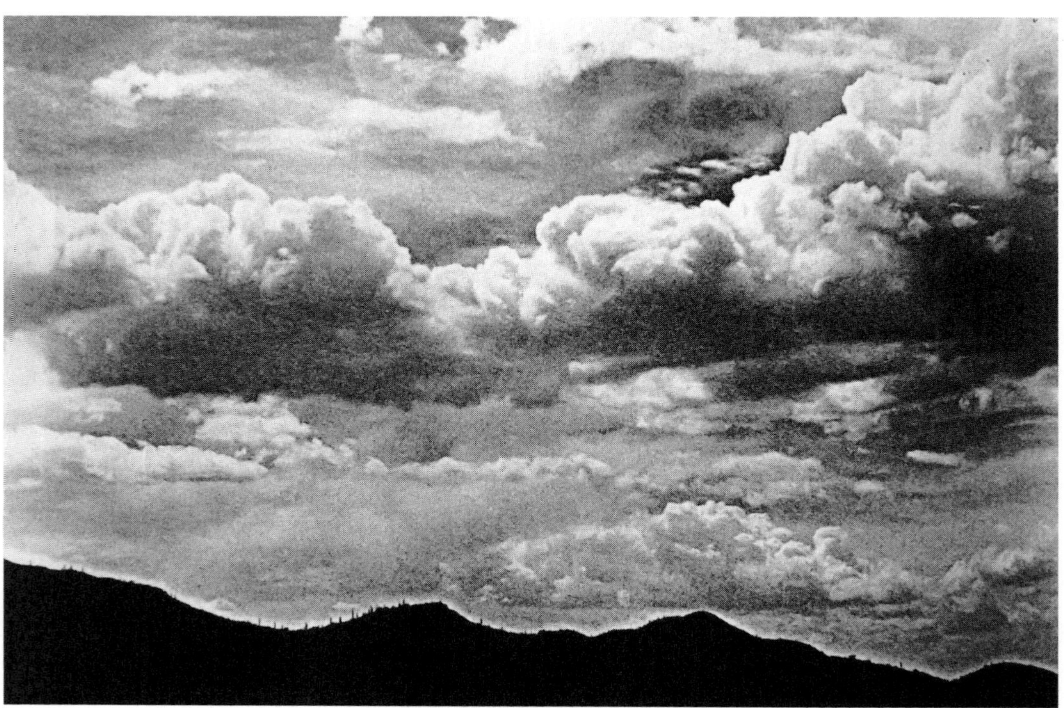



after a summer rain (11); "four Sonoran red-spotted toads in the damp earth," sleeping "head to head, each with its rear-end pointed in one of the four directions" (12), creating a fantastic natural mandala of the four sacred directions and earth and sky; the "big pottery jar full of water" placed on her great-grandmother's grave because she had belonged to the Water Clan (15); "sandstone . . . natural basins and pools that hold rain water" (18); sacred "natural springs and fresh-water lakes" that hold power because they are believed to be the "entrances to the four worlds below" (20); and the "giant water snake named Ma'sh'ra'tru'ee" (23), who lived in the lake and served as a mediator, carrying "the prayers of the people to the Mother Creator below" (24). Again, Silko resists having the photograph illustrate the text. Accompanying her description of the "natural basins and pools" is a photograph of rocks (fig. 2.9). Although rock formations may hold rainwater, it is not clear from the photograph where the "natural basin" about which Silko speaks might be. The photograph does remind the reader, however, of Silko's fascination with animate rocks that move throughout the land, primarily by the force of flashfloods.

Ironically, in the hottest parts of the summer, the threat of drowning increases for animals and humans. When "the water holes dry up, thirst drives the creatures to try to reach water no matter where the water may be" (33). Silko tells of finding "an elf owl floating face down in a

     Literature-Based Image-and-Text Forms

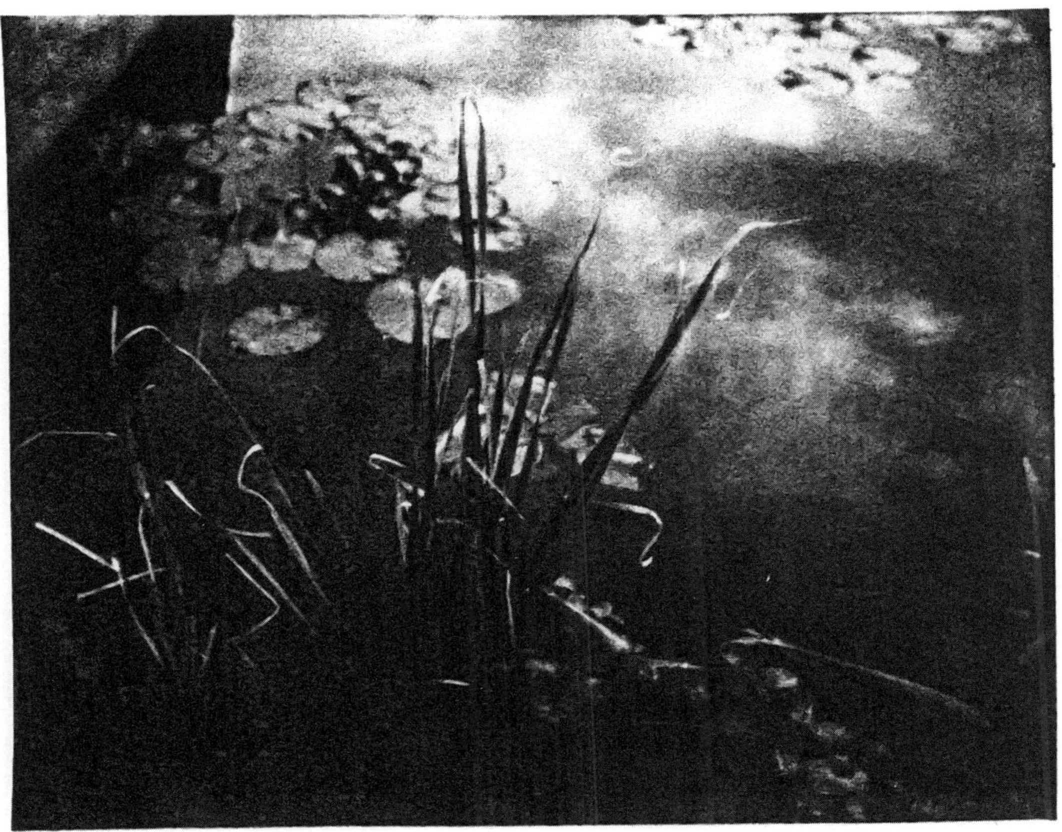

water barrel" (33); it had been unable to get out. Young children die from drowning in the many backyard swimming pools. Summer thunder-storms may cause flashfloods that can sweep away homes, people, and especially macho motorists "driving four-wheel-drive vehicles" (34). Without intelligent run-off systems, like Felipe Riley's "arrangement of stone check dams" that "conformed to the natural contours" of the land at Laguna Pueblo, homes and crops would be flooded (45). The federal government finally installed "giant storm drains" at Laguna (46), but Silko prefers more natural solutions like Riley's or "the rain water" col-lection practices she learned about in Ketchikan, Alaska, and that she uses at her ranch house. She "routes all rain water from the roof" as well as "run-off from a gravel-covered slope" into "a concrete pool" (52).

Silko seems to portray an all-beneficent world of intimate and loving interrelationships. Even the dead bless the people "when they return as rain clouds" (17). But the network of harmonious natural relations can be, and has been, disturbed—and even life-giving water can be deadly in the wrong circumstances. In an old story, jealous neighbors ruined the "beautiful lake"; when the lake dried up, "the giant water snake was

FIGURE 2.8. Leslie Marmon Silko. *Water Lilies after Rain (Sacred Water*, 1993, 4). (Photographer: Leslie Marmon Silko. Image from *Sacred Water* by Leslie Marmon Silko. Copyright © 1993 by Leslie Marmon Silko, used by permission of The Wylie Agency LLC.)

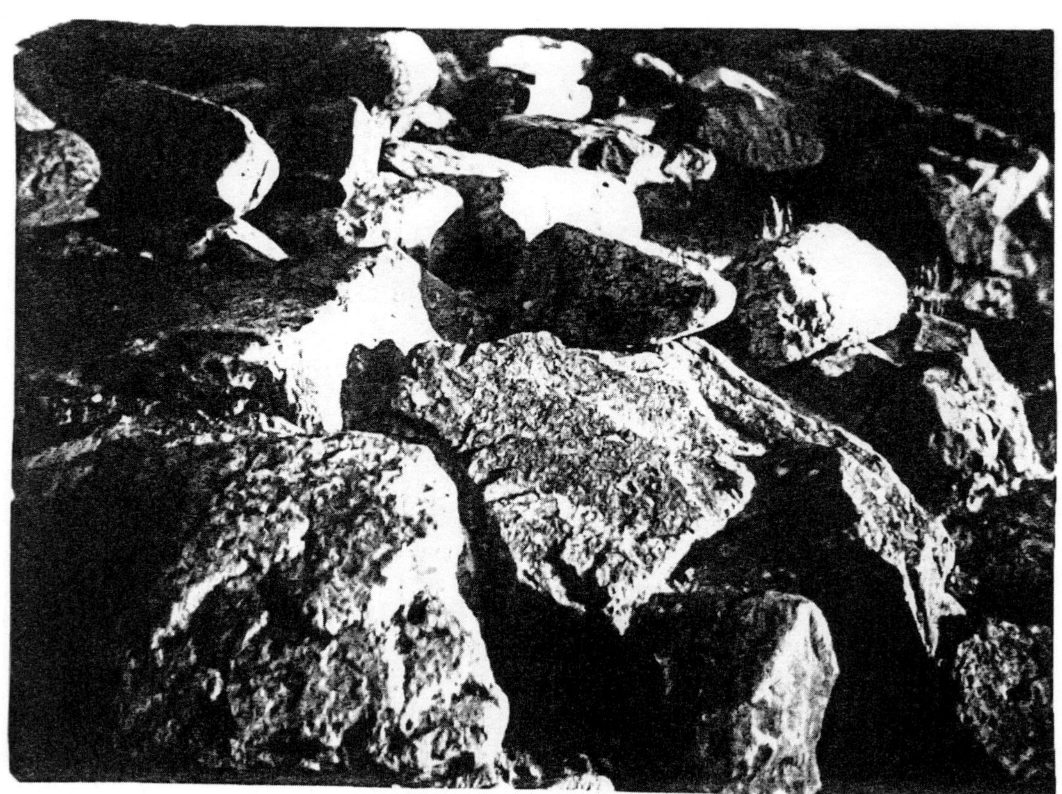

FIGURE 2.9.
Leslie Marmon
Silko. *Rocks* (*Sacred
Water*, 1993, 19).
(Photographer:
Leslie Marmon
Silko. Image from
*Sacred Water* by
Leslie Marmon
Silko. Copyright
© 1993 by
Leslie Marmon
Silko, used by
permission of The
Wylie Agency LLC.)

never seen" again (27). When the Spaniards came, they mistook coiled snake glyphs as directing the way to "buried treasure the Indians had hidden," rather than as a guide to freshwater, the true "treasure" (29). In a more contemporary anecdote, Silko tells of inviting a man and his sons to dinner. After the meal, the boys and dog went outside for some fresh air. When Silko and the man joined the boys, just "a few minutes later," they "found them with the dog by the rain water pool. Strewn all around the pool were the remains of toads smashed flat by the boys and the dog" (64). Like the Buddhist priests "shot execution-style" for no comprehensible reason, the toads are "smashed flat" systematically. The boys' senseless violence silenced the "night-long choirs of multitudes of toads" (66). Ominously, as Silko has explained, hurting toads and frogs—"the beloved children of the rain clouds"—can bring disaster. Silko speculates that the "Chernobyl nuclear reactor disaster" that "occurred not long afterward . . . may also have effected [*sic*] the toad population" (66). The photograph of a lovely water lily on the opposite page almost belies the destruction Silko's text describes, perhaps offering a glimpse of hope or a reminder of cycles of destruction and creation. The return of pollywogs, survivors of "radioactive fall-out and the boys with the dog" (66), offers some vision of renewal and continuance.

     Literature-Based Image-and-Text Forms

Although the pollywogs are a hopeful sign, Silko's rainwater pool continues to deteriorate, "a strange red algae" smothering the plants. Rather than a life-giving source of sacred water, the red algae-covered pond becomes a deathtrap for animals that try to walk on what appears to be its solid surface, only to drown. Just before she is about to surrender and fill in the pond, Silko tries a few new plans to save it. She dumps gravel to filter the water and provide an escape route for animals; she plants various water plants—"duck weed, water lettuce, or water lily"—with no luck. Finally, with a "critical mass" of water hyacinths, "the water in the pool began to clear" (72). A reader unfamiliar with botany would assume that the captionless photocopied photograph of a flower on the opposite page would surely be a water hyacinth—the flower she writes about in detail. "Water hyacinths," Silko explains, "digest the worst sorts of wastes and contamination: decomposing rodents and dead toads . . . [and] remove lead and cadmium from contaminated water" (72).[21] But, in fact, true to her interest in "photographs that obscure rather than reveal . . . , photographs that . . . do not illustrate the text . . . , but form a part of the field of vision" ("As a Child" 168–69), the flower depicted on pages 71 and 73 is a datura. While Silko is singing the praises "of the lowly water hyacinth, purifyer [*sic*] of defiled water" (*Sacred Water* 71), the visual field on the right is dominated by a datura, a plant to which the reader will be introduced when she or he turns the page.

"Only the datura," claims Silko, "has the power to purify plutonium contamination. . . . [It] actually removes the plutonium from the soil so that the soil is purified and only the datura plant itself is radioactive" (75). Best known to the West as a dangerous poison and hallucinogen and to indigenous people in the American Southwest as a sacred substance, datura, Silko claims, has the possibility of purifying the earth of pollutants. Indeed, some scientific studies have concluded that datura has potential for removing the "organic load from wastewater" (Vaillant-Gaveau et al. 1328). Datura, Silko suggests, sacrifices itself because it recognizes that "all water is sacred" (*Sacred Water* 75). In a 1994 interview, Silko explains that the "earth itself is rebelling against what's been done to it in the name of greed and capitalism" (Boos 144). She catalogs the toxic wastes—from uranium mines, underground nuclear tests, and abandoned excavations—that threaten to destroy sacred water. But Silko concludes *Sacred Water* as she did *Almanac of the Dead*: "Human beings desecrate only themselves; the Mother Earth is inviolable. Whatever may become of us human beings, the Earth will bloom with hyacinth purple and the white blossoms of the datura" (76).

Each of Silko's photo-text autobiographies deploys diverse image-text relations. *Storyteller* is an assemblage of text—in the form of stories, gossip, poems, letters, and journals—and photographs; *Sacred Water* is a

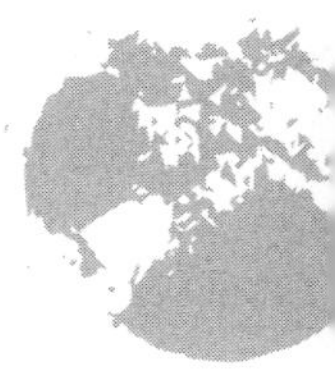

series of photo-and-text juxtapositions. Throughout *Storyteller* the photographs and text are in dialogue. In *Sacred Water* the grainy black-and-white photocopied photographs (remember that Silko printed her photographs on a laser copy machine in photo mode to deconstruct the highly constructed images) resist illustration of, sometimes even correspondence to, the text. They serve, instead, as part of "the field of vision" ("As a Child" 168–69) that itself is constructed from both text and image. With their relational, contextual, and temporal interfaces, both of her photo-narratives underscore her thematic focus on Pueblo subjectivity as it is generated in relation to community, time, a specific location in the natural world, and stories of all types. Silko celebrates the continuity of personal and collective Pueblo identity as stories, embedded in specific land sites, that endure against all odds.

Leslie Marmon Silko's deceptively simple photo-text narratives challenge readers-viewers' expectations about reference and reading conventions: they demand that readers pay attention, question assumptions, and consider the entire book as a visual and verbal field. Silko juxtaposes photograph and text to derail expectations of any seamless correspondence between them, turning the photographs into a sense of all-permeating place into which the reader-viewer enters and coercing the reader-viewer to experience the relation between images and texts as an entire field, an assemblage of interpenetrating moments. Through a "subtle resonance" between words and images, Silko thematizes and illustrates an indigenous time-space continuum that constitutes a Native subjectivity. Grounded in place, particularly the land where the Pueblo people have lived for thousands of years or the desert ecosystem of her ranch, Silko's time is cyclical; the past is not lost but very much a part of the present — alive in the stories embedded throughout the land.

# Art Spiegelman's Graphic Memoir *Maus*

## "One Is Left with What Remains, the Ruins
## That Are Sifted Over Endlessly"

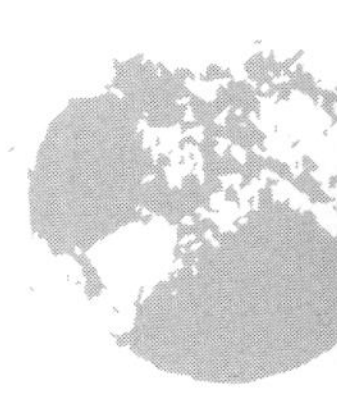

Comics has been defined as a sequential art form, the art of telling stories with pictures, a narrative series of cartoons, and imagetexts. Autobiographical comics are also called graphic memoirs. Although not all comics have words, those that do often have an equitable relation between text and picture. Words can function as images or sounds, as well as do the work of reportage, narrative, and dialogue. Pictures can convey what remains unwritten. The conventions of the comics format permit the representation of multiple, simultaneous times and places, allowing for nuance and complexity.

Chapters 1 and 2 focused on Peter Najarian's and Leslie Marmon Silko's innovative incorporation of text and image (in the form of drawings, painting, and photographs) to share an autobiographical narrative in book form. This chapter considers the comics form (in this case, drawings, text, and photographs), which by design is a more complete union of image and text. In his autobiographical comics book *Maus*, Art Spiegelman experiments with several visual-verbal interfaces: the relational interface in which neither image nor text is subordinated to the other but rather exist in dialogue; the contextual interface, particularly as it refers to a political context that "draws on scenes of collective memory" linking personal experience to a community (Smith and Watson, *Interfaces* 26); the temporal interface in which moments of self-reflection "unfold as process" (34); and the spatial interface—"when surfaces project through canny juxtapositions, disparate histories, images, identities, all co-existing in the same space" (31). Spiegelman's spatial interface intermingles maps, photographs, diagrams, masks, and innovative frames that suggest multiple shifting identities. In this imagetext form, Spiegelman interweaves multiple stories, extending the autobiographical "I" to include mother, father, extended family, and culture. Spiegelman presents himself as narrator, artist, amanuensis, son, husband, and father. Rather than a singular autonomous "I," then, the autobiographical subject is profoundly relational. Last, Spiegelman offers self-reflexive commentary on the autobiographical process and struggles to find a suitable conclusion to his family story.

The Nazi genocide of Jews—and of Roma, homosexuals, the disabled, and political dissidents—known as the Holocaust, or Shoah, has claimed preeminent status as the unimaginable collective trauma of the twentieth century, a century overburdened by the violence of world wars.[1] Holocaust studies focuses on a fundamental paradox: the unspeakable horror that must be spoken. Survivor testimonies reiterate that what they are about to say is too horrible to tell. But given the fact that those who died can never bear witness to their experience, the ethical responsibility lies with those who survived to do so—to tell personal experiences that may also illuminate the dark fate of those who did not survive. Whether they speak or are silent, survivors are tormented by their choice. If they are silent, are they reneging on the responsibility to speak for those who cannot? Are they complicit with attempts to erase the dire acts, to expunge them from historical records? If they do speak, how can they describe with integrity what they experienced, witnessed, and did? Now, a new generation—children of survivors—struggles with the ethics of representing the Shoah, grappling with ongoing questions about who is entitled to speak about it and in what forms.[2]

In her classic study of psychoanalytical concepts of trauma, Cathy Caruth describes "what it means to transmit and to theorize around a crisis that is marked, not by a simple knowledge, but by the way it simultaneously defies and demands our witness" (5). From the Greek *trauma*, meaning wound, trauma today includes psychic wounds. Not fully capable of comprehending the traumatic event itself, a trauma victim may experience a deferred understanding; it emerges over time in repeated and unbidden manifestations of the trauma—in the form of nightmares, phobias, flashbacks, hypervigilance, dissociation, and related phenomena. Most scholars understand trauma, then, as "an exceptional form of memory" (Traverso and Broderick 5). If a trauma victim is to heal and not merely endure the repetition of the horror, he or she must bear witness to the traumatic experience(s) in the form of testimony. In psychoanalytical terms, to tell the story is to place trauma into a comprehensible narrative. But there is a desperate conflict at the center of such stories of trauma. According to Caruth, testimonies of trauma engage in "a kind of double telling, the oscillation between a *crisis of death* and the correlative *crisis of life*: between the story of the unbearable nature of an event and the story of the unbearable nature of survival" (7, emphasis in original). Which is the true trauma: facing brutality, torture, terror, or death or living with the memory and repercussions of that experience? Is surviving merely a modified extension of the original trauma?[3]

Trauma studies has focused on the psychological consequences to individuals and groups who have suffered violence, humiliation, and subjection at the hands of oppressors and who often relive these experiences continually as a result of the psychic wounds inflicted. The study of transgenerational trauma, however, examines how an individual's or group's personal experience of trauma may be passed on to the next generation and beyond, through "postmemory" (M. Hirsch) and in the form of "haunting legacies" (Schwab). Hirsch argues that "postmemory" is distinct from "memory by generational difference and from history by deep personal connection." A special form of memory, postmemory focuses more on "imaginative investment and creation" than recollection (Hirsch, *Family Frames* 22). Postmemory "characterizes the experience of those who grow up dominated by narratives that preceded their birth" (22), powerful narratives that threaten to eclipse their own life stories. The parents' traumatic experiences are "transmitted to [the second generation] so deeply and affectively as to *seem* to constitute memories in their own right" (Hirsch, *Generation of Postmemory* 5, emphasis in original). "For children of survivors . . . , the knowledge of that forbidding event was transmitted in very intimate ways. It was passed on through private stories, through family speech, or indeed family silences" (Hoffman 5). The articulation "was often incoherent, fragmented, broken; it came in encapsulated, explosive phrases; it was speech under the pressure of great pain" (Hoffman 5). As a consequence, the second generation experiences "malaise at being neither here nor there" (Brodzki, *Can These Bones Live?* 203). But it is left to the children of survivors, the second generation, to shape the fragments and omissions, mediated as they are, into narrative.[4]

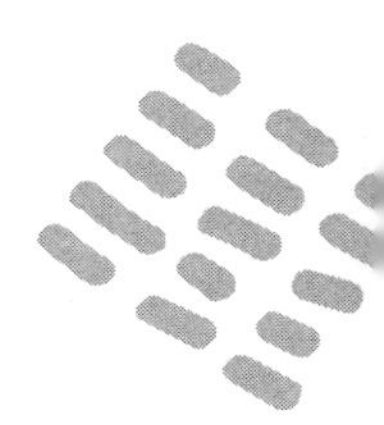

. . . . . . . . . . . . . . . . . . . . . . . . . . . . . . . . . . . . . . . . . . . . . . . . . . . . . . . . . . .

Just as Peter Najarian situates the Armenian genocide as the heart of his family narrative and Theresa Cha (see chapter 5) focuses on the consequences of the Japanese occupation of Korea, so Art Spiegelman places transgenerational trauma at the center of his graphic memoir. Spiegelman attempts to narrate his parents' histories and the global politics that shaped them, as well as his own complex subjectivity in relation to his traumatic family history. He illustrates how his parents' experience of the Holocaust is the dominant and dominating formative force not only in their lives but, in different ways, also in his. Spiegelman attempts to understand and translate his parents' trauma and to comprehend the effects of the legacy of torment and perpetual loss that has been passed on to him. He emphasizes the challenges of trying to extract a coherent narrative about the war from his father, of attempting to comprehend the haunting absence left by his mother's suicide and the destruction of her journals, of struggling to understand the enormity of the Holocaust, of trying to represent the unrepresentable, and of grappling with the anxiety and distrust he has inherited simply by being a child of survivors. Spiegelman uses imaginative combinations of image and text, often using a "cinematic style" (Geis, introduction 2), to narrate his stories and, at the same time, to reveal the challenges and processes of self-articulation. He struggles to bring his graphic memoir to a definitive conclusion. In fact, he performs this difficulty by staging multiple, competing endings.

## A Note about Comics and Cinematic Techniques

For obvious reasons, the form of comics is often compared to film.[5] Both film and comics are composed of a sequence of static frames, but in film viewers "transform a series of still pictures into a story of continuous motion" (McCloud, *Understanding* 65), while comics requires readers-viewers to participate in "closure"—a process that requires readers "to connect these moments and mentally construct a continuous, unified reality" (McCloud 67). This occurs in the gutter—the space between comics frames that "activates the medium" (Spiegelman, *Comix* 100)—where "human imagination takes two separate images and transforms them into a single idea" (McCloud 66). Closure in comics, then, involves "observing the parts, but perceiving the whole" (63). Scholars agree that, more than film, comics requires active reader-viewer participation, "allowing a reader to be in control when she looks at what and how long she spends on each frame" (Chute, *Graphic Women* 9). Like Cha, Spiegelman uses a filmic style, but his is grounded in comics conventions, rather than experimental video and performance art. He uses camera angles (such as close-ups and long shots), creates successions of linked frames that spatialize time and action, and manipulates the gutter. Last, unlike film, comics visualizes simultaneous temporalities and spaces through techniques of juxtaposition, overlay, and framing.

Until the fairly recent rise of scholarly work on comics, the comics form had had a profoundly undervalued position in U.S. culture.[6] The most common assumptions were that comics were written for pubescent, hyperhormonal boys; that they focused on humor of the silliest and grossest kind; and that they dealt with science fiction, fantasy, and superheroes. In short, the comics form could not be a medium for serious literary or artistic concerns.

A misnomer itself, since there is nothing necessarily funny about the form, the term "comics" has been inadequate almost since its inception. In Italy, for instance, the word for comics is *fumetto* (little cloud), referring to its dialogue bubbles; in France, it is *bande dessinée*, referring to the drawn strip or panel format (Horn).[7] Unlike the U.S. word, both the Italian and French terms focus on the formal qualities of comics rather

   Literature-Based Image-and-Text Forms

than the supposed content. In an attempt to define comics more precisely, to formulate a vocabulary for comics, and to argue for comics as a form capable of artistic and literary merit, comics artists and scholars have defined comics in a variety of ways. Emphasizing the sequence of frames in a panel, Will Eisner defines comics as "sequential art" (*Comics and Sequential Art*); highlighting the narrative, Scott McCloud defines them as "the art of telling stories with pictures" (*Making Comics* 3); and insisting on their seamless combination of image and text, W. J. T. Mitchell refers to comics as "vernacular composite forms" or "image-texts" (89, 93).[8] Others use the term "graphic novels" (Gravett), a term usually reserved for comics books, not strips, with serious literary and artistic intent. "'Graphic novel' can usefully designate a certain type of comic: a single-author, book-length work, meant for a grown-up reader, with a memoirist or novelistic narrative, usually devoid of superheroes" (Batuman 23). On the other hand, many comics artists ridicule the term as a pretentious and disingenuous attempt to rebrand comics in order to elevate their cultural status. Certainly "graphic novel" is meant to replace the term "comics," but its definition is too capacious for what I focus on here: graphic memoir. Scholars have introduced a neologism — "autographics" — in order to underscore "the tensions between 'auto' and 'graph' in the rapidly changing visual and textual cultures of autobiography" (Whitlock and Poletti v). "Autographics" may be a product: a "life narrative fabricated in and through drawing and design using various technologies, modes, and materials" (v); or it may be a practice: "of reading the signs, symbols and techniques of visual arts in life narrative" (v). By 2011 an accumulation of competing labels had developed: "autobiographix, graphic memoir, and autography" (Chaney 5). No matter what it is called, "comic art" is "a literary medium in transition from mass popularity and cultural disdain to a new respectability as a means of expression and communication" (Witek 5). Since the late twentieth century it has been necessary to view "comics as a differentiated medium and not as one indivisible block of para-literature" (Christiansen and Magnussen 24). Explaining that "definitions [of comics] are more like indications rather than recipes," Art Spiegelman prefers to use the *American Heritage Dictionary* definition of comics: "'a narrative series of cartoons'" (*MetaMaus* 166).

The comics form, as it is generally understood in the United States, was established in mid- to late nineteenth-century newspapers.[9] But it was not until the "underground or alternative comix" (spelled "comix" to emphasize the co-mixing of image and text) movement of the 1960s, most often associated with R. Crumb and dated from the publication of his comics books *Zap #0 and Zap #1* (1967) and *Snatch* (1968), that the form broke loose to focus on "overtly sexual work," "more philosophical" topics (Horn 224), and, as is now well established, more autobiographical content.[10]

In the late twentieth century, the two-volume *Maus* (1986, 1991) by cartoon artist Art Spiegelman was one of several graphic narratives to elevate the form of comics from children's to adult literature, from fantastic to serious content, from fantasy to nonfiction.[11] In their call for a "polycentric aesthetics" (that is, a non-Eurocentric aesthetics) for the study of visual culture, Ella Shohat and Robert Stam describe the "aesthetics of garbage," an artistic movement that demanded "a strategic redemption of the low" (51) that originated in Brazil in the 1960s. While this sounds suspiciously like the nineteenth-century romantic movement, which idealized the poor and rural as well as the forms associated with them (for example, the ballad), or like the modernist art practice that elevated everyday objects—known as readymades or found objects or outsider art—into art galleries, various literary and art scholars have attempted to reexamine inherited dictums in order to see anew visual forms that had been categorized into degradation or invisibility. When Art Spiegelman was awarded a Pulitzer Prize for *Maus*, volume I, in 1992, the first graphic narrative to be so acknowledged, the comics form was legitimated overnight. Since that time *Maus* has become canonical in university literature departments throughout the United States.

In *Maus: A Survivor's Tale* (vol. I: *My Father Bleeds History*, 1986, and vol. II: *And Here My Troubles Began*, 1991), Art Spiegelman (re)tells the stories of his father Vladek's survival of Auschwitz; his process of recording, translating, and shaping his father's story; his troubled relationship with his father; and his own anxiety about being the son of survivors. Throughout I refer to the author as Art Spiegelman or Spiegelman and to Spiegelman's autobiographical persona as Artie. Like many others before and after him, Spiegelman has contributed to the literature of witness arising out of the Holocaust. Unlike others, however, he narrates these multiple stories in comics form; highlights the difficulties of recording and translating the past, including the omissions, multiple interpretations, uncertainties, and outright lies; and performs the process of attempting to apprehend the near incomprehensible horror of the Shoah as well as the process of trying to represent the unrepresentable—all the while grappling with questions about the ethics of representation generally but also in comics form specifically. In short, throughout *Maus*, Spiegelman performs the central conflicts debated in Holocaust studies and by children of survivors: Is it ethical to try to represent the Holocaust? Who is entitled to speak about it? Is it possible to represent the unrepresentable? What is an appropriate form for such a representation?

Although in *Comics Books as History*, Joseph Witek claims that Spiegelman's use of animals to convey his narrative "can defamiliarize his too well known story and can sidestep the 'already told' quality of the Holocaust" (103), it is the comics form itself that demands a new way of seeing the Holocaust. Accustomed to documentary photographs of emaciated bodies in concentration camps or mass graves, readers-viewers of *Maus* are jolted out of any previous visual orientation to the topic. Spiegelman establishes the cast of characters of his animal fable quickly: the Jews are mice, the Germans cats, French frogs, Poles pigs, Americans dogs, English fish, Roma Gypsy moths, and Swedes reindeer. The use of animals recalls the long history of animal comic strips, often providing a critical commentary on the foibles of humans, and emphasizes the dehumanizing reduction of human identity to types. They are at various times more, or less, human. Actually, the characters are hybrid humans with animal heads or, as Spiegelman describes them, "anthropomorphized mice" (*Comix* 17). The hybrid animals in *Maus* represent nationalities except in the case of the mice, who are Jewish whether they are Polish, German, or French. The animal as visual metaphor of identity in *Maus* raises central questions: If it is not national, is Jewish identity based on religion or culture or biology? Spiegelman's choice of mice, of course, echoes Adolf Hitler's call to eradicate Jews, whom Nazi propagandists called "dirty and filth-covered vermin."[12]

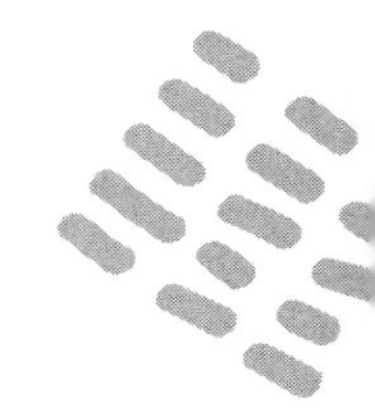

Yet although Spiegelman represents the Jewish people as they were viewed by Nazis—as "vermin"—he also draws them as they saw themselves: small and innocent-faced, watching with large, sad eyes as the Nazi agenda spreads over Europe. In contrast, Spiegelman draws the cats (Nazis) with large heads and vicious facial expressions, many strong lines, and deep shading, visually highlighting their power and brutality. The fact that Spiegelman's selection of animals imitates, in some regard, their behavior in the natural world troubles his visual metaphor. Just as cats chase, torment, and kill mice, so the Nazis hunt down, torture, and kill Jews. Just as dogs chase cats, so Americans pursue Nazis. The animal world offers a powerful reference for human behavior. On the other hand, the fact that cats instinctively want to destroy mice suggests an inevitability, a genetically coded impulse to destroy another species. If cats are programmed to hunt mice, are we to conclude that, disturbing as it may be, it's just natural? Where is the possibility of change or resistance to what might be seen as an overwhelming instinct, a biological imperative? Of course, crosschecking the behaviors of the animal characters with animals in the natural world is in itself a flawed approach, about as helpful as fact-checking memories represented in an autobiography. Nonetheless, it raises questions about representations of identity and the power relations that determine them—a key point articulated by Spiegelman throughout the two volumes.

Spiegelman himself calls attention to the artifice and limits of his

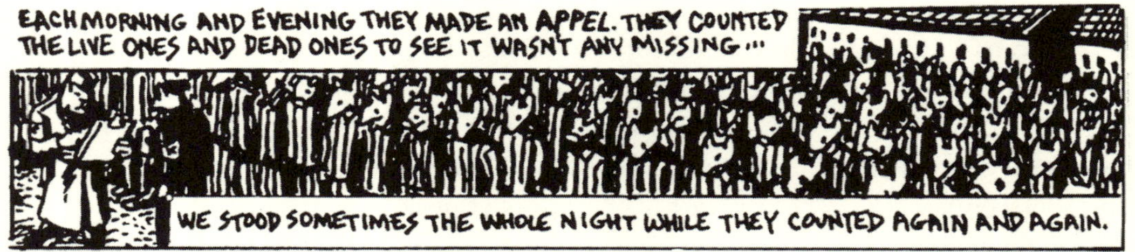

EACH MORNING AND EVENING THEY MADE AN APPEL. THEY COUNTED THE LIVE ONES AND DEAD ONES TO SEE IT WASN'T ANY MISSING...
WE STOOD SOMETIMES THE WHOLE NIGHT WHILE THEY COUNTED AGAIN AND AGAIN.


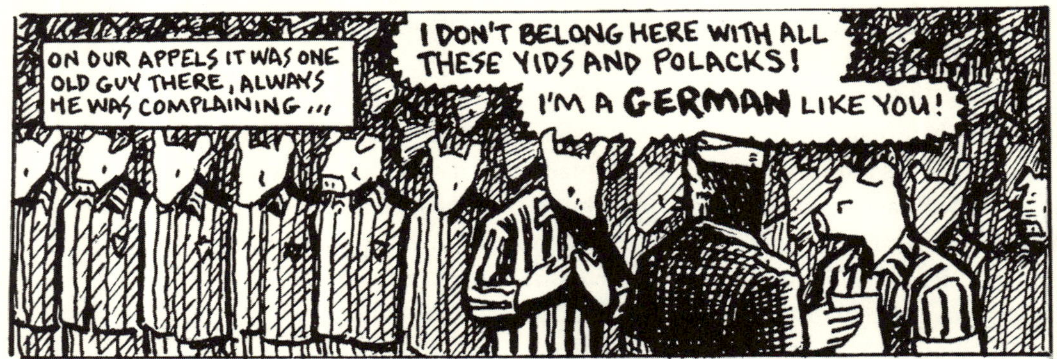

ON OUR APPELS IT WAS ONE OLD GUY THERE, ALWAYS HE WAS COMPLAINING...
I DON'T BELONG HERE WITH ALL THESE YIDS AND POLACKS! I'M A GERMAN LIKE YOU!


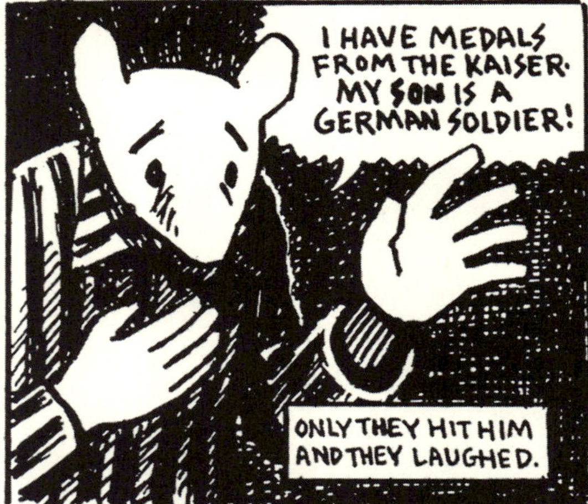

I HAVE MEDALS FROM THE KAISER. MY SON IS A GERMAN SOLDIER!
ONLY THEY HIT HIM AND THEY LAUGHED.


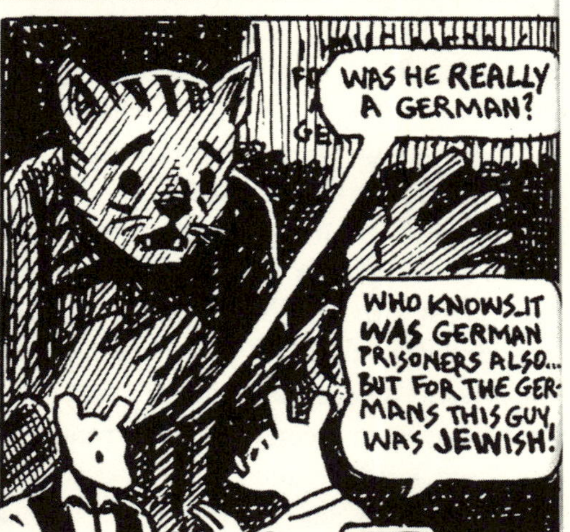

WAS HE REALLY A GERMAN?
WHO KNOWS... IT WAS GERMAN PRISONERS ALSO... BUT FOR THE GERMANS THIS GUY WAS JEWISH!


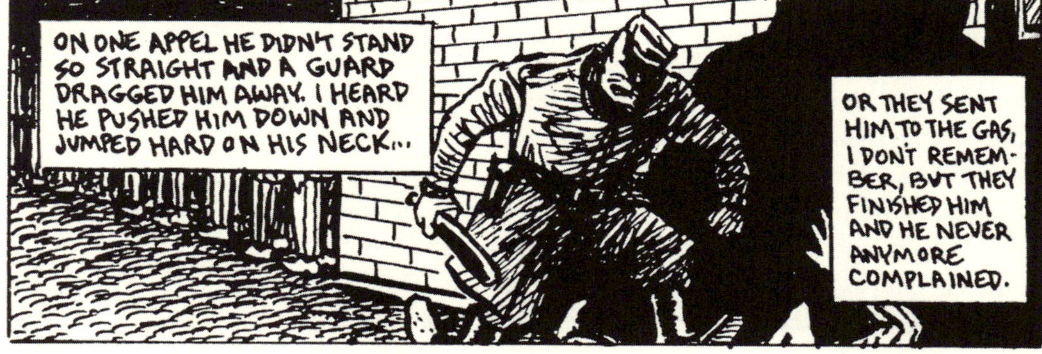

ON ONE APPEL HE DIDN'T STAND SO STRAIGHT AND A GUARD DRAGGED HIM AWAY. I HEARD HE PUSHED HIM DOWN AND JUMPED HARD ON HIS NECK...
OR THEY SENT HIM TO THE GAS, I DON'T REMEMBER, BUT THEY FINISHED HIM AND HE NEVER ANYMORE COMPLAINED.

animal schema at various self-reflexive moments throughout *Maus*. Spiegelman's autobiographical persona, Artie, wears a mouse mask to question his Jewish authenticity, while his parents, Vladek and Anja, use pig masks to try to pass as Poles. When Anja sees a rat while hiding in a basement, Vladek assures her, falsely, that it's just a mouse. Spiegelman shares his speculations about how to represent his French wife, who converted to Judaism (is she a rabbit or a mouse?). When Artie visits Dr. Pavel, whose office is "overrun with stray dogs and cats" and includes a framed photograph of Pavel's pet cat, he directly addresses the reader-viewer: "Can I mention this, or does it completely louse up my metaphor?" (*Complete Maus* II.203). Spiegelman's self-reflexivity is forthright and ironic. To be authentic, in this instance, means to expose the fragile apparatus used to convey the story.

Even though he uses animal characters to represent national identities, then, Spiegelman is deft at ensuring that identity is not reducible to nationality or any other supposedly fixed idea. He does this most explicitly in his use of masks. In one scene (I.66) Vladek wears a pig mask and speaks boldly to a Polish train official about the "stinking Nazis" in an attempt to pass as Polish. Only when he is hiding in a coat closet to remove his mask is Vladek drawn as a sad-eyed mouse. Similarly, when Vladek and Anja flee, Spiegelman depicts them wearing pig masks to pass as Polish. When Vladek tells Artie that he could pass as Polish readily, "But Anja—her appearance—you could see more easy she was Jewish" (I.138), the reader-viewer sees a mouse tail protruding from Anja's coat. As he often does, Spiegelman relies here on a single visual detail, in this case Anja's mouse tail, to convey important information: to reveal her identity as Jewish.

In volume II, written after *Maus* I's critical success, Spiegelman highlights not only the historical problems of identity but also his difficult decisions about representing it. The volume begins with a sketch of his sketchbook serving as the opening panel, one of his many self-conscious representations reminding readers-viewers of the problem of representation. On the sketchbook, Artie is experimenting with drawing different animals. He presents a conversation with his French wife, Françoise, about how best to depict her. Should she be a frog or a rabbit? Finally, she says, "But if you're a mouse, I ought to be a mouse too. I CONVERTED didn't I?" (II.171). Being Jewish cannot be reduced to a national identity, and Françoise's status as a converted Jew underscores the multiplicity, complexity, and permeability of formulations of Jewish identity.

Spiegelman continues his exploration of Jewish identity in his depiction of Vladek's life in the Nazi camps (fig. 3.1). He retells Vladek's story of a man, depicted as a mouse in the second panel, who complains: "I don't belong here with all these Yids and Polacks! I'm a GERMAN like

(OPPOSITE)
FIGURE 3.1.
Art Spiegelman.
*Jewish Identity
and Nazi Power*
(*The Complete
Maus* II.210).
(Graphic novel
excerpt from THE
COMPLETE MAUS:
A SURVIVOR'S TALE
by Art Spiegelman,
*Maus*, Volume II
copyright © 1986,
1989, 1990, 1991
by Art Spiegelman.
Used by
permission of
Pantheon Books,
an imprint of the
Knopf Doubleday
Publishing Group,
a division of
Penguin Random
House LLC. All
rights reserved.)

Time flies...

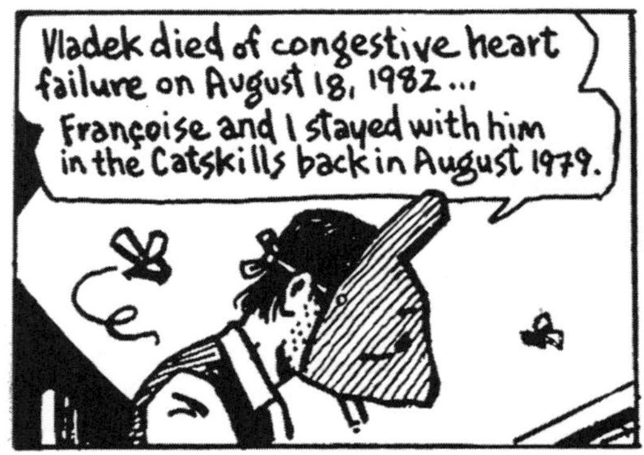
Vladek died of congestive heart failure on August 18, 1982...
Françoise and I stayed with him in the Catskills back in August 1979.

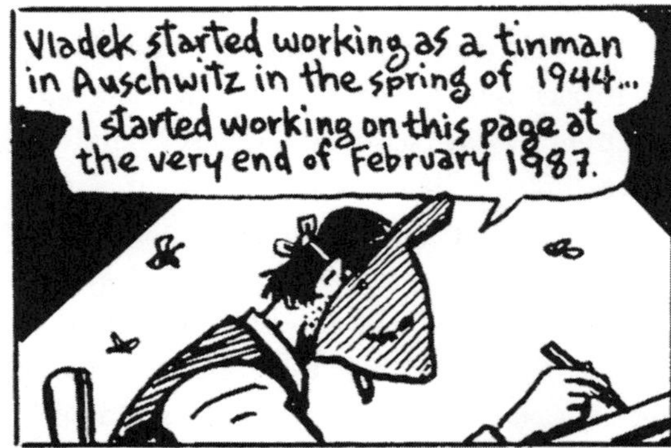
Vladek started working as a tinman in Auschwitz in the spring of 1944...
I started working on this page at the very end of February 1987.

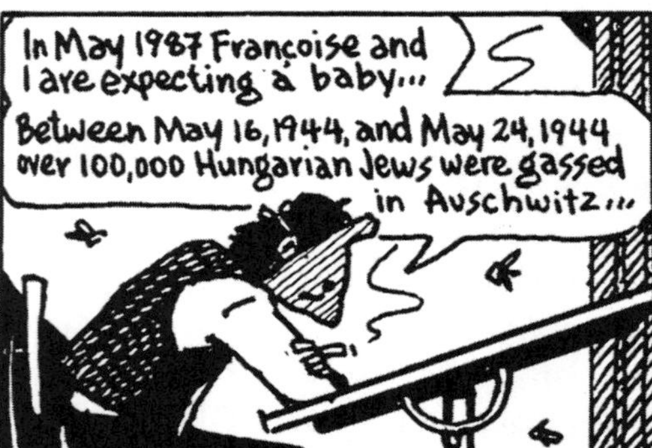
In May 1987 Françoise and I are expecting a baby...
Between May 16, 1944, and May 24, 1944 over 100,000 Hungarian Jews were gassed in Auschwitz...

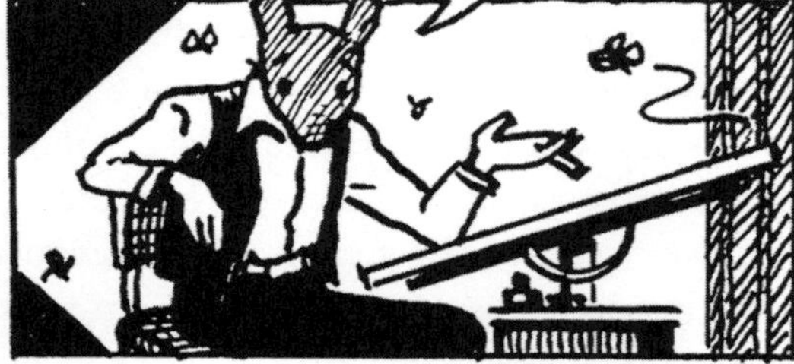
In September 1986, after 8 years of work, the first part of MAUS was published. It was a critical and commercial success.

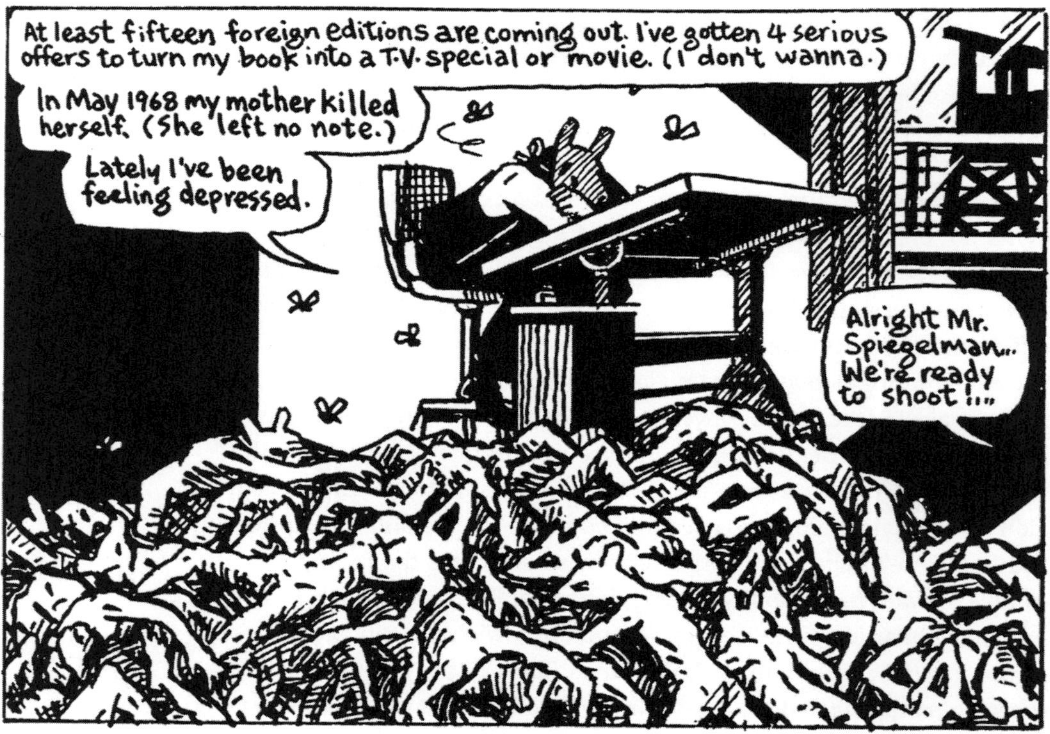
At least fifteen foreign editions are coming out. I've gotten 4 serious offers to turn my book into a T.V. special or movie. (I don't wanna.)
In May 1968 my mother killed herself. (She left no note.)
Lately I've been feeling depressed.
Alright Mr. Spiegelman... We're ready to shoot!...

you!" (II.210). No one listens or seems to care. The third panel is divided into two frames. In the left frame, a mouse protests: "I have medals from the Kaiser. My son is a German soldier!" (II.210). Vladek's commentary, inset into the frame in a rectangle, explains: "Only they hit him and they laughed" (II.210). In the right frame, almost the same image is depicted, only now the man is drawn as a cat, as if superimposed over the left frame, where he was presented as a mouse. Inset into the front of the frame is a drawing of Artie and Vladek as they converse in the present. The dialogue bubble in the present obscures the cat-man's words, "I have medals," underscoring visually how the Nazi soldier ignores them as well as how clear answers about what happened in the past are inaccessible in the present. In fact, it is Artie's question itself that blocks the cat-man's words. Artie asks, "Was he REALLY a German?" Vladek replies, "Who knows—it WAS German prisoners also. . . . But for the Germans this guy was JEWISH!" (II.210). The final panel depicts a guard killing the man, whose identity is never really determined. In one short sequence, Spiegelman represents the indeterminacy of identity and its subjection to power. It doesn't matter who you think you are, who you say you are, or who others identify you as. The only thing that matters is that those in power, in this case Nazi soldiers, can define you in any way that suits their purposes.

Volume I opens with a two-page prefatory scene, the only time in the two volumes that Spiegelman narrates an event from his childhood. This single event serves as a synecdoche—a part that stands for the whole burden of transgenerational trauma. Young Artie falls down when his roller skate comes loose, and rather than rally to his aid, his friends run off without him. When Artie returns home in tears and explains the situation to his father, Vladek responds: "FRIENDS? Your friends? . . . If you lock them together in a room with no food for a week. . . . THEN you could see what it is, friends!" (I.6). In this short introductory scene, Spiegelman shows vividly and concisely how the emotional aftershocks of trauma are passed on from the generation of survivors to their children. Rather than a word of comfort, a hug, or a conversation, little Artie is confronted with the overwhelming selfishness and evil of human nature as well as the enormity of his parents' suffering.

Spiegelman develops the consequences of his inheritance of trauma in his adult life most vividly in some of the most famous scenes in *Maus* II, chapter 2, "Auschwitz (Time Flies)" (fig. 3.2). The two frames of the first panel show a profile of Artie sitting at his drawing desk wearing a mouse mask. Spiegelman here suggests that Jewish, or any, identity is unstable, at the very least situational. A few flies hover around him. The text provides a concise historical overview, providing dates for recent events (Vladek died in 1982; Catskills vacation 1979) and links to the

(OPPOSITE)
FIGURE 3.2.
Art Spiegelman.
*Artie at His Drawing Desk*
(*The Complete Maus* II.201).
(Graphic novel excerpt from THE COMPLETE MAUS: A SURVIVOR'S TALE by Art Spiegelman, *Maus*, Volume II copyright © 1986, 1989, 1990, 1991 by Art Spiegelman. Used by permission of Pantheon Books, an imprint of the Knopf Doubleday Publishing Group, a division of Penguin Random House LLC. All rights reserved.)

distant past (Vladek worked as a tinman in Auschwitz in 1944). Juxtaposing life (the birth of Spiegelman's first child in 1987) and death (the gassing of one hundred thousand Jews in Auschwitz in 1944) in the second frame of the second panel and noting also the "commercial success" of *Maus* I, Artie turns to look directly at the reader-viewer. From this angle, Artie looks like a man with a mouse face, not like a man wearing a mouse mask. Is he an imposter, using his parents' Holocaust experiences to find profit and fame and an identity as a Jew? By the third and final panel that fills half of the page, the perspective shifts as if the camera is pulled back for a long shot. For the first time, readers-viewers see Artie's complete studio. There, heaped at the base of his desk, the source of his creativity and grief, are the crumpled bodies of Jews massmurdered in the extermination camps. Outside his window is a camp guard tower—found also on the inside back covers of each volume—as if to indicate that the death and horror of the camps are near at hand, a torment to the living, who have to decide what, how, and if to remember and to record. On the next page a sequence of international reporters wearing dog, cat, and mouse masks (in this case, the mouse is an Israeli) and a deathlike mask, representing a bottom-feeding corporate marketer, ask the shrinking Artie questions: What message do you wish to convey? Why should young Germans today feel guilty about the past mistakes of their government? How would you depict Israeli Jews? How about marketing *Maus* commercial products for profit ("*Maus*. You've read the book, now buy the vest!")? Was making *Maus* "cathartic"? By the final panel, Artie is reduced—literally Spiegelman draws him as a tiny mouse—to a small child crying for his "Mommy" (II.202).[13]

Finally left alone, the tiny Artie climbs down from his chair and heads to see his psychiatrist, Dr. Pavel, "a survivor of Terezin and Auschwitz" (II.203). The mouse mask returns, as do the corpses. This time the dead bodies are not just at the foot of his desk; they cover the streets of New York. Artie must walk atop them, prefiguring (in *Maus*) but echoing (in life) the scene in which Vladek has to walk on the typhus victims in the camp (II.255). The visual commentary suggests that for a child of a survivor it is impossible to escape the ever-present trauma of the Holocaust.

### Telling Details and Visualizing Postmemory

Relying on visuals to carry the story forward, to comment on a scene, to create a mood, or to generate a dialogue with text are all aspects of graphic narratives. A complex tripartite narrative such as Spiegelman's risks confusion about how to distinguish past and present, to clarify who is speaking, and to relate, not obfuscate, the various stories. But even for readers unfamiliar with the conventions of comics (generally comics are read left to right, top to bottom), the distinction between past and present in *Maus* is clear. Text in dialogue bubbles inside a frame indicates conversation in the past or present; text in rectangles at the top or bottom of a frame indicates Vladek's narration in the present. In fact, the "comics form makes possible . . . the representation of multiple yet simultaneous time-scapes and competing yet coincident ways of knowing, seeing, and being" (Chaney 5). Emphasizing that comics is "an art of compression that breaks narrative events down to their most necessary moments," Spiegelman has explained that a page is "a unit of space and time" (*MetaMaus* 168 and CD-ROM, later the CD-ROM is replaced with a DVD-R). It is up to the artist-writer to break the page into decipherable units, usually in the form of frames and panels. Relying on two distinct metaphors, Spiegelman compares the page both to an architectural structure, "as if each page was some kind of building with windows in it," and to "a paragraph with each panel or tier of panels like a 'sentence'" and the page as "a visual paragraph" (*MetaMaus* 166–67).[14] Spiegelman decided on a basic template, then proceeded to vary it to provide a combination of narrative variety and coherence. He varies his standard frame by breaking the frame or using tilted frames, frames within frames, and occasional vertical panels. Another set of variations emphasizes important or dramatic moments. For example, Spiegelman presents a half- or whole-page tableau rather than an individual frame within a panel or insets such as windows or the spotlight-moon used as interior frames or focalizing points.

Throughout *Maus*, Spiegelman uses visual detail to make important points not included in the text in the form of narration, dialogue, or reportage. He underscores the diverse population within the death camps, for instance, without using a single word. Suffering from typhus, Vladek has to walk over dead and dying bodies to get to the toilet. In the third panel at the bottom of the page, Spiegelman shows a close-up of Vladek's human feet walking atop a couple of mice, but also a cat and a pig (II.255). Spiegelman simply shows us, without commentary, that non-Jewish Germans and Poles also perished with Jews.

Other notable examples of this characteristic comics technique of conveying crucial information with visual details rather than with writing include the horizontally divided second panel in volume I, page 14. Artie and Vladek are conversing about Artie's plan "to draw that book" about Vladek's life. Vladek sits atop the stationary bicycle. Without any text describing Vladek's experience as a Holocaust survivor or any conversation that mentions it explicitly, a visual detail tells it all. In the lower right panel, a tattooed camp number is visible on Vladek's left forearm. Later, Vladek and Anja flee from the ghetto of Srodula and wonder where

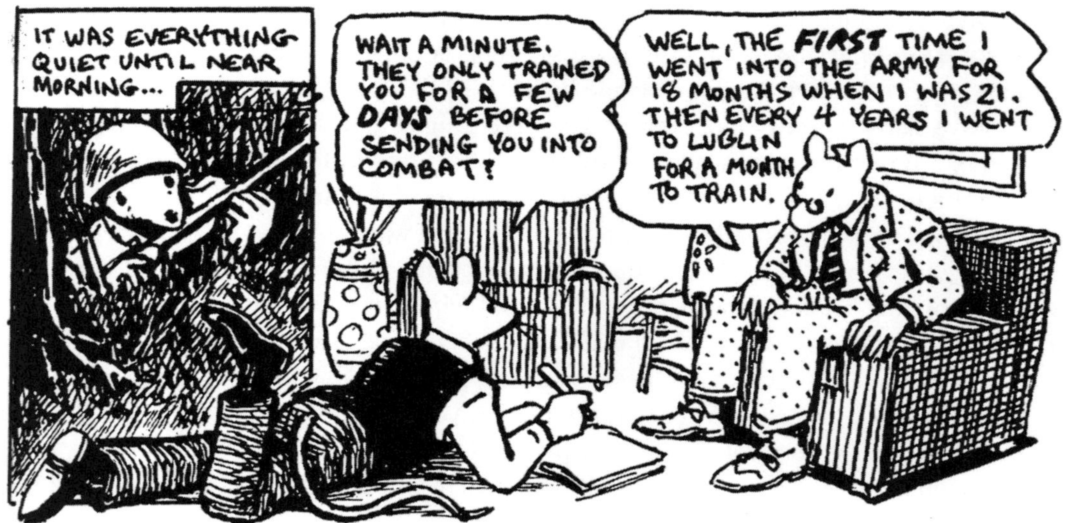



FIGURE 3.3. Art Spiegelman. *As Amanuensis, Artie Links Past and Present* (*The Complete Maus* I.47). (Graphic novel excerpt from THE COMPLETE MAUS: A SURVIVOR'S TALE by Art Spiegelman, *Maus*, Volume I copyright © 1973, 1980, 1981, 1982, 1983, 1984, 1985, 1986 by Art Spiegelman. Used by permission of Pantheon Books, an imprint of the Knopf Doubleday Publishing Group, a division of Penguin Random House LLC. All rights reserved.)


to go next. In the large frame of the third panel the couple "walked in the direction of Sosnowiec" (I.127). What dominates the image is the swastika, which is drawn as the road on which they travel, an apt visual metaphor for showing that no matter where Vladek and Anja run, their fate is determined by the terrifying grip of Nazism that has overtaken the land. Both the tattooed number on Vladek's forearm and the road rendered as a swastika work as a visual shorthand, a concise and powerful visual metaphor of the overwhelming experience of the horrendous expanse of Nazi power and Vladek and Anja's entry into Nazi control.

But more impressive than Spiegelman's mastery of the succinct visual detail that provides information or tells a story is his visual representation of how the past penetrates and permeates the present, how his parents' experience of the Holocaust shadows his everyday life. In short, he depicts the transmission and experience of transgenerational trauma, how the past persistently intrudes on the present, and how Artie's second-generation postmemory functions. A good example of this occurs in volume I, page 47 (fig. 3.3).

At the top of the first frame in the first panel, Vladek's storytelling voice begins the episode about his military service: "It was everything quiet until near morning." The drawing beneath is sketched with intensive dark lines and heavy shading in scratchboard style, underscoring this as a place and time of danger. Framed between his army helmet and rifle, Vladek's innocent face shines in the midst of a dark forest. In the next open frame,[15] Artie interrupts his father's storytelling to ask incredulously: "Wait a minute. They only trained you for a few DAYS before sending you into combat?" The second panel continues the father-son conversation, providing information about how Vladek's father, who

     Literature-Based Image-and-Text Forms

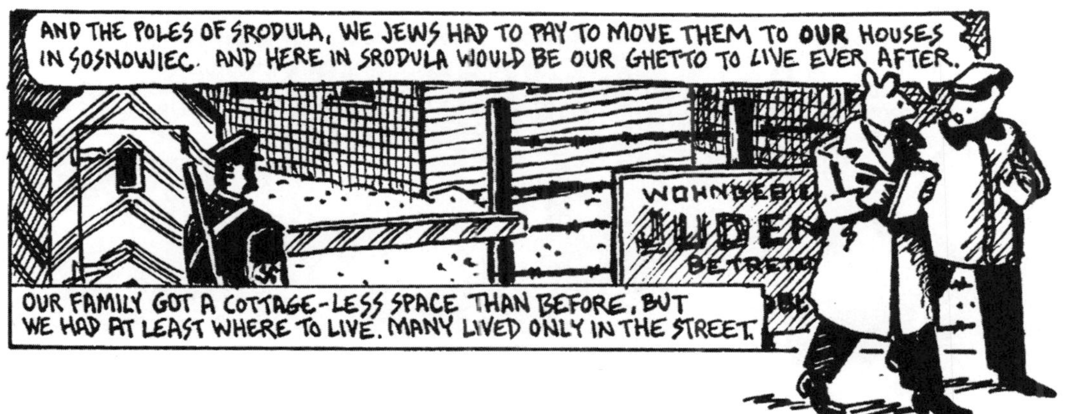


suffered in the Russian army, attempted unsuccessfully to save his sons from army service. The first frame of the first panel on this page is the only visual depiction of the past in this exchange between Artie and Vladek. Significantly, in the borderless frame in the first panel (see fig. 3.3), Spiegelman draws Artie lying on the floor, the upper half of his body facing Vladek, the lower half of his body bleeding out of the second frame and into the first.[16] The dark, striated shading of Artie's pants blends into the scratchboard shading of the forest in the lower part of the first frame. Visually, Artie is the link, the bridge between the past and the present, between Vladek's story and Spiegelman's representation of it. Spiegelman visually highlights his role as amanuensis, revealing part of the process of hearing, recording, and shaping his father's story. Just as important as how Artie is extracting his father's story from the dark and dangerous European woods is how Vladek's story transports Artie back in time. Literally, Artie straddles two worlds. This image, then, uses a visual shorthand to depict postmemory and transgenerational trauma.

Spiegelman illustrates how the overdetermined trauma of his family's past is alive in the present and how historical trauma is passed on from one generation to the next in many drawings throughout *Maus*. Two more examples will characterize the range of those representations. In volume I, page 107, Artie asks again about his mother's missing diary. After Vladek assures Artie that he will look for it later, father and son walk to the bank (fig. 3.4).

In the third panel, they walk together in Vladek's New York neighborhood and Artie asks, "What happened to you and Anja after the big selection at the stadium?" Vladek begins his response, but in the fourth panel at the bottom of the page, the scene behind them is transformed from New York to a ghetto in Srodula, where Jews were placed after being forced to leave their homes in Sosnowiec. The transformation of the background shows visually how Vladek's story transports them (and


FIGURE 3.4.
Art Spiegelman. *The Past Intrudes upon the Present* (*The Complete Maus* I.107). (Graphic novel excerpt from THE COMPLETE MAUS: A SURVIVOR'S TALE by Art Spiegelman, *Maus*, Volume I copyright © 1973, 1980, 1981, 1982, 1983, 1984, 1985, 1986 by Art Spiegelman. Used by permission of Pantheon Books, an imprint of the Knopf Doubleday Publishing Group, a division of Penguin Random House LLC. All rights reserved.)

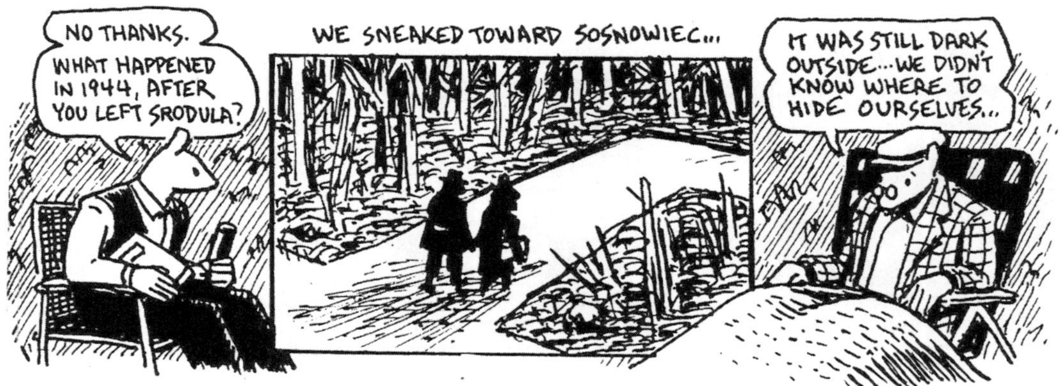




FIGURE 3.5.
Art Spiegelman.
*Framing the Past*
(*The Complete
Maus* I.135).
(Graphic novel
excerpt from THE
COMPLETE MAUS:
A SURVIVOR'S TALE
by Art Spiegelman,
*Maus*, Volume I
copyright © 1973,
1980, 1981, 1982,
1983, 1984, 1985,
1986 by Art
Spiegelman. Used
by permission of
Pantheon Books,
an imprint of the
Knopf Doubleday
Publishing Group,
a division of
Penguin Random
House LLC. All
rights reserved.)


readers-viewers) to the past and, in addition, how the memories of Jewish suffering overtake life in the present. Artie, notebook and pencil in hand, and Vladek appear as if walking out of the frame, out of that past that haunts them both: Vladek because he cannot forget, Artie because he has no Holocaust memories of his own and cannot really access his parents' suffering, much as he earnestly wishes to do so. His father's stories are fragmented and diluted; his mother's stories have been obliterated altogether. As a child of survivors, Artie, finally, has only postmemory—mediated memories imagined from his father's fragmented accounts. Spiegelman offers a metacommentary about this vexed position throughout volume II.

Late in volume I, Spiegelman presents a different scene in which he illustrates the past as alive in the present as well as the tension between him and Vladek (fig. 3.5). After an interlude outlining the troubled marriage of Vladek and his second wife, Mala, Artie returns to his interviewer role. Spiegelman's positioning of the two men is telling. In the first open frame of the fourth panel, Artie asks: "What happened in 1944, after you left Srodula?" In the third unframed frame in the fourth panel, his father answers: "It was still dark outside." The second or middle frame shows Vladek and Anja as they "sneaked toward Sosnowiec" (I.137). Again, Spiegelman breaks the frame and re-creates it.

Instead of a collection of conventional comic strip frames, Artie and Vladek serve as bookend open frames. Between them is the past. The central frame looks almost like a screen onto which Vladek's (and Anja's) past is projected. Vladek sits in front of the screen, his blanket obscuring the bottom right corner. Artie sits slightly behind the screen. The layering suggests not only generational difference but differential access to the past. Vladek has a front-row seat, whereas Artie's view is compromised, as if he is looking not directly at the past but behind the scenes.

Spiegelman thus depicts visually how the past simultaneously links and separates Artie and Vladek. The past is what brings them together—Artie is trying to understand his parents' lives—but it is also what comes between them, disrupting their understanding of each other. Artie can never really know what his father experienced at Auschwitz.

In an interview, Spiegelman explains that interviewing Vladek allowed him to have a relationship with his father, but that he used "the microphone to keep him at bay" (*MetaMaus* DVD-R). Here also Spiegelman provides an image of how the past is produced collaboratively by the two men. Vladek speaks, answers, and remembers. Artie listens, questions, and imagines—punctuated with times that Vladek digresses, complains, or resists, while Artie directs, gets frustrated, or becomes resentful. History, as Spiegelman illustrates it, is produced through active engagement and dialogue, often halting and fragmented, that continues to be revised through the distortion inherent to translation.

In addition to innovative and diverse visual and framing devices, Spiegelman uses visual-verbal echoes or repetitions to reveal how the trauma of the past endures in the present. Spiegelman depicts Vladek's account of a Belgian boy named Felix (fig. 3.6). Worried that he will be selected to be killed, Felix has terrible nightmares, crying and screaming, "AAWOOWWAH!" (II.219) Hyperbolic handwritten letters erupt from Felix, spill over the bed, fill up the room, and extend beyond the frames—the visual style suggesting the sound of irrepressible terror mingled with grief. Although the text is handwritten throughout, this is an example of text that works also as image: a visual sound to represent trauma. In one of his rare moments of empathy and kindness, Vladek tries to comfort the boy. The next day Felix is taken away, never to be seen again.

Fifteen pages (but more than thirty years) later, Spiegelman repeats the image (fig. 3.7). Artie and his wife, Françoise, are in the Catskills vacationing with Vladek. Relaxing on the deck after a long, frustrating day with Vladek (who, in addition to his well-established miserliness, insensitivity, and selfishness, has revealed himself to be a racist, believing in stereotypes of African Americans just as Germans were taught to accept dehumanizing stereotypes of Jews), they hear "AAWOOWWAH!" a visual-textual repetition of the Felix prison camp scene, this time wafting out the window and onto the deck. Readers learn that Vladek has always moaned in his sleep. "When I was a kid I thought that was the noise ALL grown-ups made while they slept" (II.234), Artie tells Françoise. Even fifty years later, Vladek seems to be suffering from post-traumatic stress disorder. Without any explicit commentary about the aftereffects of surviving camp, Spiegelman makes the point that the horror is never left

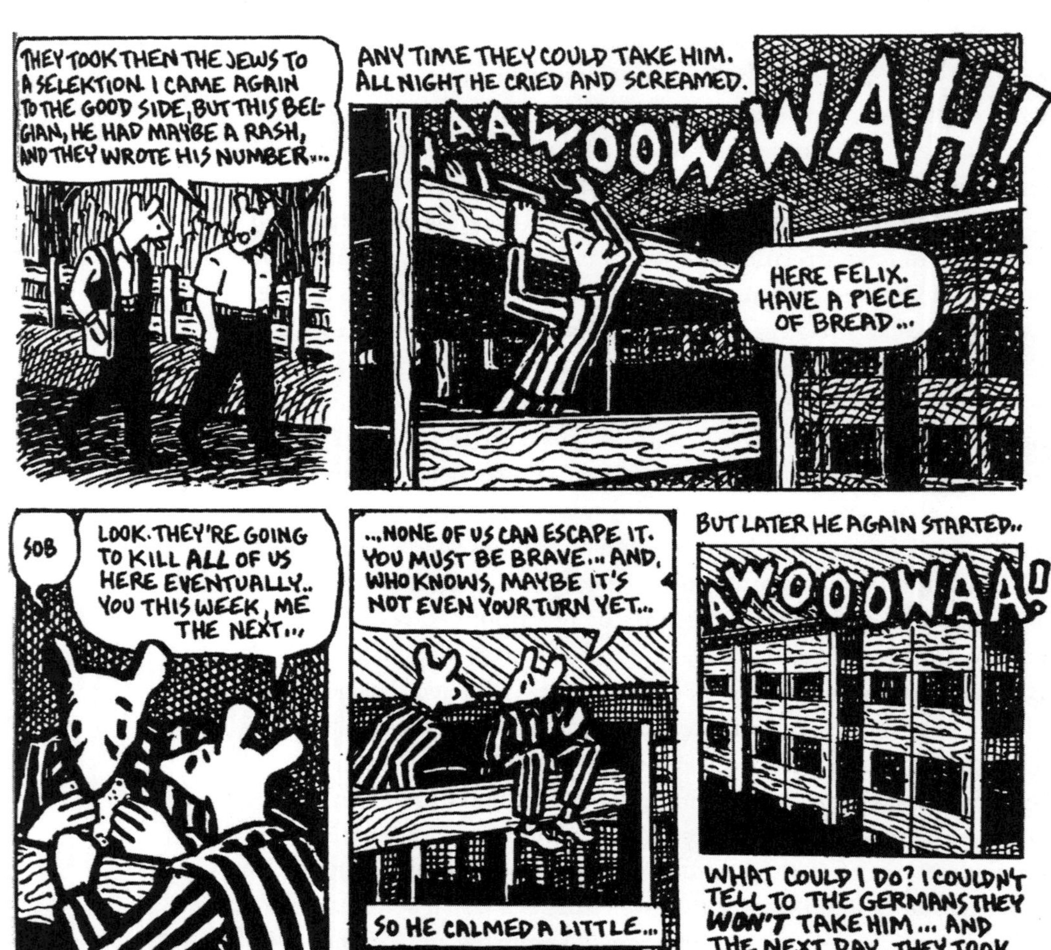


behind, but is carried on, even if it remains unnamed. To add a rather morbid irony, in the next frame Artie sprays insecticide on the hordes of mosquitoes that are beginning to torment them, a not-so subtle allusion to the Nazi gassing (with the insecticide Zyklon-B) of Jewish "vermin."

### Re-Presenting Photographs

In part, *Maus* is a lengthy Holocaust comics family photo album, documenting the profound losses in Artie's life—the death of Richieu during the war; his mother's suicide ("she left no note"), compounded by Vladek's destruction of her notebooks; and the extermination of grandparents, uncles, and aunts during World War II. As has been well established by critical essayists Susan Sontag, Roland Barthes, and others, photographs are associated with death, with loss, with what once was but is no more. "Photographs state the innocence, the vulnerability of lives heading toward their own destruction," writes Sontag, "and this link between photography and death haunts all photos of people" (70). Photographs create a "scene of mourning" for those who look at them. The Holocaust photograph, then, is doubly (or multiply) associated with death because it functions as both an "atrocity document" and a "family photo" (Hirsch, *Family Frames* 21).[17] "The horror of looking is not necessarily *in* the image," explains Marianne Hirsch, "but in the story the viewer provides to fill in what has been omitted" (21, emphasis in original). The "inability 'to take it in' is perhaps the distinguishing feature of the Holocaust photograph" (21). The photographs in *Maus* are documents of memory (the memory of survivors) and postmemory (the memory of children of survivors), which is "mediated not through recollection but through an imaginative investment and creation" (22).

It is significant, then, that Spiegelman reproduces only three photographs in the two volumes of *Maus*: a snapshot of Artie and Anja at the beginning of "Prisoner on the Hell Planet," a portrait of Richieu as a young boy at the beginning of volume II, and a souvenir photograph of Vladek wearing a camp outfit (fig. 3.8).

Together, these three historically and geographically disparate photographs compose a "complete" family portrait: the four Spiegelmans, who should have been a nuclear family, can be pieced together only from separate times and places, a fitting emblem of families torn apart during the Holocaust as well as of the Jewish diaspora. The photograph of Anja and Artie shows a smiling Artie kneeling at his mother's feet. Anja's face is pensive, her hand protectively on her son's head. Ten years later, she would commit suicide. Fittingly, this mother-son photograph is in the title frame of "Prisoner on the Hell Planet," the comics within *Maus* that tells the story of Artie's mental collapse, his return home from the mental hospital, his mother's suicide, and his wrenching guilt. The photograph of Artie with his mother underscores both his sense of closeness to her—he tells Françoise that when he was a child he imagined which of his parents he would save from the camps and it was always his mother (II.174)—and the pain of separation.

The photograph of Richieu, Artie's older brother, who was poisoned before he could be taken to a camp, serves as a portal to volume II. Richieu was never a part of Artie's daily life except as the image hanging on the wall of his parents' bedroom of the perfect son that Artie could never hope to be. Richieu's photograph is framed at top and bottom by Spiegelman's dedication. At the top, the dedication reads: "For Richieu." Below the photograph, the dedication continues: "And for Nadja." The double dedication brings together past, present, and future: the deceased older brother and the Spiegelmans' young daughter, whose future is yet to be determined. To testify to the trauma of the dead and the living

(OPPOSITE)
FIGURE 3.6.
Art Spiegelman.
*Text as Image
and Sound:
AAWOOWWAH!
(The Complete
Maus* II.219).
(Graphic novel
excerpt from THE
COMPLETE MAUS:
A SURVIVOR'S TALE
by Art Spiegelman,
*Maus,* Volume II
copyright © 1986,
1989, 1990, 1991
by Art Spiegelman.
Used by
permission of
Pantheon Books,
an imprint of the
Knopf Doubleday
Publishing Group,
a division of
Penguin Random
House LLC. All
rights reserved.)

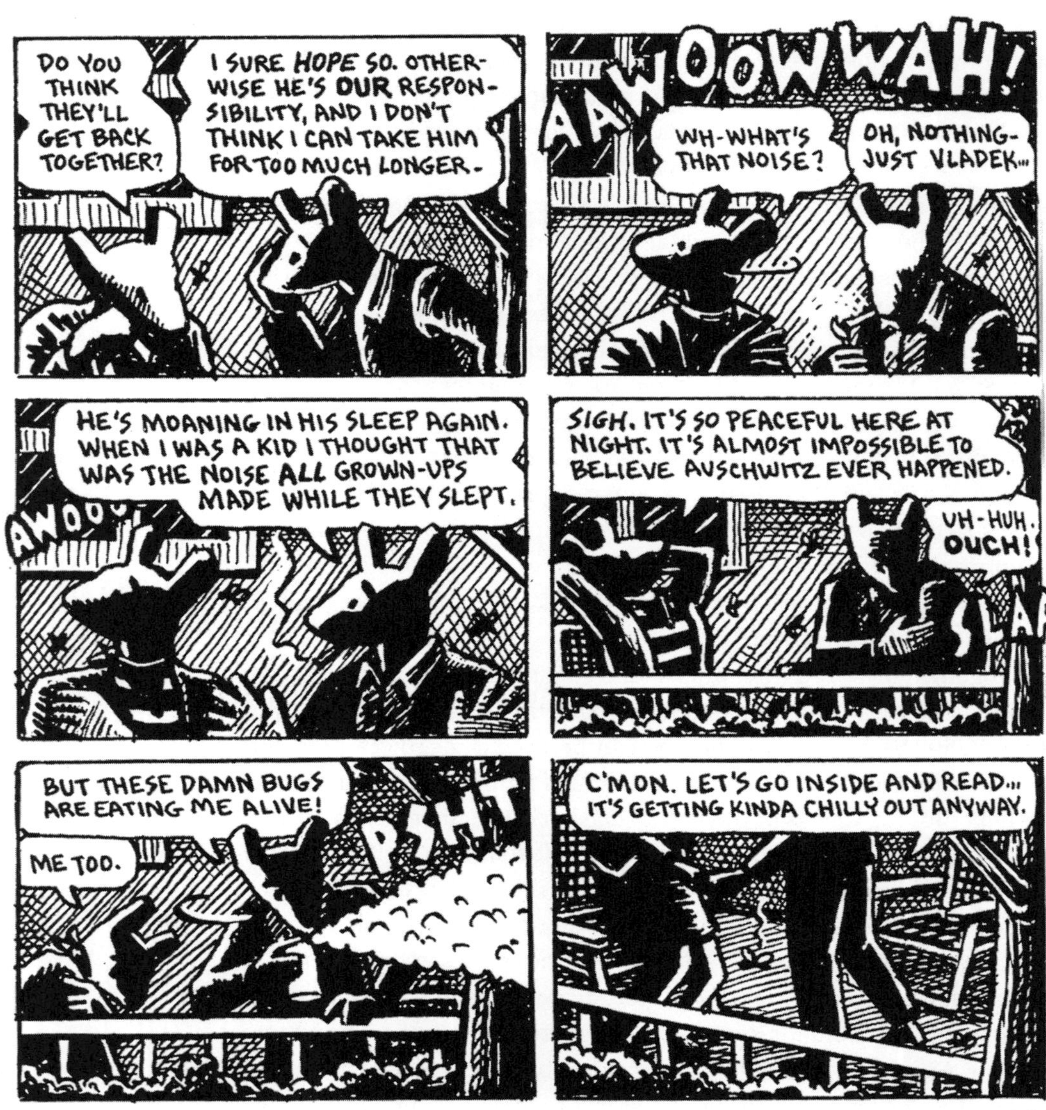


is to address the past (those who have been lost), present (listeners, readers), and future (those, like Nadja, who shall hear and inherit the story some day).

The third and final reproduced photograph is of Vladek wearing a souvenir camp uniform. When Anja is shown Vladek's photograph sent to announce his return from Auschwitz, she exclaims, "And here a picture of him! My God—Vladek is really alive!" (II.294). Unlike Richieu's photograph, which is merely evidence of having been, Vladek's photograph functioned for Anja at the end of the war as a document of his still being. The three reproductions of photographs emphasize the brokenness of the family. Just as important, they break dramatically the visual scheme of hand-drawn mice, reminding readers of the many levels of mediation—representations of representations of representations as well as formulations, reformulations, and imaginings about the past—through which Spiegelman is relaying this story. In contrast to a traditional family photo album that documents generations, important events, and sometimes everyday life, Spiegelman fragments the family photo album, underscoring how, after the Holocaust, it takes conscious and determined historical research to bring stories and images of the family together.

Near the end of *Maus* II, Artie and Vladek sit on the couch looking at old photographs from Poland. In this instance, rather than reproducing the photographs, Spiegelman redraws them as mice, extending his animal tale scheme to documentary forms of representation (fig. 3.9).

Spiegelman uses his redrawn photographs to emphasize visually a double storytelling—Vladek's memories of his past intermingled with Artie's postmemory as well as Spiegelman's attempt to shape the images into a story. Using the snapshots as individual frames (either within a panel or positioned on another single frame at an angle), Spiegelman lays them over the dominant rectangular panel, illustrating how the rendered photographic image bursts out of the frame. Just as Spiegelman describes his first depiction of the entrance to Auschwitz, so the memories here are "too big to be contained" (*MetaMaus*, DVD-R) in a single frame, a single panel, or even a single page. Discussing each photograph, Vladek catalogs the many dead. By the final panel, hanging his head and obscured by photographs of deceased relatives and friends, Vladek seems exhausted, as if the past and the massive loss it entails overwhelm him. "Anja's parents, the grandparents, her big sister Tosha, little Bibi and our Richieu. . . . All what is left, it's the photos" (II.275), says Vladek. The photographs spill out of his hand onto the floor, outside the frames and off the page. The photographs in *Maus* "protrude like unassimilated and unassimilable memories" (Hirsch, *Family Frames* 29). The photos show intact families and shared activities; their distinction from any other family photograph is that they document whom and what was lost in the Holocaust. The faces staring back at us are mere traces of having once existed. For Vladek's side of the family the story is even more grim: "So only my little brother, Pinek, came out from the war alive . . . From the rest of my family, it's *nothing* left, not even a snapshot" (II.276). Vladek's loss of any tangible trace of family, "not even a snapshot" (II.276), is echoed in the destruction of Anja's notebooks and the lack of a suicide note that make Artie's access to his mother's life impossible. Anja, in fact, functions "as that which will forever escape representation and at the same time requires it: the silence of the victims"

(OPPOSITE)
FIGURE 3.7.
Art Spiegelman.
*Repetition of Trauma (The Complete Maus*, II.234).
(Graphic novel excerpt from THE COMPLETE MAUS: A SURVIVOR'S TALE by Art Spiegelman, *Maus*, Volume II copyright © 1986, 1989, 1990, 1991 by Art Spiegelman. Used by permission of Pantheon Books, an imprint of the Knopf Doubleday Publishing Group, a division of Penguin Random House LLC. All rights reserved.)

FIGURE 3.8.
Art Spiegelman.
*Reproduced Family
Photographs* (*The
Complete Maus*
I.102, II.n.p., 294).
(Graphic novel
excerpt and
"Photograph of
Richieu" from THE
COMPLETE MAUS:
A SURVIVOR'S
TALE by Art
Spiegelman, *Maus*,
Volume I copyright
© 1973, 1980,
1981, 1982, 1983,
1984, 1985, 1986
by Art Spiegelman.
Volume II copyright
© 1986, 1989,
1990, 1991 by Art
Spiegelman. Used
by permission of
Pantheon Books,
an imprint of the
Knopf Doubleday
Publishing Group,
a division of
Penguin Random
House LLC. All
rights reserved.)

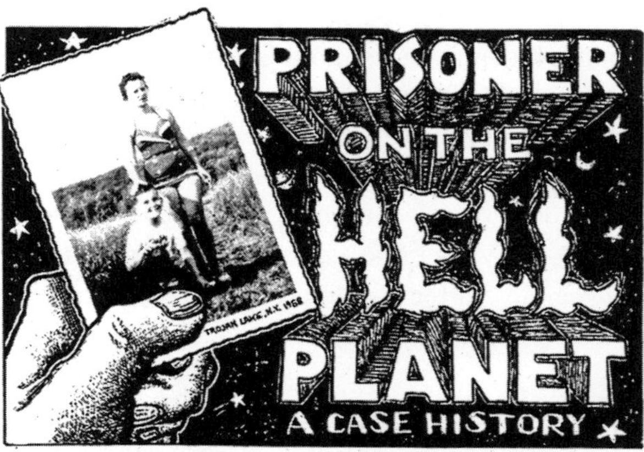


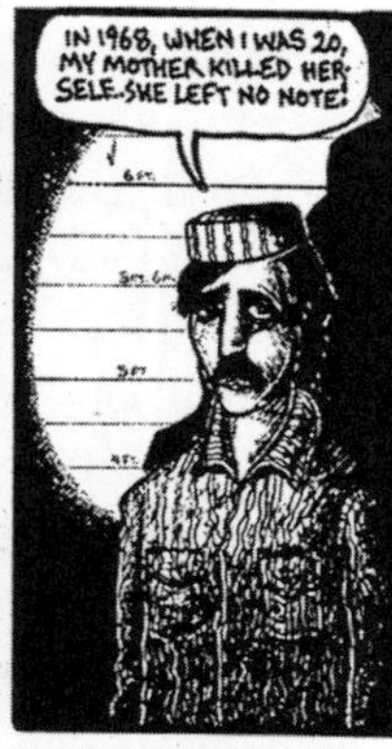


FOR RICHIEU

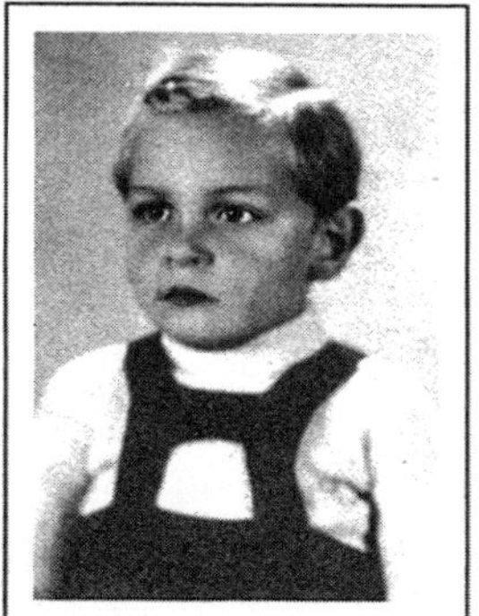

AND FOR NADJA
AND DASHIELL

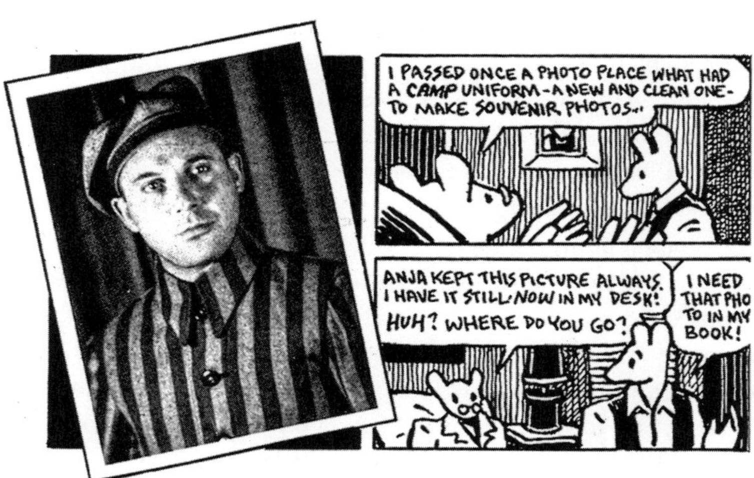

(Miller, "Cartoons of the Self" 52). Like Anja's lack of textual existence, Vladek's family's lack of photographic existence emphasizes the enormity of loss that haunts *Maus*.

## Conclusions: "A Place to Stop"

There has been considerable discussion of the problem of closure for the story of the Holocaust since its aftershocks continue daily and are reformulated and passed on to new generations.[18] And, here, I define closure not as Scott McCloud's notion of the conceptual synthesizing process required by the comics' gutter, but simply as a process of bringing to conclusion, of coming to a full stop. The problem of closure has been discussed also in autobiography studies. Because the true end of any autobiography is death, no one can tell a complete life story. Deciding on a conclusion, a temporary stopping point, is one of the many fictions inherent in the autobiographical endeavor.

Aware of this dilemma, Spiegelman presents at least four potential sequential conclusions to *Maus* II, each linked to a point of view, which in turn signals a level of narration as well as a particular kind of past. The first (fig. 3.10, first panel), from Vladek's perspective (imagined and re-created by Spiegelman, of course), of how others might see his reunion with Anja after surviving the camps, represents the *historical past*, but one that is right out of a Hollywood romantic film.

Reunited, Vladek and Anja embrace. Backlit and reframed by a harvest moon (or perhaps a spotlight), reminiscent of the iris, a filmic convention from the 1930s and an image used earlier in *Maus* to highlight the Nazi swastika, Vladek exclaims: "Anja, Anja, my Anja!" In the narrative inset, he says: "More I don't need to tell you. We were both very happy, and lived happy, happy ever after" (II.296). Of course, readers-viewers know that this is a complete fantasy. Vladek and Anja were both tormented, and Anja committed suicide in 1968. Just as early in *Maus* I, Vladek wants to edit out what he perceived as a digression from his son's Holocaust focus—his love affair with Lucia (24)—so he tries to force his story into an autobiographical narrative formula that includes a linear progression with conflict (the pogroms, removals, mistreatment, and mass murder) and resolution (release from the death camps and return to loved ones).

A second possible conclusion is found in the second frame of the third panel in figure 3.10. Here the narration emphasizes Artie's point of view and the *historical present*. Spiegelman shifts a possible conclusion from Vladek just liberated from Auschwitz and returned to Anja in Poland to Vladek with his son in New York. The ailing Vladek is in bed.

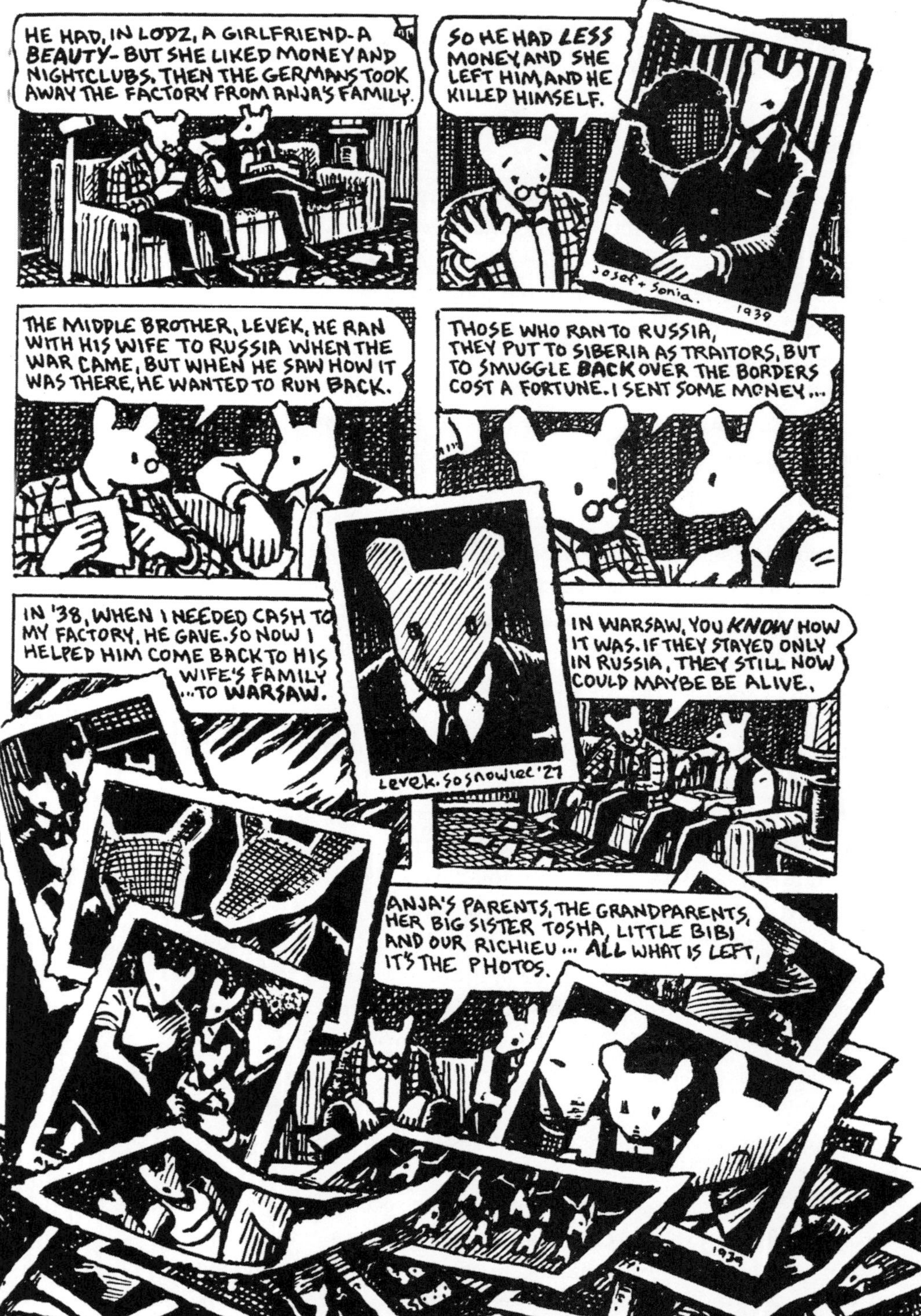

HE HAD, IN LODZ, A GIRLFRIEND-A BEAUTY- BUT SHE LIKED MONEY AND NIGHTCLUBS. THEN THE GERMANS TOOK AWAY THE FACTORY FROM ANJA'S FAMILY.
SO HE HAD LESS MONEY AND SHE LEFT HIM, AND HE KILLED HIMSELF.
Josef + Sonia.
1939
THE MIDDLE BROTHER, LEVEK, HE RAN WITH HIS WIFE TO RUSSIA WHEN THE WAR CAME, BUT WHEN HE SAW HOW IT WAS THERE, HE WANTED TO RUN BACK.
THOSE WHO RAN TO RUSSIA, THEY PUT TO SIBERIA AS TRAITORS, BUT TO SMUGGLE BACK OVER THE BORDERS COST A FORTUNE. I SENT SOME MONEY ...
IN '38, WHEN I NEEDED CASH TO MY FACTORY. HE GAVE. SO NOW I HELPED HIM COME BACK TO HIS WIFE'S FAMILY ... TO WARSAW.
Levek. Sosnowiec '27
IN WARSAW, YOU KNOW HOW IT WAS. IF THEY STAYED ONLY IN RUSSIA, THEY STILL NOW COULD MAYBE BE ALIVE,
ANJA'S PARENTS, THE GRANDPARENTS, HER BIG SISTER TOSHA, LITTLE BIBI AND OUR RICHIEU ... ALL WHAT IS LEFT, IT'S THE PHOTOS.
1939

Artie sits on the bed with the tape recorder on his lap. Vladek turns over to rest and says, "I'm *tired* from talking, Richieu, and it's enough stories for now" (II.296, emphasis in original). Close readers have noticed that Vladek calls Artie by his dead son's name, essentially, and ironically, erasing his second son. Gabriele Schwab describes Artie as one of the most famous "replacement children," children of survivors who are often in an impossible "tacit competition with a dead sibling" (37). Michael Levine interprets this as the scene in which Artie is "effectively killed by his father's address" (97). Linking this paternal scene of erasure with the maternal scenes of abandonment, Hamida Bosmajian argues that Artie's is "an orphaned voice" (26–43) throughout *Maus*. Naomi Mandel goes even further, describing Artie as a "speaking corpse," a literary figure she identifies in Holocaust testimonies and studies.[19] Multiply murdered—textually and orally (Anja's lack of a suicide note, Vladek's destruction of Anja's diaries, and Vladek addressing him by his dead brother's name), Artie is, perhaps, no more a survivor than Vladek and Anja. This scene of misrecognition does not merely depict Vladek's confusion and senility but also is another way that Spiegelman represents how the past can powerfully dominate, even obliterate, the present. Last, this potential conclusion illustrates Spiegelman's transgenerational trauma and his growing uncertainty about whether the aftershocks will ever end.

The drawing of the Spiegelman gravestone is a third conclusion (see fig. 3.10), again told from Artie's perspective and focusing on the *narrator's present*. Spiegelman describes the tombstone as "my version of a *yahrzeit* candle, a memorial" (*MetaMaus* 235). Noting both Vladek's and Anja's birth and death dates provides a kind of frame (as does the drawing itself) to contain the story of their survival. But even the span of his parents' lives is not sufficient to hold the story. Arising between the inscriptions for Vladek and Anja is smoke from a flame. The smoke is perhaps a conventional symbol on tombstones symbolizing the "eternal flame," but it also recalls Spiegelman's depictions of the smoke from his ever-present cigarette, which mingles with smoke from the crematoria of the camps, an ominous image of the traumatic memory and post-memory that wafts throughout the two volumes.

Last, as a fourth conclusion (at the bottom of fig. 3.10), from artist-writer Spiegelman's point of view, is a *postpresent history*, in which Spiegelman figures himself buried beneath his parents. Spiegelman's signature and the dates he worked on *Maus* serve as another frame, another alternative conclusion to the never-ending consequences of historical trauma. This autographic depicts the lifespan of the memoir's autobiographical persona as well as the author-artist's years of commitment to the project.

(OPPOSITE)
FIGURE 3.9.
Art Spiegelman.
*Re-presented Family Photographs* (*The Complete Maus* II.275). (Graphic novel excerpt from THE COMPLETE MAUS: A SURVIVOR'S TALE by Art Spiegelman, *Maus*, Volume II copyright © 1986, 1989, 1990, 1991 by Art Spiegelman. Used by permission of Pantheon Books, an imprint of the Knopf Doubleday Publishing Group, a division of Penguin Random House LLC. All rights reserved.)

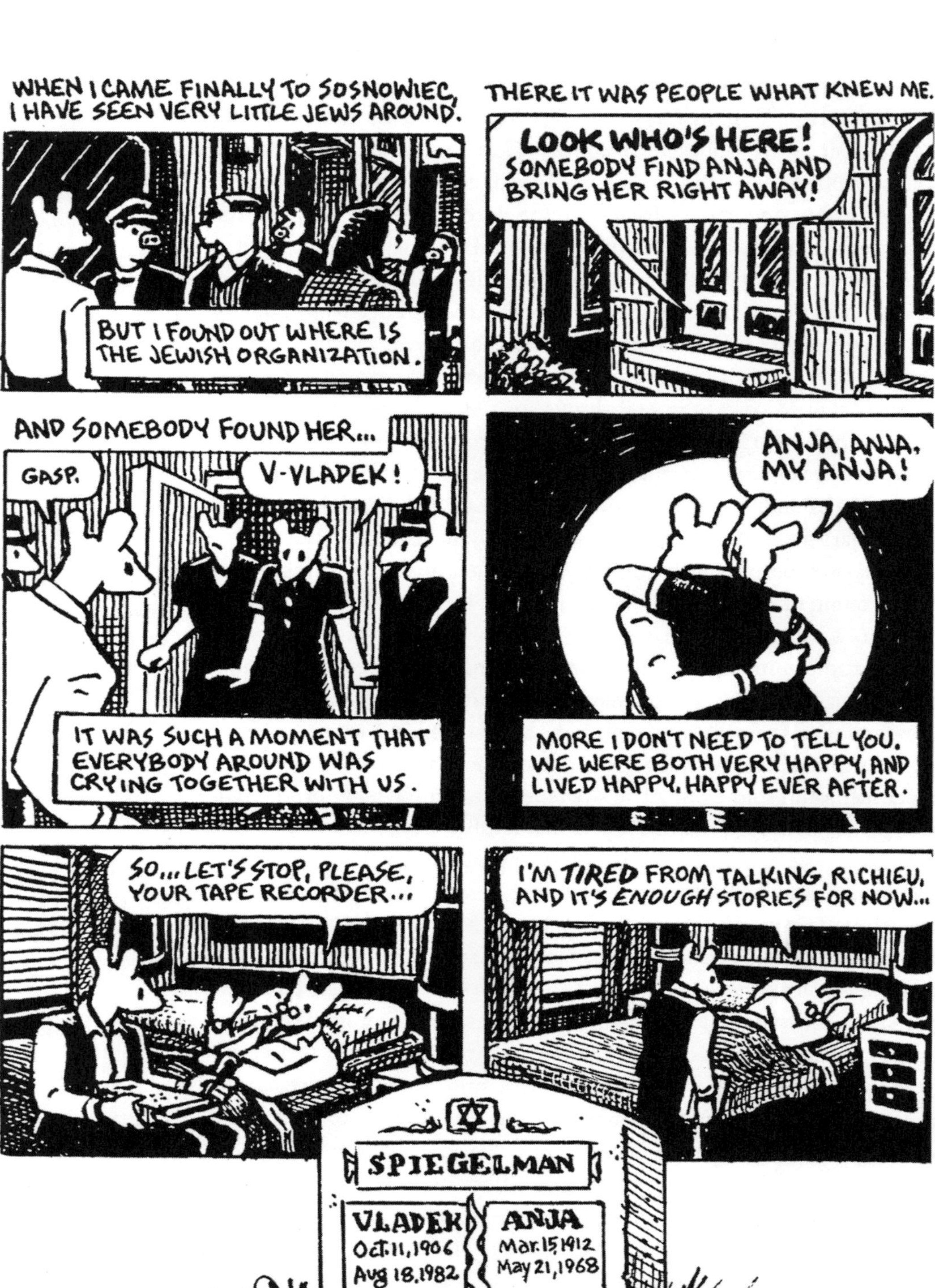

WHEN I CAME FINALLY TO SOSNOWIEC, I HAVE SEEN VERY LITTLE JEWS AROUND.
BUT I FOUND OUT WHERE IS THE JEWISH ORGANIZATION.
THERE IT WAS PEOPLE WHAT KNEW ME.
LOOK WHO'S HERE! SOMEBODY FIND ANJA AND BRING HER RIGHT AWAY!
AND SOMEBODY FOUND HER...
GASP.
V-VLADEK!
IT WAS SUCH A MOMENT THAT EVERYBODY AROUND WAS CRYING TOGETHER WITH US.
ANJA, ANJA, MY ANJA!
MORE I DON'T NEED TO TELL YOU. WE WERE BOTH VERY HAPPY, AND LIVED HAPPY, HAPPY EVER AFTER.
SO.... LET'S STOP, PLEASE, YOUR TAPE RECORDER....
I'M TIRED FROM TALKING, RICHIEU, AND IT'S ENOUGH STORIES FOR NOW...
SPIEGELMAN
VLADEK
Oct. 11, 1906
Aug. 18, 1982
ANJA
Mar. 15, 1912
May 21, 1968
— art spiegelman — 1978-1991

Spiegelman is reported to have "tried between fifty and sixty endings" (Bosmajian 41). None of the four conclusions he selected, however, is conclusive. Although Spiegelman has not revised the two volumes, he continues to develop and expand an impressive archive that contextualizes his creative research and process, thus extending the life of *Maus*. In 1994 Spiegelman published *The Complete Maus* as an interactive CD-ROM.[20] The CD-ROM includes the entire two volumes of *Maus*; video clips of Art Spiegelman speaking about the process of researching and making *Maus* and of his visits to concentration camps; transcripts and audio clips of excerpts of Vladek's recorded interviews; examples of precursors to *Maus* as well as post-*Maus* comics; and archival materials. In 2011, thirty-eight years after the publication of volume I, Spiegelman published *Meta-Maus: A Look inside a Modern Classic*, Maus. The volume expands the material covered in the CD-ROM/DVD-R. It includes interviews with Spiegelman, his wife, and their children; background materials; rejection letters from publishers; and a DVD-R. Spiegelman cannot conclude his family's Holocaust story, but he returns to it as if stirring the story's ashes will produce an ember that might spark a flame of understanding. Among other things, that recurring return to the original trauma suggests the compulsive repetition of trauma by children of survivors who live with the consequences of transgenerational trauma.

In my readings of Spiegelman's multiple conclusions, I have isolated each one, frame by frame, in order to offer a focused individual interpretation. But, in fact, these conclusions proliferate on a single, final page (see fig. 3.10). What if we consider the final collection of frames and panels as a page, as a "unit of space and time"? In that case, Spiegelman seems to be collapsing and juxtaposing both space (Poland and New York) and time (post–death camp, end-of-life, post-death, and present)—a prime example of a spatial interface in which juxtapositions and associations convey layers of multiple meanings. It is as if he is trying to depict the jumbled intersections and ruptures, the potential for a new life and the end of life with reflections on what, if anything, it may mean. The final page is a synthesis that illustrates the impossibility of synthesis or finality.

Perhaps fittingly, an image that was never a part of *Maus* offers both a presage and a coda. "The Past Hangs over the Future" (from *4 Mice*, a portfolio of lithographs published in 1992) shows the autobiographical persona, Artie, sitting on a living room floor, his hand gently on the shoulder of his young daughter, Nadja (fig. 3.11). Both are portrayed as mice. Toys are strewn about the floor. Nadja holds a stuffed Mickey Mouse–Maus. On the chair behind Artie is a pet cat similar to the one in Dr. Pavel's office (II.203). But most dramatically, the top two-thirds of the page is dominated by the dark shadows of mice hanging from ropes—

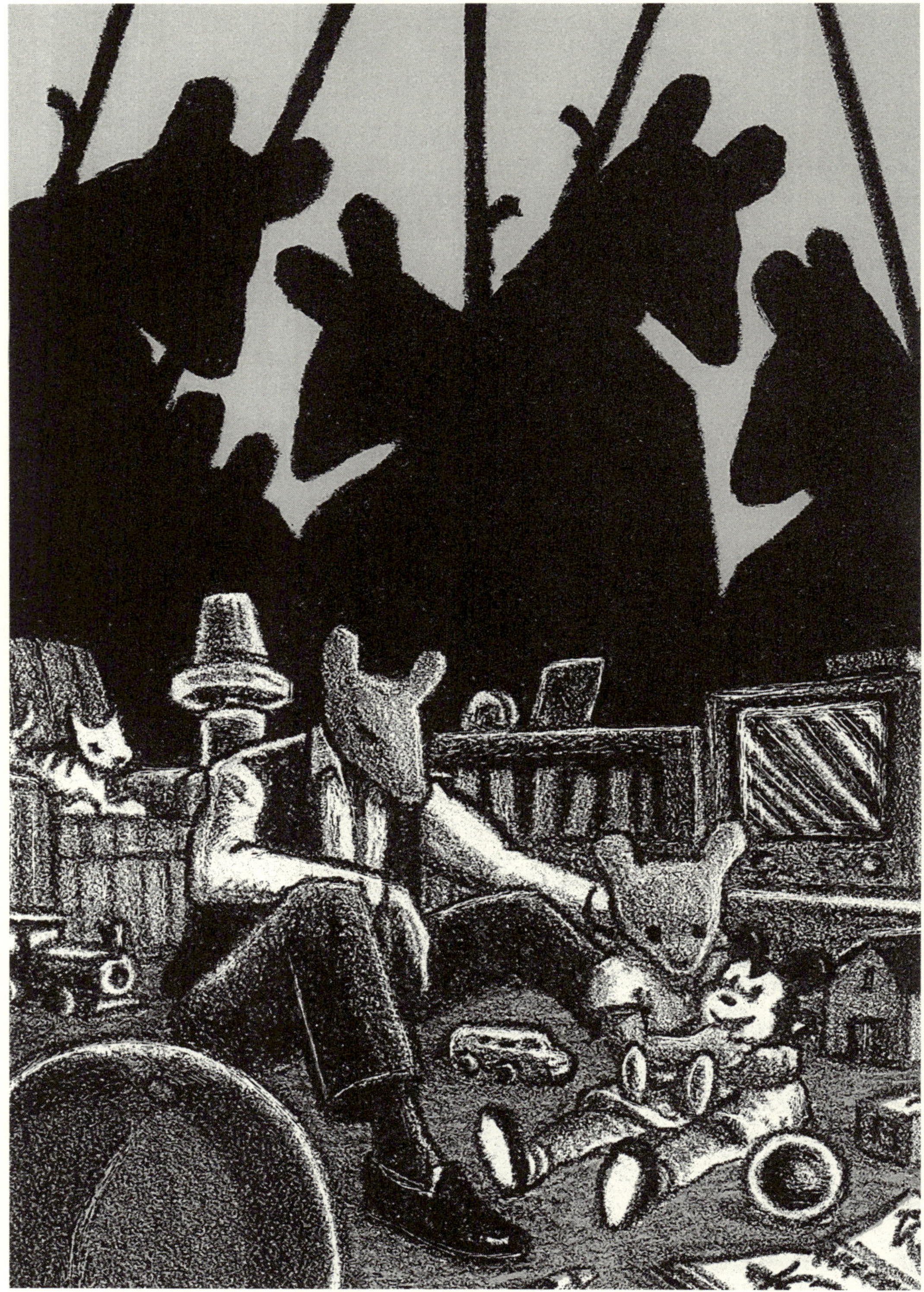

a scene straight out of *Maus* (see vol. I, chap. 4, "The Noose Tightens,"
73, 85–86) that, like the guard towers depicted outside Artie's studio,
haunts the family. Here, with Spiegelman's characteristic visual detail,
subtlety, and mastery, the message is that the reverberations of the Holocaust will never be over. There is no conclusion, only a series of variable
transmissions, morphing from one generation to the next.

...........................................................................

In *Maus*, Spiegelman depicts his deep longing for understanding the
past and his family's Holocaust experiences. Like Peter Najarian and
Theresa Hak Kyung Cha, he attempts to access a traumatic past that
began its painful wounding before he was born and that crossed continents and generations. He desires to access his parents' experiences
but encounters an essential inability to do so. Throughout the graphic
memoir, he emphasizes the gaps, ruptures, and omissions of his father's
story and his own process of representing it. Compelled by his personal
experience of the consequences of transgenerational trauma, he visualizes the desire for, and impossibility of, closure.

(OPPOSITE)
FIGURE 3.11.
Art Spiegelman.
*The Past
Hangs over the
Future,* 1992
(*MetaMaus* 72).
(Graphic novel
excerpt from
METAMAUS: A
LOOK INSIDE A
MODERN CLASSIC,
MAUS by Art
Spiegelman,
copyright
© 2011 by Art
Spiegelman. Used
by permission of
Pantheon Books,
an imprint of the
Knopf Doubleday
Publishing Group,
a division of
Penguin Random
House LLC. All
rights reserved.)

# Hinge Image-and-Text Forms

# Julie Chen's Artists' Books

## "The Constant Search for Meaning in the Chattering of Time"

Artists' books are not books about art or on artists, but books *as* art. —LUCY LIPPARD ("Conspicuous Consumption" 49)

Artists' books are art objects that reference the structure of the book—the binding, the page, the spine, the text, and the layout. They are visual and sculptural objects in which text and image function coequally. Julie Chen's artists' books are books "in which the elements of visual content, materials, text, illustration, format, and structure all work . . . together to create a unified whole" (Chen, "Books in Balance" 1).

Unlike the hybrid image-text autobiographical narratives of Peter Najarian, Leslie Marmon Silko, and Art Spiegelman, artists' books may or may not be in the form of conventional Western books. Even so, artists' books are created fundamentally in relation to the historical structure of the book. This chapter begins our shift from visual-verbal relations originating in book form to image-text relations that arise in artwork. In this case, artists' books refer to concepts of the book as both a material form and a time-based medium.

### A Brief Introduction to Artists' Books

For quite some time, artists' books were unrecognized in the world of art and literature, considered craft in the art world and scarcely considered in the literary world, except in the collaborations of poets and artists that produced lavish books of illustrated poems.[1] Even now that many artists and scholars have attempted to define book art and to elevate it from craft to art, a suspect distinction itself, a variety of definitions compete.

Many scholars begin a discussion of artists' books by defining what constitutes a book before making any distinctions about artists' books. A book is a "collection of blank and/or image-bearing sheets usually fastened together along one edge and trimmed at the other edges to form a single series of uniform leaves" (Klima 27). Books are "a collection of surfaces to receive writing for the purpose of communicating ideas" (Avrin 1). A book is "an inhabitable universe of image and thought and language, a mute space of unrealizable dreams and manifest desire for form. The book is a passage of time, an expandable space, a fluid sequence of elements whose discrete identity becomes absorbed into the reality of a seamless experience, a static set of units whose unresolvable differences return the viewer to the cells of its interior spaces in a contradictory act of engagement and transcendence" (Drucker, *Century of Artists' Books* 363). Others emphasize the basic elements of the book: *the binding*, which determines the type of book (Western codex, so-called oriental fold book, fan, venetian blind, and so on); *the pages* (each page is a unit of space and time, both literal and implied); *the text and/or pictures*; *the act of turning pages* (which suggests linear movement, temporality, tactile experience, and point of view); and *the display* (which concerns point of view) (K. Smith 73, 96). All emphasize key elements of traditional Western codex books—the page, the binding, the text, the images—in order to begin to articulate how artists' books differ.

The early claim that artists' books are "books and booklets authored by an artist" (Phillpot, "Books by Artists" 33) has long been discredited. Such a provocatively simple definition is insufficient because "artists' books are not books about art or on artists, but books *as* art. They can be all words, all images, or combinations thereof. At best they are a lively hybrid of exhibition, narrative, and object—cinematic potential co-existing with double-spread stasis" (Lippard, "Conspicuous Consumption" 49, emphasis in original). Artists' books are "books as visually and conceptually whole as paintings or sculptures" (Lippard, "Artist's Book Goes Public" 46). Artists' books are a form of "intermedia"—"works which fall conceptually between media that are already known" (Higgins, *Horizons* 23). Significantly, an artists' book is "a book done for its own sake and not for the information it contains. That is: it doesn't contain a lot of works. . . . It *is* a work" (Higgins 11, emphasis in original).

Stefan Klima distinguishes among several kinds of artistic books: an "art book" is a "book of which art or an artist is the subject"; "book art" is "art that employs the book form"; "bookwork" is "artwork dependent upon the structure of the book"; and a "book object" is an "art object that alludes to the form of the book" (27). Actually, however, artists' books come in a variety of forms; book art, bookwork, and book object may all be considered types of artists' books.

The conventional relation between image and text in which one illustrates the other, "most often in service of a linear narrative," has "been revamped in artists' books and a new form of visual literature has been created" (Rice 59), one that, like comics, creates a "fusion of word and image" (Phillpot 122). This may be true for some artists' books, but

    Hinge Image-and-Text Forms

it is not always true. Rather than fuse image and text, artists' books may juxtapose them, and certainly, there are artists' books (just as there are comics books) without any text at all.

Johanna Drucker dismisses the many attempts to define artists' books as "hopelessly flawed" or "too specific" (14). Artists' books are simply too creatively experimental for any rigid definition to suffice. They "take every possible form, participate in every possible convention of book making, every possible 'ism' of mainstream art and literature, every possible mode of production, every shape, every degree of ephemerality or archival dura-bility" (14). Given this difficulty, Klima concludes that the "determination to define artists' books, and its failure to do so, in many ways, serves as a metaphor for the still insecure position of artists' books in the world" (21). Although artists' books have become more thoroughly investigated since Klima's 1998 statement, they still have numerous flexible forms. "This mercurial condition" itself "defines the nature of the artists' book" (Tousley 5).

Although competing definitions of artists' books still abound, it is clear that artists' books are informed by sculpture, architecture, paint-ing, photography, film, printmaking, typography, installation art, con-ceptual art, and even performance art. What distinguishes artists' books is "that they sit provocatively at the juncture where art, documentation, and literature all come together" (Phillpot 33). The best artists' books are "multinotational": "Within them, words, images, colors, marks, and silences become plastic organisms that play across the page in variable linear sequence" (Lyons 7). Artists' books are important because they formulate "a new perceptual literature whose content alters the con-cept of authorship and challenges the reader to a new discourse with the printed page" (Lyons 7). Drucker eschews a single rigid definition and describes artists' books as participating in "a zone of activity," a sphere that is formed at "the intersection of a number of different disciplines, fields, and ideas" (1). What sets artists' books apart from art books, books about art, or *livres d'artistes* (usually fine art books) is that the author-artist must be "self-conscious about the structure and meaning of the book as a form" (Drucker 4); that is, there is a self-reflexivity as the artist-author investigates the book structure "through its examination of its material, thematic, and formal properties" (93).

What is known today as the artists' book "emerged in the 1960s" (Drucker 64), but the artists' book has a long history. Although many scholars cite medieval illuminated manuscripts as an origin, Drucker, emphasizing "genuine precedents" for the conceptual basis of artists' books, offers a briefer history. Such precedents include poet-artist William Blake's eighteenth-century illuminated printings and painted books; late nineteenth-century poet-designer William Morris's Kelmscott Press, which revolutionized typography and emphasized "the book as a whole" (28); symbolist poet Stéphane Mallarmé's insistence that "the letter was the basic element of the book" and experimentation with "typography and layout" (36); realist novelist Gustave Flaubert's "anxiety about the impossibility of completeness" in a book, part of "the philosophical extension of theory about the nature of the book" (39); and poet Edmund Jabès's focus on "the idea of 'The Book' within the cultural legacy of the Jewish religion and its interpretative practices" (39). In the early twentieth century, the Soviet and German avant-garde art world experimented with photographic representation in books. Later, Dieter Roth, informed by "graphic design combined with concrete poetry" (73), "focused on the book as a physical form" (74). Ed Ruscha's famous photo-text *Twenty-Six Gas Stations* is often noted as "the founding instance of artist's bookmaking" (76) but was, according to Drucker, only one important moment of many points of origin.

Several institutions and book presses have been crucial to the development of book art. In the 1950s and 1960s, book artists were involved in creating what would in the 1970s come to be known as the "artists' book as democratic multiples" (Drucker 81), a form of cheaply reproducible and widely circulated productions accessible, at least theoretically, to all.[2] Each founded in 1976, both Printed Matter Bookstore and Franklin Furnace were important sites for publication and dispersal of this artistic democratic mode. Visual Studies Workshop, which offers a site for artists and book artists to work, and the workshop's press, which publishes "process-based and experimental books" (www.vsw.org), were founded in 1969; and Nexus and its press, associated with Atlanta Contemporary, began in 1973 to support "cutting-edge contemporary art" (www.thecontemporary.org), including artists' books. Brighton Press, established in 1985, was also an influence. Founder and director of Brighton Press Bill Kelly phrases the goal simply: "break the square" (quoted in Ollman). Brighton Press proposes that "a book is, fundamentally, a confluence of relationships—between text and image, type and the page, form and function, writer/artist and reader, space and time, poetry and music, prints and passion, potential and actuality" (Ollman n.p.). Brighton Press books "embody a peculiarly tight fusion of intentions, content, form and design, a democratic union of words, images, and structure, sculpture and literature" (Ollman n.p.). In contrast to the "democratic multiples" form of artists' books, Brighton Press focuses on "limited-edition artists' books and broadsides" (www.ebrightonarts.com), expensive pieces made for libraries and collectors.

Although there are many book artists who have produced complex, beautiful, and explicitly autobiographical work (Susan King, Joan Lyons, and Genie Shenk come to mind), Julie Chen makes conceptually nuanced, meticulously rendered, acutely self-aware, and obliquely autobiographical artists' books. In "Books in Balance," her 1989 MFA thesis, Chen articulated her artistic vision. For each artists' book, her aim is to make "a book in which the elements of visual content, materials, text, illustration, format, and structure all work . . . together to create a unified whole" (1). Striving to keep a balance between craftsperson and artist, she wants her books to be both "visual and sculptural objects" that bring text and image together so that neither overshadows the other.[3] Like others, Chen is invested in "reader/viewer interaction with [her] books" as readers embark on the visual journey of reading that includes the "tactile experience of turning the pages" (3) and the experience of an "intimate" and "sensual" environment created by various papers, fonts, and images (6). Echoing definitions of artists' books that emphasize their metacritical experimentation with formal structure, Chen creates books that are "more than beautiful settings for texts" but books that are "compelling objects in their own right" (9). She never loses sight of "the book as a physical object and a time-based medium" (www.flying fishpress.com). In this chapter I examine a selection of her wide array of artists' book forms, including flag books, tunnel books, boxed books, rotating books, pop-up books, accordion books, concertina-bound books, and slat books.[4]

Julie Chen's artists' books neither narrate linear stories nor reveal explicit personal details, but they are profoundly autobiographical in their revelation of consciousness. She creates books that mirror structures of cognition and offer readers an experience of her interiority. In the process of learning how to read each of her works—where to start, how to proceed, when to linger, what to open—readers enter Chen's imaginative and analytical mind; they learn to see through her eyes. Chen explains that "the book is an extension of my consciousness" (Chen conversation); so seeing through Chen's eyes is seeing and thinking "through the structure of the book." Chen creates structures that combine relational, temporal, and spatial visual-verbal interfaces and force readers to have a unique visual, tactile, kinesthetic, and temporal engagement with the book form that results in an enhanced awareness not only of reading but also of cognition itself.

Like Leslie Marmon Silko, Chen's central and enduring theme is time as it relates to subjectivity. She returns, again and again, to the inevitable and relentless passage of time that is associated with incremental and insistent loss and consequent mourning; she celebrates time by slowing it down, focusing attentively on a single moment and thus stretching a singular act of attention into a temporal meditation. In both her writing and image-text layouts, Chen insists on the reader-viewer's acute attentiveness to the moment at hand and requires a mindful and self-reflexive reading-looking. Chen renders time spatially. She places herself and readers within time that is also within space: the refashioned space of the page, the reading environment, and sometimes a specific site, as in her later environmental work. Throughout, Chen's autobiographical persona is a disembodied, deracialized, dehistoricized, almost ungendered subjectivity that ranges free of material referents.

In her 1992 artists' book *Listening,* Chen emphasizes various modes of listening, paying attention, being mindful.[5] After opening the lid of a five-inch-by-four-inch box from right to left, the viewer finds a small walletlike structure made of paper on the left. Inside the packet is an accordion book—one piece of folded paper that can be viewed both as one unbroken surface and as discrete pages. The reader can either pull the paper to the left to unfold the accordion book or can simply turn the pages like a regular codex book. Inspired by music and playfully imagining the accordion books as "a headdress in three variations," Chen presents each variation, evoking "the rhythm, tempo, and me / lodic expression of a / movement of / music." A second piece of this work is found in a tiny envelope tucked into a slimmer-than-matchbook-size compartment. It contains two colored ribbons folded into textless pages and adorned with beads, suggesting a couple of stray notes. The most dominant structure within this bookspace is on the right: a flag book that has been printed on thick paper or cardboard and can both stand independently as a sculpture—spread out or shaped into a circle on a table—and be read like a Western codex (fig. 4.1). Chen has reconfigured the traditional page by cutting the page in two horizontally and leaving a slight space between the top and bottom portions. In this way she breaks the recurrent images of hands, here associated with voice, in half, visually and structurally emphasizing the essential gap between speaker and listener.

Hands rise and fall like musical notations or a mellifluous voice, filling (almost) each page. The continuous gap between the top and bottom halves of the page and the contrasting colors of each half are linked by the continuous imagery—a structural expression of the challenges of dialogue. In addition, Chen adheres the top half of the page to the front part of the binding and the bottom half of the page to the back part of the binding, highlighting the linked doubleness. Rather than place the text on the page proper—overlaid on the images of hands—she prints the text on what she refers to as the spine because it is part of the concertina binding that needs to be integrated into the overall book. Chen's entire first-person commentary, addressed to an unknown departed other, takes place off the center stage of the page on the book's spine, which in Western codex form is nothing more than a site for an identifying title

     Hinge Image-and-Text Forms

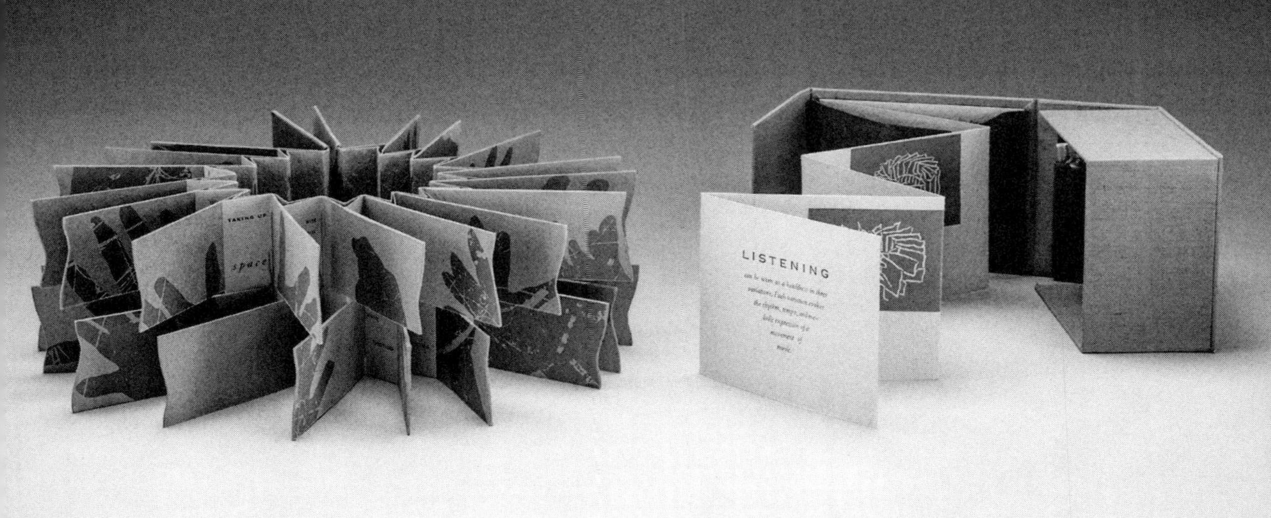



but here is translated into a kind of page. When the book is completely open, the text is hidden; only the visible hands communicate, underscoring Chen's examination of gesture and voice.

Chen varies the font throughout, using capital letters to raise the volume and lowercase letters to reduce it, bold fonts for emphasis and italics for quieter points. She arranges the words artfully to create a visual-textual rhythm of fluctuating silence and sound, space and emptiness. Throughout, hands are associated with speaking, becoming a metonym for voice: "You raise your / HANDS / And you begin to / SPEAK / and I am / LISTENING / LISTENING / To / THE / VOICES / OF / YOUR / HANDS." The hands are:

RISING

AND

FALLING

ALL

TALKING

AT

ONCE

SPEAKING IN A
language

of SILENCE
&
sound

FIGURE 4.1.
Julie Chen.
*Listening*, 1992
(flag book).
(Photo by Sibila
Savage. Courtesy
of Julie Chen.)

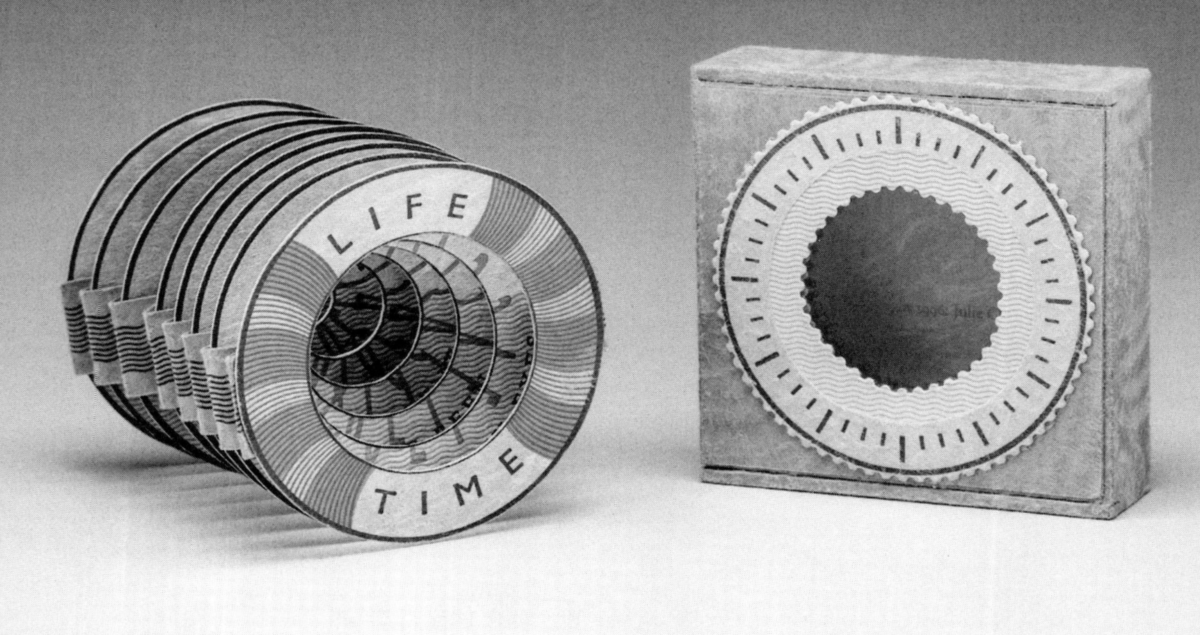



FIGURE 4.2.
Julie Chen. *Life Time*, 1996 (tunnel book with concertina binding). (Photo by Sibila Savage. Courtesy of Julie Chen.)

The variable font in this book works as image as well as text. In addition, its size and shape provide visual and sonic emphasis, like a musical score that helps the reader to see and hear, not merely read, the speaker's voice. The persona addresses a generic "you," perhaps a friend or lover, but more likely the reader herself, who, mirroring the image on the page, raises her hand to turn a page and "speaks" to the "speaker," who is "LISTENING / LISTENING / TO / THE VOICES / OF / [THE] / HANDS." Thus Chen designs a self-reflexive dialogue with her readers in which reading is an act of reciprocity.

Four years later, Chen produced a tiny book about an expansive idea: *Life Time*. The title may be interpreted as lifetime, such as the span of one's life, or as two distinct nouns, Life and Time, which will be considered in relation to each other. Nestled in a three-inch by three-inch light teal box is a circle-shaped book visible through the circular Plexiglas window in the lid (fig. 4.2). The tunnel-book consist of eight pages in the form of circles with cutout centers held together by concertina binding, a binding made of a small strip of paper folded back and forth to serve as the spine. The top circle-page has the largest cutout section, the second circle the next largest, and so on, so that the next circle is visible beneath it, creating a sense of perspective or a sense of telescoping or moving through layers to a smaller and smaller focal point.

At that final focal point is an image that is indecipherable when looking from the title page. The title, *Life Time*, is playfully ironic, professing to tell the story of a lifetime in eight tiny pages yet concisely conveying —

    Hinge Image-and-Text Forms

in words, image, and book structure—the way time overtakes everyday life. Chen uses the top and bottom of each page for the text:

MY LIFE IS PASSING
RIGHT BEFORE MY EYES

COULD IT BE THAT
I HAVE BEEN

CAUGHT BENEATH
THE CURRENT

OF MY DAILY
ROUTINE AND

AM DROWNING
SLOWLY

DAY BY
DAY

What lies between each line of text on every page is a void, a passage from one page-image-text to the next, as if viewers, like the speaker, are being pulled into the center bit by bit. Whereas in *Listening* voice is pictured as hands, here time is symbolized by water. The speaker is "caught beneath the current of [her] daily routine" and is "slowly drowning," being pulled into oblivion. At the center of the focal point is a printed image of a man diving into the water. He is fully visible only by peering between (unnumbered) pages 6 and 7. What viewers see as the pinkish object at the focal point of the book is revealed as the man's chest. As readers-viewers follow the seductive wavy lines printed on pages in teal, pink, and gold, suggesting fluidity or water or the passage of time, they are wooed to discover the man diving headlong into oblivion—a fate shared by all. Even though Chen provides no details about what constitutes the autobiographical persona's obliterating "daily routine," she underscores its consequences: a slow death. On the back of the book is an image of a clock, Chen's final wink to the reader, another personal commentary on mechanical time and human mortality.

Chen produced another playful and charming, but serious, artists' book two years later, *Bon Bon Mots: A Fine Assortment of Books* (1998). Chen's title is a pun. *Bon bon* is French for candy and *bon mots* is French for a good word or clever saying. *Bon Bon Mots* plays with both; Chen emphasizes this by presenting her book collection packaged as a box of fancy chocolates (fig. 4.3).

*Bon Bon Mots* is actually a collection of five distinct, but interrelated, artists' books (fig. 4.4). In this collection, Chen's autobiographical per-

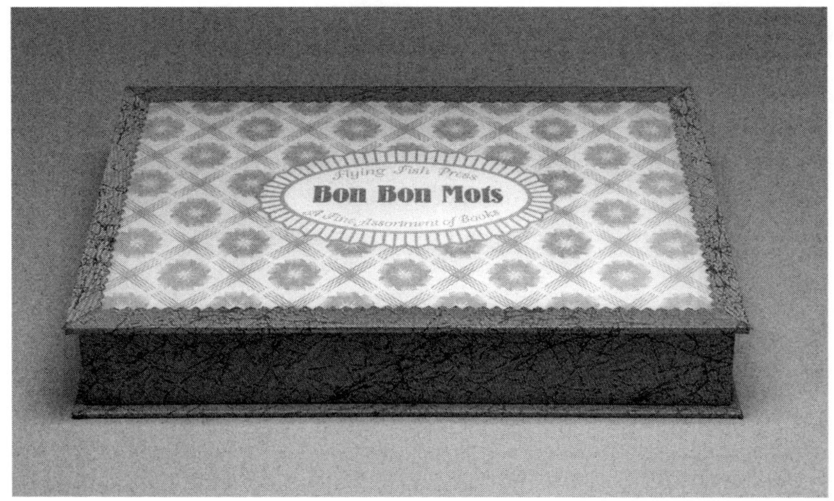


sona continues to be abstract, but she provides a bit more insight into not merely her musings about time and subjectivity but also her feelings and the pressures of societal expectations. Overall, all five books focus on the relation between time and self: life as a journey (*Labyrinth*), a cycle (*Life Cycle*), or a process of self-erosion or slow decline (*Elegy*). In one book, she breaks time into discrete units in order to record precisely her feelings and behavior on a daily basis (*Either/Or*). In another, she ponders the limits of the social self (*Social Graces*). In each book, Chen makes palpable the pressure of time passing, of life diminishing.

Inside the cover are outlines of each of the five artists' books included inside — just as the chart inside a box of chocolates identifies and maps the sweets within: *Either/Or, Social Graces, Elegy, Life Cycles,* and *Labyrinth*. There is no prescribed order in which to read these books. Rather, like selecting a chocolate from a candy box, the reader chooses according to what strikes his or her fancy (fig. 4.5).

*Labyrinth* (fig. 4.5, second from left, front) is found within a $2\frac{1}{4}$-inch by $2\frac{1}{14}$-inch box with an ornamental spiral on the top lid. Inside is a small box "book" with a see-through Plexiglas window that reveals a poem in the shape of a labyrinth. The poem functions as a textual path upon which the reader embarks on the cyclical journey of the labyrinth, traveling away and then returning, ending in the center with an indented red dot. The text uses the common metaphor of life as a journey: ". . . walking so slowly, every step becomes a journey emerging into the light, a shadow of my future self. . . ." The ellipses at the beginning and end of the sentence suggest a continuous, circuitous journey in which the autobiographical persona loops back and moves ahead, spiraling into her "future self." In each of the four corners of the box are tiny round indentations surrounded with a printed circular frame. Five small brass

   Hinge Image-and-Text Forms

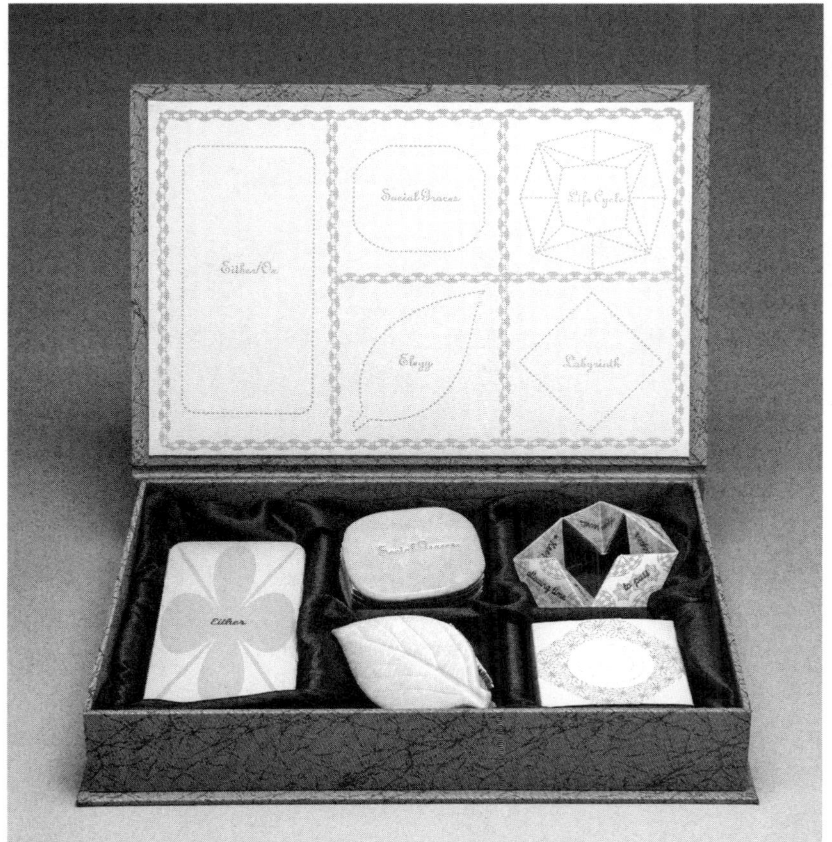



FIGURE 4.4. Julie Chen. *Bon Bon Mots: A Fine Assortment of Books*, 1998 (box open). (Photo by Sibila Savage. Courtesy of Julie Chen.)

balls roll around in the box, and, as in one of the inexpensive children's games, the reader can, with patience and skill, roll the balls into the five indentations. Here Chen's design makes the book highly interactive. Not only do readers take the labyrinth journey, a walk often associated with meditation and reflection, through time and into "a shadow of [a] future self," but they tilt, shake, and manipulate the book in order to align the balls, associated with randomness, into possible resting places— temporarily creating order out of chaos.

*Life Cycle* (fig. 4.5, front right) is a unique book made of a single paper folded into eight-sided angles and linked together to create what Chen calls a "rotating book" (Chen conversation). The entire book fits into the palm of a hand (and measures 2½ inches by 2½ inches). There are eight pages for each of the four sides. On the tiny pages, which Chen has transformed into four spreads (two pages treated as one), she has printed four related reflections. Because it is easy to miss the inside pages until the viewer learns that the tiny book can be rotated, Chen cues the reader where to begin with an asterisk at each level:

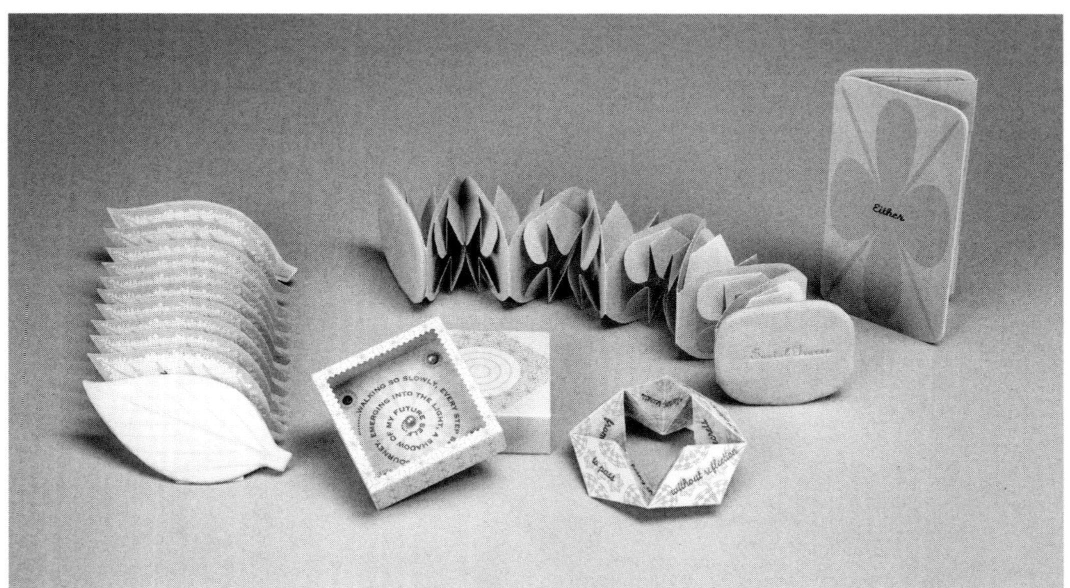



FIGURE 4.5.
Julie Chen. *Bon Bon Mots: A Fine Assortment of Books*, 1998 (five individual books inside box). (Photo by Sibila Savage. Courtesy of Julie Chen.)

Top level: "*Over and over / always the same / one thing / after another"

Outside: "*I observe myself / allowing time / to pass / without reflection"

Bottom: "*Keeping secrets / from myself / being the keeper / of your secrets"

Inside: "*Treading / in circles / waiting for life / to begin"

Again, Chen thematizes time, playing with the ideas of repetition ("over and over") and routine ("always the same") that seem to obstruct self-awareness ("allowing time / to pass / without reflection") and hinder life itself ("Treading / in circles / waiting for life / to begin"). Self-critically, the speaker laments her perpetual and enduring capacity to waste time with mindless routines; time passes while she waits for an ever-deferred life to begin. The architectural book—with its circular shape, multifaceted surfaces, rotating pages, and seamless continuity—mirrors the cyclical passing of time while suggesting hidden or secret spaces of the psyche. Again the autobiographical persona is an amorphous questioning and observing "I," an Every Woman reflecting on self and other in the web of time.

*Either/Or* (fig. 4.5, far right, back) is a two-page book (4¾ inches long and 2¼ inches wide) made to look like a checklist or personal journal. Here Chen plays with familiar forms: to-do lists and records of behavior. Within the book, she compares and contrasts negative thoughts, emotions, and self-judgments with positive ones. Printed in the center of the front cover, atop a lovely peach-colored flower on a gray back-

    Hinge Image-and-Text Forms

ground, is: "Either." The back cover has the same design with the colors reversed; printed in the center is: "Or." Inside is a hand-drawn grid and checklist printed onto the page. The two halves of the record book mirror the internal struggle of its owner. Chen addresses competing emotions and tries to be aware of them in order to better manage them. In calendric style, she breaks time into manageable units, separating the day into a.m. and p.m. In the tradition of self-help books dating back at least to Benjamin Franklin's plan for moral perfection and his fastidious record keeping of his failures, Chen keeps track of the number of mornings and afternoons she is afflicted with "worry," "guilt," and "anxiety" on page 1 and how many times she can claim "calm," doubt," comfort," "sleep," "pain," "thinking," memory," growth," "risk," "wonder," and "humor." "Wonder" and "comfort," it seems, are the rarest experiences. Chen plays with duality and opposition in book theme and structure, with the front and back of the books and pages 1 and 2 in thematic and structural opposition. Chen is aware that "every side is a front when the codex book is opened, and only *while* it is opened to that position. When the page is turned, that front becomes a back" (K. Smith 17, emphasis in original). Chen plays, also, with notions of evidence as she inserts two papers with the words "The Evidence," as if the checkmarks in her daily record book are incriminating proof of her interior struggles, as if she is documenting her unruly subjectivity in an autobiographical archive.

The plastic front and back covers of *Social Graces* (fig. 4.5, just left of *Either/Or*) look like a small (2 inches long by 2¼ inches wide), pale pink soap bar. The title, *Social Graces*, is engraved on the front in a graceful font. The book opens to five pages on the first side and four pages on the back side, actually eighteen conventional pages, but she uses the two pages as a single surface. Across the recto and verso, she has inserted a lavender paper printed with a design onto which the text is printed and which has been folded to look like a blossom, reminiscent of a pop-up book. The blossom page spreads across the two pages, turning recto and verso into a single surface known as a spread. She has numbered each page in the upper left and bottom right. An ornamental design mirrors the page number (one stamped-printed design for page 1, two designs for page 2, and so on). The text appears to be drawn from clichés of social conventions: "Avoiding the backward glance / Learning to lose without a struggle / Letting bygones be bygones / Keeping a positive attitude / Always looking your best / Smiling in the face of adversity / Forgiving and forgetting / Putting your best foot forward / Never speaking out of turn." While practicing these bits of advice may smooth social relations, they may also invite hypocrisy—being so polite that you never express what you really feel. "Always looking your best" and "Never speaking out of turn" are highly gendered, female-specific pieces of advice used to keep women attractive and compliant, or at least silent. The decorative pages enhance the positive affirmations, making them seem harmless or, perhaps, merely superficial. This collection of social conventions suggests a masking of genuine subjectivity. The autobiographical persona of *Either/ Or* documents her "doubt" and "fear," but in *Social Graces* she is silenced.

Finally, the 3½-inch by 1½-inch book *Elegy* (fig. 4.5, far left) has a plastic book cover in the shape of a leaf; the covers have been molded to resemble leaf veins. Paper pages, also in the shape of a leaf and printed with leaf veins, have been adhered to the inside of each cover, and all the leaves of the pages are bound with a folding strip of paper, concertina style. The leaf pages refer ironically to the leaves of a book, but also to a fallen leaf—a notion associated with death and suitable for an elegy, a poem or song of mourning. In this instance, Chen's lament seems to be for a generalized sense of lost time, for time passing without the auto-biographical persona's acute awareness, for her forgetting to notice the world and herself and their many and continuous transformations:

> I
>
> kept
>
> a leaf
> from the
> tree that
> died
>
> an
> ambiguous
> gesture
> of remem-
> brance
>
> .  .  .
>
> for
> the way
> things might
> have been but
> weren't
>
> disregarding
> how I
> continually
>
> forgot
> to notice
> its presence

     Hinge Image-and-Text Forms

year
after year
how
I
forgot
to notice
myself

A brittle
reminder of
the passage
of time

and the
changes that
come with
time

each branch
a measure
ment of
loss

each twig
the echo of
a voice

whispering
I am,
I am,
I am.

Although the traditional trajectory of an elegy mirrors stages of loss—
grief, praise for the deceased, and finally, consolation for the living—
Chen's poem is a more generalized lament about the passage of time.
The act of keeping the leaf is "an ambiguous gesture of remembrance."
Although it may be forgotten or trivialized, the leaf serves as a token for
the poetic speaker, a "brittle reminder" of the passing of time and continuous change. Although the speaker never idealizes the dead, the second stage of Western elegy, she concludes with a sense of affirmation:
the voice "whispering I am, I am, I am." As time passes relentlessly,
leaving a wake of loss, the poetic voice insists on affirming her own being
in the present moment.

Considered as a whole, *Bon Bon Mots* offers an aesthetic sampling of
artists' book forms even as they, sometimes seriously, sometimes playfully, thematize the insistent passage of time, the journey of life, the

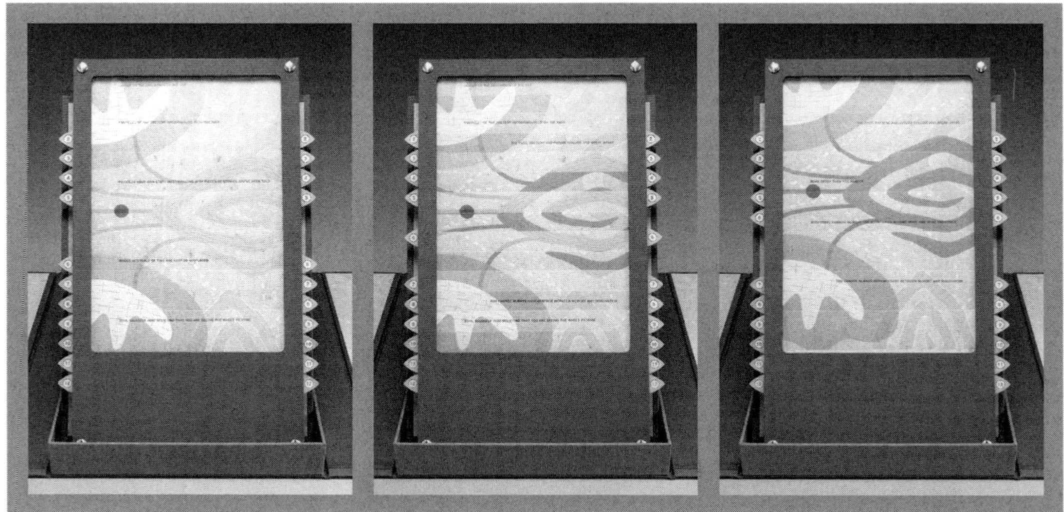



human obsession with self-improvement and desire for self-awareness, the ever-present background noise of social expectations, and the possibility of renewal after profound loss. The autobiographical persona observes, ponders, and reflects, sharing not a life story but a consciousness in process.

Since 2000, Chen's artists' books, which have always been brilliantly conceived and beautifully made, have become even more elegant, complex, and monumental. In 2004, she made *True to Life*, a handsome tablet book or slat book that offers numerous hypertextual pathways through the book (fig. 4.6).[6]

The book is housed in a large rectangular box covered in a rich wine-colored fabric. Printed on the inner bottom of the box are instructions: "How to Work This Book." Chen advises the reader-viewer how to pull up and prop the book on a hinge so that it stands upright; she explains that "to change the page that shows through the plexiglass window, simultaneously push upward on both the left and right wooden handles. . . . Sections of the new page will slowly slide into view over the previous page. . . . You may view pages out of order, as well as view combinations of sections of two or more pages." There are fourteen "text or image strips" (in the form of about 2-inch-high by 7-inch-long strips of paper) for each of the eleven tabs (numbered 2–12). Fourteen strips constitute a page. Each page also functions as a display. The pages alternate in color between a light terra-cotta and a soft teal; if tabs are pulled up only partially, the resulting page includes portions of two separate pages in both colors. Like hypertext—"segments of text electronically linked in a network in such a way that the reader has freedom of movement within that network" (Gaggi 102–3)—the organization of the material pages of

   Hinge Image-and-Text Forms

*True to Life* invite readers to experiment freely with how to read. A hybrid page entirely recontextualizes the text and images, resulting in multiple alternative readings. As well as allowing, or encouraging, varied reading and viewing possibilities, the tablet form creates both a single visual field and fourteen distinct "image and/or text strips" simultaneously. Slat or tablet books "take the discrete unit of the codex page and put it into a new syntagmatic arrangement," enabling the page surfaces to function "as part of a whole image or field" (Drucker 131) as well as an individual page. The result is the creation of at least two fields of vision at once and the possibility for the reader-viewer to navigate multiple paths through the book. In her highly interactive text, Chen offers not "a clearly delineated path, but a textual [and visual] space . . . for exploration" (Gaggi 123).

In addition to the reading instructions, Chen includes a key for deciphering the recurring images. It is important to note that the reader-viewer needs to spend some time simply becoming acquainted with and oriented to the experimental book form, just the first step of the interactive reading experience that artists' books necessitate. Chen uses a set of glyphs, a kind of "invented writing" (Drucker 227), to provide a visual symbol with a textual meaning. Such "marks are imbued with meaning but seem to belong to a secret realm which charges these invented signs with power and value" (227). The glyphs challenge the reader to decode and understand them. Chen, though, provides a key to understanding her symbols: the interwoven ribbons stand for "unspoken longings"; the African shield shape means "emerging questions." The spiral represents "difficult transitions," while the dark circle translates as "episodes of conflict." The four-petaled form stands for "bursts of understanding," and the star symbolizes "unexpected moments of joy." Chen disperses these glyphs profusely throughout *True to Life,* forcing the reader-viewer to look to the key or to remember the glyphs, to consider the relations among them (for example, what does it mean to have three circles, two stars, a shield, and a spiral on the same surface?) as well as in relation to the text. The glyphs, like free-floating thoughts or embedded seeds of stories, circulate throughout the book, providing a visual, intellectual, and emotional backdrop to the text as well as a counterpoint to the narrative.

With the fourteen "text-image strips" on each tab serving as both autonomous discrete pages (onto which some text may be printed) and a continuous surface (onto which some images are printed, often moving across pages) and with the dispersal of glyphs (invented language) throughout, there are many interpretive possibilities. There is still a story to be told textually. Again, Chen addresses the passage of time, difficult transitions, woundedness, and memory, but this time she also thematizes how human beings formulate and articulate their life stories. Directly addressing the reader, the autobiographical persona muses about how you "turn events into a story that you can tell yourself and others," how you edit your life story–often lying to yourself, changing "the words ever so slightly," omitting "shameful scenes" and "painful exchanges" even as you tell yourself that you are "preserving the truth." At the same time, you "reinvent the details . . . , allow the story to replace . . . actual memories." Here Chen explicitly summarizes key points in autobiography studies about the slippery distinction between truth and imagination, between self-protective fiction and outright lies, and between self-fashioning and refashioning. Just as an autobiographer makes strategic choices about how to construct a life story, Chen designs her book of musings to highlight her acute awareness of the many choices involved in self-representation and to provide flexible interpretations. Readers-viewers are also forced to make choices as they navigate the book and co-create the story.

After these reflections on autobiographical editing, Chen moves to larger questions about the nature of time, truth, and subjectivity—concerns central to autobiography studies. She writes about "particles of the present intermingling with the past / pieces of your own story intermingling with pieces of stories you've been told"; she notes how "the past, present and future collide and break apart / . . . with every passing moment the boundaries become more and more indistinct / you cannot always differentiate between memory and imagination." She charges the "you" she addresses to "sift through the pieces," to attempt "to separate fact from fiction," to "reassemble a patchwork," and, most important, to question if anything like "absolute truth" exists. After a sequence debunking any possibility of a "true" self-history ("revise your history to suit the person you believe yourself to be / splice together things that happened at different times," admit that "you can no longer remember the exact sequence of events"), Chen reasons that "chronology is meaningless" and that it is impossible to "stand firm . . . against the flow of time." "Where does the past end and the future begin?" she asks. With the intermingling of past, present, and future, the inadvertent and inevitable omissions and misrememberings, how is it possible to concoct a narrative of one's life? Chen concludes that "a life story must be invented and reinvented even as it is being told." A life story, as is well known in autobiography studies and by anyone who has attempted to formulate one, is all process and flux, never fixed and stable. The very structure of *True to Life*—with its coexisting imagetexts, its simultaneity of part and whole, its ever-shifting narrative pathways—mirrors the conflation and reassemblage of past, present, and future. Time and space merge as the page becomes a point in space; the pages become a continuous, yet

    Hinge Image-and-Text Forms

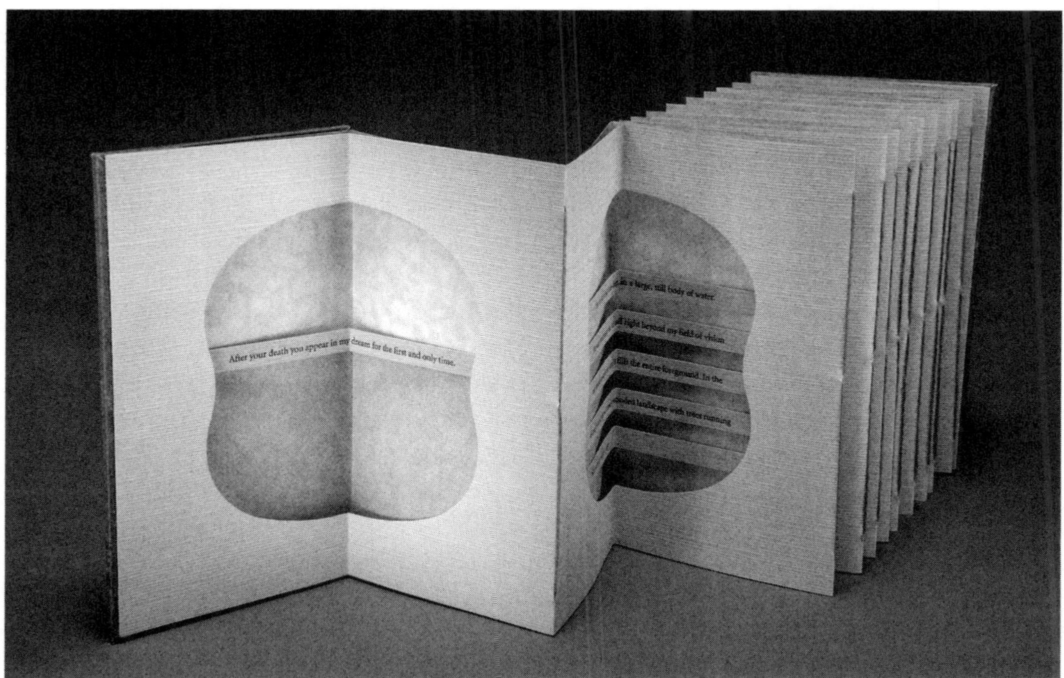



changing, surface; and the representation of subjectivity is both troubled and enabled.

In *View* (2006), Chen expands her consideration of space and time to include dreamscape and dreamtime, life and afterlife and the amorphous point at which they might meet. The paired narratives are within a rectangular box covered with gold silk fabric. Opening first the left and right flaps, then the front and back flaps, reveals this statement: "We dream the answers before we ask the questions," an ambiguous introduction to what lies within. Opening the top of the box (lifting it up and back) reveals the title page and publication information, and, on either side, a small book: volume 1, *Mise en Scène*, an accordion book, on the left and volume 2, *Afterimage*, on the right. Both books can be read as traditional books—turning the pages—or as a continuous sculptural surface. Volume 1 describes a dream about seeing a deceased loved one becoming aware of his own death and the effect it will have on his father.[7] In volume 2 the autobiographical persona-witness tries to imagine the deceased meeting his father.

Volume 1, *Mise en Scène*, French for positioning on stage or placing in a scene, literally sets the stage and the mood for the two narratives. Each page has a cutout in the shape of a wide oval with matching indentations on either side and below (fig. 4.7). Inside the cutout is sheer paper that lets light through. The top is a marbled light gray, the bottom half a dappled pale sage green, evoking the colors in the dream from

FIGURE 4.7. Julie Chen. *View*, volume 1: *Mise en Scène*, 2006 (cut-out book with opaque inset). (Photo by Sibila Savage. Courtesy of Julie Chen.)

sky, woods, and lake. The last four pages extend the sky to about the top two-thirds of the page and confine the lake to the bottom third of the page. The text is printed onto strips that are overlaid upon, but not connected to, the sheer paper. The text strips range from a single one at the beginning to six, varying throughout. When the accordion book is extended, light, filtering through the sheer paper, softly illuminates the pages, enhancing the retelling of the dream by generating a dreamlike atmosphere.

The speaker directly addresses a loved one who has died: "After your death you appear in my dream for the first and only time." The text strip is positioned in the exact middle of the page (see fig. 4.7), obstructing the demarcation between gray and green paper, between cloudy sky and lake, and highlighting the dissolving boundaries between life and death in the dream. The speaker views the scene from a distance, and like Theresa Cha (see chap. 5), Chen uses cinematic language to describe it. Under an overcast sky, the deceased is "standing, knee-deep, in a large, still body of water . . . [that] stretches to the left and right beyond my field of vision. . . . In the distance . . . is a densely wooded landscape." "You are positioned slightly to the right of the center of the visual frame with your back to me. Your attitude suggests intense contemplation of the distant tree-lined shore." When a figure appears in the distance, the man turns and walks through the water in that direction. "As you move towards the distant figure" [long shot], the narrator notes, "my viewpoint moves with you, following you so closely that I can see your face quite clearly" [zoom in to close-up]. "Your expression is one of deep grief tinged with shock and confusion." As well as narrating and visualizing the dream, the speaker describes her own growing awareness: "In the midst of the dream I have a sudden understanding that in the scene I am witnessing, you are only just coming to the realization of your own death. You are bewildered and scared. You are inconsolable." She realizes that the figure in the distance is the deceased man's father. The dead man faces his father "with an expression of utter anguish," but his father turns to look with a "bright and untroubled smile." In this scene, the placement of the text emphasizes the initial gap between father and son and slows down the father's revelation that he already knows of his son's death. In the text strip near the top of the page, up in the sky, the narrator explains: "He reaches out to draw you closer to him and he says to you," and at this point, the reader-viewer must drop to a text strip near the bottom of the page, at the meeting point of water and sky, before the narrator continues with the father's words: "'Don't worry, we already know.'" The placement of the text emphasizes both the distance between the father and son and the dissolution of boundaries of time and space as the son

    Hinge Image-and-Text Forms

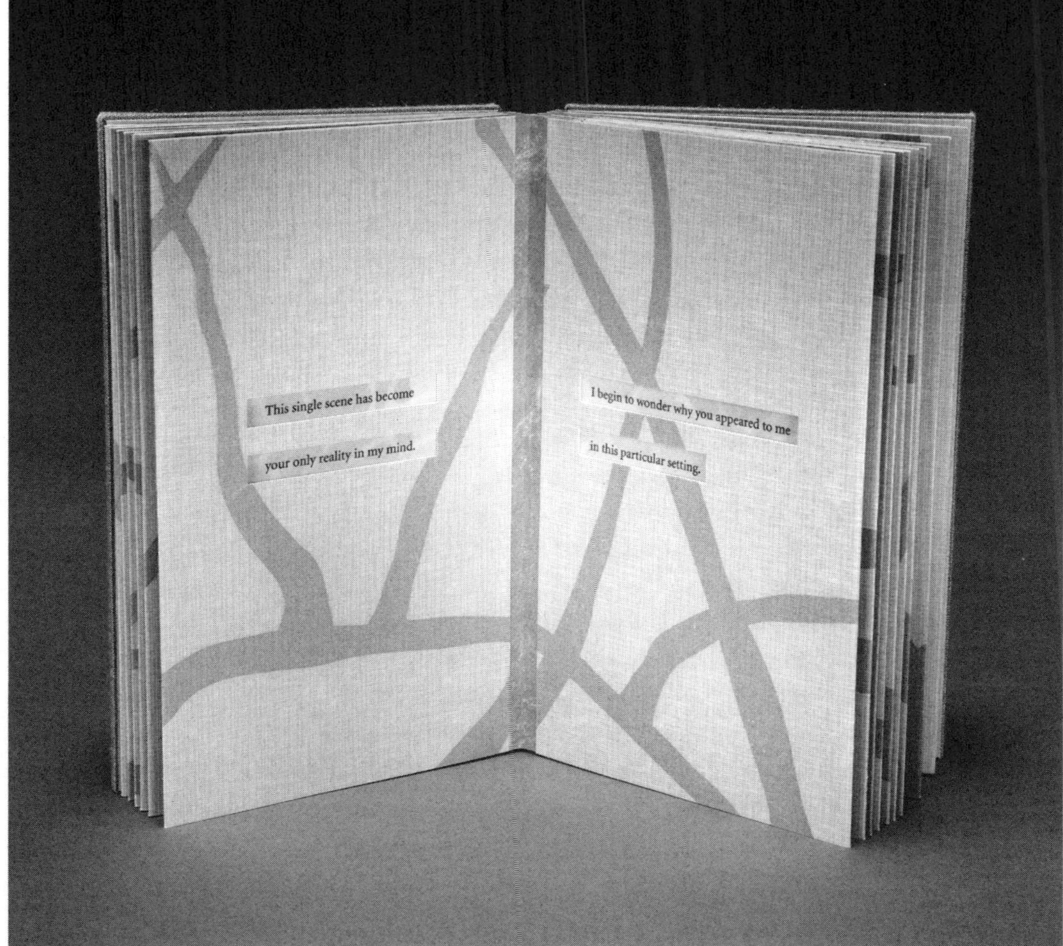


FIGURE 4.8. Julie Chen. *View*, volume 2: *Afterimage*, 2006 (handmade book with inset text). (Photo by Sibila Savage. Courtesy of Julie Chen.)

realizes and accepts his transition from life to death. As the father embraces the son, the son's expression of grief becomes "astonishment," followed by "relief." As the dream concludes, the speaker, like Peter Najarian in chapter 1, wakes "with an overwhelming sense of longing / for something that [she] cannot name or comprehend."

Volume 2, *Afterimage*, continues the narrator's reflections about her dream (fig. 4.8). In this volume, the pages are more substantial than the first, with silhouettes of bare gray-green tree trunks and branches printed onto yellow-green textured paper. The text appears now in printed strips on sheer paper embedded within, not overlaid upon, cutout sections of the page, as if the autobiographical persona has absorbed the meaning of the dream and is speaking from deep within.

An afterimage refers to an impression of a vivid sensation or image that lingers after the original stimulus stops. In photography, an afterimage is an optical illusion generated by the biological structure of human vision, an image that continues after exposure to the original has ended. A different type of afterimage "occurs when someone sees an image that is very emotionally charged," "an image that the viewer cannot get out of his or her mind." This type of intense, often traumatic, memory is distinguished from "the simple memory of an image . . . that tends to fade over time" (www.photo-graphic-image-arts.com). Here the narrator grapples with "waking recollections" of the dream, fading memories of images of the "pearly grayness of the sky" merging with "the silvery grayness" of the water" and of the "dark shapes of the trees," which are like "spectators / watching [him] from their vantage point"; how the deceased's "footsteps create agitated ripples / in the water," "how [his] legs struggle to overcome the resistance of the water," and "how the sound of the water" transforms from chaotic to "a sense of unwavering resolution." What remains for the dreamer is one image of commingled sky, water, and woods. With this single scene, distilled from all the other images of the dream, imprinted upon her mind, the speaker, haunted by lingering ethereal sensations, begins an endless cycle of anguish, wondering—why the loved one appeared "in this particular setting"; where was he before and "to where will [he] return"? Addressing her loved one, she muses: "It is as if time no longer exists for you." To free herself from this cycle of distress, she tries to "imagine / what happens next."

From this point on, the speaker speculates about what happens to her deceased loved one once he leaves his father's embrace. In a series of parallel repetitions, the speaker envisions several possible outcomes: "I imagine you leaving your father's embrace" and finding him "no longer necessary to your own understanding" of your transition to death; "I imagine you standing alone in the water, taking in the absolute stillness . . . then turning . . . to gaze at the distant shore"; "I imagine you hesitating for a moment / before striding towards the land"; "I imagine you slipping through the sheltering / trees and disappearing from view"; "I imagine that you are entering into a new / existence outside of time and worry"; "I imagine that you are now a stranger / no longer knowable or reachable." Chen concludes with a final vision, a description that returns to the original dream but moves it forward in time: "A man stands alone, knee-deep / in a large, still body of water." In contrast to the original dream, in which he was distraught, not yet fully comprehending his death and mortified at having to break the news to his father, the man "is standing in a relaxed manner, . . . not remembering / or caring how he came to be in this place. / He breathes deeply, taking in the stillness / of his surroundings." Finally, "he turns and begins to walk / towards the now familiar shore." The deceased man, having become familiar with his transition, is ready to travel to the other side. And, of course, the dreamer, the one left behind, releases him—the deceased, who, unlike

     Hinge Image-and-Text Forms

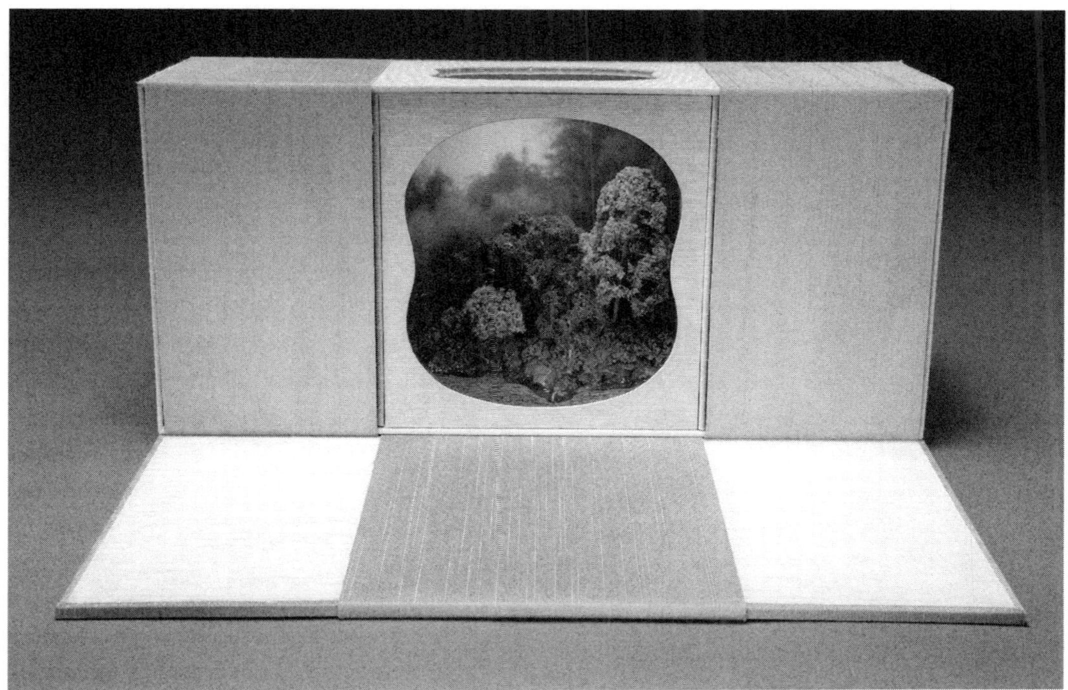

her, has become freed from time. Although the story focuses on the recently deceased man's transition, it is really about the dreamer's processing of death, of loss, of the collapse of past, present, and future, and the process of letting go.

Even after reading volume 2, however, the story has not yet ended. In fact, such a story has no ending—only the arbitrary artistic closure. In this instance, at the bottom of the compartment holding volume 2, is printed the following:

### INSTRUCTIONS

After reading both MISE EN SCÈNE and *AFTERIMAGE*, replace the books in their compartments and close the box lid. With the lid closed, tilt the box towards you until the lid is perpendicular to the surface of the table and the box is resting on its side. Pull the top edge of the lid downward until the lid is resting on the table, revealing the contents of the central compartment.

Following these instructions, the reader-viewer realizes that while she or he has been reading the dream narrative, inside the center compartment is a diorama of a wooded landscape nestled up to a grayish lake (fig. 4.9). On the back wall a misty photograph continues the imagery of gray sky meeting the woods. This is a mysterious, interior place of imagination.

FIGURE 4.9. Julie Chen. *View*, 2006 (internal diorama). (Photo by Sibila Savage. Courtesy of Julie Chen.)

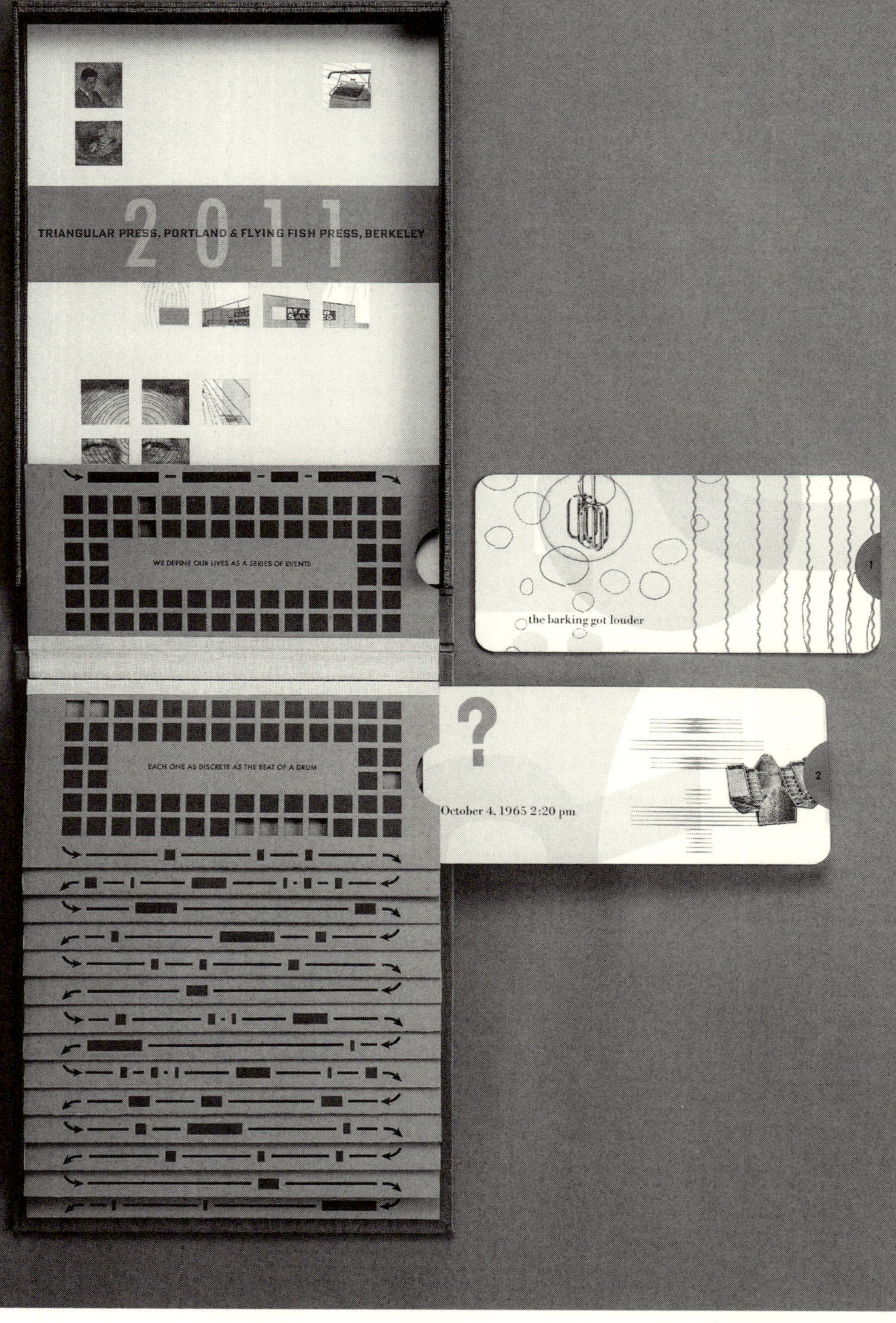
2011
TRIANGULAR PRESS, PORTLAND & FLYING FISH PRESS, BERKELEY
WE DEFINE OUR LIVES AS A SERIES OF EVENTS
EACH ONE AS DISCRETE AS THE BEAT OF A DRUM
the barking got louder
1
?
October 4, 1965 2:20 pm
2

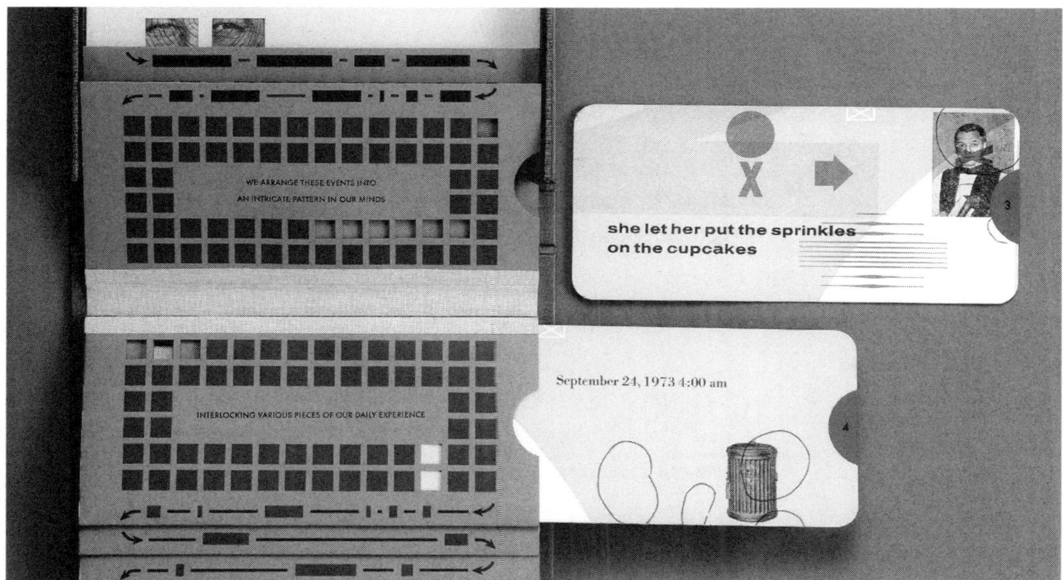


The dreamscape is hidden in the center of the structure—between the two imagetexts that frame the site, serve as its bookends, and narrate its story and symbols—suggesting the power of the dream, the difficulty of accessing it clearly, and the painful processing of loss that relates the two stories.

In the elaborately conceived artists' book, *Glimpse* (2011), a collaboration between Julie Chen and Barb Tetenbaum, Chen returns to a self-reflexive consideration of subjectivity and the challenges of comprehending and representing it.[8] Inside a box covered with brown silk is the book. Affixed to the bottom half of the box are fifteen sleeves that contain heavy cards with various printed images of household machines—hand mixers, old typewriters, parts of machines. The sleeves are arranged so that they cascade from top to bottom: only the top sleeve is fully visible; the rest peek out from beneath the one on top (fig. 4.10).

Onto the bottom half-inch visible section of the top sleeve and the top half-inch section of the bottom sleeve, Chen has printed arrows, lines, squares, and rectangles to guide the reader through the book. Onto each rectangular sleeve are printed eighty-four brown squares (six rows of fourteen squares). A few of the squares on each sleeve have been cut out to reveal a glimpse of the printed card within.

The book has two sets of texts—one on the sleeve by Chen and one on the card inside the sleeve by Tetenbaum. Text, uppercase and centered, is printed onto the top and bottom surfaces of the sleeve on front and back. In the external sleeve text, Chen muses again about memory, subjectivity, and autobiography:

(OPPOSITE)
FIGURE 4.10.
Julie Chen and
Barb Tetenbaum.
*Glimpse*, 2011 (title
page of flap book
with inserts).
(Photo by Sibila
Savage. Courtesy
of Julie Chen and
Barb Tetenbaum.)

(ABOVE)
FIGURE 4.11.
Julie Chen and
Barb Tetenbaum.
*Glimpse*, 2011
(inside).
(Photo by Sibila
Savage. Courtesy
of Julie Chen and
Barb Tetenbaum.)

WE DEFINE OUR LIVES AS A SERIES OF EVENTS

EACH ONE AS DISCRETE AS THE BEAT OF A DRUM
WE ARRANGE THESE EVENTS INTO
AN INTRICATE PATTERN IN OUR MINDS

INTERLOCKING VARIOUS PIECES OF OUR DAILY EXPERIENCE
IN ORDER TO FORM A PLEASING COMPOSITION

·   ·   ·   ·   ·   ·   ·   ·   ·   ·   ·   ·   ·

WE TELL OURSELVES THAT THIS PATTERN IS OUR HISTORY

THIS IS WHAT MAKES US WHO WE ARE
WE CONVINCE OURSELVES THAT CERTAIN PARTS OF THE PATTERN
ARE PREDETERMINED AND OUTSIDE OF OUR CONTROL

WHEN IN FACT WE OURSELVES CHOOSE
WHAT TO INCLUDE AND WHAT TO DISCARD
THE SPACES BETWEEN EVENTS OFTEN GO UNEXAMINED

IGNORED OR SIMPLY FORGOTTEN
WE THINK OF THEM AS INTERRUPTIONS

OR AS NON-EVENTS DEVOID OF CONTENT
WE FAIL TO REALIZE THAT IT IS DURING THESE SPACES

·   ·   ·   ·   ·   ·   ·   ·   ·   ·   ·   ·   ·

WHEN OUR THOUGHTS ARE FOCUSED ELSEWHERE
NOT AT THE INSTANT OF THE DRUMBEAT

BUT DURING THE INTERVAL BETWEEN ONE BEAT AND THE NEXT
THE MOMENT THAT WE THINK OF AS SILENCE

MAY CONTAIN THE ENTIRE LIFETIME OF
THE SOUND THAT CAME BEFORE

BUT IT PASSES SO QUICKLY THAT WE BARELY NOTICE ITS
     EXISTENCE

BEFORE OUR ATTENTION IS DIVERTED BY THE
CONSTANT SEARCH FOR MEANING IN THE CHATTERING OF TIME

Once again, Chen continues her "constant search for meaning in the chattering of time." The speaker fears disappearing in all-enveloping Time. She critiques the human tendency to identify individual events, to arrange these events into patterns and sequences, and to claim that such a construction is "our history," "ourselves." In the determination to shape our lives, we assume that some experiences are "predetermined

     Hinge Image-and-Text Forms

and outside of our control," but, Chen insists, we always select "what to include and what to discard" from our experiences. In the process, "the spaces between events often go unexamined." That the "spaces between" are important is accentuated by the structure of the book: Chen presents this concept at the very center of the book where the gutter—the space where the page disappears into the binding, the space that is hidden yet holds the book together—is most pronounced. "The spaces between events"—what happens off the page—are construed as "interruptions" or "non-events," but Chen declares that it is in the interstices "when much of life is actually lived."

Inside each sleeve is one printed card (fig. 4.11). The fifteen cards are printed on both sides, making them two pages. To turn the page, the reader flips the card up (not to the right).

The pages are numbered with tabs on the right-hand side of the card that are visible while the card is in the sleeve. The reader must pull the card out of the sleeve from the right-hand side. Each of the pages has a specific date and time, moving chronologically in leaps and bounds from March 13, 1957, 9:25 a.m., to July 15, 2010, 5:00 p.m. Julie Chen's co-author, Barb Tetenbaum, produced cards that echo earlier artists' books made of random letters, designs, and shapes—all in dialogue with one another but not really telling a story or revealing much personal information. There are numerous printed letterpress letters, stamps of domestic machines (for example, a Sunbeam hand mixer, what looks like an old adding machine, a typewriter, and a metal milkshake mixer) and household tools (including a metal garbage can, assorted plumbing, a cooking pot, a toolbox, a mallet, and a notebook binder), and seemingly random images such as a scuba diver, an ice cream sundae, a factory building, and a soccer shoe. All of these images of prefabricated objects suggest a daily world cluttered with mass-produced technology. In addition, there are stamped circles, arrows, wavy lines, hands with a finger pointing, and Xeroxed photographs, all common directional notations, but here placed randomly. In contrast, hand-drawn red spirals and lines that are less polished than the stamped and printed images reveal a human hand. Following the date and time and intermingling with the various images is the text. Rather than a developed narrative, Tetenbaum presents evocative fragments:

March 13, 1957 9:25 a.m.
the barking got louder

October 4, 1965 2:20 p.m.
she let her put the sprinkles / on the cupcakes

·   ·   ·   ·   ·   ·   ·   ·   ·   ·   ·   ·   ·   ·   ·   ·   ·

August 30, 1996 9:00 p.m.
we are out of sweet vermouth

.   .   .   .   .   .   .   .   .   .

July 15, 2010 5:00 pm
I put cumbia on the cd player

Collecting these fragmentary memories mirrors the process of memory in which bits and pieces of experiences and images may come to mind, rather than complete and coherent scenes and stories. The fact that each memory byte is tied to a precise time and date emphasizes how life stories are constructed out of a capacious collection of discrete moments. Within each partial memory is embedded a story, a latent autobiographical narrative.

Chen's text serves as a filter for Tetenbaum's, which, in turn, serves as another filter for the underlying images, which appear dissociated, out of context, and random. Chen and Tetenbaum use the autobiographical process of selecting, omitting, and filtering events not to shape the past into a coherent narrative but to highlight omissions, gaps, spaces, and partial glimpses of those "unimportant events" that make up daily life. In the process, they illustrate the difficulty of accessing and shaping a comprehensible or conclusive life story.

Sculptural and architectural objects that place image and text in innovative relation to each other, Julie Chen's artists' books disrupt readers' expectations about reading conventions. Like hypertexts, they require readers to pay attention to the structure, to explore multiple surfaces, and to consider the entire book as a visual-verbal field, a collection of interfaces with multiple sites of interaction. They require an intensely interactive engagement. Overall, they offer "a confluence of relations—between image and text, type and the page, form and function, writer/artist and reader, space and time" (Ollman n.p.). Through this interrelationship of image and text, Chen thematizes and spatializes time and its influence on subjectivity. Like Leslie Marmon Silko, she reflects on the passage of time, but focuses more on the unceasing erosion of life and the inevitable accumulation of loss. Chen shares her personal experiences obliquely—no explicit linear life stories but instead an assemblage of interpenetrating moments and processes of consciousness. Rather than autobiographical details, then, Chen constructs architectural structures of cognition. As readers navigate the unique pathways of her books, they journey through Chen's musings and an array of finely crafted sensory processes. Focusing on the book as a time-based medium and experimenting with the book form and the page, Chen manipulates the

     Hinge Image-and-Text Forms

reader's temporal experience, emphasizing her preoccupation with ever-flowing linear time, which erodes the structures of self, inevitable second by inevitable second. At the same time, she ponders not only the nature of subjectivity, but its construction and representation. Just as it is not possible to stop time, it is not possible to limit the self to any fixed set of characteristics or one's life story to a finite selection of moments. By design, Chen heightens the reader-viewer's awareness of each singularly precious present moment and emphasizes the importance of bringing full consciousness to it. The act of navigating her artists' books requires nothing less.

# Theresa Hak Kyung Cha's *Dictée*

## "A Series of Metaphors for the Return"

Informed by her experimental video, mail art, and performance art, Cha uses a cinematic technique, juxtaposes image and text, and deconstructs the word on the page as part of a multidimensional art practice in book form.

For more than five decades the publication of autobiographical narratives bearing witness to trauma has burgeoned. Anguished stories of surviving political and domestic violence, genocide, colonization, and other forms of physical and psychological abuse abound. Not surprisingly, "the desire for return to origins and to sites of communal sufferings has progressively intensified" in the late twentieth and early twenty-first centuries (Hirsch and Miller 3). Theresa Hak Kyung Cha participates in this literary and cultural phenomenon of return, of looking again at the past in order to testify about its continuing aftershocks. Like Peter Najarian and Art Spiegelman, in her radically experimental visual autobiography, *Dictée*, Cha addresses themes of historical violence, displacement, memory, transgenerational trauma, and the difficulty of articulating a complicated legacy of loss. She seeks to understand her parent's traumatic experience during the Japanese occupation of Korea and to convey its consequences in her own life as an immigrant who searches for her past—a history, a language, a culture, and a home—to which she cannot return. Like many Asian American immigrant subjects, Cha seeks to find her place within both the United States and "global, transnational, and diasporic matrices" (Lim 16). The phases of Cha's work, in fact, prefigure the transition that had taken place in Asian American studies by the mid-1990s, from a focus on national (U.S.-based experience) to transnational (multiply national or diasporic experiences).

Using a cinematic style, Cha incorporates many personal and historical stories in a complex assemblage. In some sections, she creates detailed storyboard narration in which each camera angle is determined; conceives of the page as both a unit of space and time and a screen; and juxtaposes diagrams, letters, documents, archival photographs, and film stills with textual narrative. Cha's autobiographical persona is a narrator, filmmaker, and daughter, but most profoundly, like Julie Chen (see chapter 4), she is a witnessing, interpreting consciousness. She is everywhere but nowhere in the text—a disembodied female voice struggling to visualize embodied speech on the page. Cha offers a self-reflexive commentary on the autobiographical process and struggles to find a suitable conclusion to her narrative of trauma. Although Cha desires to return to her homeland, language, and culture, her return is endlessly deferred even as she perpetually performs the attempt through acts of memory that become, finally, memorialized in the book.

### *Dictée*

Born in Pusan, Korea, Theresa Hak Kyung Cha (1951–82) was twelve years old when she and her family left South Korea for Hawaii—the fundamental displacement that she would thematize throughout her work. One year later, she and her family moved to San Francisco. Throughout the 1970s, Cha participated in the lively San Francisco Bay Area art community, contributing her unique vision and voice to the conceptual arts scene. Cha worked in a variety of modes: the then-emerging form of performance art, film and video, handmade books, mail art, mixed media installations, and experimental literature.[1]

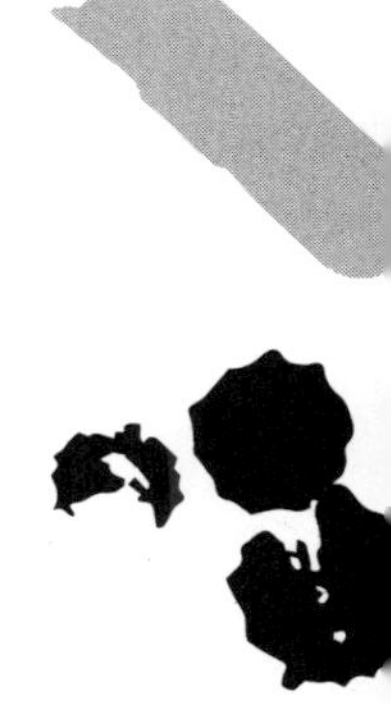

In her MFA thesis, Cha envisioned the artist as an alchemist, a medium whose "vision belongs to an altering, of material, and of perception." Through the transformative promise of art and art making, "the perception of the audience has the possibility of being altered, of being presented a constant change, Re-volution" ("Paths" 3). She links the possibility of transforming audience perceptions to the notion of collective consciousness, a "kind of meta-Confucianism" (Rinder 28). In short, Cha believed that art can elicit not merely an individual revelation but also a collective transformation.

My focus here is on Cha's radically experimental visual autobiography *Dictée*, but I also discuss some of her other creative work—experimental film, performance art, and mail art—as it informs my reading of *Dictée*. Cha incorporates many kinds of cultural stories: official history, personal narrative, stories of parents remembered and imagined, black-and-white photographs, government documents, handwritten and typed letters, lists, diagrams, and maps. "An experimental anomaly in Asian American literature" (Lamm 43), the multilingual *Dictée* is written primarily in English and French, but also includes Chinese characters and Pinyin, Latin, and one instance of Hangul, the Korean written script. *Dictée* has been discussed as an epic poem in the modernist tradition of Ezra Pound, but with an emphasis on "transpacific connections" (J. Park 22), but a more credible description of *Dictée* is as "an explosion of high-wire techniques and wide-ranging influences, a feat of historical imagination, a multimedia display, an eloquent stutter. . . . Language breaks down, starts up, transposes itself from French to English, becomes a deadpan grammar lesson. It ends near glossolalia" (E. Park 9).

With *Dictée*'s emphasis on process, its laying bare the limitations of language, and its innovative typography and cinematic vision, Cha challenges not only the conventions of autobiography as focused on an individual subject with a linear story in writing but also those of the form of the book itself and, consequently, the process of reading. Like Peter Najarian and Art Spiegelman, who struggle to form historical narratives from the fragments of their parents' memories, Cha wrestles with the fragments of her family's past and both remembers and imagines stories: of displacement—her mother's removal from Korea to Manchuria, the family's from Korea to the United States; attempted erasure—the Japanese outlawing the Korean language in Korea, insisting that Koreans speak Japanese in its place; and death—the Japanese soldiers shooting down student demonstrators. Mirroring her attempt to piece together a violently ruptured past, the collection of fragments in *Dictée* bump up against each other uneasily. Words are broken into component bits; sentences are liberated from punctuation or arranged in nonlinear relations; images float free of labels; images and text are juxtaposed. Similar to Chen's artists' books, fragments of text and image create a collection of counterpoints, variously bouncing off one another or intersecting, requiring readers to navigate the dynamic interfaces.

Cha intermingles the Western forms of epic (focused on a grand national scale) and lyric (devoted to a personal voice) to retell the intermingled histories of Korea, Japan, and the United States, the personal histories of her family members, and her own struggles with a sense of being a "perpetual exile" (*Dictée* 81). Unlike the predominantly assimilationist immigrant autobiographies of the late nineteenth and early twentieth centuries in which immigrants write to convince readers of their successful transformation into the new culture and their belonging, Cha's image-text performs the challenge of translating herself to another language, culture, and identity.[2] Unlike many other autobiographers, Cha does not assume an essential wholeness from which she derives or to which she returns. "In the prism of *Dictée*, representativeness (founded on the identity of single type) and authenticity (predicated on original, unmediated essence) are refracted and returned as difference and mediation" (Wong, "Unnaming the Same" 104). Similarly, "*Dictée* is not interested in identities," but "it is profoundly interested in the process of *identification*" (Cheng 141). The female figures in *Dictée*, in particular, continually attempt to translate themselves but always struggle with the fragments of ever-elusive words and images with which to do so. Cha's autobiographical persona, situated as the organizing intelligence of disparate and partial female voices, is fundamentally collective and relational.

## Visual Organization

To prepare for a close consideration of Cha's treatment of gendered and politicized language and dictation themes, visual and cinematic techniques, and serial conclusions, an overview of the structure of *Dictée* will be helpful. Number symbolism is a dominant aspect of Cha's visual organization. Cha's design for the overall structure of *Dictée* uses three iterations of the number nine, each with its own set of referents and associations, and each repeated variably throughout. Organizing *Dictée* into nine sections, she invokes and alters the Muses from classical Greek literature: Clio, Calliope, Urania, Melpomene, Erato, Elitere, Thalia, Terpsichore, and Polymnia. Cha replaces the sixth Muse, Euterpe, with one she invented, Elitere, perhaps a combination of "elite" and "literare" (Wong, "Unnaming the Same" 115). It is telling that Euterpe, the single Muse Cha banishes from *Dictée*, has a name that translates as rejoicing well or bringer of delight, suggesting that rejoicing and delight have no place in Cha's project.

A related organizing device is her repetition of the number nine in a Catholic context, particularly through references to the novena, the "recitation of prayer and practicing of devotions during a nine day period" (*Dictée* 19). The *Catholic Encyclopedia* reports that according to Saint Jerome, "'The number nine in Holy Writ is indicative of suffering and grief'"; the novena itself is associated with "hopeful mourning," "yearning," and "prayer" (www.newadvent.org). This tone of yearning—for a lost past, homeland, and identity—permeates *Dictée*.

Finally, the ten Chinese characters on page 154 are translated into English on page 173 as the ten aspects of the Chinese universe:

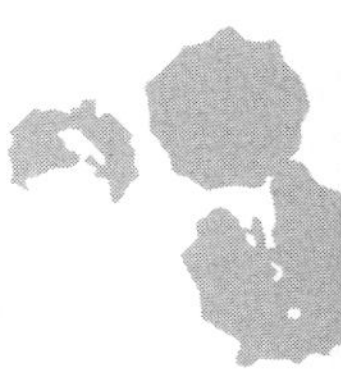

TAI-CHI  First, the universe.
LEUNG YEE  Second, Ying [*sic*] and Yang.
SAM CHOY  Third, Heaven, Earth, and Humans.
SAY CHEUNG  Fourth, the Cardinals, North, South, East, West.
NG HANG  Fifth, the five elements, Metal,
    Wood, Water, Fire, Earth.
LOK HOP  Sixth, Four cardinals and the Zenith and Nadir.
CHUT SING  Seventh, seven stars, the Big Dipper.
BAT GWA  Eight, the Eight Diagrams.
GOW GEE LIN WAN  Ninth, Unending series of
    nines, or nine points linked together.

The list begins with undifferentiated wholeness and moves to increasing multiplicity and specificity. Beginning with the universe, the second splits into two—binary, yet complementary, opposites—Ying [*sic*] and Yang. The third divides into three—heaven, earth, and humans who link them, while Say Cheung, the fourth, stands for the four cardinal directions. Not surprisingly, the fifth refers to the five elements and the sixth to the four cardinal directions and up and down. The seventh moves into the heavens to note, more specifically, the seven stars of the Big Dipper, while the eighth, referring to the *I-Ching* (*The Book of Changes*), notes the *Bagua*, or Eight Diagrams, that depict the eight natural phenomena: sky, earth, thunder, wind, water, fire, mountain, and lake. The ninth, itself the final link of nine, also stands for an "unending series of nines" that are embedded in the tenth, "a series of concentric circles" that contain the universe in all its numerous complex manifestations.

These ten Chinese aspects of the universe recall the nine Muses and Sappho (who is often noted as the tenth Muse). Considered together, the repeated references to the number nine (encircled by ten) provide an elaborate transcultural-linguistic-spiritual structure for Cha's interpenetrating themes of domination, loss, and hope for redemption (associated with the Catholic nine) through expansive creative expression (associated with the nine Muses and Sappho) in relation to the universe (associated with the Chinese cosmos).[3]

### Language and Dictation: Visualizing "Speech under the Pressure of Great Pain"

In *Dictée*, as in much of her other artwork, Cha is both fascinated and frustrated with language. She focuses on language not merely as product—print on the page—but also as physical process. That is, she emphasizes language being shaped by the tongue and lips, language emerging from the cavernous and fluid recesses of the body and being transmitted outward or thwarted. More dramatically, Cha visualizes speech, illustrating in text and image the process of making sound. In a "Statement of Proposed Study—Holland," Cha writes: "The main body of my work is with Language, looking for the roots of language before it is born on the tip of the tongue. . . . Certain area(s) that continue to hold interest for me are: grammatical structures of language system itself, by function or usage, and how transformation is brought about through manipulation, processes as changing the syntax, isolation, removing from

     Hinge Image-and-Text Forms

context, repetition, and reduction to minimal units. These concerns are experimented with in book-making, with written texts and images."

Throughout *Dictée*, Cha liberates language from its imprisonment in proper "grammatical structures." She removes words from their contexts, sometimes presenting them in isolation (for example, "Until."). She breaks words into syllables to expose multiple meanings or to unearth fossilized associations (for instance, "From A Far" or "uni formed soliders"). She shatters words into phonemes to emphasize their sound value and the sometimes halting, strangling process of articulation. At times, language is defamiliarized so that even writing, broken into marks on the page, is seen as image. Cha repeats words, phrases, and concepts with slight variation (for example, "What nationality / or what kindred and relation / what blood relation / what blood ties of blood / what ancestry / what race generation / what house clan tribe stock strain / what lineage extraction / what breed sect gender denomination caste") to create a network of meaning and allusion. Her creative play with language is also an experiment with time. She contracts and expands time to encompass two levels of the past—history and mythology—and their relevance in the present, a point to which I will return near the end of this chapter. Cha's obsession with language is not surprising given that the "Third World immigrant experience in the U.S. is punctuated by everyday reminders of the ideological and institutional intimacy of language, identity, and social legitimacy" (Kang 73).

All through *Dictée*, Cha thematizes language, visualizing its spoken and written production, potential translation, and attempted transmission. The title itself is illustrative. *Dictée*, a French feminine noun, can be translated as dictation or as the act of dictating; as a verb, it may be translated as dictate. Throughout *Dictée*, Cha plays with the notion of translation—linguistic, cultural, and physical. Dictation is literally an old-fashioned form of language instruction in which the student writes down what the instructor speaks, something Cha experienced in Catholic school classes. On page 1, Cha writes a teacher's dictation in French: "Aller à la ligne C'était le premier jour point." The second paragraph is the student's English translation of the French dictation. By mimicking "perfectly" and "literally" the teacher's words, the student mocks the translation exercise: "Open paragraph It was the first day period" (1). By writing "Open paragraph" and "period" rather than using the standard notation for punctuation, Cha emphasizes the imperfection of translation and, more important, the possibility of resisting being dictated to or being translated into a compliant subject. "The menace of mimicry," explains Homi Bhabha, "is its double vision which in disclosing the ambivalence of colonial discourse also disrupts its authority" (88). Al-

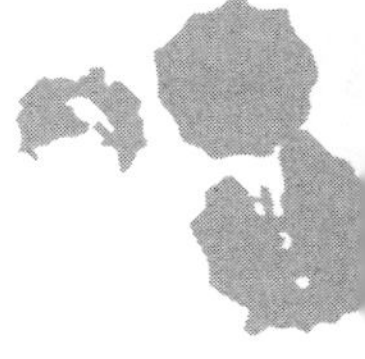

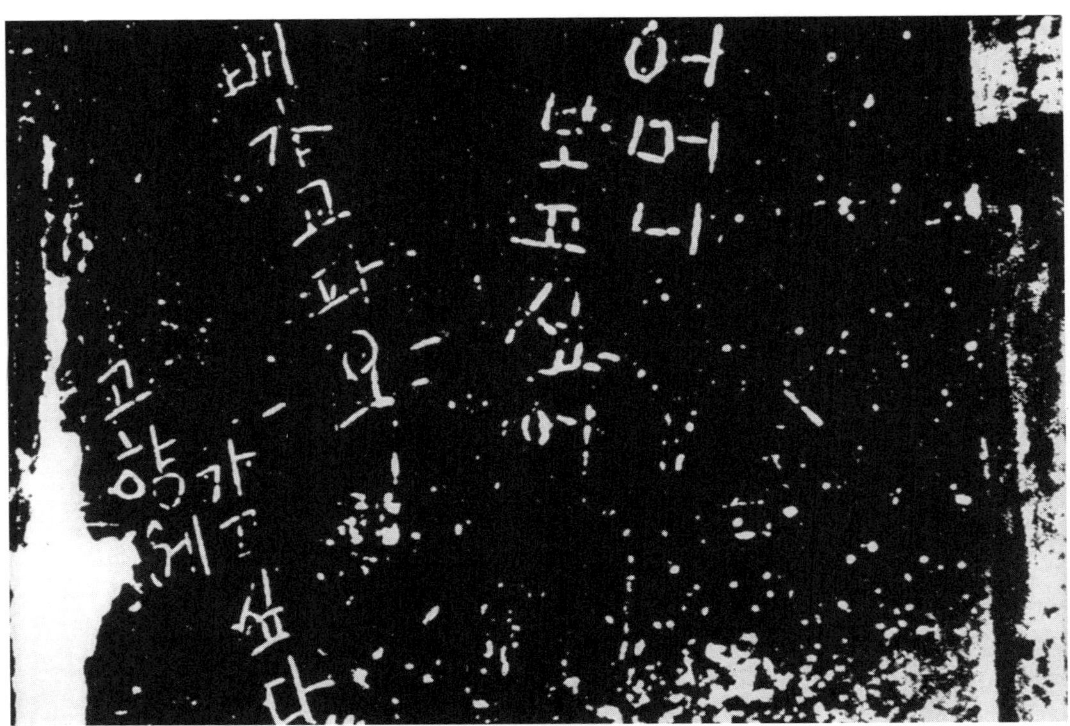



though in this instance French is not the colonizer's language, it is associated with the language of authority, the language of an/Other that Cha wishes both to speak and to note her distance from. Allan deSouza claims that by moving between and mixing English and French, Cha forces the reader into "the position of the colonized learning the colo- niser's tongue" (75). It may be more accurate to say that, with the inclu- sion of English, French, Chinese, Latin, and Korean, most readers will find themselves positioned as Other at some point in *Dictée*. In fact, read- ing *Dictée* can be considered as a lesson in reading a multiply inflected cultural and linguistic "otherness" (Twelbeck 187). Cha's use of multiple languages and stylistic innovation disrupts readers' expectations. We are forced to rethink how to read, how to look, how to interpret.

Significantly, Cha includes only a single instance of Korean writing in *Dictée* (see fig. 5.1), and she does not translate it. The gateway to *Dictée*, in fact, is an image of Korean characters carved into a wall or tunnel by Koreans who had been forced into labor in Japan. The writing translates as: "Mother, I miss you / I'm hungry / I want to go home [to my native place]" (Kim 10, 25n9; Wong, "Unnaming the Same" 107).[4] In the 1995 Third Woman Press edition of *Dictée*, this writing appears on the page before the title page. In the 2001 University of California Press edition, the Hangul appears as the second image, but on the verso page next to the title page. Both editions retain the centrality of the anonymous, oppressed, and homesick Korean voices through which the reader enters the work. For readers unable to read Korean, the Hangul text serves merely as image, as marks on a surface. That Cha does not explain or translate this imagetext underscores the haunting nature of an inaccessible mother tongue and a tortured Korean history in *Dictée*.

The French dictation is followed by a section entitled "Diseuse," a term that refers to a female speaker (nct exactly the autobiographical persona) who, as a woman with a voice, is "fundamentally disruptive" (Wong, "Unnaming the Same" 121). The female speaker, like the student taking dictation, "mimicks the speaking." Her words "resemble speech. . . . Bared noise, groan, bits torn from words" (3). Cha describes how the woman's speech is rendered physically: "The entire lower lip would lift upwards then sink back to its original place. She would then gather both lips and protrude them in a pout taking in the breath that might utter some thing" (3). Cha returns to *diseuse* and a consideration of language a hundred pages later: "Dead words. Dead tongue. From disuse" (133). Here, Cha presents aural punning on "diseuse," which in English sounds similar to "disuse"—a single word-image that contradicts itself— a female speaker who has a "dead tongue" "from disuse" (133).

Cha thematized the physical process of articulation, visualizing sound and perhaps language in her earlier work as well. In her eight-minute black-and-white video, *Mouth to Mouth* (1975), Cha performs her insistence on the physicality of language (fig. 5.2). She presents a series of images that depicts the process of articulation: here is a voice that is not heard but visualized.

With the sound of water or static in the background, the title, "m o u t h to mouth," rolls onto the screen from right to left. Out of the grainy film an image emerges; slowly viewers recognize a mouth speaking. Cha "silently mouths the eight Korean vowel graphemes" (Lewallen 9).[5] Close-up shots of the mouth reveal an almost ritual-like articulation of Korean vowels.[6] With Cha's emphasis on the bodily production of language, viewers are forced to notice slight alterations of the lips, teeth, and tongue as each vowel is voiced. The mouth is difficult to see because "video snow nearly obliterates the image" (9). While this depicts "'a loss of language over time'" (Rinder 9), it also, more important, emphasizes the moment when language as a symbol system is enacted as voice, the "I," but also the fundamental difficulty of speaking and being heard and, for Cha, the challenge of speaking a language that has been wrested from her. In addition, the video snow serves as a dissolve—the ironically silent speaking mouth moving in and out of the visual field. The video concludes with the mouth dissolving into a grainy screen. The first letter of the Korean alphabet is a consonant that functions as a vowel at the beginning of a word, a point that resonates with Cha's preoccupation with

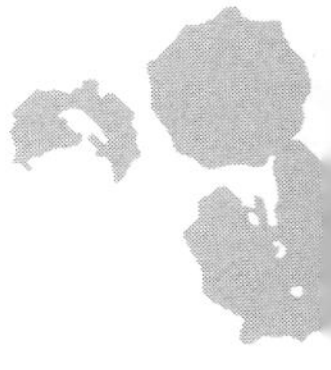

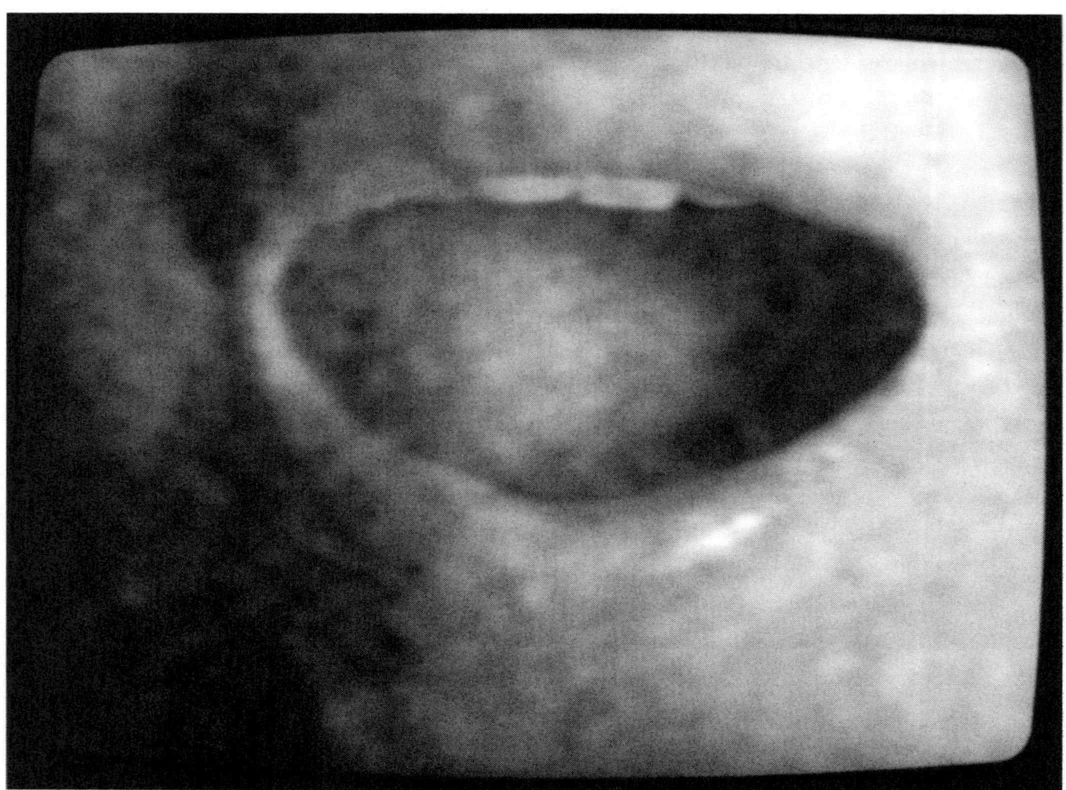



the absence of sound, the state of pre-enunciation, and the trace of language.[7] Last, techniques from Cha's experimental video *Mouth to Mouth* inform her cinematic style in *Dictée* in such practices as isolating parts from contexts, extreme close-ups, repetition, and dissolves rather than linear transitions, to name a few.

In *Dictée*, Cha presents language or speech as image, a kind of mediazation of speech. She emphasizes the physicality of language, the embodied voice, by providing detailed descriptions of characters who are speaking (or attempting to speak) and by including charts that map the physical formation of language in the throat, on the tongue, and on the lips (fig. 5.3).

In these charts, readers can locate the literal physical locations of speech—glottis, epiglottis, nasal passage, oral passage, pharynx, larynx, trachea, esophagus, lungs, diaphragm, and so on. On the page to the right, the recto, Cha describes the physical process of articulation:

One by one.

The sounds. The sounds that move at a time

stops. Starts again. Exceptions

　　　Hinge Image-and-Text Forms

stops and starts again

all but exceptions.

Stop. Start. Starts.

Contractions. Noise. Semblance of noise.

Broken speech. One to one. At a time.

Cracked tongue. Broken tongue.

Pidgeon. Semblance of speech.

Swallows. Inhales. Stutter. Starts. Stops before

starts. (75)

Cha breaks down the production of sound before it is organized into speech: "One by one. / The sounds." They stop, start, stop, and start again. What emerges are not complete sounds but "contractions," not words but "noise," not even noise but "semblance of noise." Midway through the page, Cha identifies this as "Broken speech. . . . Cracked tongue. Broken tongue"—a tongue that can merely "stutter." Cha depicts the difficulty of speaking as a woman, an immigrant, a person exiled from her homeland and forced to speak an alien language. The voice depicted here communicates the tortuous process of speaking, especially speaking in an alien tongue—the stops and starts, the bits and pieces of broken language, what Ed Park refers to as Cha's "eloquent stutter"—a hybrid, fragmented immigrant and diasporic subjectivity reeling in the aftershocks of trauma. Not surprisingly, these visual and verbal descriptions of the difficulty of speaking are followed by a map of Korea divided into North and South—a broken land that has given rise to a "cracked" and "broken" tongue (75). Fittingly, the image of a divided Korea serves as the entry to the "Melpomene/Tragedy" section.

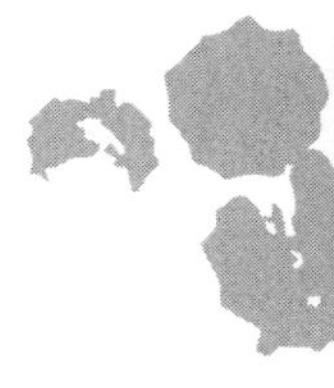

Cha's representation of embodied speech focuses not only on the painful obstacles to self-articulation but also on the process of the emerging of sound from within the body, moving up through interior cavities, then onto the tongue and lips and flowing forth as speech. She also emphasizes the embodiment of language when she compares giving blood to writing: "It takes her seconds less to break the needle off its body in attempt to collect the loss directly from the wound" (65). Here the needle creates the wound from which it draws blood, but Cha links the wound not only to the body but also to the past that she attempts to access directly. The blood becomes the ink with which to write the trauma of the past. Cha continues: "Something of the ink that resembles the stain from the interior emptied onto emptied into emptied upon

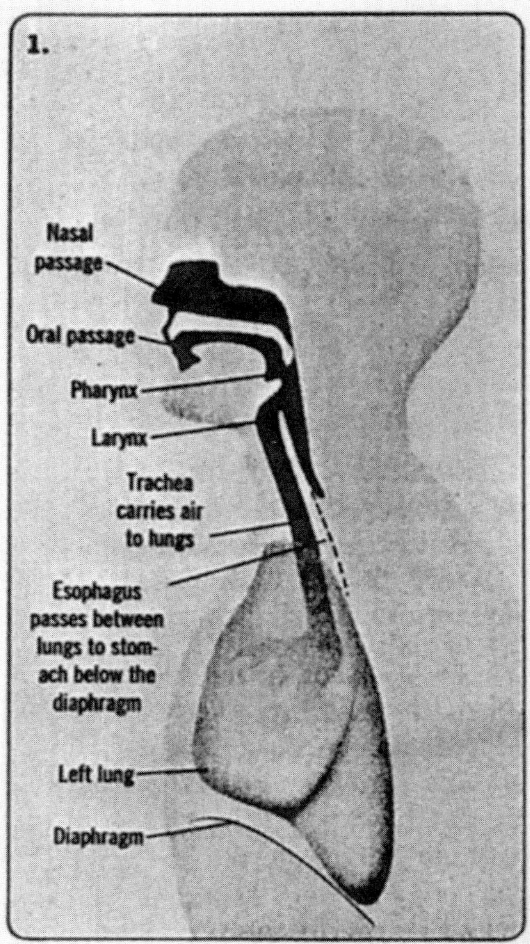


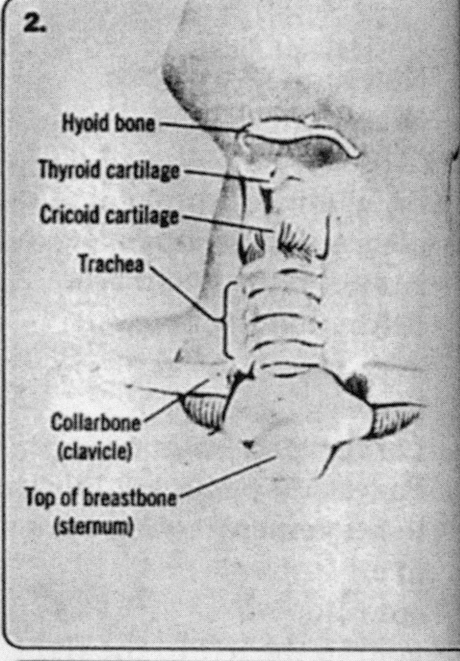


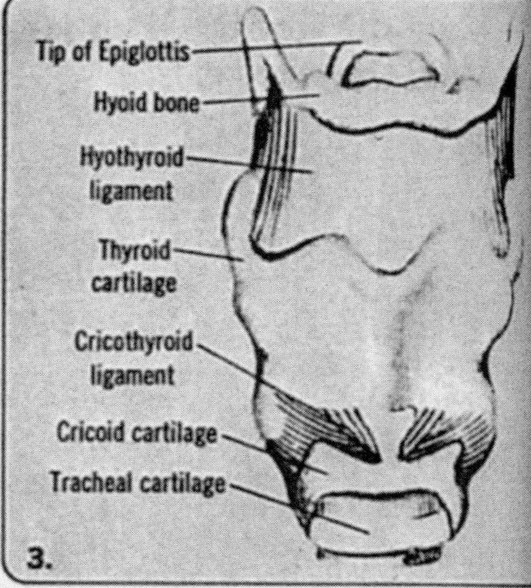


FIG. 1   Side View of Air Passages and Lungs

FIG. 2   Position of the Larynx in the Neck

FIG. 3   Front View of the Larynx

FIG. 4   Superior View of Larynx and Vocal Folds

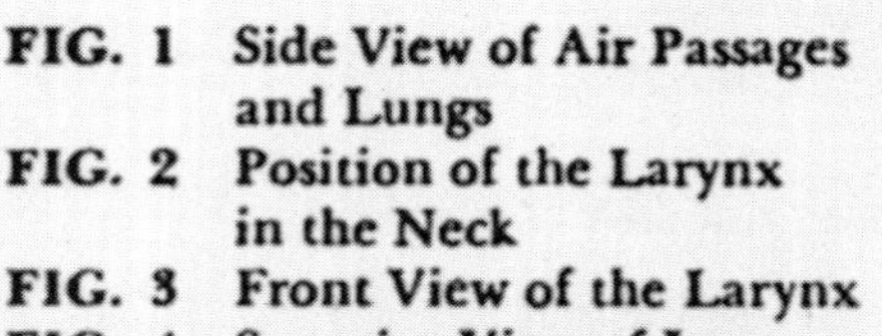

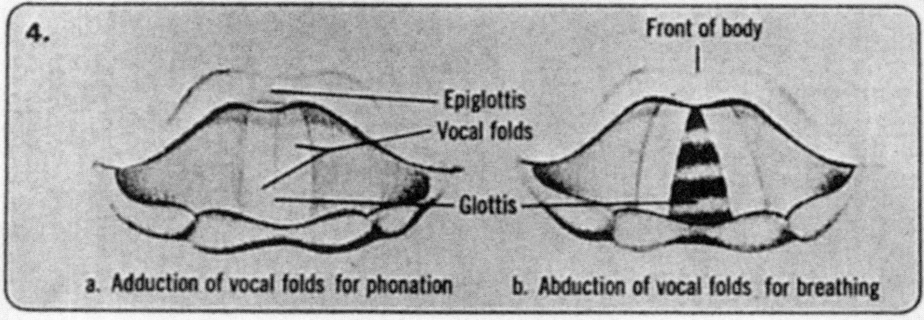

this boundary this surface. More. Others. When possible ever possible to puncture to scratch to imprint. Expel. . . . Sang. Encre" (65). Implicit in English, the link between blood and ink is explicit in French; "Sang" translates as blood and "Encre" as ink. Once again, the attempt to access and express the trauma of the past is difficult: the ink "resembles the stain from the interior" that is "emptied" onto, "punctured," "scratched," "imprinted" upon "this boundary this surface," the page. The image of bodily fluids spilling onto the page is linked with Cha's images of body cavities, such as the mouth and lungs, that enable utterance. Speech, for Cha, is associated with internal pain. Stirring inside is "the pain of speech the pain to say," but even worse is "the pain not to say." The desire, necessity, and pain inside fester like a "wound" that must break open to be healed. Throughout *Dictée*, Cha evokes "barren cavities" that "make swollen"—a kind of false pregnancy. The female speaker "allows others. In place of her" (3). "The others each occupying her" (3) like cancerous tumors. Her selection of the word "occupying," of course, invites readers to consider that the occupation is not only of the female body but of Korea. When the weight of these others is too heavy, when the pain of speaking their language or, worse, not speaking at all is too much, "She gasps from its pressure, its contracting motion" (4)—like birth pangs expelling speech. Punning on "delivery," the female speaker makes her "delivery"—a speech and a birth. Through visualized utterance, "speech under the pressure of great pain" (Hoffman 5), the autobiographical persona gives painful birth to herself.

## Language, Image, and Female Subjectivity

As discussed earlier, *Dictée* enacts taking dictation, but it also refers to being dictated to—by the French language instructor, by the Catholic Church's male authorities, and by the Japanese who colonize Korea. Like Julie Chen's persona, Cha's autobiographical persona is a (mostly) disembodied voice of loss, a woman seeking agency in a myriad of oppressive systems. In a series of narratives in the "Erato/Love Story" section, Cha tells the story of two women, one subservient to a husband and one to God, also figured as male. The women, perhaps a collective female autobiographical persona, are depicted as bereft of agency. Cha describes the husband and wife: "He is the husband, and she is the wife. He is the man. She is the wife. It is a given. . . . You only hear him taunting and humiliating her. She kneels beside him, putting on his clothes for him. She takes her place. It is given" (102). Later, "It is the husband who touches. Not as husband. He touches her as he touches all the others. But he touches her with his rank. Gratuity is her body her spirit. Her non-body her non-entity. His privilege possession his claim. Infallible is his ownership" (112). The woman is always "wife," never "woman," while the husband is always "man" even if he is also "husband." He "touches" her not with his individual desire or humanity but with his "rank," his social position as inherently superior to females. Like the seemingly all powerful Japanese colonizers who assumed authority over Koreans and enacted their will, the man in this scene is the one who acknowledges and claims his right to subjectivity, agency, authority, and ownership.

The husband's unlimited and unquestioned domination of his wife is echoed in a Christian God's power over humans. The voice of an abject aspiring female martyr is linked to the story of the dominated wife. Cha resurrects the voice of Thérèse of Lisieux (1873–97), a French Carmelite nun known as Saint Thérèse of the Child Jesus and the Holy Face and "The Little Flower of Jesus." Thérèse believed that, as a woman, she was powerless to perform great deeds but that she could prove her love of God by doing even the smallest actions with great love. Cha quotes from Thérèse's autobiography, *The Story of a Soul*, in which Thérèse explains her rationale for her love of God: "'I am only a child, powerless and weak, and yet it is my weakness that gives me the boldness of offering myself as VICTIM *of your love, O Jesus!*'" (111). Both the wife of man and the wife of Jesus are situated as subservient to the higher power of their male consorts. Here Cha critiques both Korean and Christian patriarchy as well as positions the Korean motherland as a victim of Japanese power. Unlike Saint Thérèse, Cha does not position herself as victim, but she does assume the role of a long-suffering diasporic subject longing for home.

To underscore her multilayered critique of male power, Cha frames this section with photographs of two martyred saints, neither identified.[8] Beginning this section is a photograph of Thérèse of Lisieux, who was canonized in 1925. Concluding it is a still close-up of the anguished face of Renée Jeanne Falconetti, the actor who played Jeanne d'Arc in Carl Theodor Dreyer's silent film *La Passion de Jeanne d'Arc* (1928), which depicts Jeanne's trial, incarceration, torture, and burning at the stake (fig. 5.4). Jeanne d'Arc (1412–31) was canonized in 1920.

In Cha's cinematic method of assemblage and allusion, both women are celebrated as female martyrs for God and country (though Jeanne was executed and Thérèse died of tuberculosis); both are patron saints of France. In this manner, Cha underscores the martyrdom of women more generally. More important, the women's martyrdom to man and God parallels the experiences of the Korean people colonized by Japanese forces who, like the dominating husbands—man and God—demand absolute submission from the conquered Koreans. Cha aligns Thérèse and Jeanne d'Arc, then, with another female martyr introduced earlier in *Dictée*: Yu Guan Soon (1903–20), a Korean patriot who "forms a resistant group with fellow students and actively begins her revolutionary work"

   Hinge Image-and-Text Forms

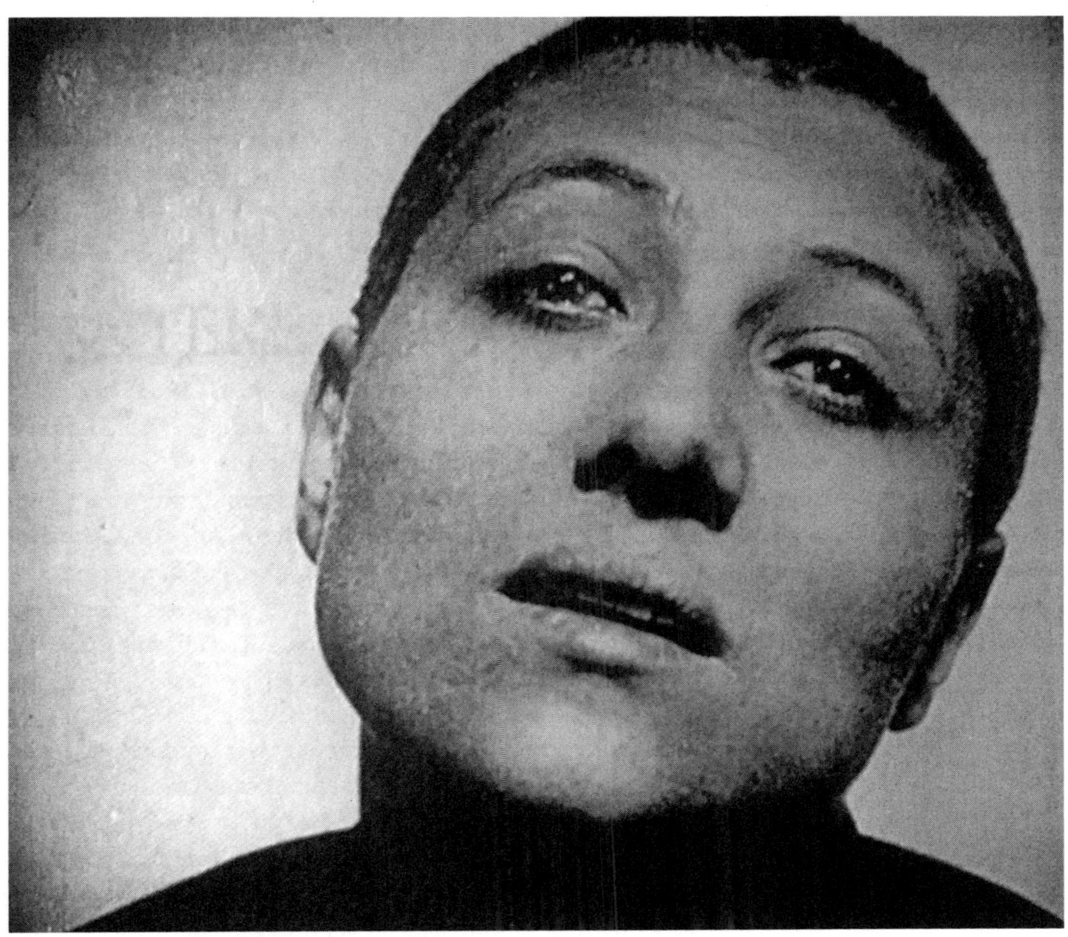

against the Japanese occupation (30). Much like Jeanne d'Arc, Yu Guan Soon is tortured and killed at the age of seventeen. The gallery of martyred women haunts the book. Throughout *Dictée*, then, Cha links the dominated bodies of women to the colonized country of Korea, female martyrdom to Korea's suffering. Cha goes so far as to compare herself to Yu Guan Soon—"the imperiled female nationalist in Korea . . . and the immigrant identity presented in the text, which seems similarly threatened by imminent erasure" (Mukherjee 197).

## Unidirectional Communication and Audience Reception

As she did in her postcard mail art, Cha addresses questions about speakers and writers and their addressees at several points throughout *Dictée*. How does one get through to an audience? How does one know? Cha's intimate interest in her audience is expressed clearly in *Audience Distant Relative* (1977):

FIGURE 5.4.
*Close-up Still Shot of Renée Jeanne Falconetti as Jeanne d'Arc in La Passion de Jeanne d'Arc* (1928), a silent film directed by Carl Theodor Dreyer. (Theresa Hak Kyung Cha. *Dictée* [Berkeley: University of California Press, 2001], 119; public domain.)

you are the audience
you are my distant audience
i address you
as i would a distant relative
as if a distant relative
seen only through someone else's description

neither you nor i
are visible to each other
i can only assume that you can hear me
i can only hope that you can hear me (n.p.)

Cha's mail art is about addressing the audience, expecting and desiring a response, but never being certain that the message is ever received. This, of course, is akin to any artist trying to reach viewers but never being certain that he or she is understood. More important, Cha's correspondence art underscores the gaps, limits, and dead ends of human communication.

Cha translates this theme of long-distance communication that may or may not find its intended reader in *Dictée*. Throughout, Cha uses fragments as well as a type of unidirectional, and therefore incomplete, correspondence to perform, resist, and lament the challenges of transpersonal communication and, to some extent, of self-narration. She incorporates into *Dictée* scripted utterances: two letters, one typewritten and one handwritten—with neither context nor response, neither narrative nor explanation—that never reach their addressees. She introduces the first letter with a description of an oral communication. The "Thalia/Comedy" section begins with a female character who "decides to take the call" (139). After the woman accepts that initial call, the text moves to a meditation on the past, pain, time, and the desire to use writing to "displace real time," to "display it . . . and become its voyeur" (140).[9] This desire may serve as an overall description of Cha's experiment throughout *Dictée*—how to make the past accessible in the present, how to fix time long enough to see any moment or oneself clearly. The acceptance of the call and the meditation on time are followed by a typewritten letter to Laura Claxton (1915). Written by H. J. Small in a formal, educated voice, the letter explains that the postcard that Mrs. Claxton wrote to Mr. Reardon has not reached him. He has moved with no forwarding address (142). Several pages later, a second letter to Mrs. Claxton (1921?), handwritten with scrawled writing and several misspellings, reports on the sorry state of Mrs. Claxton's sister, who is "in an awful shape," threatening to kill her family, unable to eat, afraid that she is going crazy. Spending money on doctors rather than food, the family is "broke." The anonymous letter writer (the letter is signed "A Friend"), finally, asks for

     Hinge Image-and-Text Forms

financial help (146–47). Neither letter has a respondent. Both letters are about an addressee who has not or may not have read the original letter and who cannot respond.

Cha includes several more unidirectional communications in *Dic-tée*. These communications include official histories that report the facts of war and trauma in neutral tones that obliterate any sense of human passion and suffering and thus elicit no humanitarian response, such as the unanswered "Petition from the Koreans of Hawaii to President Roosevelt" in which they implore U.S. help to "see to it that Korea may preserve her autonomous Government and that other Powers shall not oppress or maltreat our people" (35–36), as well as reports by language teachers who expect rigid compliance with their dictation. Through these documents, Cha counters the unitary with the multiple. In place of a single, autonomous subject or authority, she opts for a proliferation of fragmented perspectives, emphasizing multidirectional communications that challenge "uni-form" vision and unmediated reception.

## Cinematic Techniques

Arising from her avant-garde art practice and requiring committed reader engagement, Cha's cinematic style consists of her incorporation of diagrams, historic photographs, stills from early films, and typewritten and handwritten letters into her narrative. Just as important, her cinematic style arises from her own experimental videos and mail art, as well as her notion of the page as a screen onto which she projects her story and into which she places some of her characters. As part of her experimentation in language to create a new kind of autobiography and reshape the book form into an interart mode, Cha presents both filmic influences and structural innovation. In the "Erato/Love Poetry" section, she presents one facet of her cinematic style, what can best be termed a filmic or camera-angle description of the scenes. This is complicated because readers are sometimes behind the camera, sometimes in front of it, but always aware of its ever-shifting perspectives—close-up, long shot, panning, slow-motion, and so on. "The cinema—so often a metaphor of ideological inscription of subjectivity, and so often an image of fantasy and the subject's psychic reality—is a crucial textual and visual arena for understanding *Dictée's* portrayal of exile" (Lamm 46). Through textual representation of the cinema, Cha simultaneously projects and disrupts her desire for mother tongue and home. In one highly cinematic scene, Cha provides a lengthy verbal description of the unnamed woman who enters the theater, purchases her ticket, waits in line, presents her ticket to the usher, and walks up the steps into the room: "The whiteness of the screen takes her back wards almost half a step. Then she proceeds

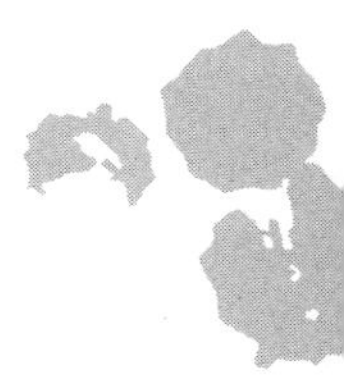

again to the front. Near front. Close to the screen. She takes the fourth seat from the left. The utmost center of the room" (94). Playing with the moviegoer's position in the theater, front and center where the woman can best enter the filmic fantasy, and her identification with the images on the screen, Cha describes the woman's actions: "She enters the screen from the left, before the titles fading in and fading out. The white subtitles on the black background continue across the bottom of the screen. The titles and names in black appear from the upper right hand corner, each letter moving downwards on to the whiteness of the screen. She is drawn to the white, then the black. In the whiteness the shadows move across, dark shapes and dark light" (94). Explicitly associating the white screen and the white page, Cha calls attention to the moment before inscription, to the process of making images and words, of manufacturing meaning. She exposes the film's images as merely the play of light and dark as "shadows move across" the screen, reminiscent of how she deconstructs language into black-and-white marks on the page.

In a style suggestive of a combination of storyboard and screenplay, Cha describes in detail the camera angles through which viewers see the woman who entered the theater, then entered the film.

> Extreme Close Up shot of her face. Medium Long shot of two out of the five white columns from the street. She enters from the left side, and camera begins to pan on movement as she enters between the two columns. . . . Medium Close Up shot of her left side as she purchases the ticket. . . . Camera holds for a tenth of a second. The camera is now behind her. . . . Long shot. Cut to Medium Close Up shot of her from the back. She turns head sharply to her left. cut. . . . She selects a row near the front. . . . Medium Close Up, directly from behind her head. . . . Camera pans left. . . . Camera pans back to the right. . . . The screen fades to white. (96)

The film described, we realize, is a storyboard retelling, reenvisioning of the woman entering the theater, buying her ticket, finding her seat, yet another repetition of the scene, but with a cinematic descriptive lens.

In a third explicitly cinematic scene, Cha positions readers as behind the camera, scanning and zooming in as the filmmaker-writer determines. The title, "The portrait of [a woman]," the narrator tells us, sets up expectations that the woman in the film will be "beautiful" (98). Cha describes the anticipation of the audience waiting to see the woman, a viewing that is, of course, constantly deferred. "One imagines her already," explains the viewer, "Already before the title. She is not seen right away" (98). The "music on the sound track" prepares viewers for "her entrance." But rather than reveal the much-anticipated woman, the camera shows "the house in which she lives, from the outside" (98). Then, slowly, the camera moves into the woman's home: "Then you, as a viewer and guest, enter the house. It is you who are entering to see her. Her portrait is seen through her things, that are hers. The arrangement of her house is spare, delicate, subtly accentuating, rather, the space, not the objects that fill the space. Her movements are already punctuated by the movement of the camera, her pace, her time, her rhythm. You move from the same distance as the visitor, with the same awe, same reticence, the same anticipation" (98, 100).

Cha's depiction of the room arrangement—"spare, delicate, subtly accentuating, rather, the space, not the objects that fill the space"—is analogous to Cha's word arrangement. Cha is mindful of the spatial dimensions of the page, using abundant white space to provide a visual frame for the precise and unusual layout of the words.[10] The fact that the beautiful woman is seen only indirectly through the design and ordering of her belongings is an autotopographical trope that emphasizes how personal objects and spatial arrangements can reveal aspects of identity.[11] The fact that the woman is never seen, not even in a photograph or painting, underscores that representations in image or text are necessary mediations that disallow, or at least displace, any unmediated access to a subjectivity that is always situational and shifting anyway. Finally, Cha's insistence that we see the woman "without actually seeing, actually having seen her," we "see only her traces," is a metaphor for the autobiographical and historical process—the attempts to recover a past that can, in truth, reveal only its traces.

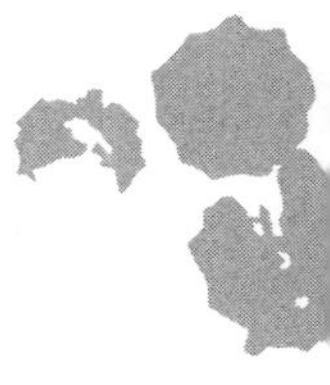

Throughout the "Erato" section, Cha presents a veritable cubist presentation in words, a visual style showing multiple perspectives simultaneously on the two-dimensional surface of the page. Just as Cha breaks down action into cinematic frames ("Close Up, "Medium Shot," and so on), freezing and focusing on a single object or scene, so she breaks down language (such as sentences into fragments and words into syllables), forcing a deeper look at voice and the constituent parts of visual-verbal representational systems. Like Dreyer's camera, which slowly scans, then moves into a close-up and lingers on the raw anguish of Falconetti's suffering face (see fig. 5.4), Cha's cinematic technique forces readers to look slowly, deeply, closely. Overall, Cha demands more of her readers than most authors because she observes neither the conventions of life writing (linear narrative, complete sentences and paragraphs, standard punctuation) nor the customs of self-portraiture (representations of self, captioned images). Instead, like comics (but without its conventions) and like artists' books (but without their structural innovation), she breaks down and reassembles both language and image, reformulating defamiliarized fragments into new allusive networks of meaning.

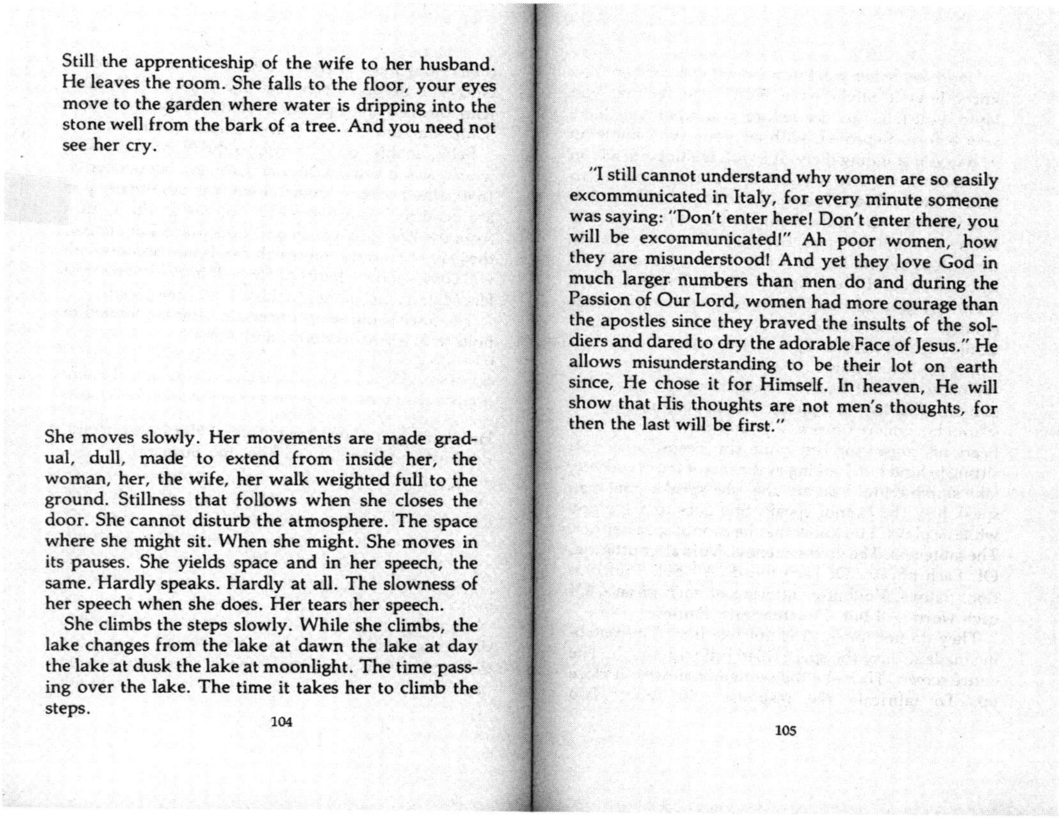

FIGURE 5.5. *Interlocking Narrative.* (Theresa Hak Kyung Cha, *Dictée*, 104–5.)

Just as challenging as Cha's cinematic style for many readers is her structural innovation. Like Spiegelman, Cha treats the page as a unit of space and time, altering that space and time to her will. Like book artists, Cha reimagines the relation between text and the white space of the page. Some of her text has line breaks that resemble poetry; other text appears in the form of lists. Certain narrative sections disrupt readers' expectations of linear narrative. Like the camera person forcing a viewer's point of view, Cha directs the reader to follow her reorientation of text and white space. Before readers can ask, "What is she talking about?" they must grapple with a more fundamental question: "How do I read this?" Again, the "Erato" section is the best example. As readers move from one page to the next, we find the idea that we have been following dropped and replaced with another; the sentence we have been reading disappears; we search to find a linear, logical, coherent flow of language, only to find a void of white or to be called to a full halt at the precipice of an incomplete sentence (fig. 5.5). The conventional modes of reading in the West are disrupted and readers-viewers are required to read and look differently, to engage more consciously with the page-screen.

One way to read this section is to cheat a little and read the left page sequentially, then the right page. While this way of reading clarifies a narrative flow, it violates Cha's purposeful linkages of the dual narratives—the wife's submission to her husband and the nun's submission to God. A more appropriate way to read this is to treat two pages as one in which "recto and verso narratives interlock, the text of one page fitting erotically into the white space on the other" (E. Park 9). This hypertextual reading practice (eyes moving from left to right across both pages, then down, apprehending multiple texts and images on a page spread, and so on) allows the entangled narratives to comment on, refer to, bleed into each other. While the same reading tactic is required for pages 94–95, for instance, the dialogue between verso and recto is not between two oppressed wives (of man and God) but between the thick description of the film (verso) and the repeated phrases, much like a Greek chorus (in the recto). This multiply conscious reading tactic is what visual texts often require in different ways, depending on their distinctive visual-verbal sets of relations.

Early in *Dictée*, Cha asks:

> Why resurrect it all now. From the Past. History, the old wound. The past emotions all over again. To confess to relive the same folly. To name it now so as not to repeat history in oblivion. To extract each fragment by each fragment from the word from the image another word another image the reply that will not repeat history in oblivion. (33)

Echoing Christian notions of resurrection, Cha emphasizes remembering and retelling as redemptive, though necessarily limited, actions. Just as Christ's martyrdom and resurrection are depicted as excruciating, Cha's process of resurrecting the past is presented as tortuous. Depicting history as an "old wound" emphasizes the trauma associated with it. To return to "the old wound," to "relive the same folly," to "extract each fragment" of the visual-verbal record, Cha seems to conclude, is both necessary and impossible. Those who have not experienced the "same oppressions" simply "cannot know" (32). Like Holocaust survivors finding no words to represent the unrepresentable, Cha concludes: "Unfathomable the words, the terminology: . . . recording . . ." (32). Reports of this, delivered in the same words and images, have been "neutralized to achieve the no-response . . . , to submit to the uni-directional correspondance" (33). The words cannot adequately represent the core of trauma so it is "necessary to . . . invent anew, expressions for this experience, for this *outcome*, that does not cease to continue" (32, emphasis in original). Like the trauma of the Holocaust or the Armenian Genocide, the pain of the Japanese occupation and colonization of Korea "does not cease to continue" but is passed on to the next generation. Throughout *Dictée*,

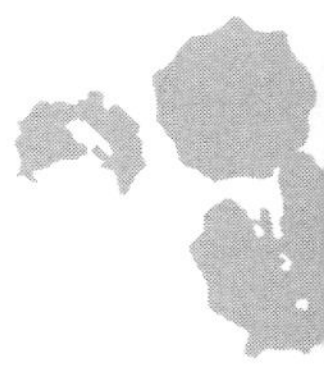

Cha struggles magnificently with the remnants of the past, of cultures, and of languages. She refuses T. S. Eliot's grand modernist declaration in *The Waste Land*: "These fragments I have shored against my ruins." Rather, Cha's postmodern performance enacts the process of rummaging through the shards of personal, family, and global history and the impossibility of making a unified vision out of the fragments of diasporic displacement. And yet, she does make a book—informed by film, installation art, performance art, and correspondence art—that memorializes all of these.

### Serial Conclusions and Endlessly Deferred Return

In her "Personal Statement and Outline of Postdoctoral Project," Cha writes: "My work, until now, in one sense has been a series of metaphors for the return, going back to a lost time and space, always in the imaginary. The content of my work has been the realization of the imprint, the inscription etched from the experience of leaving" (2). The concept of return requires a notion of origin. For Cha, the desire to go back to Korea is linked to nation and language and, ultimately, home. Home, then, is a central concept for Cha, as it is for many Asian immigrants who find themselves with multiple sites of belonging or, on the contrary, altogether homeless.[12] In his often-cited essay "Imaginary Homelands," Salman Rushdie sums up the experience of being between two worlds (cultures, languages):

> It may be that writers in my position, exiles or emigrants or expatriates, are haunted by some sense of loss, some urge to reclaim, to look back, even at the risk of being mutated into pillars of salt. But if we do look back, we must also do so in the knowledge—which gives rise to profound uncertainties—that our physical alienation from India almost inevitably means that we will not be capable of reclaiming precisely the thing that was lost; that we will, in short, create fictions, not actual cities or villages, but invisible ones, imaginary homelands, Indias of the mind. (10)

Although Rushdie refers to India, what he says is equally true for Cha's search for Korea (the mother language or nation) or any diasporic "people who regard themselves as part of dispersed communities in relation to a lost or idealized homeland" (Simal and Marino 15). Usually home is an endpoint, a destination, a place to which one may return even if one chooses not to do so. In *Dictée*, the "contested and contesting terrain is home" (Wong, "Unnaming the Same" 109). Cha seeks endlessly for home but finds it nowhere. Home, for Cha, is homeland—

South Korea. Home is language—Korean. Home is mother-motherland, mother tongue. Home is return—to Korea (45). Home is what eludes her. This is part of Cha's thematics of displacement that includes forced removal, physical displacement, and linguistic rupture. Such displacement generates a fundamental fracturing so that Cha's only hope of self-representation is through reassemblage and imagination, but always, like Peter Najarian, with a performative melancholy.

Although Cha desires to return to her homeland, language, and culture, her return is endlessly deferred as she perpetually performs the attempt through acts of memory that become, finally, memorialized in the book. Like Najarian, who struggles to say good-bye to his mother, and Spiegelman, who has difficulty finding an appropriate conclusion for the story of the Holocaust, Cha experiments with several conclusions for her story of the transgenerational consequences of Japanese colonization of Korea and its attendant erasures and displacements. Although Kirsten Twelbeck claims correctly that "*Dictée* is a text without an ending" (197n20), Cha narrates an almost hopeful myth of return at the beginning of the "Polymnia/Sacred Poetry" section. The photograph that introduces this first conclusion is of ancient ruins, a mysterious relic of human existence that reminds us of Cha's focus on language as a trace, the past as inaccessible. Borrowing from fairy-tale motifs and mythic archetypes, Cha retells "the Korean myth of princess Pali" (Shih 156): the young girl who ventures out on a quest to save her mother, overcomes the hardships of the long and arduous journey, and encounters a wise woman guide who gives her "special remedies for her mother" as well as "instructions on how to prepare them" (169). When the girl stops to rest near a well on her journey home, she meets the woman, who seems to have been waiting for her. The well, symbol of life-sustaining water and of the womb of earth, which dispenses it. is a fitting site for healing. The image of the hollow cavernous well also echoes Cha's images of the womblike caverns of the body that give rise to words (via saliva, blood, and ink). Echoing the importance of the number nine, the woman gives the girl nine packets of medicine for the girl's mother and a tenth pocket and a porcelain bowl for the girl herself.[13] The girl follows the woman's advice "to go home quickly, make no stops, and remember all she had told her" (170). The story concludes: "As she came nearer to the house she became aware of the weight of the bundles and the warmth in her palms where she had held them. Through the paper screen door, dusk had entered and the shadow of a small candle was flickering" (170). With its tone of longing, this is a tale of hope and healing. It is significant, however, that the girl, like Cha, never really returns home. Rather, she remains on the threshold, on the outside of her home, looking into the paper screen door, ever poised to enter. Perhaps standing on the thresh-

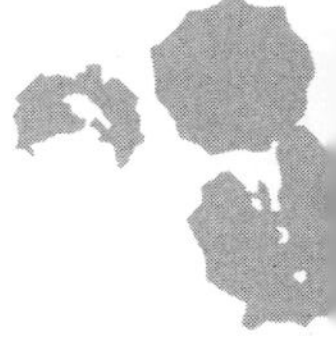

old emphasizes artistic, if not literal, entry. Furthermore, the paper screen door is reminiscent of a screen or a page upon which only the flickering shadows of the past can be suggested, just as the black marks and uncaptioned images on the pages of *Dictée* offer only traces of Cha's history and subjectivity.

While remaining poised forever on the threshold of home would make a poignant ending to *Dictée*, the myth of (near or endlessly deferred) return is followed by a second conclusion: the translation of the ten Chinese aspects of the universe discussed earlier. The ten universal phenomena echo the nine medicine bundles and the tenth medicine bundle in the porcelain bowl—"a circle with a circle, a series of concentric circles" (173). This ending emphasizes interrelatedness, inclusive of all time and place, as well as multiplicity, but suggests a sense of metaphysical wholeness that *Dictée* both presents and resists.

Cha's penultimate conclusion is a poetic commentary on language and time: "Words cast each by each to weather / avowed indisputably, to time. / If it should impress, make fossil trace of word, / residue of word, stand as a ruin stands, / simply, as mark / having relinquished itself to time to distance" (177). After all the words, photographs, and diagrams, what remains, perhaps, is an impression (such as words made by a printing press), a "fossil trace," a "residue," a "ruin," a "mark"— some reminder of having existed. Like the photograph's association with death, words, like historic ruins, carry the weight of what has been but is no longer.

In the fourth and final conclusion of *Dictée*, Cha intersperses a child's command ("Lift me up mom") with adult descriptions ("The ruelle is an endless path turning the corner behind the last house"), interweaving past and present, and fracturing point of view into multiplicity. The relatively unpunctuated paragraph is organized by variable repetition: "Lift me up mom to the window . . . Lift me up to the window . . . Lift me to the window" (179). The window serves as another image of a screen or a page through which, or upon which, the child will see as well, perhaps, an image of the viewer-voyeur-reader who witnesses Cha's process. But all the girl deciphers is "a blur now darks and greys mere shadows lingering above her vision" (179). The shadows grow into night. Just as Cha has tried to access the past through women (her mother and the female martyrs), so the girl asks her mother to lift her, but the mother cannot lift her daughter–the reader high enough to get a clear view out the window. "There is no one," explains the narrative voice, "inside the pane and the glass between" (179). As if relinquishing her demand to see, Cha moves from the sense of sight to the sense of sound: "Lift me to the window to the picture image unleash the ropes tied to weights of stones first the ropes then its scraping on wood to break stillness as the bells fall peal follow the sound of ropes holding weight scraping on wood to break stillness bells fall a peal to sky" (179). Throughout *Dictée*, visuality is emphasized by photographs, innovative page layouts, and recontextualizing print into marks on the page, but here seeing gives way to hearing—yet another displacement. Significantly, what is heard is not words, not descriptions, explanations, or answers. What remains is pure sound: "a peal to the sky" or "appeal" to the heavens. These are two different acts. The first ("a peal") is a sound wafting into the sky, while the second requires an agent to make an "appeal" to the heavens. Not surprisingly, Cha's visual representation of the words insists on their coexistence.

......................................................................................................

Even though a romantic nostalgia for a lost and broken past, for an inaccessible homeland, for a mother tongue, permeates *Dictée*, Cha thematizes the relentless fragmentation of the present and the impossibility of concocting a coherent autobiographical story in both form and content. She focuses on discontinuities, disruptions, and contradictions. Cha emphasizes the attempted obliteration of (Korean) cultures and bodies. She tries to translate personal, family, and cultural narratives, acutely aware of how little she can locate any clear or unifying sense of subjectivity or story. Cha performs a desire to return—not so much literally—though Cha visited Korea a couple of times to research her screenplay *White Dust from Mongolia*—as imaginatively. The impulse to, and the impossibility of, return, then, serves as a metaphor for understanding, as the potential not to redeem the past but to make the past visible and maybe even bearable. Yet rather than narrate a romantic, nostalgic return, Cha visually and textually *performs* its impossibility in the pages of *Dictée*.

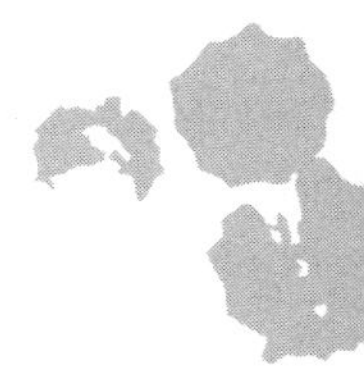

# Art-Based Image-and-Text Forms

# Carrie Mae Weems's Photo-(Auto)biographies

## "Work That Is Essential to Our Cultural Dialogue"

...................................................................................................

Carrie Mae Weems's photo-(auto)biographies develop from photo-text sequences hung on gallery walls to elaborate architectural installation pieces that require viewers to enter and navigate the narrative visual-verbal space with its many surfaces and interfaces.

...................................................................................................

Photographer Carrie Mae Weems examines in image and text the nature of memory and history, insisting on an intense critique of the wrongs of the past as part of a process of self-formulation. Like the other artists and writers explored in this volume, Weems examines the relation between individual life stories and collective historical narratives. As a storyteller-artist, she envisions the artist as the "narrator of history" (Weems, "Interview" 79). In the process of showing and telling through photographs and texts, she represents the historical legacy of racial violence to provoke readers-viewers to become aware of injustice and the false narratives that enable it. Focusing on African American and Native American racial and cultural histories, Weems is deeply self-referential and unapologetically political. In dialogue with social documents and visual archives, she creates visual-verbal sites of personal engagement and political intervention. In the process, Weems sets up the conditions for an intersubjective or affiliative mode of looking—a type of looking that values interrelatedness. Finally, in constituting her personal and collective histories, Weems engages in a process of refiguration; in her photo-(auto)biographies, she couples photographic images and text—in the form of commentary or story or dialogue—and creates a sequence that hangs on a gallery wall. In her later work, she enlarges and projects digital photographs onto fabric surfaces that are designed as interactive architectural sites. Rather than walking by the exhibit, the reader is forced to enter into it.

Best known as a photographer-activist, Carrie Mae Weems was trained as both an artist and a folklorist. A visual storyteller for more than thirty years, Weems uses photographs to critique class and race in U.S. society, to comment on the human condition, and to document her experiences as a woman of color. In the process, she both continues and increasingly challenges the tradition of documentary photography. Like

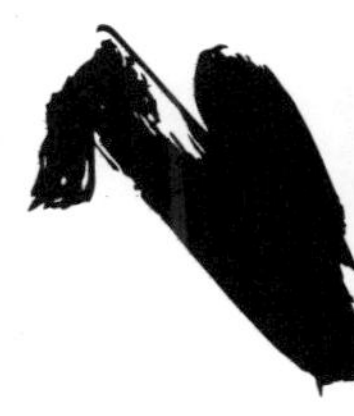

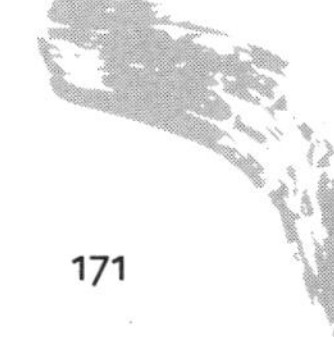

participant-observer anthropologists, Weems actively engages with the people and communities she records and imagines. Rejecting the supposed objectivity of photographers and "traditional discourses of documentary photography" that maintain a distance from their subjects, she asks viewers to question claims about "objectivity" and "outsiderness" (Sterling 20). In almost all of her work Weems interweaves or juxtaposes image and text "in order to expand upon layers and levels of meaning" (Piché 14). In relation to the photographs, "the text takes on a double-voiced character, combining the direct speech of an active participant and the third-person reportage of an omniscient observer" (Piché and Golden 15), self-reflexively narrating, describing, and interrelating subject positions and voices. Weems is known, in particular, for provocative works that "examine and subvert the relationship between conventional photographic representation and racist and sexist ideologies" (Sterling 20). Weems rises to the challenge articulated by bell hooks in 1992: "Challenged to rethink, insurgent black intellectuals and/or artists are looking at new ways to write and talk about race and representation, working to transform the image" (2). Like other political photographers and artists, Weems uses art in the service of social critique as well as individual and collective identity formation.[1]

For African Americans, "from the twentieth century onward, photography as a political tool and movement strategy is unavoidable" because "the political stakes of cultural representation and the cultural terrain of political representation are . . . never very far apart" (Raiford 27). Founded in New York in 1963 by a group of African American photographers who sought to correct the dearth of black photographers in the art world, the Kamoinge Workshop has influenced Weems's work.[2] *Kamoinge* translates as "a group of people acting together." Kamoinge photographers work to represent everyday lives of black people from their own perspectives, part of the ongoing project of African American self-reclamation, historical correction, and sovereignty. According to Leigh Raiford, "For African Americans, photography necessitated an opportunity and a challenge to reclaim, repair, remake, reimagine, and redeem" (8).

Like Faith Ringgold's fabric paintings (chapter 7), Weems's photographs are in constant, complex dialogue with the long history of racist representations of black people that overshadow, if they do not negate, their humanity. "I produce work," says Weems, "that is essential to our cultural dialogue" ("Interview" 78). Dealing with "the critical role of representation, both socially and in the work of art," Weems makes "representations of people of color to stand for the human multitudes," rather "than as degraded symbols of blackness" (80). Weems actively rejects the assumption, however, that because she is African American, she should



Art-Based Image-and-Text Forms

focus only on blacks. "I'm black and Native American," Weems explains, "but I don't know any more about being Indian than I know about being African. . . . I assume that I have the right to speak about any—and everything affecting you, me, us, and them" (80). One of her goals is to represent "colored peoples [who] can and must stand for humanity" (80), not just for their particularized conditions.

As well as critiquing racialized and racist representations, a practice of "critical black memory, a mode of historical interpretation and political critique" (Raiford 16), Weems's work "examines the nature of memory and history" (McInnes vii)—both personal and collective history. She focuses on re-membering the past, reassembling historical narratives from a variety of overlooked voices and visions, and reanimating the historically silenced into a multiplicity of voices that challenge historical stereotypes. For Weems, remembering includes not only researching the "facts" of the past but also reimagining the significance of those facts in the present. Weems's "reclassification of history occurs at the intersection of multiculturalism, postcolonial theory, and feminist criticism" (McInnes 2) and reflects tensions between the Black Arts Movement and the later development of black aesthetics, between feminism and multiculturalism, and between traditional and conceptual photography (Piché and Golden 31).

In her early *Family Pictures and Stories* (1978–84), Weems combines photographs, captions, and audiotaped family stories told in the first person. Using a contextual (documentary) visual-verbal interface, Weems uses the textual to "situate the visual within a context of social and cultural meaning" (Smith and Watson 25). With a temporal interface she provides serial juxtapositions that tell a personal story. Weems conceived this photo-autobiography, in part, as a refutation of the 1965 Moynihan Report, which claimed that African American families were dysfunctional, due in part to absent fathers and a matriarchal system. Based on intensive research in Harlem that he generalizes to the condition of all poor, urban blacks, Moynihan asserts that "Negro Americans" will soon "go beyond" requests for "civil rights" to demand "equal opportunities" for which, as a group, they are not well equipped to compete. Blacks cannot compete with whites at this time, says Moynihan, due to "the racist virus in the American bloodstream" and because a broken black family structure does not support children to develop into well-prepared citizens. Moynihan sees absent fathers and husbands, illegitimate children, divorce, female-headed households, and high rates of public assistance and welfare dependency as a nearly complete "deterioration" of family structure, one of the devastating consequences of "three centuries of exploitation" of blacks. Insisting that the heterosexual, nuclear, male-headed family is the "basic social unit of American life," Moynihan

warns that the "crumbling" of the black family unit leads to perpetual social inequity; and he calls for federal policies to enhance "the stability and resources of the Negro American family."[3]

In her photo-text, spoken-word family history, Weems challenges Moynihan's assumptions about African American families. She narrates four generations of her family's experiences, including their migration from south to north, encounters with racism, and struggles with poverty. Rather than present an idealized African American family to counter Moynihan's representations of lower-class African American matriarchal (that is, "dysfunctional") family, Weems presents the men and women in her family with a full range of human strengths and flaws, noting affection as well as violence, resilience as well as vulnerability, in order to create "a multidimensional portrait" (Kirsh 12) that defies any essentializing definition of the black family. Stylistically, Weems eschews formal portraiture and studio poses, favoring instead informal family snapshots and spontaneous engagement. Rather than situating herself as an objective documentary photographer, she positions herself as a family and community member—both inside and outside of the photographic image. This affiliative looking recognizes the relationship between the photographer and the photographed and resists false claims to objective representation.

The photograph *Dad and Son-Son*, for instance, shows the father seated at a table, his son standing behind his father's chair. Both look at the photographer matter-of-factly—no smiling or mugging for the camera. The narrative accompanying the photograph explains that although the two really love each other, when they have been "drinking things have been known to get out of line, ya know." One time when "they were on 'full,' . . . they'd both whipped out pistols and boom!! Fired on one another!" (*Carrie Mae Weems* 41). In a lively and informal voice, Weems shares a scandalous family anecdote, one that is likely to get passed on to future generations as an example of how her "folks can get way crazy" (41). Rather than analyze or judge her family's behavior, Weems, as participant-observer and family member–photographer, merely reports or describes it.

In *Van and Vera with Kids in the Kitchen* (fig. 6.1), Weems captures a completely different kind of family encounter: a moment of intense engagement between her two sisters, who face each other, not the camera. In the text-voice accompanying the photograph, Weems explains: "It amazes me that even in the midst of a bunch of crazy wild kids, my sisters still manage to carry on a half-way decent conversation." Standing in the kitchen, an overdetermined female space that underscores their domesticity, the sisters are caught in midsentence. The one on the left holds a baby in one arm, while her free hand gestures emphatically.

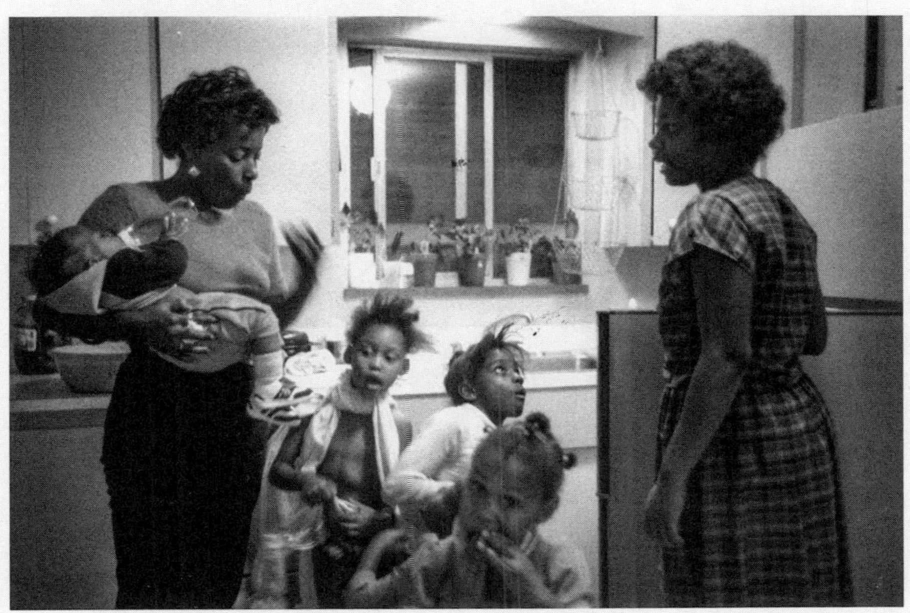


In striking contrast to Weems's sisters' intense focus on each other, the three children create a swirl of dynamic activity between them, their motion rendering them slightly out of focus. While the mothers talk to each other, two of the little girls look in opposite directions. The third little girl, center and forefront, looks directly at Weems, the camera, the viewer, breaking the fiction of the observed-observer divide and acknowledging the link between them.

*Family Pictures and Stories* was followed by three photo-projects that boldly challenge racist stereotypes in word and image: *Ain't Jokin'* (1987–88), *American Icons* (1988–89), and *Colored People* (1989–90). Like Faith Ringgold disassembling and reimagining racist images of Aunt Jemima in order to clarify her own story as an African American woman artist, Weems exposes racism in a variety of cultural productions. Inspired by her studies of folklore with University of California, Berkeley, professor Alan Dundes, who assured her that urban life and jokes were legitimate topics of folkloric study for what they revealed about cultural beliefs and practices, Weems created *Ain't Jokin'*. In this series of photographs and text, Weems used a large-format camera to create square photographs with typeset text beneath each, an example of the relational visual-verbal interface in which image and text are equally important, generating a

FIGURE 6.1.
Carrie Mae Weems.
*Van and Vera with Kids in the Kitchen.*
*Family Pictures and Stories*, 1978–84.
(Silver print,
8½ × 13 in.
© Carrie Mae Weems. Courtesy of the artist and Jack Shainman Gallery, New York.)

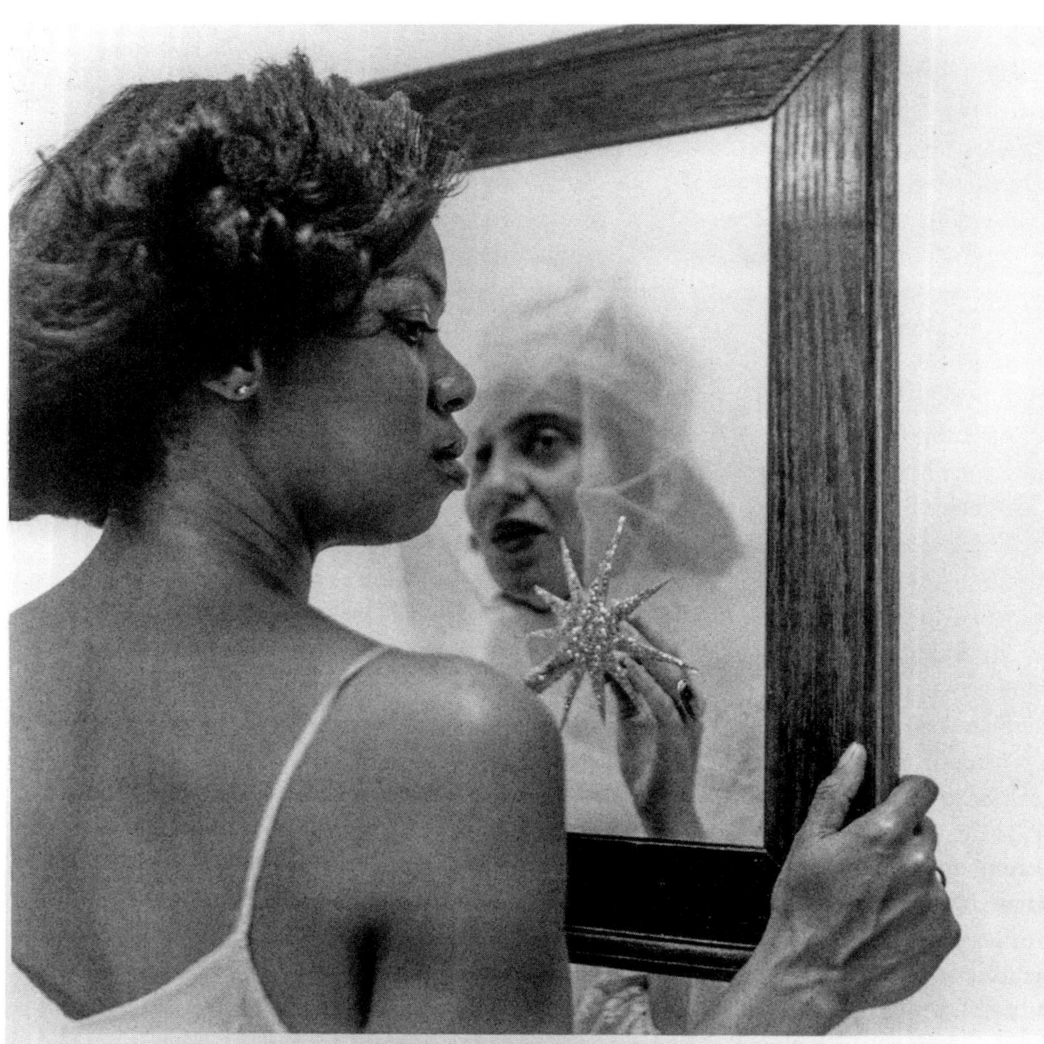



dialogue between them. The photo-text series retells racist jokes and children's verses and revisits Western fairy tales, moving them from the generally private realms in which they are shared to the full glare of public exhibition. In this photo sequence, Weems "sets out to make us understand that racial prejudice occupies some of the deepest structures within the American psyche" (Sterling 23).

In one photograph, an African American man wearing a plaid sport coat and baseball cap stands on the porch of his home. He stares intently,

    Art-Based Image-and-Text Forms

and with a certain serious dignity, at the camera. Below the photograph, the caption asks: "What are the three things you can't give a black person?" The response is written in a small font below. "Answer: A black eye, a fat lip and a job." Part of the uncomfortable humor is based on viewers believing that they are overhearing a racist joke, perhaps even feeling guilty or angry, then having the orientation switched at the last moment when the comment shifts from racialized and racist physical characteristics to social critique from a black perspective about African American unemployment.

In *Mirror, Mirror* (fig. 6.2), Weems riffs on the classic fairy tale *Snow White*. In this photograph, Weems reenacts and revises the famous scene in which the Queen—Snow White's evil stepmother—looks into her magic mirror and asks, "Mirror, Mirror on the wall, who's the fairest one of all?" Here the African American woman asks, "Mirror, Mirror on the wall, who's the finest of them all?" Weems replaces "fairest" with "finest,' seemingly deemphasizing color (the fairy-tale princess, of course, is renowned for her skin as "white as snow"). But the fact that a black woman asks the question forces viewers-readers to see the unacknowledged racial bias in the tale. Inside the mirror, the magic mirror persona is depicted as another, slightly older black woman wearing a white veil. Her virulent response to the question ("Who's the finest of them all?") is a shock: "SNOW WHITE, YOU BLACK BITCH, AND DON'T YOU FORGET IT!" Is this an example of internalized racism? Of an older generation warning a younger generation about the constricting consequences of racism? Of the unexamined privilege of whiteness? Or of black woman as universal? If Snow White and the Queen represent aspects of universal womanhood and good and evil, why can't Weems's characters? The woman's face is averted from the mirror. She looks away and down, seemingly pondering what she has just heard. In this example, the African American woman who dares to look for an affirmation of her reflection in the always, already European mirror is denounced, reminded that in western European narratives, she is seen only through racist lenses. Throughout *Ain't Jokin'* viewers are exposed to, implicated in, and only rarely exempted from the racist ideology embedded in such common cultural productions.[4]

Having exposed and critiqued racist visual and narrative regimes in the United States and western Europe, generally, Weems turns again to a more personal story that places her at the center. In contrast to her earlier *Family Pictures and Stories*, with its sense of spontaneity, intimacy, and autobiographical focus, Weems's *Untitled (Kitchen Table Series)* (1990) presents a series of highly staged and formalized black-and-white photographs, each presenting a tableau. Although the visual-verbal interface is primarily temporal since it tells a story through serial juxtaposition, it is also contextual in its documentation of sociopolitical contexts. Using a dining room table and an overhead light, reminiscent of an interrogation light or a surgery room light, as the setting for each, Weems varies who is at the table, what items are on the table, and what images and objects are in the room.[5] The text, written in both standard English and vernacular African American English, reappropriates cultural narratives and tells the story of an African American woman and her relationships with her man, her child, her friends, and, ultimately, herself. Weems's focus is on relations among African Americans, especially interactions between male and female. Weems herself performs the black woman whose story she narrates. Although the woman may be considered Weems's autobiographical persona, she stands for every black woman who has struggled with relationships and, ultimately, given Weems's insistence on claiming African American experience as universal experience, for every woman who has wrestled with deep longing and profound loss. Throughout the photo-narrative, the viewer is positioned at the end of the kitchen table, looking into the scene as if from a front-row seat.

Weems reappropriates song lyrics, literary quotations by Zora Neale Hurston and James Baldwin, popular advertisements, hymns, twentieth-century pop songs, and children's rhymes and games into her stream-of-consciousness narrative. The story moves from the woman's experience of the tenderness and hope of new love to growing conflict and disappointment, to her ambivalent relationship with her child, and to her ultimate aloneness. The kitchen table is the stage for all of it. This is where the lovers share food and drink, newspapers and cigarettes, conversation and conflict. With a few shifting props, Weems suggests the highs and lows of relationships as well as loneliness and longing. A deck of playing cards suggests luck, or lack of it, in love and life. A birdcage appears in the background of at least two of the scenes, the caged bird bringing to mind the loss of freedom associated with domestic life and, of course, Maya Angelou's 1969 autobiography *I Know Why the Caged Bird Sings*.

Three photographs summarize the trajectory of the story. Stage One: New Love. *Untitled (Man smoking)* conveys the intensity and uncertainty of new love (fig. 6.3). Weems's character sits at the end of the kitchen table, looking intently at the man sitting diagonally across from her. He looks at her, one-fourth of his face exposed. They mirror each other imperfectly in their off-centered symmetry. Sharing a bottle of whiskey and a bowl of peanuts, the lovers play cards. She holds her cards face down and seems to try to assess what hand he holds. Smoking, he looks directly at her, but does not reveal his hand. His cards, however, are partially visible to viewers. He holds a four of hearts, a four of clubs, a two of diamonds, and a king of clubs, while a fifth card is not visible.

    Art-Based Image-and-Text Forms

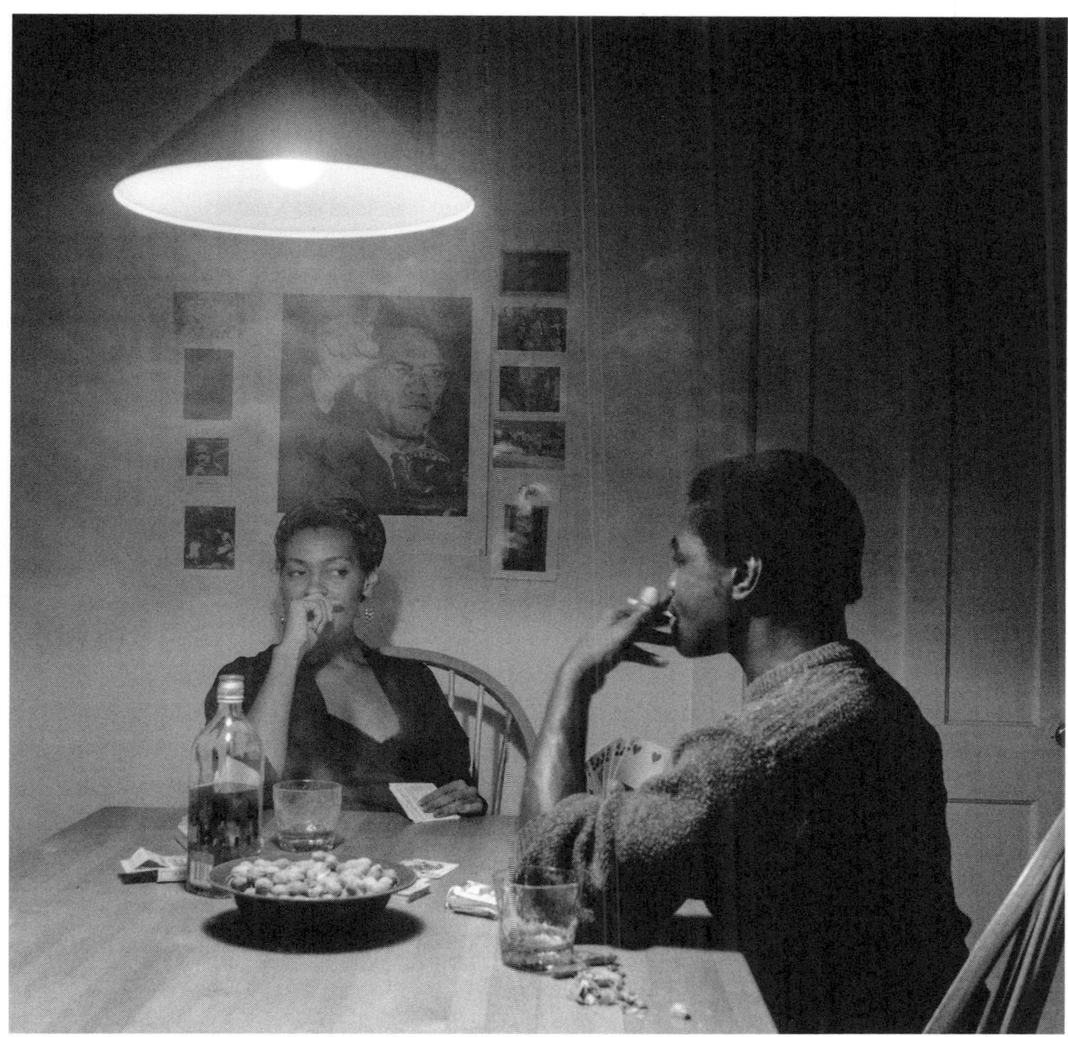

If this is a poker game, he has a weak hand, foreshadowing the downfall of their relationship. More than trying to assess a card game, the woman seems to be trying to calculate the possibilities for their relationship. Love, like a game of chance, the tableau suggests, is impossible to control. On the wall behind the woman a poster of Malcolm X looms large, framed on either side by a series of photographs. While Malcolm X was a voice of militant Black Nationalism, he became an emblem of heroic activism for political and spiritual seekers globally. His image underscores Weems's Afrocentric humanism.

The text associated with this photograph tells the story of the lovers' powerful attraction: "They met in the glistening twinkling crystal light of August/September sky. They were both educated, corn-fed-healthy-Mississippi-stock folk. . . . Together they were falling for that ole black

FIGURE 6.3. Carrie Mae Weems. *Untitled (Man smoking)*. *Untitled (Kitchen Table Series)*, 1990. (Silver print, 27¼ × 27¼ in. © Carrie Mae Weems. Courtesy of the artist and Jack Shainman Gallery, New York.)

magic. In that moment it seemed a match made in heaven. They walked, not hand in hand, but rather side by side in the twinkle of August/September sky, looking sidelong at one another, thanking their lucky *stars* with fingers crossed" (66, emphasis in original). An idealized fairy tale ("They met in the glistening twinkling crystal light of August/September sky"), Weems's account of new love is cliché-ridden ("a match made in heaven," "thanking their lucky stars") and inflected with popular and African American culture ("that ole black magic").

Stage Two: Love and Compromise. In the next photograph, depicting an intimate meal, the photograph of Malcolm X has been replaced by a still-life painting of flowers. A birdcage has appeared in the corner. Both the painting and the caged bird suggest a shift toward shared domesticity, the birdcage an emblem of a containment of passion that the woman, not inclined to monogamy, believes should be free.

Stage Three: Love Lost. *Untitled* (*Woman and phone*) presents a minimalist image of heartbroken despair (fig. 6.4). The woman sits alone at the end of the table, her head bowed to her knees as she endures the pain of separation. A half-empty bottle of wine next to a single wine glass and a full ashtray suggest a long evening of solitude. Front and center of the photograph, however, is the focal point that informs all the rest: the telephone. In a gendered and clichéd image of an abandoned lover, the woman waits for the man to call or resists the impulse to call him. The accompanying text summarizes, from both of their perspectives and in both of their voices, how "trouble lurked" in "their daily life" (72):

He said that she was much too domineering. He didn't mind a woman speaking her mind, but hey, she was taking it a tad too far. Accused her of talking too loudly, being a little too wild in public places. No matter what the subject, she had to get her two cents in, ruined dinner parties with her insistent demand that everything . . . be viewed politically. He was tired of the base and superstructure white-boy-book-shit! Arguing til blue in the face bout them theories. Couldn't be cool or back-down just once. Naw!! She had to have the last word, had to be right. Plus she was always in the streets, running. Oh, and the way she was dealing with the kid! He didn't dig it at all. Something had to give.

She insisted that what he called domineering was a jacket being forced on her because he couldn't stand the thought of the inevitable shift in the balance of power. She assured him that the object of her task was not to control him, but out of necessity — freedom being the appreciation of necessity — to control herself. She went on to tell him that in face of the daily force

     Art-Based Image-and-Text Forms

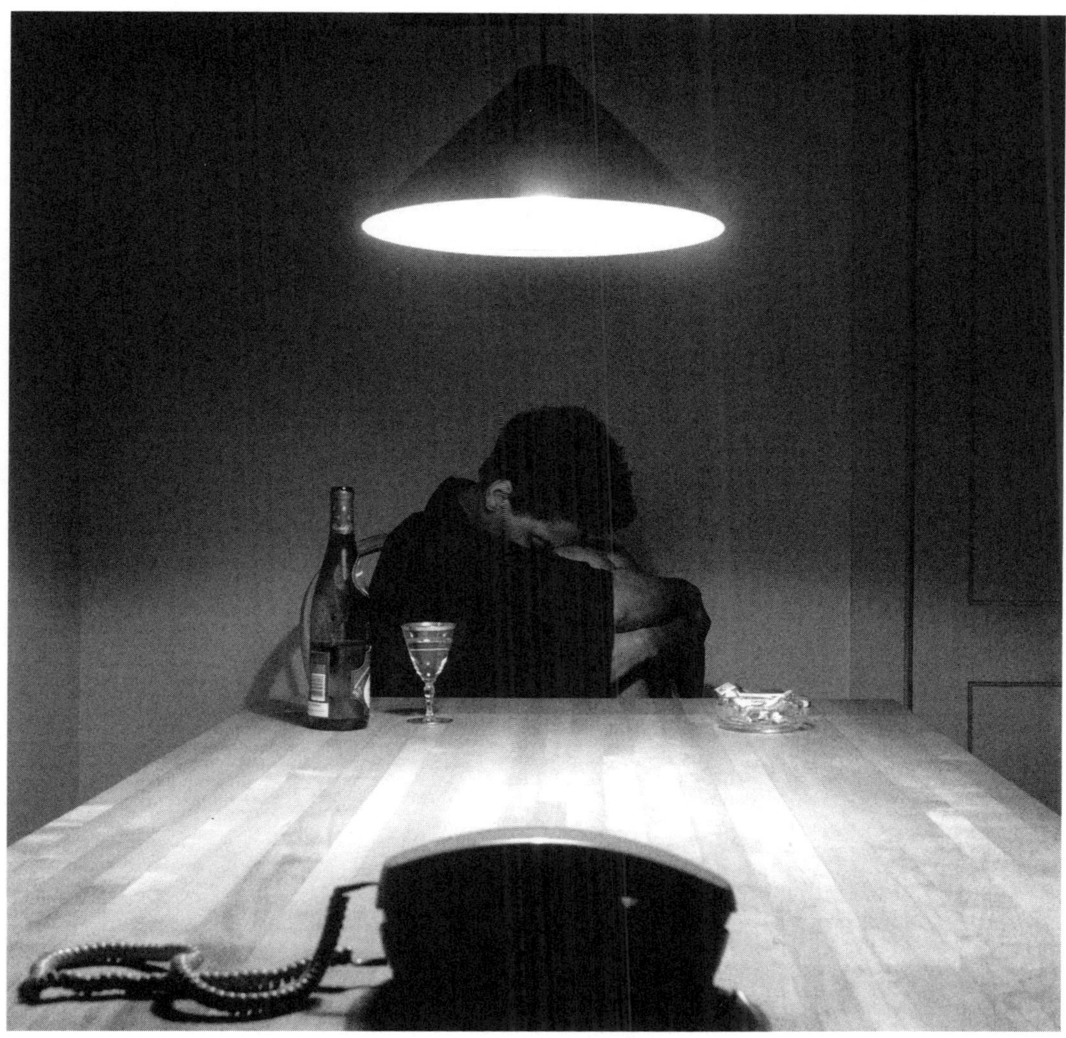

she understood his misgivings. But they were in a 50–50 thing. Equals. She wasn't about to succumb to standards of tradition which denied her a right place or voice, period. She was trying to be a good woman, a compadre, a pal, a living-doll and she was working. How could he ask for more!! She was really getting tired of him talking out of both sides of his mouth about the kinda woman he wanted. Fish or cut bait. (72)

Both speakers begin with a declaration in standard English and move into slang and vernacular African American English as their anger and fear increase. The academic tone and language with which she begins to articulate her position—"the inevitable shift in the balance of power"—

FIGURE 6.4. Carrie Mae Weems. *Untitled (Woman and phone)*. *Untitled (Kitchen Table Series)*, 1990. (Silver print, 27¼ × 27¼ in. © Carrie Mae Weems. Courtesy of the artist and Jack Shainman Gallery, New York.)

is precisely what her lover denounces as "white-boy-book-shit." Enacting the trajectory of an argument, the voice in each paragraph becomes increasingly agitated; each concludes with an ultimatum. "Something had to give," he exclaims. "Fish or cut bait," she demands. Significantly, by allocating a separate paragraph to each, Weems highlights that although this is presented as a record of a dialogue, there is no empathic exchange—just a recitation of the individual grievances and rebuttals of the two disenchanted lovers.

Their relationship deteriorates, in part, because she is "working, making long money" and he is not and it is "truly messing with his mind." Although the photography focuses on the woman, the text presents an empathetic stream-of-consciousness account of the man's feelings:

> He was starting to feel like a Black man wasn't supposed to have nothing, like some kind of conspiracy was being played out and he was the fall guy, like the mission was impossible, like it ain't a man's world, like just cause she was working and making so much dough, she was getting to where she didn't love him no mo, like he had bad luck, like he didn't have a dream, like he needed a night in Tunisia, like he needed to catch a freight train and ride, like if he felt tomorrow like he did today, come Sunday he'd pack up and make a get-away, like if he stayed, the kid would hate him for sure, like he just might have to contribute to the most confusing day in Harlem, like he had a tomb-stone disposition and a grave-yard mind. Like maybe a Black man just wasn't her kind. (84)

This emotional outburst is depicted in only two sentences. The first is a long, run-on sentence in which clauses pile up, one after the other like jazz riffs, gaining in intensity until they arrive at his "grave-yard mind." In this example, Weems creates a black man's blues out of popular phrases, literary bits, song lyrics, and internal rhymes. Rhyming with the first sentence, the second and final sentence functions as a coda: "Like maybe a Black man just wasn't her kind." Cataloging his insecurities, fears, disappointments, resentments, gender expectations, and depression in the first sentence, the man concludes that his woman maybe doesn't really want a(n oppressed) black man at all. With this, Weems makes clear that the couple's problems are not merely personal but profoundly socially and culturally generated. In picturing the pain of intimate relationships, Weems invites viewers-readers not just to gain insight into African American relationships but also to empathize with the human condition in general.

Coda. *Untitled* (*Woman standing alone*) (fig. 6.5) is a strong counter-

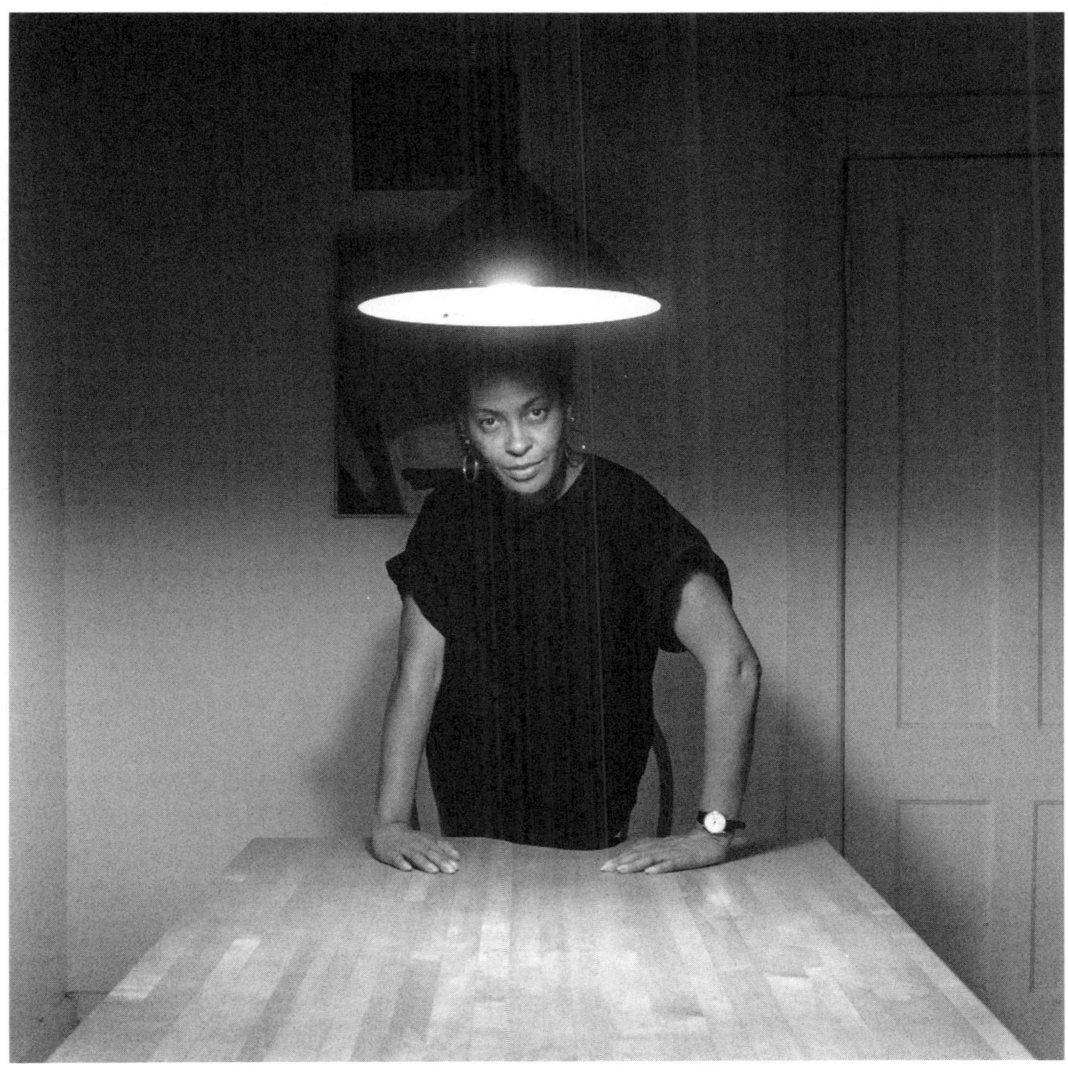

point to *Woman and phone*. Here Weems's character stands tall, leaning with both strong hands at the end of the kitchen table. With the light illuminating her face below the eyebrows, she stares directly into the camera. Her body language and facial expression convey a strong woman who will not break or back down. The kitchen table is clean and clear of all props, as if the slate has been wiped clean, as if she is free of baggage. Behind her is neither a photograph of Malcolm X nor a still-life painting of flowers but rather an abstract painting open to multiple interpretations.

Although the photograph of the strong, defiant woman would make a triumphant conclusion to Weems's tale of love found and lost, she does not end here. Weems's woman has struggled all along with conforming

FIGURE 6.5. Carrie Mae Weems. *Untitled* (*Woman standing alone*). *Untitled* (*Kitchen Table Series*), 1990. (Silver print, 27¼ × 27¼ in. © Carrie Mae Weems. Courtesy of the artist and Jack Shainman Gallery, New York.)

to traditional gender roles. She is not a compliant and monogamous wife, a polite and soft-spoken female, or a happily domestic woman. She has fierce passion and ferocious opinions that she is not afraid to articulate. Certainly, the unnamed woman is a figure of women artists grappling with societal expectations. Fittingly, the final image of the series is the woman playing solitaire.

## Reframing the Photographic Archive at Hampton Institute: Leaving the Wall, Entering History

While her earlier work looks more like straightforward family history, political critique, or photo-documentary, in her later work Weems ramps up her photographic and storytelling skills to reexamine U.S. history, particularly the racist and colonizing practices visited upon African Americans and Native Americans. Her exhibits become more historically expansive and more conceptually complex. Weems translates, repositions, and rematerializes her photographs into different structures and onto varied materials. She lifts photographs off the walls and onto fabric banners suspended from ceilings. She enlarges basic photographic images from two-by-three-inch, four-by-five-inch, and eight-by-ten-inch parameters in frames to larger-than-life-size images that flutter frameless. In the process, she re-situates viewers from engagement with a single image or sequence of images hanging statically on a wall to interactive participants who move through a palimpsest of images, each in lively dialogue with the others. Photo-histories such as *Ritual and Revolution* (1998–99), *The Hampton Project* (2000), and *The Jefferson Suites* (2001) actively involve viewers in the coproduction of meaning and feeling from encounters with photographic images, text, and audio. I will focus here on *The Hampton Project*, a photo exhibit that Weems was invited to produce and one that continues her lifelong commitment to questions of representation, justice, memory, and history.

Founded in 1868 by Samuel Chapman Armstrong, an 1862 graduate of Williams College and the leader of the Ninth U.S. Colored Troops in the Union Army, Hampton Normal and Agricultural Institute (Hampton Institute) was established to provide vocational training for newly emancipated Negroes.[6] Ten years later, in 1878, fifteen Native American men, referred to as "warriors" in much of the documentation, who had been captured in what was then Indian Territory, were admitted to the school. At the same time, many Native men who had been fighting the U.S. military incursion into their nations were arrested and sent to prisons.[7] Certainly, going to school was better than going to prison, but the fifteen young men who went to Hampton might be considered prisoners of war in another kind of institution.



Art-Based Image-and-Text Forms

Hampton Institute was a carefully constructed colonial contact zone.[8] Native students from a variety of nations traversed cultural borders with each other, free blacks, and the white teachers and administrators. Hampton was a site where the multinationed Natives were reshaped into uninational American subjects and where nationless African Americans were educated into "citizens" under emerging Jim Crow laws. Hampton Institute's official narrative was about creating possibilities for two groups of an underclass: free blacks and captive Natives. Education served an uplift agenda for blacks and an assimilationist agenda for Natives, one associated with the infamous Richard Henry Pratt philosophy of "kill the Indian . . . , save the man."[9] Literacy, of course, has had different associations historically for African Americans and Native Americans. Long associated with liberation for African Americans, reading and writing helped develop what by 1895 was called the "New Negro." In contrast, literacy for Native Americans is associated more often with broken treaties, stolen land, and cultural and linguistic erasure. Not surprisingly, Hampton's pedagogical practices were structured around the comparative racial understandings of the day. Donal Lindsey describes Hampton as the place "where English North American's two major minorities had their first encounters" (back cover), encounters strategically orchestrated by school officials.[10]

In 1899, Hampton Institute commissioned Frances B. Johnston, a Washington, D.C., photographer, to photograph the school and its students. Johnston's elaborately staged photographs served as part of Hampton's promotional materials, advertising its success and seeking financial support. The photographs were displayed in the *Exhibit of American Negroes* at the 1900 Universal Exposition in Paris. The exhibit assured "an American audience that free blacks could be counted on to take their place in the agricultural economy of the South" and an international audience that U.S. race relations were under control (Przyblyski 68). Johnston took great care in arranging her photographs into "carefully staged tableaus" (Glenn 63) (fig. 6.6), depicting African Americans and Native Americans as "domesticated" and thus underscoring the assimilationist project of converting "slaves and wild Indians into self-respecting, self-supporting Americans" (Guimond 31).[11]

Notice the carefully constructed composition, the balance of bodies at work. Six well-dressed and groomed male students pose in various acts of manual labor, their bodies arcing in consonance with the architectural angles as if they have been assimilated into their surroundings or have become extensions of the structure itself. They clean, polish, hammer, and build as they install the stairway, embodying the goal of Hampton graduates: to assimilate into American society and join the labor force as self-supporting workers. Johnston's Hampton photographs "sublimate

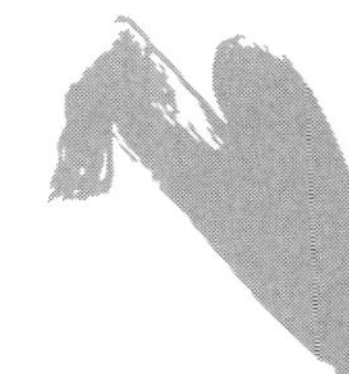

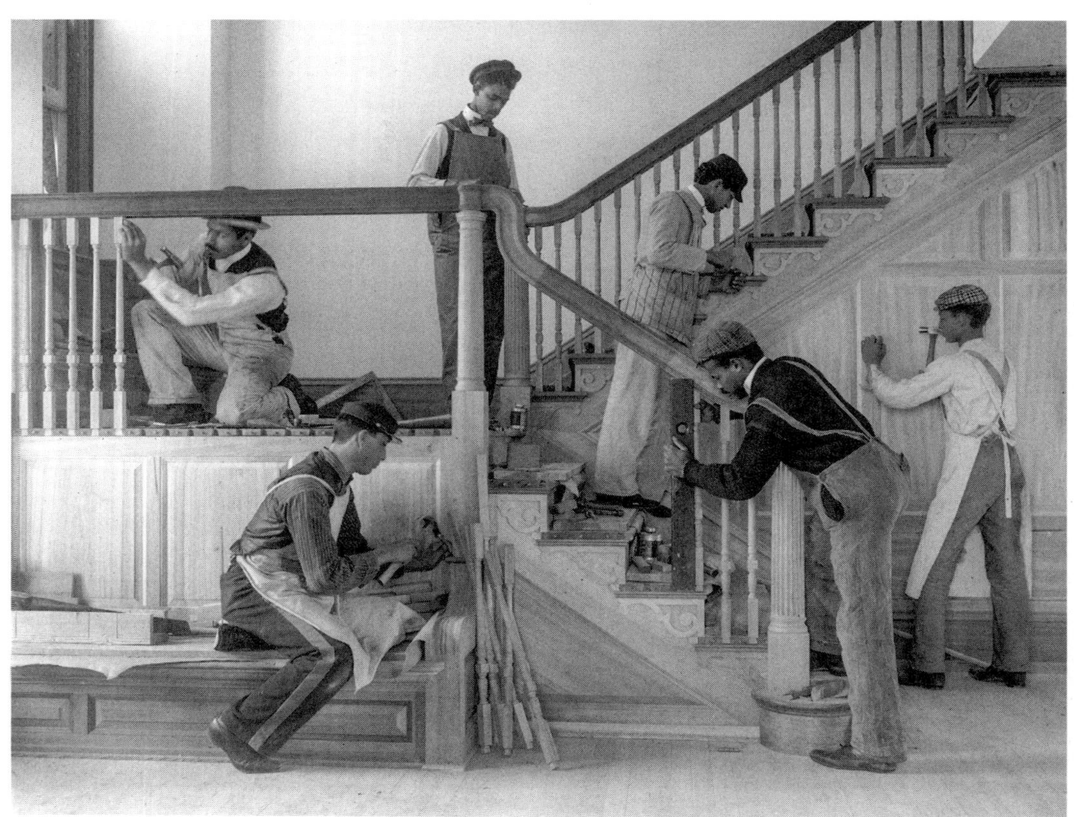



all marks of domestic racial struggle into the appearance of social harmony" (Wexler 129). They were, in fact, "a public relations assignment" (131), burying "their art in a façade of inevitability" (133) rather than acknowledging a series of purposeful choices to construct the image.

One hundred years later, the director of Williams College Museum of Art[12] asked Carrie Mae Weems to provide a contemporary artist's perspective on Frances Johnston's Hampton photographs.[13] The outcome of Weems's engagement with the Hampton visual archive was *The Hampton Project*, consisting of a series of digital photographs and texts transferred onto large-scale (four by five feet to eight by ten feet) sheer muslin banners that hang suspended from the ceiling, accompanied by five digitally enlarged photographs printed onto large pieces of stretched canvas hung high on the walls of the gallery. An audiotape, entitled *Before and After*, adds music and poetic narration, a provocative and "evocative counterpoint to the imagery" (Patterson, "The Hampton Project" 32). Although several of Johnston's photographs are included, Weems's photographs are gleaned from a variety of sources: thirteen images from a fifty-year period at Hampton Institute; one nineteenth-century photograph taken by William Larrabee; some photographs attributed to a stu-

    Art-Based Image-and-Text Forms

dent camera club at Hampton; an Edward S. Curtis photograph; a famous photograph of an Indian baptism owned by the Church of Jesus Christ of Latter-Day Saints; a news image of 1960s racial violence in Birmingham, Alabama; her own photographs—of a detail of Augustus Saint-Gaudens's Shaw Memorial, a Boston memorial to the "first troop of black soldiers to have been permitted to enlist in the Union Army" (Patterson, "The Hampton Project" 33); a sculpture of Sappho found on an architectural detail in Florence, Italy (33); a Ku Klux Klan parade float; and others. Weems, then, mingles formal images of Hampton life staged by Johnston with informal photographs taken by Hampton students and nineteenth- and twentieth-century photographs of memorials and domestic and political scenes. In the process of reappropriating and juxtaposing images from the nineteenth and twentieth centuries, she revisits Native and African American histories and stages a dialogue between present and past. Riddled with well-intended but colonizing misrepresentations, official histories—of education in the United States, in this example—render African and Native Americans as unschooled children who need to be guided or as wild primitives who need to be civilized. Weems exposes the Hampton project for what it was: cultural genocide. Rejecting Hampton's official narrative, Weems unapologetically depicts an alternative story, part of an ongoing process of decolonization and self-reclamation.

Vivian Patterson refers to *The Hampton Project* as the third of a "trilogy of fabric suites" (22)[14] or "fabric environments" (25) because the project itself becomes an architectural structure. Interested in getting her photographs off the wall and into new forms, Weems enlarges and prints them onto fabric. The see-through series of hanging fabrics creates a palimpsest of images and words, each filtering the others, suggesting again the layering of people, events, and stories associated with place. *The Hampton Project* becomes a memorial, a material manifestation of painful histories, and a scene of haunting—the diaphanous fabric creating a spectral vision. The banners may be likened to pages as well, so that the viewer-reader literally enters the story. The hanging imagetexts are arranged so that the viewer must walk through them, creating a spatial visual-verbal interface into which viewers are not merely invited but required to enter. It is as if viewers enter the past, journeying among the larger-than-life images and reading and hearing Weems's challenge to the official Hampton narrative of assimilationist uplift. Richly evocative, the diaphanous banners also refer to the "veil of race," so aptly described by W. E. B. Du Bois, through which people of color are viewed by others. In addition, they serve as a metaphor for the inevitable mediation of looking at the past through the filter of the present moment and for the way that the past is always shaped and constructed, if not reinvented.

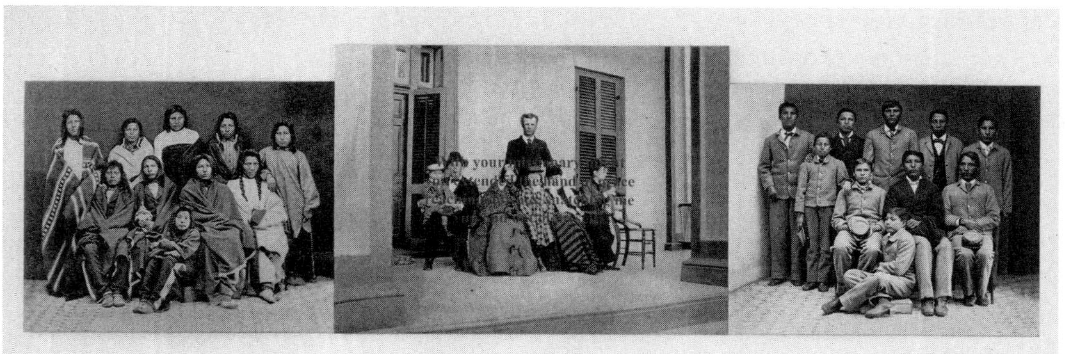





The Hampton story of before and after is represented in images like the first and third of these in figure 6.7. The photograph on the left, taken in 1878, documents the arrival of a group of American Indians at Hampton Institute. The long-haired men wear blankets and moccasins. Their facial expressions vary: anger, defiance, distrust, and curiosity. A second photograph (far right), taken three years later, in 1880, provides visual evidence of what "the Hampton method" could produce. The now short-haired Indian men wear suits, ties, and boots. Their expressions vary: resigned, defiant, detached, but, at the very least, wary. Gerald McMaster describes a similar photograph at a Canadian boarding school: "These boys represented the colonial experiment, a type of colonial alchemy: transforming the savage into a civilized human being. Yet somehow their resistance remains visible" (79). Weems enlarges these two photographs and positions them on either side of the exhibit, where they serve as visual referents to the Hampton method.

"Before and after," then, is a key framing device for Weems's exhibit. One of Johnston's famous photographs depicts a young American Indian man dressed in buckskin, wearing a feathered headdress, and holding a pipe. He stands on a bench, elevated before his class—a cultural specimen and spectacle. The other Hampton students observe dutifully. This is an example of a "cannibalistic moment" in which a photographic subject is devoured by the photographer, in contrast to "'intersubjective time' where the emphasis is on interaction and communication" (Lippard, *Partial Recall* 37). Given Weems's history of interacting with the subjects of her photographs, of placing herself both behind and in front of the camera, her photographic practice has always countered cannibalistic photography. Here Weems implicitly critiques the process of how a human subject becomes an anthropological object, showing how the forces of history, and in this case U.S. education, shape who we are allowed to be. Her accompanying text elaborates on the violently transformative Hampton agenda:

   Art-Based Image-and-Text Forms

**At Hampton you arrived**

**as prisoners of war & freed-slaves**

*You arrived and*

**displaced and dislocated**

*acquiring the ways of the patriarch*

**Leaving blankets and chains at the door**

*became your practice*

**you checked in one way**

*assuming its name*

**and came out another**

*your fate, your progress now measured*

**but your Missionary instruction**

*by your successful distance*

**would *not* be**

*from your past*

**to Conserve a Legacy**

*God and education*

*had posed as the perfect package deal*

*& your soul was the price of the ticket*

*Educated away from yourself*

*you gave up Ogun, Ife, Yemoja,*

*Obatala & Wankan alike*

*for a single and alien god*

*Ashe floating by on a red cloud*

(Patterson, *Carrie Mae Weems* 72)

Weems's text, shaped into prose poetry lines, can be read at least three ways. It may be read as two separate "prose poems": a short poem in bold font and a longer one in italics. In addition, it can be read interlinearly, such that the lines in bold and italics are read sequentially, with their meanings interpenetrating like a palimpsest of words transferring the meanings and images between and across the lines: "*You arrived and /* **displaced and dislocated** / *acquiring the ways of the patriarch.*" In this example, the boldfaced "displaced and dislocated" inform readers about the conditions that led to having "arrived" and of "acquiring the ways of the patriarch." Displacement and dislocation—both literally and psychologically—dominate the experience of the colonized and oppressed as well as the awareness of the reader. One of Weems's motivations is to reveal the "unbridled reality" (79) of historical forces that forged contemporary identities, including her own. Her photo-narrative intermingles references to Native and African histories of violent encounter with the West. She translates her mode of visual interweaving and juxtaposition to text as she mixes Native and African touchstones—"prisoners of war," "freed-slaves," "blankets," "chains"—in this banner. "Educated away from" themselves, the Hampton students "gave up" their particularized cultures, languages, and gods; the price of assimilation was their very souls.

In *The Hampton Project*, Weems appropriates photographs by Johnston and others, recontextualizing them visually in a process that critiques their original agenda and reclaims some sense of agentive voice and vision one hundred years later. Yet, ironically, at times Weems relies on the very kind of representational practices she critiques. For example, in at least one instance, she treats human beings as interchangeable: an unidentified European American Hampton administrator stands in for any number of others. To be sure, in the process of correcting historical misrepresentations and critiquing an oppressive Other, it is easy, perhaps necessary, to be lured into using reductive binary oppositions—true representations versus false representations, us versus them, or good versus bad. It may be challenging to avoid using an oppressor's representational tactics—simplifying, generalizing, caricaturing—to counter the original misrepresentations. Relying on representation and re-representation to critique representation is not an unproblematic practice.

In one photograph of an unnamed Hampton administrator (presumably the founder) and his family (fig. 6.7, center), Weems overlays the family photograph with bold red text: "With your missionary might / you extend the hand of grace / reaching down and snatching me / up and out of myself." Weems does not identify this family, using them merely as the representation of missionary outreach, educational rebranding, and discursive violence. With the exception of the man standing, the faces and figures are obscured, if not obliterated, by Weems's textual overlay. Symbolically, Weems reclaims power one hundred years later. Hers is the dominant text, the voice of the present echoing back to condemn and obscure, if not erase, the Hampton administrator, just as nineteenth-century colonial discourses rendered indigenous students invisible. The

     Art-Based Image-and-Text Forms

man in this photograph, it turns out, is not the founder but the treasurer of Hampton Institute. But Weems is concerned with critiquing historical wrongs, not with trying to present a seemingly balanced perspective inclusive of European American and African and Native American perspectives. For most of U.S. history, those oppressed by the dominant colonizing agenda have had no or little power of representation. Weems does not apologize for speaking truth to power.

Incorporated into one of the final banners is David Wojnarowicz's well-known photograph of bison being driven off a cliff (fig. 6.8). Produced in the 1980s while he was struggling to survive the emerging AIDS epidemic, Wojnarowicz's photograph alludes both to the violence of a nation willing to sacrifice callously those dying of AIDS and to the foundational violence upon which the United States has been constructed. The buffalo photograph, argues John Sevigny, is "the photographic equivalent of Allen Ginsberg's *Howl*, an indictment of a sick nation reeling in riches and hubris even as it feasted on the weakest, cast the mentally ill out into the streets, and blamed death on the dying."[15] The image of bison being destroyed is decidedly Native. The purposeful destruction of the bison was one way the federal government stopped Native people from traveling to hunt in order to feed and clothe themselves. In addition, as Kiowa writer and artist N. Scott Mcmaday notes, destroying the buffalo was a form of deicide. For Wojnarowicz, this image is an exposé of the violence that the sanitized image of the United States belies. The federal government destroyed the physical and spiritual sustenance of Native peoples in order to claim the land for itself. Generations later, the U.S. government is slow to set up medical research programs and allows thousands to die of AIDS, blaming the ill for their own suffering and doom.

As she often does, Weems incorporates herself into the image (see fig. 6.8). In *The Hampton Project*, she is telling not her personal or family story but the history that precedes and shapes her own. This historical narrative is a central part of her story just as it is foundational for her viewers. Here she depicts herself as the artist, standing and looking, as *historical witness*, but, more importantly, as she says, as *"the narrator of history"* (Fogg and Ramzy, "Interview" 79, my emphasis), not the object or subject of others. With her back to the audience, Weems becomes the medium for viewers to look *through* a black body, through her point of view. Weems's artistic practice, then, is a form of artist-activist double consciousness that enacts a "critical black [and Native] memory" (Raiford 16) and that enables the formation of new subjectivities less burdened by official discourses.

Although the *image* of the slaughtered bison evokes Native history (for example, the literal destruction of indigenous sustenance) and African American history (for example, the nineteenth-century Negro mili-

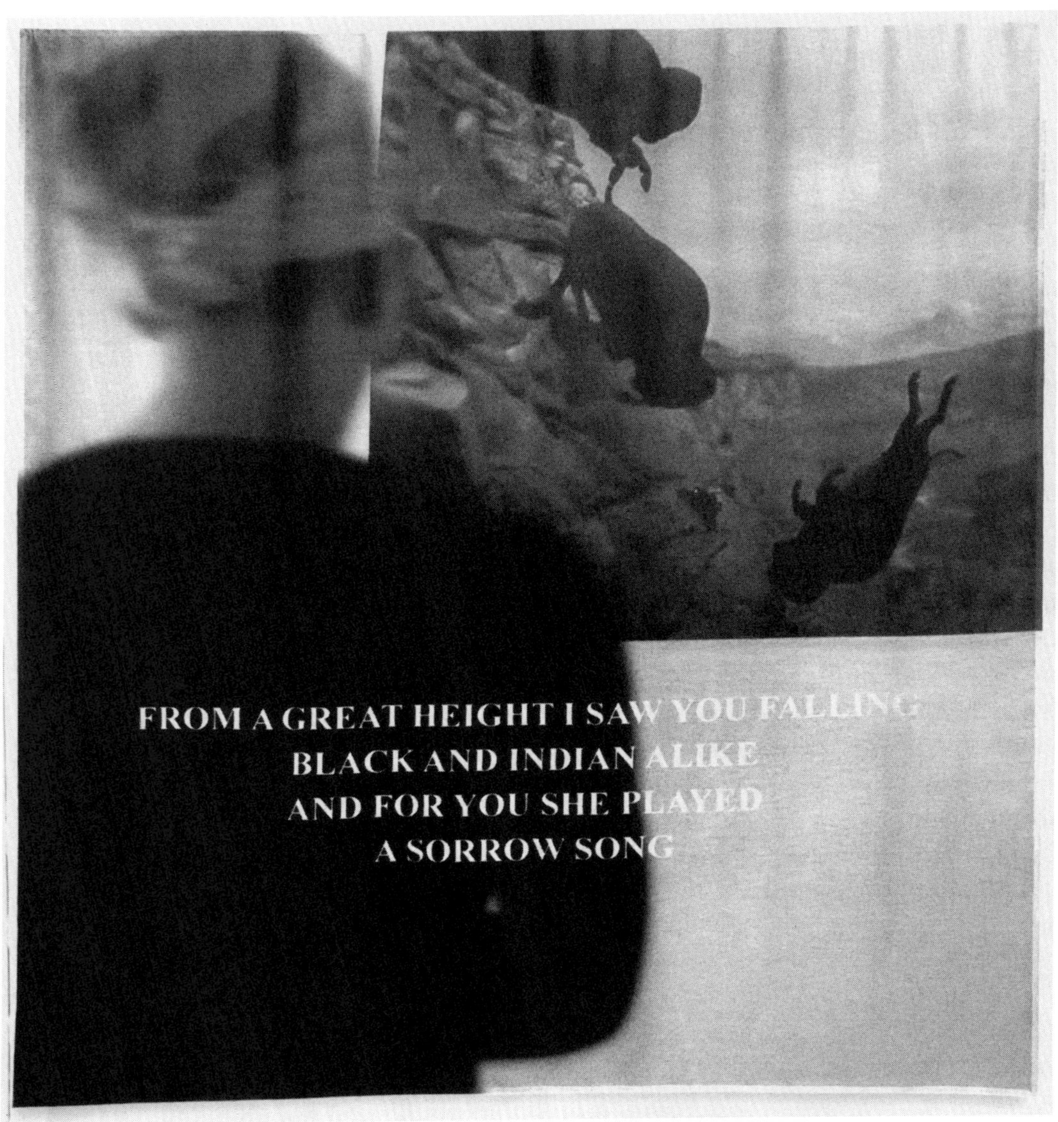


tary men known as Buffalo Soldiers who fought against Native people), the *text* overlaid upon this image has clear African American referents. The artist-witness-narrator of history plays a sorrow song, precursor to the blues, for the African and Native Americans who are seen in the midst of being undone and remade by the Hampton educational process. Viewing "women as the weepers of history" (Fogg and Ramzy, "Interview" 79), Weems shares and passes on the burden of remembering those whose lives were lost or transfigured through a colonial education. The penultimate banner-page in the photo-history is a prayer of remembrance and grief, punctuated with the names of twenty-three Native students Weems found on headstones in Hampton's Native American cemetery:

     Art-Based Image-and-Text Forms

*VIRGINIA MEDICINE-BULL*

*ARMSTRONG FIRE-CLOUD*

*LOUISA BANKS*

*ELIZABETH KENNEDY*

*SIMON MAZAKUTE*

*JOSEPH TASUNKA-WASTE*

**And against the odds**

*ENOCH CONKLIN SAVARPKS*

**I saw you become many things you**

*BENJAMIN BEAR-BIRD*

**were not supposed to be**

*MAHPIYA-MANI*

**and to my horror I saw**

*OLIVE MADISON*

**some of you die trying**

*GEORGE NORCROSS HIPOYA*

**For those of you**

*EDITH YELLOW-HAIR*

**whose remains**

*FRANCIS RENCONTRE*

**remain here**

*LORA BOWED-HEAD SNOW*

**the ancestors are still weeping and**

*MARY TURNER*

**calling out your names**

*NICK PRATT*

*THOMAS NOBLE*

*JOHN BLUE-PIPE*

*FRANCESCA RIOS*

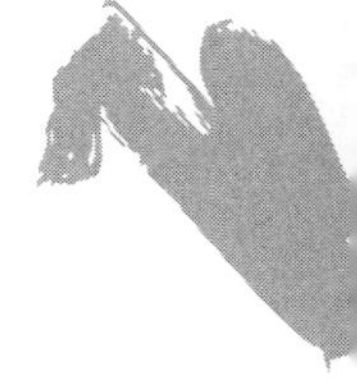

(OPPOSITE)
FIGURE 6.8.
Carrie Mae Weems.
*Weems and Buffalo Jump* (ink on muslin banner, 83 × 76 in.), *The Hampton Project*, 2000. (© Carrie Mae Weems. Courtesy of the artist and Jack Shainman Gallery, New York.)

This banner is the only one that notes the specific names of real people. The fact that the Hampton administrator's family and people in other photographs are unnamed in the exhibit has drawn ire from Jeanne Zeidler, the director of Hampton University Museum. She points out that the man in the family photograph (see fig. 6.7) is Frank Dean Banks, "the head bookkeeper in the Treasurer's Office" (77), *not* the founder. Similarly, she notes that the generic Plains Indian student exhibiting his culture was for the edification of "Jane Worcester's class in American history"; and he has a name: Louis Firetail (from the Sioux and Crow Creek nations).[16] It is important to note that *The Hampton Project* was supposed to be exhibited at Hampton University, but Hampton, the very subject of the photo exhibition, refused to be involved and banned Weems's art show from the campus. The show traveled nationally, but never to Hampton, Virginia. Hampton University Museum administrators objected to Weems's generalizations about Hampton and its students, her appropriation of culture and history for her own political agenda, the lack of individual voices of students or administrators, and her claim that "education is conformity." Is Weems using the master's tools to dismantle the master's house? Or is she simply guilty of turning the tables—producing just another grand narrative (that still renders people invisible) to counter an official colonial history?

More often, however, Weems's work is celebrated. Weems is praised for being on "a mission of beguiling visual warfare, appropriating, enlarging, annotating her images with the spoken word and written texts to bestow the very precious gift of a renewed public persona on those who have heretofore depended on others, or submitted to them, for dignified representation and subsequent empowerment" (Patterson, "The Hampton Project" 37). Hampton officials prefer to tell a story of education as life improvement, emphasizing how a Hampton education helped young African Americans and Native Americans gain skills that would help them find jobs. They do not acknowledge their role in the larger colonial project. In contrast, Weems tells a story of education, in this case colonial education, as cultural, and sometimes physical, death. Reframing the Hampton Institute photographic archive from subaltern perspectives, she is actively "deconstructing history and photography" (Fogg and Ramzy, "Interview" 80). "Nothing moves forward without sincerely looking at the multiple levels of reality," explains Weems, "and unbridled reality is often painful" (79). In *The Hampton Project*, Weems offers a kind of visual-verbal shock therapy. She challenges viewers to acknowledge the violent history of the United States, to look at how forces of oppression have shaped contemporary identities, and to remember those who were lost in the process.

........................................................................................................

Weems chooses to highlight the politics of her art, contributing to what she calls "the cultural dialogue" by grappling with the complex issues of representation, memory, history, and subjectivity. To carry on that dialogue, she looks to historical and visual archives, figuring personal narrative and refiguring historical narrative to nudge her readers-viewers into awareness and to illustrate how artistic processes and products can redeem "the web of rape and plunder" (Najarian, *Daughters* 92). She emphasizes storytelling and truth-telling in image and text. Weems moves her photographic pages out of books, then off the walls, to hang her larger-than-life image-texts from ceilings. Her architectural form demands viewers' physically active engagement as they literally walk through the layered pages of text and photographs. Weems must counter racist stereotypes of African Americans as part of her process of self-formation, and she claims the right to present herself and African Americans generally as universal subjects whose experiences and insights are relevant to everyone. Weems returns to the wrongs of the past in order to recover silenced histories, to assess the continued influence of past oppression on the present, and to offer at least temporary redress through art.

# Faith Ringgold's Story Quilts

## "All Things American in America Are about Race"

Faith Ringgold's story quilts are painted image-text narratives on fabric. While quilts generally are used for such everyday purposes as covering a bed or wrapping around a person, Ringgold's oversized quilts are intended to be displayed in an art gallery. The quilt squares are stitched together, functioning simultaneously as individual images or texts and as part of the entire quilt. That is, each piece may be examined as part and whole. Each quilt square functions also as a page, while a series of quilt squares can function also as a frame. The sets of relations between page and frame, between image and text, are multiple and variable.

As we have seen with the work of Carrie Mae Weems, countering racist representations of African Americans has been a substantial post–civil rights project for African American writers and artists. The vigilant process of always contingent and shifting articulation—revising imposed representations and stories, whether those are textual or visual—was a necessary preoccupation for late twentieth-century writers and artists and continues to be so in the twenty-first century. Riddled with racist and sexist misrepresentations, official histories of Western art and of the United States often render women and ethnic minorities as either distorted or downright invisible. As the narrator in Ralph Ellison's *Invisible Man* says famously: "I am invisible, understand, simply because people refuse to see me. . . . They see only my surroundings, themselves, or figments of their imaginations" (7). In order to become visible as an individual and collective subject, not merely as a stereotypical representative of a racialized and gendered community, one has to expose, challenge, and correct historical misrepresentations. That is, many marginalized groups—women and African Americans among them—must intervene in a long history of textual and visual domination to simultaneously revise historical representations and generate more accurate and dynamic ones. Of course, such a corrective process is itself flawed if it is based on the assumption that there is a single true historical narrative that, once excavated, redeems everything. Like subjectivity itself, personal and collective histories are intricately interdependent and processual.

They are mutually constitutive, subject to perpetual negotiation and re-constitution.

Well known for her painted and stitched story quilts, artist Faith Ringgold thematizes race and gender in most of her work. "'All things American in America are about race'" (Roth 56), she insists. There is a great "weight placed on black cultural production to do something to alter a history and system of racial inequality that is in part constituted through visual discourse" (Fleetwood 3). Countering racist discourses and reimagining U.S. history and the history of Western art, Ringgold's work documents the experience of African Americans, offers "layers of social commentary," and reveals her "interests in the dynamics of color and issues of composition and form" (Holton 9). Like many people of color in the United States, then, Ringgold must first undo centuries of misrepresentation by others, must name and subvert the visual and verbal stereotypes. This is an especially challenging task when it comes to black women, who have been rendered doubly invisible: by both dominant racist social discourses and masculinist black discourses.[1]

Ringgold not only revises the history of Western art and its exclusion of artists of African descent but rethinks the basic materials of the artist by working with fabric. There has been a substantial tradition of story quilts in many rural and working-class communities in the United States, but nowhere has this craft been more significant than in African American communities, where women literally stitched together their family histories and life stories from discarded, found, or worn-out scraps. Early on in autobiography criticism, "stitching together a life" became a metaphor for the process of women writing autobiographically, for gathering, sorting, and shaping fragments—of memories, experiences, and materials—into a coherent life story. In the 1960s and 1970s, fiber art emerged as part of a process of postmodern experimentation with everyday materials, often reflecting a feminist intent to elevate traditional women's art forms and reveal gendered and racialized biases in the "high art" world.[2]

Ringgold employs and/or refers to the piecing process of quilting to redesign a personal and collective history that enables her, as an African American woman artist, to be visible on her own terms. Inspired by her mother's[3] fabric remnants, Ringgold joins high art with folk art, transforming the quilt form, associated with female domestic space, into a public display in art galleries.[4] In her quilts, Ringgold experiments with various relations of image and text as well. Ringgold tends to create series that naturally use a temporal interface, but with her explicit political engagement, she also creates contextual interfaces. Ringgold uses the visual and verbal and their interface, then, as a site to stage a social debate about racialized and gendered identities, including her own.

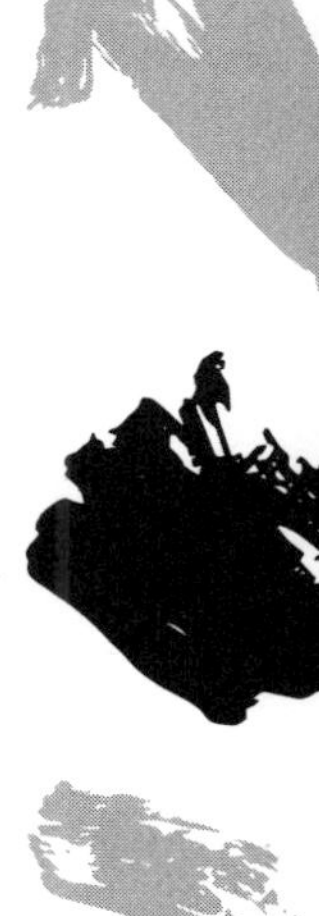

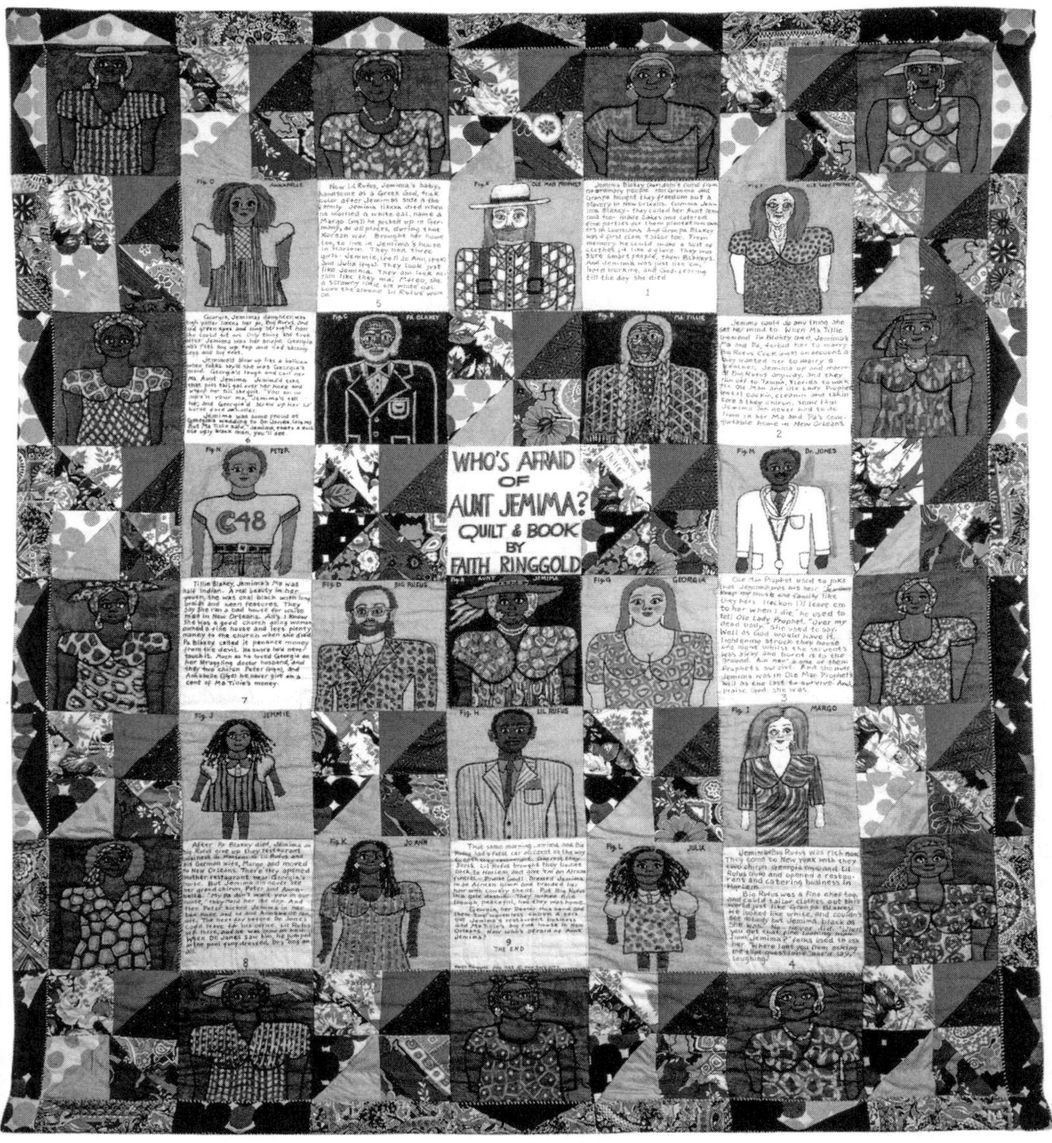

Generally, Ringgold makes two types of quilts and mixes several visual-textual interface categories. In the first type of quilt, Ringgold organizes the visual-verbal interface relationally, contextually, and temporally. Each panel contains a discrete image or text; each quilt consists of a collection of panels arranged in a series to highlight the relation between image and text. In her first story quilt, entitled *Who's Afraid of Aunt Jemima?* (1983), an ironic echo of *Who's Afraid of Virginia Woolf?* (fig. 7.1), for instance, Ringgold creates a collection of juxtapositions or a sequence of images and texts that are in dialogue with one another. In this case, the alternating text and image panels require the viewer to both look and read. In this quilt, as in other early quilts, such as those in the *Change* series, Ringgold's emphasis on individual panels highlights her book-format layout in which each panel is a page as well as a canvas.

In Ringgold's second type of quilt format, a large central canvas is made to resemble a collection of quilt pieces by stitching that suggests the quilt form and is itself framed by stitched-together pieces of fabric. These are paintings on a quilted surface. Her paintings, then, deaccentuate the boundaries of the individual panels in the service of a single, large scene (see fig. 7.2). Ringgold "speaks" in the language of "high art"—that is, through painting, but in a manner that evokes a rupture not only between the scenes, but also in the accompanying narrative. She both fuses and juxtaposes high art (painting) and domestic craft (quilting). The stitching is placed strategically to link, divide, and highlight individual sections of the painting. This quilt-as-canvas format allows for multiple simultaneous frames—binding; patterned, textual, and painted panels; and stitching—within a single painting and calls attention to the way Ringgold sutures together the personal and collective past.[5]

*Who's Afraid of Aunt Jemima?* (see fig. 7.1) is the first of her works to talk back to historical misrepresentations of African American women. Ringgold transforms Aunt Jemima from a monodimensional, endlessly reproducible brand into Aunt Jemima as a living woman with a multiplicity of selves, affiliations, and locations. Ringgold is not alone in redesigning Jemima; a number of "artists associated with the black arts movement" have even depicted Jemima as a dangerous militant (Farrington 76). "What mystified Ringgold," explains Farrington, "was the fact that, no matter who was constructing the image, Aunt Jemima seemed to be portrayed in extremes" (76). Although this quilt is not autobiographical, I want to focus on it briefly because it prefigures Ringgold's strategy and form in her later, more autobiographical work and challenges historical racist stereotypes that threaten to occlude her self-narration.

A well-known racist-sexist stereotype—the black mammy or domestic servant—Aunt Jemima is servile, willingly taking care of all the needs of her white employers. She is single and without any relations other than those with her employers; she lives to serve. But here Ringgold has invented a whole family and history for Aunt Jemima. Ringgold places Jemima "at the center of a family narrative and a migration story, the object of sympathetic sentiment rather than disgust or fear" (Sheehan 6).

Jemima, the center of the quilt both visually and thematically, is located just beneath the title page at the center of the square that is itself the center of the quilt. The four human figures that frame and surround Jemima represent her African-Native American mother, daughter, husband, and father, everyone explicitly color coded—high yellow to dark

(OPPOSITE)
FIGURE 7.1.
Faith Ringgold.
*Who's Afraid of
Aunt Jemima?
Quilt and Story
Book*, 1983.
(Acrylic on canvas;
dyed, painted,
and pieced fabric
with sequins,
90 × 80 in.
© Faith Ringgold
1983. Courtesy of
Faith Ringgold.)

black. Numbers help the viewer to follow the alternation between text and image, each in a panel reminiscent of a page in a book. The top right textual panel is numbered 1. Viewers read down, alternating between family portraits and text, to panel 4, then to the top left to locate page 5 and back down to the bottom center, page 9. Although Ringgold maintains a sense of a conventional page, she appropriates the page as a quilt square in a narrative quilt. The pages are surrounded, informed, and sometimes interrupted by family portraits. The viewer-reader is required to get up close to the quilt to read Jemima's story and must read unconventionally, top right to bottom right, top left to bottom left, with the concluding page centered in the bottom middle.

Handwritten in vernacular African American English, the writing tells a family history of struggle and triumph. Jemima Blakely "didn't come from no ordinary people" but came from former slaves who "bought they freedom." A woman who "could do anything she set her mind to" (Cameron 81, 9),[6] Jemima runs off to marry Big Rufus, gains an inheritance from her white employers after their death by lightning, develops a successful business, and, as she ages, questions the values of younger generations. By the end of the story, Ringgold's Jemima and Big Rufus die in a car accident; their bodies are returned to Harlem, dressed in African clothing, and given an African funeral. "They looked nice," explains the narrator, "like they was home" (81, 2). Ringgold, then, reconfigures the long-standing Aunt Jemima stereotype of black female servitude, gives her a story of self-sufficiency, and then kills her, figuratively at least, destroying the racist stereotype and laying it to rest with an African ritual (81, 9). It is noteworthy that home is associated not only with Harlem but also with Africa and death, all linked to a notion of return or rebirth. African American death, in this case, is a passage into subjectivity, a way of becoming legible as fully human.[7] Like nineteenth-century slave narratives in which African American speakers and writers articulate blacks as human subjects and not as property, Ringgold's Jemima story quilt wrestles with dominant racist discourse and insists on African American female specificity and agency.

Ringgold's reclamation of Jemima's image is an attempt to free herself from the distortions of racist historical lenses, a necessary precursor to her more autobiographical work. I want to focus here on *The French Collection*, a series of story quilts produced in 1990–97. Ringgold's daughter, Michele Wallace, describes it as her mother's "most revealingly autobiographical" work (*French Collection* 15). Scholars have speculated that Willia Marie Simone is "an alter ego of Ringgold's mother" or "an incarnation of Ringgold herself" (Farrington 80). This does not mean, however, that factual details of Ringgold's life are included, but rather that the driving questions of her life are explored creatively.[8] As

     Art-Based Image-and-Text Forms

I use the term, "autobiography" refers not only to explicit recounting of the experiences of individual authors but also to representations of the collective history in which a relational subjectivity is enmeshed. This collectivity is especially important for African Americans, who, since their acts of witness in slave narratives such as those by Frederick Douglass and Harriet Jacobs, have been expected to speak for their race. More important for present purposes, this quilt series exemplifies Ringgold's multiple simultaneous modes of intervention into representational systems that have erased, ignored, misrepresented, and devalued her as a woman, as a person of African descent, and as an artist. In *The French Collection*, Ringgold renarrates African American history, reappropriates art history, and in the process makes a place for herself.

*The French Collection* consists of twelve story quilts. The protagonist of this story sequence, Ringgold's autobiographical persona, is Willia Marie Simone. All autobiographies have characters, often with the same name as the autobiographer, who stand in for the writer-artist. Much has been made of the essential fiction of the autobiographical persona—a literary or artistic representation of the writer-artist.[9] By giving her autobiographical persona another name, Ringgold both gives herself creative license and underscores the fictional nature of self-narration itself. The figure of Simone serves to "demythify and historicize the nature of the split between the representor and the represented—often a gendered as well as a racializing separation—that characterized the historical avant-garde as much as it had traditional art" (Gibson 70). Significantly, Simone is an expatriate African American artist-model-wife-widow-mother-café owner. She is a woman who both creates images and herself serves as one, a woman actively engaged in a network of personal, social, artistic, and financial relations.

Ringgold tells Simone's story visually but also textually in a series of letters to her Aunt Melissa that literally frames the images. As she did in *Who's Afraid of Aunt Jemima?*, Ringgold dismembers the book form and reassembles it imaginatively. While she conceptualizes the quilt square as both a page and a canvas, she decenters the text, repurposing it to serve as a partial frame for the painting. Five quilt rectangles at the top and five at the bottom function simultaneously as pages and frames. Look for the five stitched *x*'s in the top and bottom series of rectangles. Each quilt in the series has twelve "pages" of text in the form of quilt rectangles: six pages at the top and six pages at the bottom (see fig. 7.2). The image-text interfaces are complex: relational in that the text is in dialogue with the images, contextual in that Ringgold portrays cultural contexts, spatial in that the text not only tells the epistolary story but also serves as a frame for the hand-painted images, and temporal because of its series format. Viewers are drawn first to the enormous scale, vibrant colors, dynamic

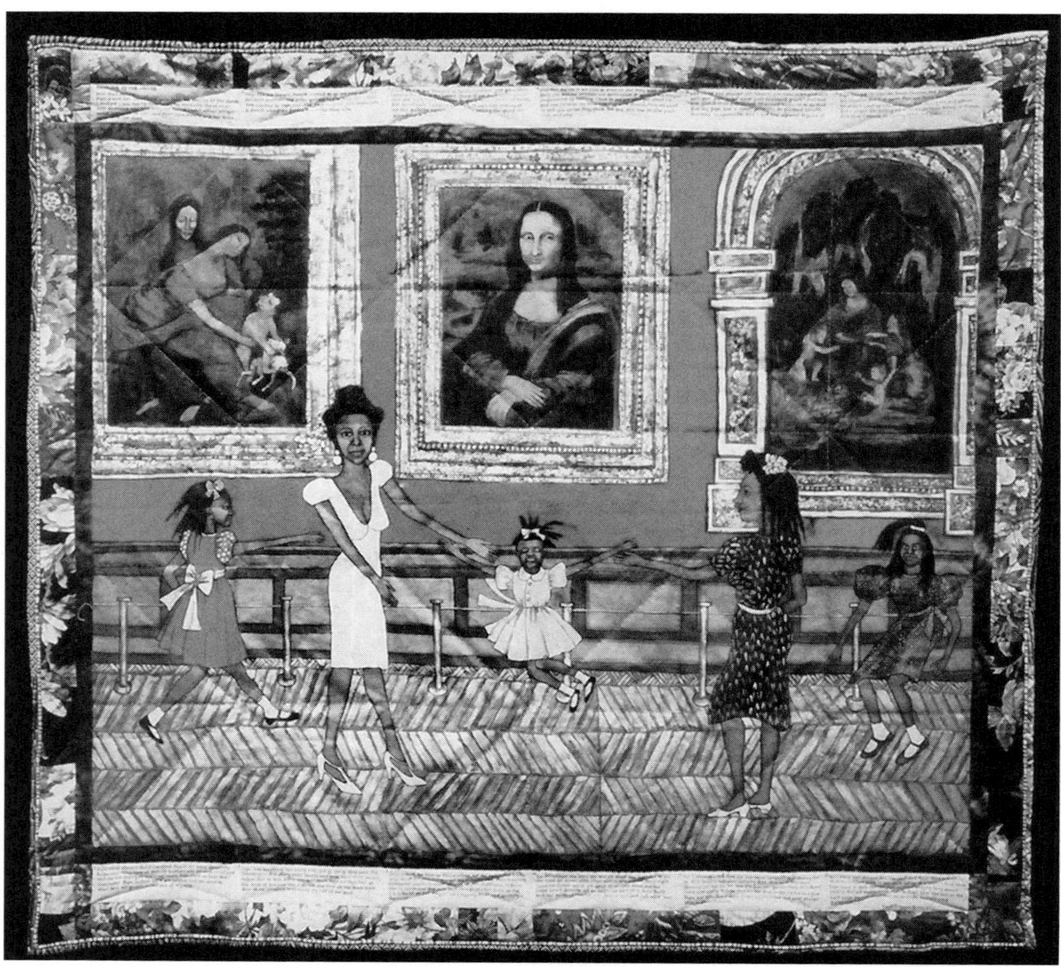



shapes, and painterly play with fabric. Only after an intense visual experience does the viewer notice the text. Even then, it is difficult to access. Because the large quilts hang on gallery walls, the pages are literally too high or too low to read easily.[10] Viewers must stretch or bend physically, exert effort, and change points of view to be able to read the text at all. Perhaps the initial textual inaccessibility is another way that Ringgold underscores the challenges of accessing the past.

Although this is Ringgold's most revealingly autobiographical collection, she cannot tell her story without refashioning history, exposing biases in the dominant formulations of "genius" and "art." Struggling with how to narrate this history, Ringgold asks what she should paint: "A black man toting a heavy load that has pinned him to the ground? Or a black woman nursing the world's population of children? Or the two of them together as slaves, building a beautiful world for others to live free?" (Cameron 132, 10). "Non!" she answers. Eschewing visual realism

    Art-Based Image-and-Text Forms

and historical literalism, Ringgold recontextualizes history and incorporates figures of African American history (Harriet Tubman, Frederick Douglass, Malcolm X, and others) and art history (among them, Édouard Manet, Pablo Picasso, Henri Matisse, and Vincent van Gogh). In each quilt, she features a famous European male artist—sometimes representationally, sometimes in the form and composition of her images. Staging dialogues through and across generations and continents and people and languages, Ringgold creates a relational subjectivity for her autobiographical persona. Simone is the result of a history of both deprivation and possibility. The subaltern, in this case, not only speaks (to invoke feminist critic Gayatri Spivak) but also paints, writes, and sews.

In the first quilt of *The French Collection, Dancing at the Louvre* (1991) (fig. 7.2), Ringgold tackles what would become a dominant concern in visual studies: modes of looking and the power relations in which they are embedded. In this case, Ringgold challenges dominant cultural conventions and institutional impositions about what we should look at and how we should look—a fitting portal through which to examine her refashioning of art history.

In this opening scene, Ringgold critiques the type of viewing associated with Western high art housed in museums. The formal, heavy, and gilded frames around the paintings (Leonardo da Vinci's *Virgin and Child with Saint Anne, Mona Lisa*, and *Virgin of the Rocks*) hanging on the wall of the museum form a backdrop to the vitality of the children dancing in front of them.[11] No matter how much museums and art galleries attempt to control our viewing—through architectural design, velvet ropes to keep us at a safe distance from the art, lighting to obscure or enhance what is visible, brochures informing viewers what they are looking at and how to interpret it, audiotaped tours, guards, and so on—there is a social component to galleries and museums that defies that visual coercion.[12] Ringgold's intervention emphasizes the folk moving into the European center of high art: the Louvre in Paris. Here, viewers' eyes are drawn to the lively children in the foreground. On the left, Simone's arms direct attention to the dancing child in the center. On the right, the woman's arms do the same. Together they provide a human frame for the child, focalizing her movement. All of the family members are outside the ornate picture frames, beyond the containment of the museum's velvet ropes. The children are more interested in their own playful interaction than in the Louvre's visual display of artistic masters.[13]

There are multiple frames in this quilt. Moving from outside to inside, the frames include the exterior black border, the colorful rectangles of cloth,[14] the text of the letters, the interior red band, the three formal gilded frames, the human frames (noted above), and the stitching that

creates a series of tilted squares, subtly framing the women: Simone and each of the three prancing children. With her simultaneous multiple frames, Ringgold both dramatically directs the viewer's gaze and highlights the constructedness of vision itself.

In addition, the oversized *Mona Lisa* is framed by two paintings of mothers with infants. Ringgold's selection of paintings targets not only high art as part of her reconsideration but also representations of mothers and their children. The Leonardos depicting idealized mother-child relationships form a visual counter to the story Ringgold is about to tell. After the death of her French husband, Simone relinquishes her two children to be raised by their aunt in the United States so that Simone can pursue her art in France. Throughout *The French Collection*, Ringgold shares the intimate history of the torturous choices Simone makes for the sake of art. At the same time, she illustrates her artistic ability by employing and deploying the masters' techniques and forms. Simone looks out of the canvas, directly at viewers, as if acknowledging the outside observers-listeners of the story she is about to narrate.

In *Wedding on the Seine*, the second quilt, Ringgold depicts what appears to be a lovely scene of a bride in a flowing gown. The text, however, narrates a more troubling story. The bride is running away, agonizing over the choice between being an artist or a wife, fretting about whether her French betrothed, a white man, loves her for herself or her exotic blackness. Simone's struggle complicates the binary opposition—artist or wife. After rigorous self-scrutiny and considerable local encouragement, she marries. Three years later, her French husband dies, leaving her "alone with her art and two babies" (Cameron 141, 14). Years later, responding to questions about why she left her children, why she stayed in Paris, she explains: "The French said, I was beautiful. . . . They called me Mademoiselle Précieuse. In America I would be just another black bitch" (Cameron 141, 14).

In the third and fourth quilts Ringgold expands her imaginative retelling of the relations among African Americans, women, and art history. *The Picnic at Giverny* (1991), quilt three (fig. 7.3), is an appropriation of Claude Monet's *Décorations des nymphéas* (1920s) crossed with Édouard Manet's *Le Déjeuner sur l'herbe* (1863), a painting of two women—one nude and one partially dressed—having a picnic with two fully clothed men, a scene that shocked the Parisian art world at the time and, some claim, heralded the arrival of modern art.

In an ironic inversion of Manet's nude woman, Ringgold depicts a gathering of fully dressed contemporary women artists and art educators and an exposed, naked Picasso (front left) looking sheepishly at the viewer.[15] At the bottom right, Willia Marie Simone stands at an easel painting the scene. In the temporal visual-verbal interface Ring-

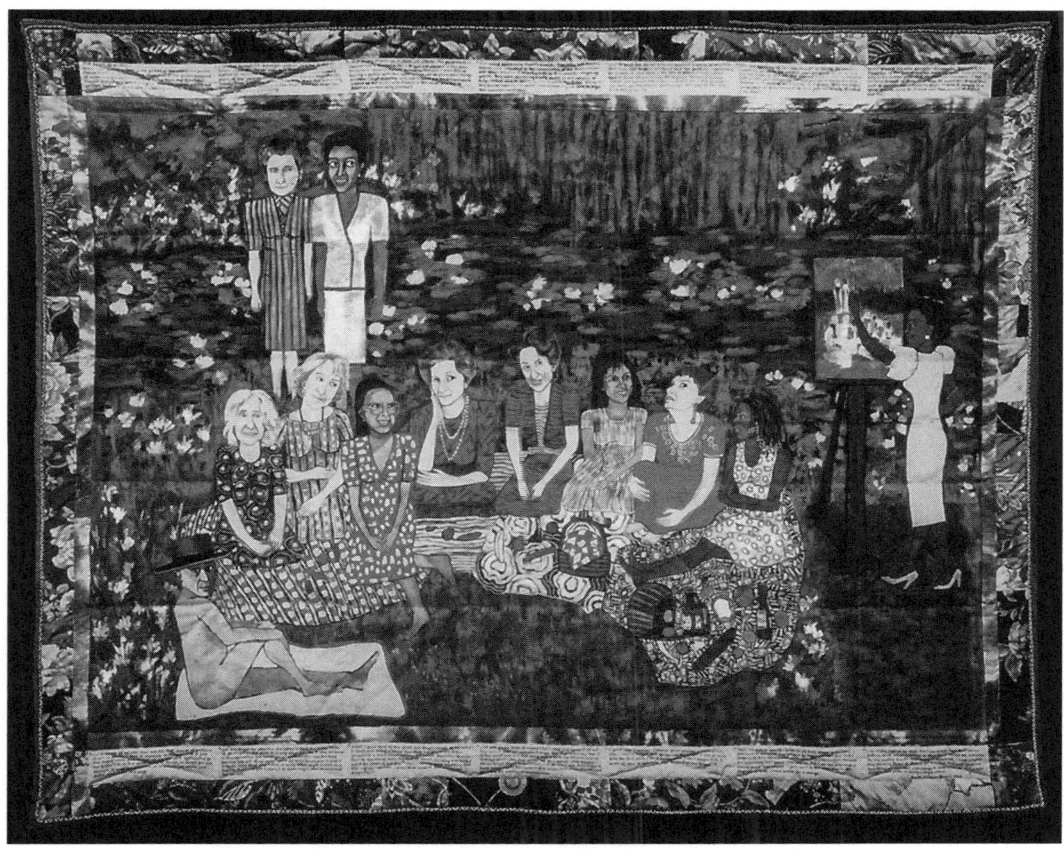

gold collapses time, simultaneously joining and juxtaposing past and present. Present-day Simone is visually aligned with Picasso; with their backs slightly turned, they frame the gathering of women. But Ringgold reverses their roles: Picasso is the model, Simone the maker of art. A woman artist, Simone creates and participates in a community—both historical (in this case, Picasso, Monet, and Manet) and contemporary (the gathering of women). More important, she is the one who holds the power and tools of representation and the one who reverses the male gaze to focus on the exposed white male body.[16]

In a similar fashion, the fourth quilt, *The Sunflower Quilting Bee at Arles* (1991) (fig. 7.4), appropriates Vincent van Gogh's famous sunflowers. This time, however, Ringgold represents not a collection of contemporary artists but an imagined gathering of historical African American women activists. Here Ringgold presents another visual compression of time, gathering nineteenth- and twentieth-century African American artists and activists. Left to right are Madame C. J. Walker, Sojourner Truth, Ida B. Wells, Fannie Lou Hamer, Harriet Tubman, Rosa Parks, Mary McLeod Bethune, and Ella Baker. This imaginary assemblage, the

FIGURE 7.3.
Faith Ringgold.
*The Picnic at Giverny. The French Collection*, Part I: #3, 1991.
(Acrylic on canvas; painted, tie-dyed, and pieced fabric, 73½ × 90½ in. © Faith Ringgold 1991. Courtesy of Faith Ringgold.)

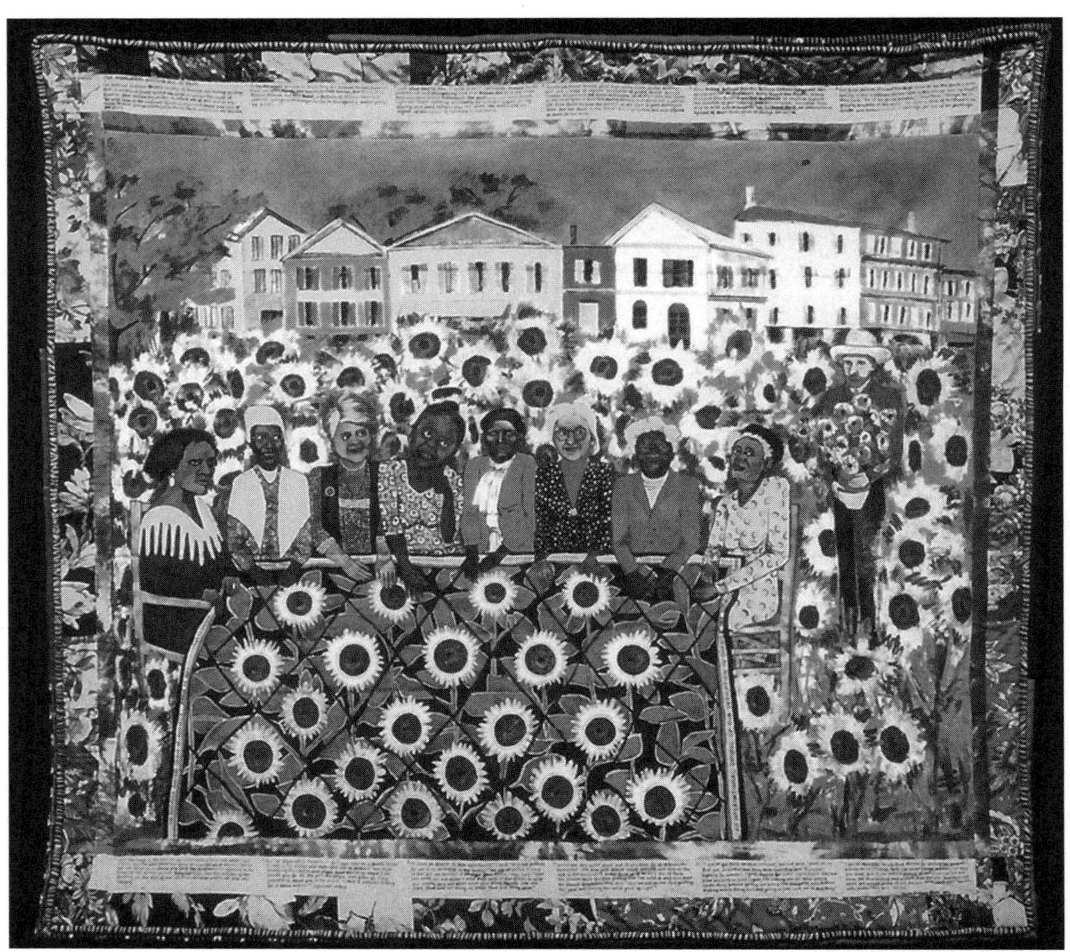



FIGURE 7.4.
Faith Ringgold. *The Sunflower Quilting Bee at Arles: The French Collection, Part I: #4*, 1991. (Acrylic on canvas; painted and tie-dyed fabric, 74 × 80 in. © Faith Ringgold 1991. Courtesy of Faith Ringgold.)

National Sunflower Quilters Society of America, has gathered in southern France to work on a quilt of sunflowers. Aunt Melissa has asked Simone to "take good care of them in that foreign country" because "these women are our freedom" (Cameron 133, 10). A shy van Gogh, who stands behind the women holding a van Gogh–ish vase of sunflowers, seems to await their acknowledgment. Van Gogh becomes a focal point not only for Ringgold's implicit invocation of Western art but for her explicit articulation of the sins of the past. When Sojourner Truth reveals that she lost a child to "a Dutch slaver in the West Indies" (Cameron 133, 10), the women ponder: Should the Dutch man be held accountable for what his countrymen had done? Concerned for the expatriate Simone, they ask whether Europe is a "natural setting" for "a black woman"? Simone explains to the women that she went to France to "seek opportunity" that was unavailable to her in the United States. The visual narrative shows that as the women discuss history, they are stitching a rep-

     Art-Based Image-and-Text Forms

resentation of a field of sunflowers in which they are sitting, which is Ringgold's representation of van Gogh's paintings of "real" sunflowers. The representational trail is elaborate, but Ringgold's "real quilting," her "real art," as one of her characters says, is aimed at "making this world piece up right" (Cameron 133, 10). Part of that process is piecing together an alternative history capacious and audacious enough to include African Americans, women, and artists and, most explicitly, African American women artists.

In *Picasso's Studio* (fig. 7.5), Ringgold continues her visual interplay with canonical artists. In this quilt, Ringgold imagines Simone posing as a model for Pablo Picasso. Alert, yet relaxed, the nude model perches atop a quilt-covered divan. Simone seems to levitate in midair directly in front of Ringgold's repainting of Picasso's *Les Demoiselles d'Avignon*. With her pose and positioning, Simone almost merges into the painting of the women. She is surrounded by reproductions of cubist paintings and drawings. To her right (top left of canvas), two African masks hang as a reminder of the original inspiration for cubism. On the bottom left, Picasso stands before his easel, about to place his mark on the blank canvas. Significantly, he stares intently at the canvas, not at his model, Simone, a not-so-subtle reminder that Picasso and other European artists imagined Africa without having really seen it. "The European artists took a look at us and changed the way they saw themselves" (Cameron 137, 5), Simone notes. Ringgold's daughter, English professor Michele Wallace, who writes about African American visual culture, claims that unlike "the positive scene of instruction of Afro-American and Euro-American music, in which mutual influence and intertextuality is acknowledged . . . , in the negative scene of instruction of Afro-American art and Euro-American art the exchange is disavowed and disallowed—no one admits to having learned anything from anyone else" (*Modernism* 45). Ringgold addresses the disavowal of African influence in Western art by setting up a dialogue between Simone and Picasso's prostitutes—depicted in *Le Demoiselles d'Avignon*—who, along with the African masks in the background, remind viewers of how Picasso, and the cubists in general, appropriated objects of African material culture, ignoring their everyday cultural and religious functions and transforming them into art, whose purpose became display and commodification. In her letters, Simone reports hearing voices, both past and present, imagined and real: Aunt Melissa, the African masks, and the prostitutes from Picasso's painting. Aunt Melissa affirms folk wisdom and African beauty and worth, despite the long history of European enslavement of Africans. The African masks, emblems of lost or stolen cultures, encourage Simone to follow her artistic vision. They tell her: "Art is the truth, not the artist" (Cameron 137, 6). Even the brothel women in *Les Demoi-*

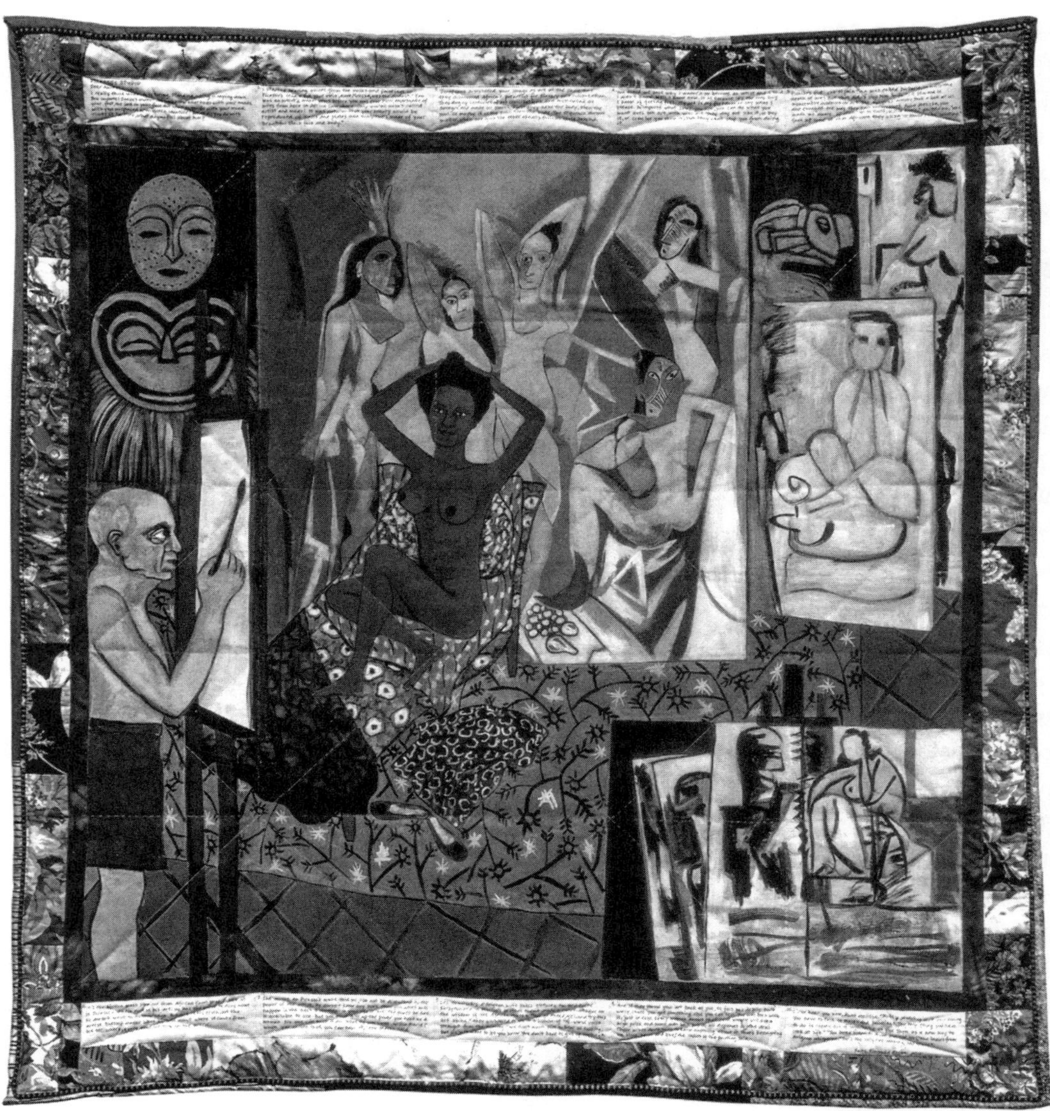

*selles d'Avignon* conspire with Simone, encouraging her to not be intimidated by renowned male artists like Picasso. For Ringgold, hardworking Aunt Melissa articulates wisdom; objects bear witness; art speaks. Collectively, in images and words, these women tell alternative histories and claim boundless possibilities for women of color artists.

Ringgold continues her fanciful historical and artistic linkages in the ninth quilt, *Dinner at Gertrude Stein's* (1991) (fig. 7.6). In this case, she depicts imaginative encounters between African American and European American writers and artists. At the back left, a shy Willia Marie Simone looks approvingly at the unlikely, but fascinating assembly in Gertrude Stein's salon. From left to right, the figures are

    Art-Based Image-and-Text Forms

Leo Stein, Willia Marie Simone, Zora Neale Hurston, James Baldwin, Alice B. Toklas, Gertrude Stein, Pablo Picasso, Richard Wright, Ernest Hemingway, and Langston Hughes. Each figure is separated from the others—no one is touching—as if they are themselves framed in isolation. It goes without saying that this particular configuration of artists and writers never sat together in Stein's home. Dominating the visual field at the center of the picture, Stein is doubled: she holds court in her salon beneath an imposing portrait of herself. The entire scene is narrated in a parody of Gertrude Steinian language with its continuous present tense, inflected with vernacular African American English: "My favorite event of the evening was Zora Neale Hurston reading from her comedic play, *Mule Bone*. Zora is being and making a classic of the black folk culture and language we are always being so ashamed of. It is the way we be being talking when there are no white people being around" (Cameron 140, 10). Mimicking Stein's mimicking of black language and injecting Hurston's language of the folk, Ringgold enacts a reversal of Stein's famous depiction of vernacular African American English in the voice of Melanctha from *Three Lives*. More important, Ringgold speculates about the creative possibilities of artistic encounters that never happened and makes visible Harlem Renaissance writers who were writing outside the hallowed bounds of Stein's salon.

Ringgold's imaginative gathering of artists culminates in *Le Café des Artistes* (1994) (fig. 7.7). As well as being an artist and model, Willia Marie Simone is a café owner, someone who designs the menu and sets the table-tableaux. Here Ringgold again depicts a variety of artists and activists, both alive and deceased.[17] Note how (almost) all eyes are on Simone, who beams happily at the acknowledgment. Notice also that, at the far right, there is a more realistic portrayal of Ringgold, who looks in on the scene with self-reflexive, playful amusement. In this venue, Simone announces "The Colored Woman's Manifesto of Art and Politics." Her manifesto, declaring a woman's right to be an artist, is met with various registers of sexist and racist objections: "'Women should stay at home and make children, not art'"; "'You should learn French cooking. It will help you to blend your couleurs'"; you will "'model for me my African maiden! Earth Mama! Queen of the Nile!'" (Cameron 142, 6, 11, 14). Ringgold both re-creates and challenges the old script that has made the artist's life difficult for women and nearly impossible for women of color.[18] It is not surprising that Simone's manifesto is presented as the penultimate quilt—a dramatic summary of her struggle to be an artist and a rationale for her decision to leave her children.

Echoing an earlier scene with Willia Marie Simone and her son, the final quilt, *Moroccan Holiday* (1997) (fig. 7.8), depicts a reunion and reconciliation between Simone and her daughter, Marlena.[19] In this

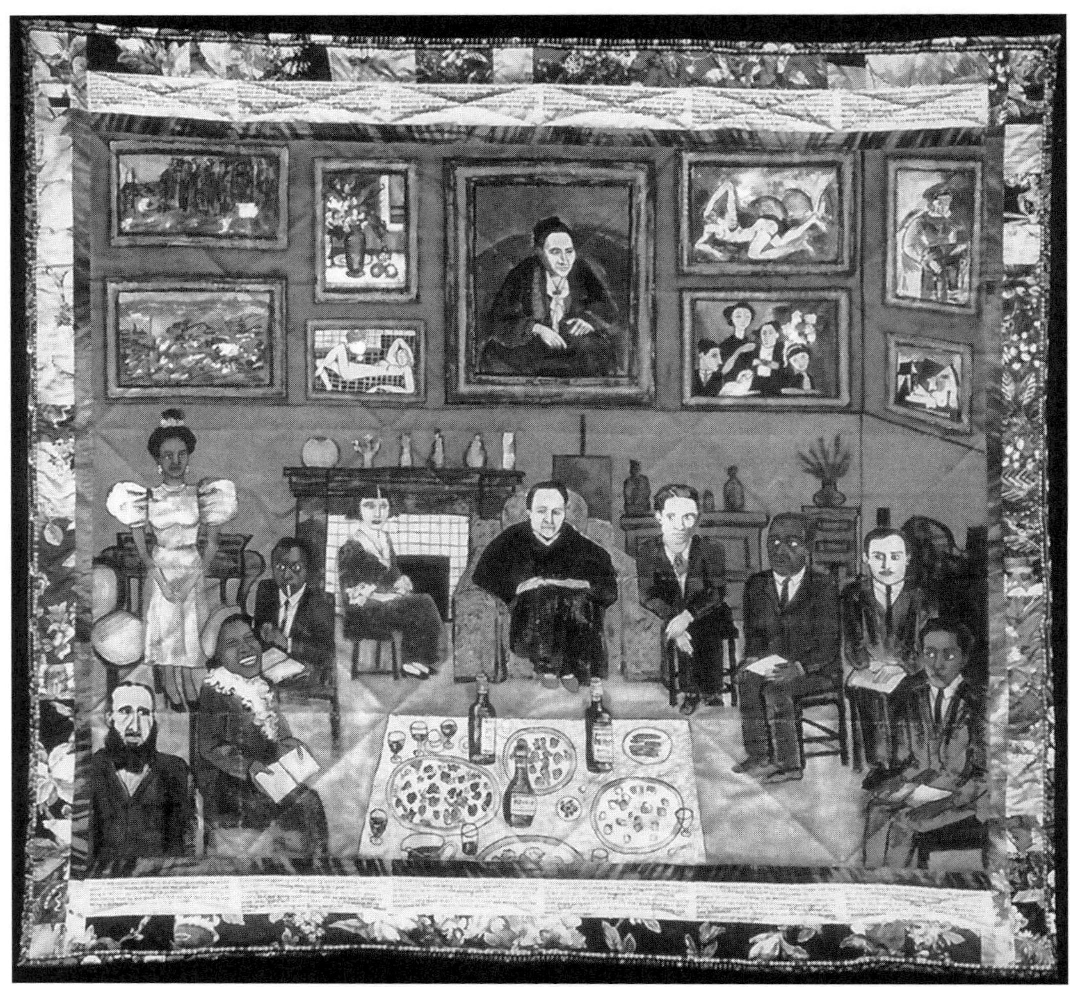



quilt, "we both hear and see Willia Marie's daughter for the first time" (Roth 56). Here, the conflict that has permeated the entire series— can a woman be both a mother and an artist?—is laid bare; here, the daughter, abandoned for the sake of art, is reconciled with her mother. Ringgold stages the reconciliation scene both spatially and temporally, creating a storied site for the encounter. Fittingly, the mother and daughter meet in Simone's studio, surrounded by the materials of her art— paints, brushes, and canvasses. Simone's art, which is what has kept her away from her children, here unites mother and daughter. There are at least two visual exchanges of energy in this quilt: horizontally between mother and daughter and vertically between the large portraits and the women. The visual field is cut horizontally with four dominant portraits of prominent African American men from history (left to right, Frederick Douglass, Marcus Garvey, Malcolm X, and Martin Luther King Jr.)

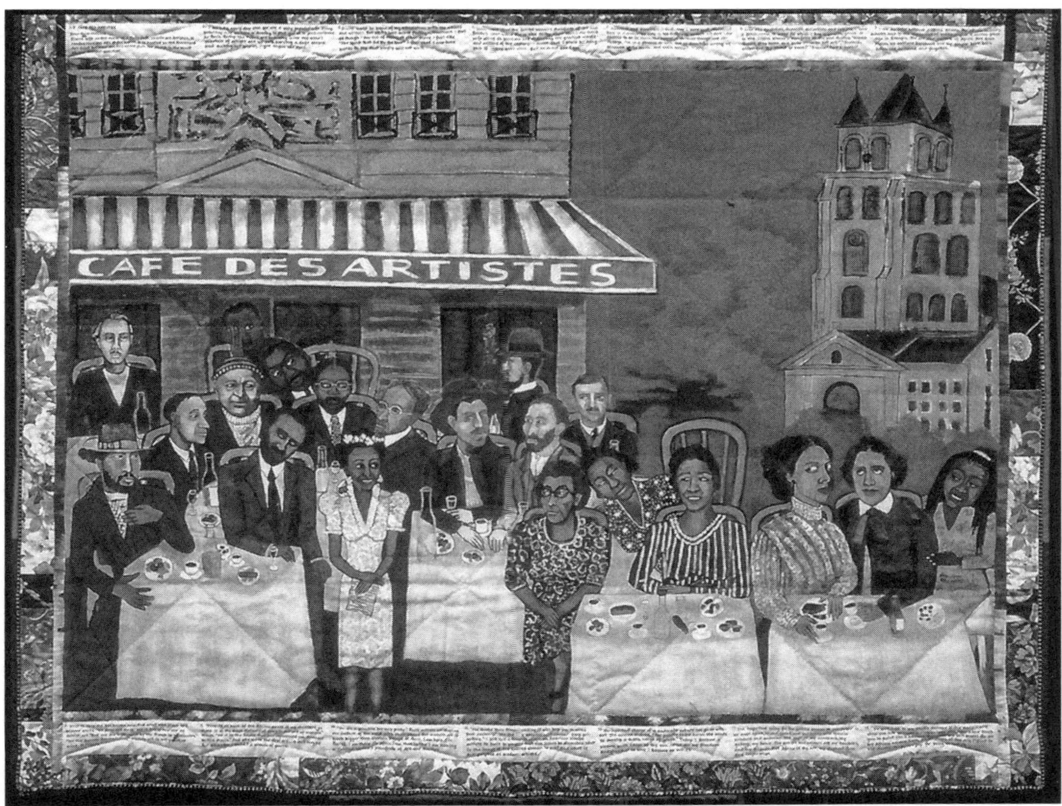



looming above the women. These towering figures of black activism serve as background and inspiration for the painful and intimate conversation between mother and daughter. Simone suggests that these great men served to inspire and enable her achievements, but daughter Marlena reminds her mother that Aunt Melissa, the woman who raised her and her brother, should be represented along with the heroic men who fought for freedom and civil rights. In the end, Marlena forgives her mother and appreciates her for showing not only "how to be a woman but an artist as well" (Cameron 144, 14).

It is important that Willia Marie Simone must enact her own displacement, leaving the relentless racialism and racism of the United States and entering the hegemonic center of art—defined here as European and male. "Power and knowledge can be found in the act of constructing and reconstructing, of reading and rereading, images both of compliance and of resistance" (Hirsch, *Family Frames* 211). Ringgold's *French Collection* reenvisions African American and art history, piecing together a personal and collective story of possibilities for women of color artists and, ultimately, for herself as an artist. Just as slave narratives enacted a black human subjectivity, so Ringgold's story quilts in-

FIGURE 7.7.
Faith Ringgold.
*Le Café des Artistes. The French Collection*,
Part II: #11, 1994.
(Acrylic on canvas; painted, tie-dyed, and pieced fabric, 79½ × 90 in.
© Faith Ringgold 1994. Courtesy of Faith Ringgold.)

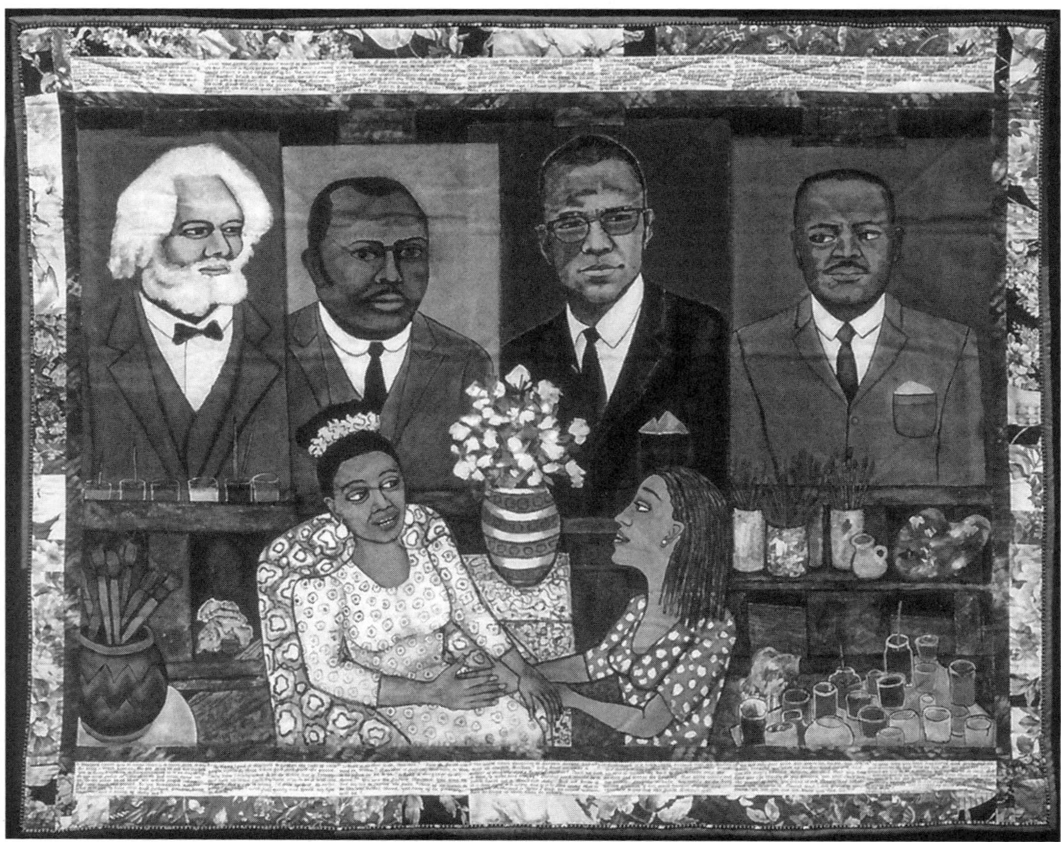



FIGURE 7.8.
Faith Ringgold.
*Moroccan Holiday.*
*The French*
*Collection*, Part II:
#12, 1997.
(Acrylic on canvas;
painted, tie-dyed,
and pieced fabric,
74¾ × 92 in.
© Faith Ringgold
1997. Courtesy of
Faith Ringgold.)

sist on an African American woman's presence and agency. At the same time, the quilts create a provocative union of female-identified American domestic arts—stitching and quilting—and predominantly European male-identified art—painting—that injects complexities of race and gender into Ringgold's retelling of art history in her visual autobiographical narratives.

Experimenting with the form of the quilt, Faith Ringgold pieces together stories about herself, art history, and the history of the United States, especially narrating the struggles of women, artists, and African Americans. In her large, vivid, and dynamic quilt series, she uses image and text to contribute to the late twentieth-century project of liberation, part of the ongoing struggle to free individuals and collectives from oppressive discourses and visual regimes. Criminalized and sexualized by the dominant society, African Americans continue daily to struggle against racist representations and prejudices. Many post–civil rights artists, like Ringgold, are committed to an ongoing interrogation of inherited artistic, historical, and cultural forms and practices. In order to articu-

     Art-Based Image-and-Text Forms

late herself, Ringgold must counter stereotypes, retell history from an African American woman's perspective, and share stories of social un-belonging, including expatriation. By reimagining the past, situating herself in relation to history, and innovating artistic forms, Ringgold makes a place for herself and other women in the creative arts.

# Hachivi Edgar Heap of Birds's Artwork

## "Native Peoples Have Chosen Art as
## Their Cultural Tool and Weapon"

Hachivi Edgar Heap of Birds's artwork is the most art-based
visual autobiography included in this book. His word paintings
emphasize the visuality of letters, the fact that words are images
that we've agreed to read in a certain manner. He challenges
conventional reading practices by giving letters color and
texture, depth and scope, by defamiliarizing words from the
conventions of syntax and paragraph, forcing us to deal with
language as marks on the page or canvas. His abstract paintings
reference shapes and hues of his home in Oklahoma as well as
his global travels. His installations and public art exhibits, which
juxtapose image and text, demand an interactive engagement.

When visitors to the Fifty-Second International Art Exhibition of the
2007 Venice Biennale arrived at Marco Polo International Airport, they
were welcomed by an intriguing billboard (fig. 8.1). The billboard is
one part of Cheyenne-Arapaho conceptual-activist artist Hachivi (pronounced *Hock E Aye Vi*) Edgar Heap of Birds's public artwork, entitled
*Most Serene Republics*, created for the Venice Biennale. The exhibit consists of "a series of text interventions" (Ash-Milby 58) placed throughout Venice: the airport billboard, sign installations, posters, and printed
tote bags given to attendees. Heap of Birds's trilingual text—in English,
Italian, and Cheyenne—exhorts viewers-readers to remember, *rammentare* in Italian. Specifically, Heap of Birds raises awareness of the Native
performers who traveled to Europe in 1890 as part of Buffalo Bill's Wild
West show and who died far from home, their remains never returned
to their homelands.

In this billboard, Heap of Birds's textual design insists that we both
look and read. The notice passes briefly as official signage—"BENVENUTI
... WELCOME TO THE SHOW," but both its content and form disrupt the
process of reading. Viewers are startled by the reference to the historic
figure of Buffalo Bill; they are baffled by the Cheyenne words—*nastona*
and *numshim*—that Heap of Birds translates respectively as "our daughters" and "our grandfathers." Below each of these Cheyenne words, he

FIGURE 8.1. Edgar Heap of Birds. *Most Serene Republics* airport billboard (Venice Biennale, 2007). (From the collection of the artist. Courtesy of Edgar Heap of Birds.)

names those who perished. The act of naming serves as an act of remembrance and a call for repatriation. The polyphony of English, Italian, and Cheyenne suggests the transnational experience of Native performers and the collision of cultures in a colonial context. Heap of Birds recalls these nineteenth-century Native losses in the expansive context of "the violent origins of most nation-states, created through the destruction or subjugation of other cultures" (Lowe 14). The trilingual text is framed all around by alternating icons: the Christian cross in the center of a shield and a "Cheyenne warrior society shield" featuring an eagle (Heap of Birds e-mail). A well-known symbol of the Christian Crusades, a bloody conquest that extended into global colonization, alternates with an image of the Cheyenne resistance to European invasion. The clash of Christian and indigenous cultures frames the text, visualizing the historic context. As a result of Christian colonization of the so-called New World, Native people lost autonomy, with some performing "Indianness" for non-Native audiences as part of Buffalo Bill's Wild West.

More than one hundred years later, Heap of Birds traveled to a prominent art world center and the prestigious Venice Biennale in Europe to communicate an indigenous account of the history and legacy of violence and colonialism. His art, like the nineteenth-century ledger book art of Native warriors imprisoned at Fort Marion, in Saint Augustine, Florida, is a form of resistance and renewal. Although there is nothing explicitly autobiographical here—we don't learn about Heap of Birds's childhood or his development as an artist, his favorite color or his family life—Heap of Birds's focus on memory, history, and community is central to his self-fashioning. He makes visible a history of Native erasure, a necessary first step in articulating a contemporary, collective, and sovereign Native identity. To enter fully into a Cheyenne-Arapaho subjectivity, Heap of Birds must renarrate colonial history from an indigenous perspective and bring home the remains of scattered ancestors.

In his artwork Heap of Birds appropriates colonial and settler discourses of place and time, transforming their meaning in the process. Like Leslie

Marmon Silko (see chapter 2), Heap of Birds insists that American land is indigenous land and that Native people have a right to narrate American history. Place (origins, home, social position) is a problem for Native Americans, but not as a generalized (post)modern symptom of alienation. Frontiers, borderlands, contact zones, and boundary cultures are not merely spatial metaphors but sites of contested and cacophonous transcultural interaction. Historically, indigenous people have been *dis*placed from homelands (cultures, languages) and *re*placed elsewhere. How does one relate to one's home when that home and land have been stolen, when one is *dis*placed, or when one's homeland has been subsumed by settler society?

In addition, the language used to describe place in mainstream discourse has come under scrutiny, its Eurocentric assumptions revealed. For many Native people such as Silko, terms such as "wilderness," "wild," "frontier," and "landscape" all reveal a colonizer's point of view: an us versus them mentality that rationalizes scopically and literally subduing the dangerous Other—figured as Native—ensconced in those zones. For a Native person with a long history of residence in one place, stories of place are both personal and cultural. Further, when people are removed from their homelands and partially or completely dispossessed of cultures and languages, stories—or revisions of stories—can help restore their relationship to home. This is not political escapism, artistic conservatism, or romantic nostalgia. Examining the African, Native, and African-Native presence in literature is part of "an understanding of literature as a process of both *emancipation* [of the enslaved black body] and *sovereignty* [of the enslaved red nation] (Holland, "'If You Know'" 337, emphasis in the original).

Noting "the intersection of a politics of location and a politics of displacement" in the 1970s and 1980s, Caren Kaplan claims that it "marks a postmodern moment in which mapping and storytelling vie as technologies of identity formation" (Kaplan, "Reconfigurations of Geography" 27). And Jean Fisher reanimates this idea almost twenty years later when she claims: it is "the task of the intellectual, the storyteller, to reconstitute cultural memory . . . to produce a new national consciousness" (39). Countering racist representations of Native Americans as anthropological specimens, who are deemed most authentic when frozen in an (European) imagined past, has been a challenge to indigenous writers and artists since at least the nineteenth century. Through his interart interventions, Heap of Birds activates "the ethics and transformative possibilities of representation" (Somerville and Justice 242) and contributes to this ongoing process of indigenous re-membering.

With the centrality of spatial metaphors in mind, I consider mapping and storytelling as technologies of Native identity formation in the work of Heap of Birds. Heap of Birds reconfigures traditional Western definitions of the autobiographical and revises U.S. history by using images and texts in innovative relation to each other, by exposing historical erasures and misrepresentations, and by reconstituting the autobiographical subject as both individual and relational, local and global. In his work, autobiography is neither a linear narrative depicting a singular subject nor straightforward self-portraiture. Instead, he maps himself in place and time through storytelling and image-making. I am not so much interested in the mapping of space as much as I am in autotopography: the precise positioning of oneself in place and time and the visual self-representations and self-narrations of such self-mapping.[1] In the artwork I discuss in this chapter, Heap of Birds, like Carrie Mae Weems (see chapter 6) and Faith Ringgold (see chapter 7), finds it necessary to revise the stories of official history embedded in literature and art in order to formulate his understanding of himself, and thus to create and claim a place from which to be seen and heard.

In the service of the settler society, official U.S. histories distorted or erased indigenous people: the inevitable disappearance of the so-called primitive was rationalized as a necessary sacrifice for the progress of nation-building. In order to become visible as Native subjects, not merely as degraded or romanticized stereotypes, Native artists, writers, and activists continue to challenge historical misrepresentations. Like many marginalized groups, they must intervene in a long history of textual and visual domination to simultaneously revise historical representations and generate more accurate and dynamic ones. Heap of Birds creates works that seamlessly blend visual-verbal interfaces. His work often includes a temporal interface as he tells a story or revises a history. Often, he creates spatial interfaces in which one surface reorients viewers to another, requiring new modes of looking. Quite often, Heap of Birds employs a contextual interface, emphasizing sociopolitical contexts. In the process, he generates a dynamic dialogue with the audience as viewers-readers are forced to grapple with new modes of looking at and reading diverse formulations of the visual-verbal interface.

Like Faith Ringgold, Edgar Heap of Birds is trained in the Western European art tradition. He made a conscious decision to articulate his personal and community history by exploring both Native North American and European art forms. As "the creator of some of the earliest and most memorable conceptual Native American art in the United States" (Lowe 11),[2] Heap of Birds has explained that he tries to work in a way that unifies both Native and non-Native modes and to resist easy pigeonholing as an Indian artist. "For today's Native artists," he writes, "it is imperative to pronounce strong personal observations concerning the individual and political conditions that we experience. At times this visual expression should speak of human rights and issues of tribal sovereignty, but most important, our art must articulate viewpoints from a deeply personal perspective" ("Of Circularity" 66). That is, like other Native American artists, Heap of Birds attempts to address past and present, local and global, individual and collective, and to insist on a contemporary—not museumized—Native identity (Heap of Birds, "Born from Sharp Rocks" 343).[3] A "headsman of the traditional Cheyenne Elk Warrior Society" (343), one of several "tribal organizations of renewal and protection" ("Of Circularity" 66), Heap of Birds considers himself a modern "warrior" who fights to keep alive Tsistsistas (Cheyenne) culture and language. "Today strong artworks with the warrior spirit, such as these from Fort Marion," he explains, "remain as a method of a more modern warfare" (*16 Songs*). Like the nineteenth-century ledgerbook artists imprisoned in Fort Marion,[4] Heap of Birds uses visual-verbal forms as a way of making visible Native people. Even though they are separated by more than a century, the pictographers and Heap of Birds share certain concerns: resisting social and cultural captivity and erasure, negotiating with and critiquing the dominant society, and retaining or reclaiming tribal community values and ideals. Heap of Birds sees himself as "on the edge of battle to re-educate non-Native peoples" about Indians (*16 Songs*). For him art is both a (multi)cultural tool and a weapon. Like Ringgold, he asks: How can any artist educate and politicize, yet resist didacticism? Or move beyond realism? "Do I make a bunch of narrative paintings of Custer killing children in the Washita River?" Heap of Birds asks (*16 Songs*).

Heap of Birds answers this question by working in a variety of forms: public art in which he asserts, simultaneously, a historical and a contemporary Native presence into the local context; word drawings; abstract paintings; and critical writing about art.[5] In each of these forms, "distinct but reinforcing aesthetic modes" (Rushing 365), Heap of Birds forces his viewers to reenvision what we thought we knew. Each of his site-specific public art projects focuses on history and place and the necessity of understanding them in order to know yourself—as an individual and a people. In one of his earliest public art installations, *In Our Language* (1982), created two years after he moved to the Cheyenne-Arapaho reservation in western Oklahoma, Heap of Birds designed a twenty-foot by forty-foot lightboard for Times Square in New York City. For two weeks, every twenty minutes the Tsistsistas (Cheyenne) "spoke" in the Cheyenne language about their views of the "white man." The lightboard illuminated about one word per minute—like a drumbeat, Heap of Birds explains:

    Art-Based Image-and-Text Forms

Heap of Birds describes this as an act of translation in which he conveys bilingually what some members of his Tsistsistas (Cheyenne) community say about the history of European American treatment of indigenous people. The form of presentation resists easy comprehension. Because just one word is displayed per minute, a viewer in kinetic and image-overladen downtown New York City could pass by without viewing the entire piece or even realizing that "Tsistsistas" translates as "Cheyenne." This emphasizes the alienation of a non-Cheyenne-speaking viewer-reader, as well as the gaps and interruptions inherent in any linguistic and cultural translation. Here, Heap of Birds turns the table on the image of Native people as nonliterate. In this installation, all non-Cheyenne-speaking people are othered. Even more significantly, the associations with Vehoe, the Cheyenne Trickster Spider, suggest that the "white man" has "wrapped up," entrapped, contained, and restrained Native bodies—with European clothing and prisons—and lands—not only with fences but with imprisonment and outright dispossession. Such images of containment suggest also how non-Native religious and political ideologies "wrap up" Native subjectivities and communities as well as curtail Native histories.

In his 1988 public installation, entitled *Native Hosts* (fig. 8.2), Heap of Birds continues his efforts to reveal the Native presence that European American history has attempted to erase. He placed twelve aluminum road signs in City Hall Park in Manhattan. As drivers and walkers commute to their destinations, they are reminded of the genocide—the absent, indigenous nations that lie beneath the cities and villages of what is now the United States. It is significant and purposeful that, in a dramatic act of appropriation, Heap of Birds purposefully employs the state and county producers of highway signage to make the signs for this installation; that is, he uses the dominant system of mapping and naming itself to criticize its own existence. The physical authoritativeness of the signs contrasts with their perplexing written messages, and, Jackson Rushing reminds us, they underscore an ironic twist on "the idea of 'Indian sign language'" (376). Like Ringgold, who mimics West-

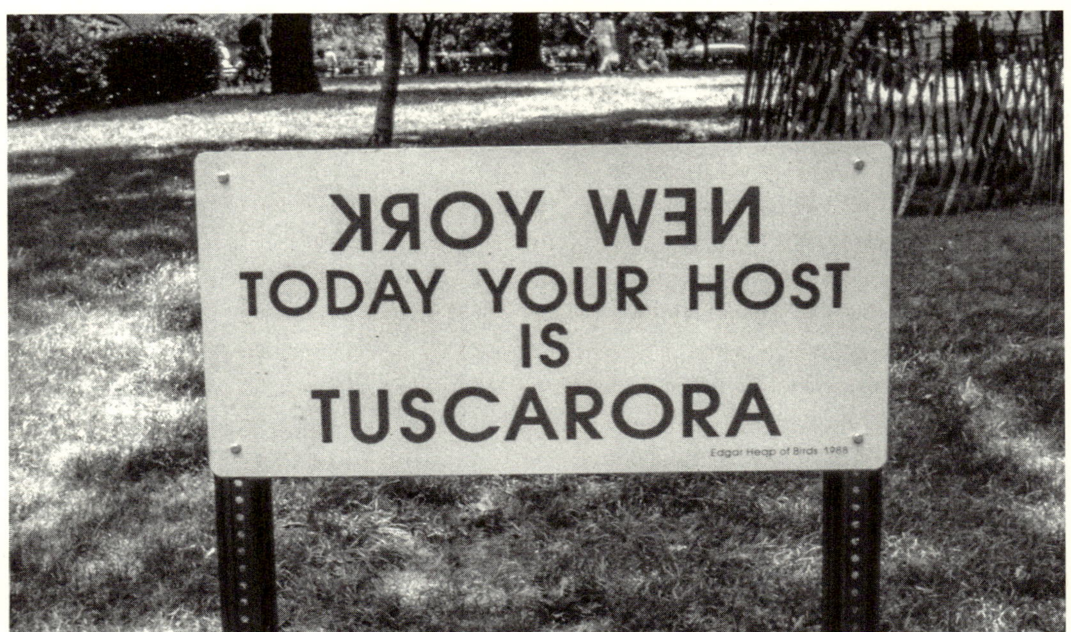




ern masters in order to prove her artistic skills and to critique omissions in art history, Heap of Birds reproduces state signs, but with a critical difference. The signs—from the modes and material of their production to their placement—reproduce exactly official state road signs. Only the message is from a radically different perspective. Rather than a sign that is overlaid upon a land—as is all colonizing mapping—announcing with assurance where you are and how far it is to where you are headed, each of these signs reverses the colonizing position. The mirrored lettering of ꓘЯOY WƎИ suggests that the city is backwards, wrong. The letters "symbolically reverse the claims of the post-Columbian city and . . . force the viewer to face (back into) the past" (Slocum n.p.). Mirrored words "disrupt legibility" (Slocum 2). In addition, the distorted words cannot be trusted; they recall the treacherous use of alphabetic literacy—broken treaties, fraudulent land deeds, enforced assimilation through boarding school education—against indigenous people. *Native Hosts* asks the question: Do you know where you are? "Manhattan," Heap of Birds reminds us, was "a nation of people, not a city on an island."[6]

Like *Native Hosts*, Heap of Birds's *Who Owns History?* is a collection of twenty-five state and federal signs (fig. 8.3). This time Heap of Birds placed the signs at historic sites where they serve as counterhistories, corrections to an official U.S. history of Native erasure. Like the public signage in *Native Hosts*, that in *Who Owns History?* coerces viewers into a reconsideration of the country's official history. Far from being an objective account of fact, the dominant history ignores or suppresses the narratives of conquest and violence that undergird it. Again appropriating official signage and using a simple technique of public sign juxtaposition, Heap of Birds exposes the silences and lies embedded in the state-sanctioned histories. What led to the Fort Pitt Museum at Point State Park in Pittsburgh, Pennsylvania, as it stands today? The official Point State Park website explains that the site "commemorates and preserves the strategic and historic heritage of the area during the French and Indian War (1754–63)."[7] Heap of Birds offers an alternative explanation: the "Anglo Saxon," fueled by their own fictions of "supremacy" and manifest "destiny," won "victory" over the land and its people and thus now have the power of representation. From New York City to Pittsburgh to Denver to San Jose to Seattle, Heap of Birds has continued his practice of researching local histories and producing site-specific artistic interventions on behalf of indigenous people.[8]

In 2007, Heap of Birds expanded the scale of his site-specific historical interventions to a global level when he represented the National Museum of the American Indian at the Fifty-Second International Art Exhibition in Venice. Heap of Birds's installation, *Most Serene Republics,* is "a public art installation of multilingual signage in Italian, English, and Cheyenne" (Gover 8). Lucy Lippard notes that the recurrent Italian word *rammentare*—"remember," but also literally "rethink"—is the key word in Heap of Birds's Venice signs. He "asked the people of Venice and the international art world to honor the American Indians who had died in Wild West shows, with the goal of bringing home their remains" ("Signs of Unrest" 31). Furthermore, exhibition curators Kathleen Ash-Milby and Truman Lowe describe Heap of Birds's installation as generating discussion not only about Native Americans but about "the creation of republics or nation-states through acts of aggression, displacement, or replacement of populations or cultures" (58)—that is, about the global proportions of European colonization of indigenous peoples. Heap of Birds's public signs play with a contextual visual-verbal interface in which location (city centers, parks, and highways, as well as gallery spaces), history, and politics are provoked into dialogue. Through his art practice, Heap of Birds exposes the treacherous history of so-called civilized nations and reveals how the lives of human beings in the twenty-first century are more interconnected than ever.

In addition to having created site-specific public projects, Heap of Birds is well known for his word paintings, which he calls "wall lyrics," underscoring their poetic rhythms as well as their visual registers. Inspired by finding, through his own research, a list of the names of all the nineteenth-century Cheyenne and Arapaho warriors imprisoned at Fort Marion between 1875 and 1878, among them his relatives, Heap of Birds created *Fort Marion Lizards* (1979), a work that is "a key early work

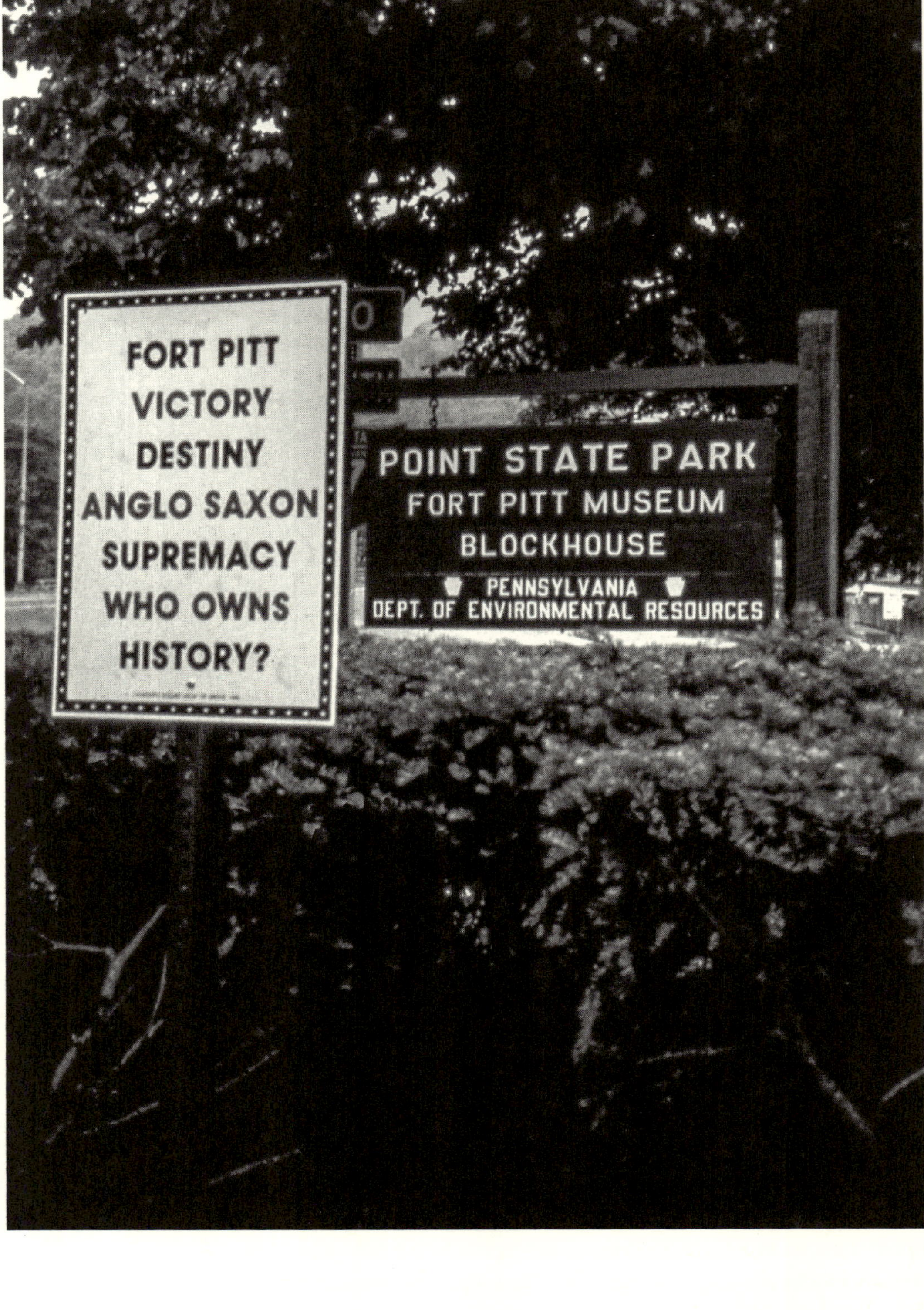

FORT PITT
VICTORY
DESTINY
ANGLO SAXON
SUPREMACY
WHO OWNS
HISTORY?
POINT STATE PARK
FORT PITT MUSEUM
BLOCKHOUSE
PENNSYLVANIA
DEPT. OF ENVIRONMENTAL RESOURCES

in terms of establishing the primacy of words in [Heap of Birds's] artistic arsenal" (Rushing 370). A movable memorial, *Fort Marion Lizards* is an eight-foot-tall word painting. The painting notates history, using words as documentary but also as image. This is "a big painting," Heap of Birds explains, "of just the words" (*16 Songs*). The red words refer to his relatives who died at Fort Marion. The choice of words over image is important because, as Heap of Birds notes, his ancestors were not merely placed in a literal prison in Fort Marion, Florida, but also situated in a larger and more enduring linguistic-cultural prison that imposed on them the English language, Christianity, and European American cultural practices. More than a hundred years later, Heap of Birds resurrects and recalls the prisoners' names, overturning a long silence and turning words from an oppressors' mode of imprisonment to a Native form of resistance and education.

Whereas nineteenth-century pictographic artists used images as narrative—and sometimes added words, often in syllabary, to translate the pictography, Heap of Birds uses words in these paintings not only as referents but also as images. In a familiar poststructuralist move, he empties the letters and words of their referentiality, at least momentarily, forcing us to attend to his black-and-white or multicolored writing as shapes and marks on the canvas. Some viewers try to read his word paintings, such as *Peru-South* (a pastel on paper, 90 inches by 110 inches) (fig. 8.4), looking for patterns, rhymes, alliteration, thematic linkages, or color coordination. Although everyone notes the dynamic vitality of each word and the collection of words overall, it is important to emphasize the processual materiality of the words as well. Heap of Birds uses many strong lines to make each letter and word, calling attention to the historically embedded layers of meaning in each.

Although there is no clear design, there are some color associations in this painting: "stars," "sun," and "corn," positive images associated with nature and life, for instance, are yellow, but in contradiction so are the less explicit "tail" and the decidedly antireferential "gray." Seemingly negative images of "knots," "cross," and "tie," words reminiscent of the Vehoe's/White Man's "wrapping up" of Native bodies and lands, are green, but so are the positive images and concepts of "pine," "fruit," "yellow," "better," and "respect." It helps somewhat to realize that this word painting is part of a four-part structure associated with the four directions—an organizing device common to many Native American ceremonial and storytelling practices—that, in fact, the piece is related to place: South (southern Oklahoma, the southern United States, and Peru). This painting, then, is one point on Heap of Birds's compass of personal and collective self-mapping that links contemporary and his-

(OPPOSITE)
FIGURE 8.3.
Edgar Heap
of Birds. State
museum sign
installation,
*Who Owns
History?*, 1991.
(From the
collection of the
artist. Courtesy
of Edgar Heap
of Birds.)

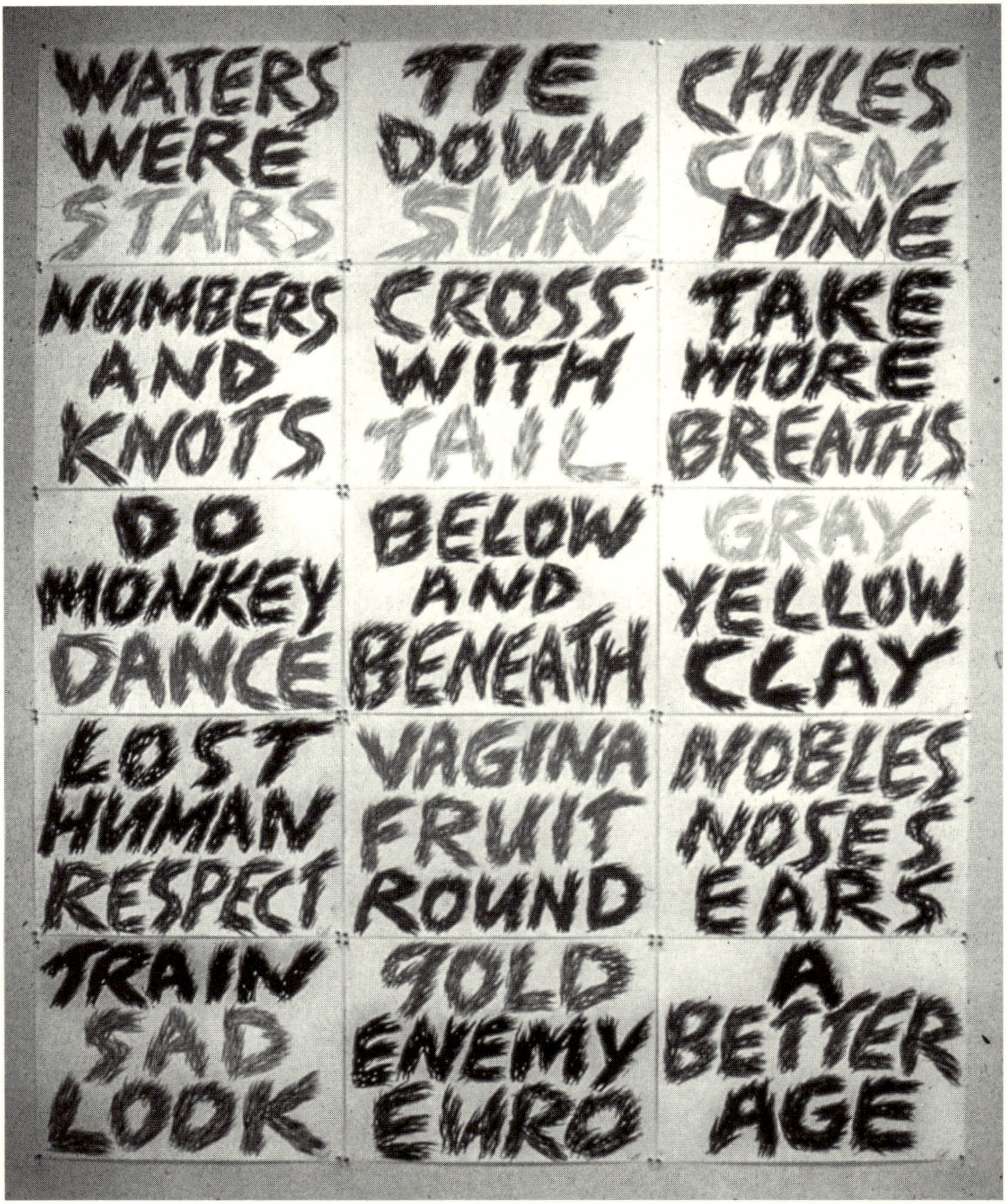

WATERS
WERE
STARS

TIE
DOWN
SUN

CHILES
CORN
PINE

NUMBERS
AND
KNOTS

CROSS
WITH
TAIL

TAKE
MORE
BREATHS

DO
MONKEY
DANCE

BELOW
AND
BENEATH

GRAY
YELLOW
CLAY

LOST
HUMAN
RESPECT

VAGINA
FRUIT
ROUND

NOBLES
NOSES
EARS

TRAIN
SAD
LOOK

GOLD
ENEMY
EURO

A
BETTER
AGE

torical representations. Displayed together, the word paintings present a diagram of self based on a Cheyenne place-specific epistemology, but through the medium of English words. Appropriating the colonizers' language as his own, Heap of Birds relies on the written word in his wall lyrics, but at the same time, he destabilizes conventional ideas about and uses of alphabetic literacy.

Another of Heap of Birds's wall lyrics, HEH WAH MAUN STUN HE DUN, or *What Makes a Man* (1987), consists of "poetic phrases drawn in pastel on rectangular sheets of rag paper" and "combined to make a composite whole" (Rushing 373). Art critics praise the "roughly scrawled, rhythmic character" (Matthews 18) of Heap of Birds's painted words, while others describe them using vivid imagery: "Some letters consist of slashing diagonal strokes, while others are wiry like steel wool or prickly like barbed wire, and still others flicker like flames or lie down like blades of grass in the wind" (Rushing 373). Dynamism, again, is a key feature of these wall lyrics. This time, however, just as Ringgold interrogates what it means to be a woman and an artist and an African American, Heap of Birds tackles the question of what it means to be a Native American man. How is it possible to dismantle colonizing gendered identities? What does it mean to be neither an anthropological specimen nor a cultural representative, neither an authentic, romanticized figure of the past nor a caricature Indian, but a contemporary Cheyenne man who is a husband, father, son, community member, artist, and individual? Significantly, in the exhibition *What Makes a Man* Heap of Birds juxtaposed his wall lyrics with some of his *Neuf* paintings (see fig. 8.5), linking gender, race, history, contemporaneity, and place within a Cheyenne epistemology that sees cyclical rather than linear patterns and place-specific self-formations. What Shanna Ketchum says about Heap of Birds's later projects *Diary of Trees* and *Wheel* is true also for *What Makes a Man*: "As a form of art in resistance to institutional ideologies, Heap of Birds succeeds in organising his body of work empowered by historical responsibility and artistic visioning. . . . The conceptual programme . . . is based . . . on Native American metaphysics of time and space" (361).

In all of his many artistic forms are embedded "coded little stories" (*16 Songs*), Heap of Birds says. But the fragmentation—reflective of postmodern deconstruction, perhaps, but also of indigenous multiplicity—is dominant. Like Ringgold's piecing and careful positioning of textual narration and description, Heap of Birds's work offers only fragments, only bits of knowledge, and it is the viewer who must find "all the pieces [to] put it together" (*16 Songs*). Heap of Birds presents story shards sharp enough to rip open official histories, challenging viewers to reformulate notions of Native American history and subjectivity. Heap of Birds's

(OPPOSITE)
FIGURE 8.4.
Edgar Heap
of Birds. Word
painting, *Peru-
South*, 1991 (pastel
on paper).
(From the
collection of the
artist. Courtesy
of Edgar Heap
of Birds.)

work might be criticized as limited to two of four "conditions that still affect the work of Native American contemporary artists and curators": the discourses of the Past, Gatekeeping, Postcolonialism, and the Center/Periphery (McMaster, "Introduction" 17). Heap of Birds, clearly, focuses extensively on the discourses of the Past and the Center/Periphery, but with an eye to a vision of a future postcolonial condition.[9] His work contributes to the reclaiming of indigenous perspectives on the past and the articulation of multiple sites of subjectivity that both reify and challenge the Center/Periphery. These are necessary steps toward the possibility of envisioning an indigenous aesthetic that encompasses the many local and global sites of indigeneity that so many contemporary Native intellectuals are positing. In fact, rather than participating in a racialized or nationalist form of gatekeeping, deciding who is Native and what Native American art should be, Heap of Birds unhinges the gates themselves. He invites Native artists to go beyond narrowly defined Indian art, still too often associated in the popular imagination with feathers and beads and anthropological notions of tradition. He demonstrates how Native artists can and should create whatever they envision—as indigenous people, contemporary individuals, and global citizens with roots in their homelands.

Although Heap of Birds stridently criticizes the colonizers of Native bodies, histories, and lands, he also offers possible routes to reconciliation with the past. Honest acknowledgment of history from an indigenous perspective is only one step. In his abstract but, ironically, more explicitly autobiographical paintings he returns to his relationship with the land, particularly Oklahoma and its landforms, lakes, and trees (fig. 8.5). "This is where my paintings come from" (*16 Songs*), he says. Just as his word paintings are resistant in their disruption of referentiality, so too are his landform paintings in that they are nonfigurative—abstract suggestions of shapes and hues, rather than explicit hills or cottonwoods. Both modes of resistant representation, he insists, are versions of his visual autobiography. In his ongoing *Neuf Series*, the shapes and colors allude to a highly personal and place-specific set of natural forms, the cedars, grasslands, and red earth of Oklahoma and, later, include sensuous water images associated with his experiences of the Great Barrier Reef off the shore of Australia.

In the Tsistsistas (Cheyenne) language *neuf* means "four," a sacred number associated with the four directions. This painting is part of a series of spiritual, cultural, and geographical self-mappings. While viewers learn nothing about the details of Heap of Birds's life, they do see a spiritual-political self-positioning, reminiscent of the painted shields of Plains Indian men, who, well into the nineteenth century, depicted their spiritual aspirations and accomplishments in a diagram of self.[10] Like

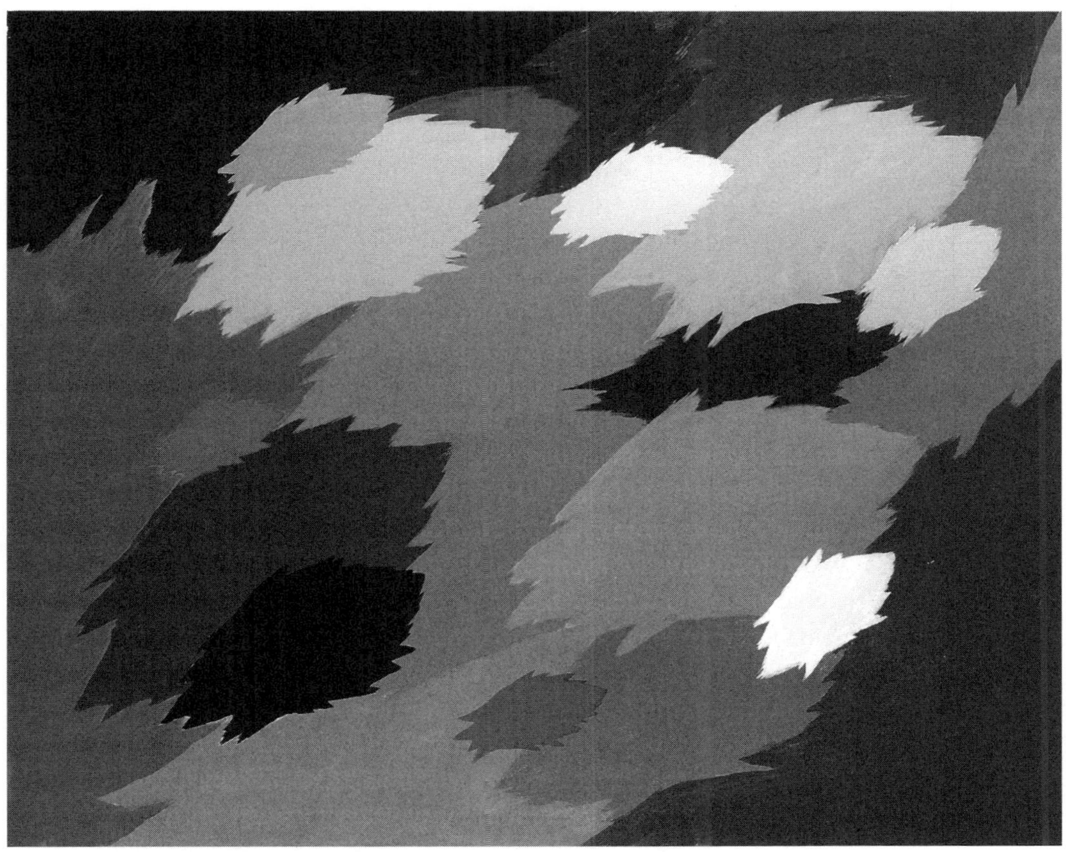

them, Heap of Birds maps himself in relation to each of the four directions as well as to his Cheyenne land—in what is now Oklahoma—and
the increasingly small globe; he positions himself in a profoundly local,
yet radically global geography, a particular place called home.

In his process of cultural, visual, and textual self-articulation, Heap
of Birds challenges stereotypes about Native Americans and attempts to
subvert the dominant discourse of American history. Like some other
male Native American artists and writers (N. Scott Momaday and Gerald
Vizenor come to mind), Heap of Birds considers himself a word warrior.
His aim is to reclaim his Tsistsistas (Cheyenne) language, name, and
nation and, in so doing, construct a contemporary Native subjectivity
capacious enough for all the contradictions and cultural crossings of a
complex contemporary world. Increasingly, Heap of Birds initiates transnational indigenous dialogues and art practices that link geographically
disparate but commonly colonized indigenous personal and communal
histories. He has traveled to Australia, South Africa, and the Americas
to meet with indigenous people who share their histories, cultures, epistemologies, languages, and political interventions in the form of artistic

FIGURE 8.5.
Edgar Heap of
Birds. *Landform*,
the *Neuf
Series*, 1990.
(From the
collection of the
artist. Courtesy
of Edgar Heap
of Birds.)

practices. In this way, Heap of Birds develops a transnational network of indigenous artists whose members, Paul Chaat Smith proclaims, are "rising to the challenge of creating [their] own visual history" (136).[11]

Edgar Heap of Birds uses image and text to contribute to the late twentieth-century project of decolonization, part of the ongoing struggle to free individuals and collectives from oppressive discourses and visual regimes. Either villainized or romanticized, Native people have all too often been objectified by the dominant society and transformed into ethnic commodities. Although his projects of self-construction may seem to be fraught with the trappings of enlightenment notions of self-invention and the dangers of identity politics or cultural and ethnic nationalism, such asserting, reclaiming, and inventing an identity is necessary for internally (or neo-) colonized Native Americans seeking cultural and political autonomy.

Pulitzer Prize–winning Kiowa writer N. Scott Momaday has said that "the greatest tragedy that can befall us is to go unimagined" ("Man Made of Words" 167). Heap of Birds suggests that it is far graver to leave yourself to the imaginings of others. In order to articulate his distinctive, contemporary, transcultural subjectivity, Heap of Birds must counter stereotypes, retell history from indigenous perspectives, and share stories of place—including displacement, removal, and relocation—with a particular focus on home or homeland. Only by situating himself in relation to history (time) and place (space and memory), only by temporalizing place (calling attention to the historical palimpsest of indigenous presence), and only by revisualizing himself in modes that require new ways of seeing-reading at the visual-verbal interface can Heap of Birds create a site of personal and collective visibility—a prerequisite for establishing an inclusive and diverse twenty-first-century global art and literature.

# Coda

## Image-Text Interfaces, Material and Digital

Although images and words have a long history of relationship and writers and artists have always experimented with them, the post–civil rights era in the United States gave rise to a period of particularly intense innovation in autobiographical expression in text and image. The coalescence of rebellion against historic modes of thought, heightened awareness of the politics of race and gender, and challenges to the artificiality of disciplinary silos resulted in a storm of innovative self-expression. In *Picturing Identity*, I have examined a broad spectrum of hybrid autobiographical forms in image and text. Produced by writers and artists alike, these self-representations and self-narrations play with visual-verbal interfaces—the coalescence, juxtaposition, or relation of image and text—in numerous and diverse ways.

As we saw, Peter Najarian's illustrated memoirs are closest to life writing supplemented with images—drawings, paintings, and photographs—clear examples of relational and temporal interfaces. Leslie Marmon Silko takes this a step further in *Storyteller*, in which personal and cultural narratives are in dialogue with family and landscape photographs. In *Sacred Water*, Silko's reflections are juxtaposed with photographic images that are purposefully degraded in order to become a part of the field of vision, creating a complex set of relational, contextual, and temporal interfaces in which neither text nor image dominate but both coexist on equal terms. With his comics, Art Spiegelman fuses image and text, presenting an intimate relational interface, an "imagetext" (Mitchell 89n9) that seamlessly blends picture and word. Julie Chen's artists' books are based on books not only insofar as they rely on the conceptualization of the book (for example, notions of binding, page, typography) but also as the concept of the book form engages with sculpture, architecture, design, and other art forms. The interfaces in her work are primarily spatial and temporal. Her artists' books highlight a confluence of relations between image and text, page and canvas, architectural surfaces and three-dimensional visuals. Theresa Hak Kyung Cha's experimental autobiography extends this by challenging conventions of book design, transforming the page to a screen, referencing experimental film, and using a cinematic technique. With its primarily spatial interface, *Dictée* disrupts usual reading practices, forcing readers to attend to language fragments and gaps, to read across two pages—a spread—

rather than conventionally, and to reenvision the page as a screen. Faith Ringgold translates the page into a quilt square and moves painting from canvas to fabric. She repurposes text as frame for her story quilts, combining temporal, spatial, and contextual interfaces. Carrie Mae Weems expands photo-narrative to retell personal and historical stories in the form of interactive installation art in photo-biographical architectures that mix temporal, spatial, and contextual interfaces. Last, conceptual artist Hachivi Edgar Heap of Birds uses words as images, words as text, and abstract images as personal narrative and political intervention. Each of these writers-artists illustrates that media is "always transmedia and not only in our current historical moment" (Chute and Jagoda 7). Each of them works across media, referencing and transforming each medium as they do. All bear witness to themselves in relation to history, society, and culture. Far from the American self-made autonomous subject, these artists envision themselves as part of the vast network of history and culture. Each emphasizes process as much as product so that what readers take away is not necessarily a book or art object, though it may be, but an *experience*—of being provoked, coerced, or seduced into looking through the eyes of another.

During this same period, profoundly new possibilities for image-text self-expression arose as the internet was developed, digital tools were generated, and social media sites were launched. More than ever before, it is technically easier to combine image and text. From memes— concise image-text communications—to Facebook, with its more elaborated prospects for writing and image sharing, the tools of image-text self-expression are readily available. Although each has its distinctive possibilities, each social media mode has an autobiographical counterpart in the predigital world. A Twitter post, for example, is reminiscent of a short diary entry, in this case, a 140-character record of feeling, observation, opinion, or experience. Taken cumulatively, Twitter feeds might in theory generate a compendium of concise textual moments over time. Similarly, Snapchat is akin to a photo album, with the capacity for a short caption or hashtag but not an explanatory storytelling voice narrating the past.

Facebook, by contrast, resembles a scrapbook as well as a journal. Users share opinions, experiences, and anecdotes as well as photographs. Facebook friends can also post messages, photographs, and videos, so the experience may also be likened to an epistolary exchange as well as a networked engagement.

Like the interart autobiographies discussed in this volume, each of these social media sites demands a high degree of *interactive engagement* between producer (of image and text) and reader-viewer. Of course, there are enormous differences as well. Digital modes are *instantaneous* communications to a *vast number* of friends, followers, or users. The intense interactivity as well as the speed and range of delivery are three crucial aspects that distinguish digital personal narrative from most earlier analog modes of self-representation and self-narration. Last, just as the structure of the book shapes the possibilities of what is written and imaged in it and the size and shape of the canvas limits what may be depicted, so the structure of the social media site—its platform, software, corporate influences, and network—create parameters of self-representation and self-narration that both shape and limit the online subject's possibilities. For instance, Facebook has a generic template used to create an online profile. It consists of a set of questions: What are your favorite movies? What music do you like? and so on. Users can answer (or not) these questions, but importantly, they cannot redesign the questions, alter the basic template designed to define them within corporate parameters. The writers-artists in this book stretch and reformulate the basic media in which they work (book, drawing, painting, photograph, sculpture). At this time, with the exception of hackers, it is still not possible for users of social media sites to make such creative interventions.

Perhaps one digital descendant of the image-text forms I've discussed in this book is e-poetry. Defined as "a poetic practice made possible by digital media and technologies," digital poetry is not just poems written on a computer but poems actively shaped by technology (Flores, "Digital Poetry" 155). Like the artists and writers discussed in this book, who are self-reflexively engaging with formal qualities of the page, the binding, the canvas, the portrait, the screen, and so forth, and like the writers of concrete poetry, e-poets create digital poems that reflect "the process of thinking through this new media, thinking through *making*" (Glazier 6, emphasis in original).[1]

It is important to note that writing and image-making in material or analog forms coexist with digital image-text self-narrations. They are not mutually self-negating. In fact, hypertext is prefigured in material ways in the sculptural dimensions of Chen's artists' books, in Weems's architectural photobiography installations, and in Cha's page as screen and disruptive text. Certainly, the eight writers and artists I discuss in this book participate in contemporary social media on many levels, but they came of age before the internet was invented and before it became ubiquitous. Although many use digital technologies (primarily photography), they do so to work with analog forms. Each of them begins in a certain literary or artistic mode (memoir, comics, or photography) but pushes or explodes its boundaries in ways that are not yet possible to expand the limits of the software that structures a social media site. For most of the artists and writers discussed in this book, the internet is a place to post a website so that their readers and viewers can learn more about them and their work. That is, the Internet functions more like photography used to — as a place to document and advertise — rather than as the material of production itself.

Much of the scholarship on digital autobiography focuses on how digital technology itself decenters, or splits or splinters, the subject — as if the technology alone determines subjectivity. "The digital era complicates definitions of the self and its boundaries," claims Laurie McNeill, "both dismantling and sustaining the humanist subject in practices of personal narrative" ("There Is No 'I' in Network" 65). As we have seen, the life narrators in this book, working primarily with material modes — writing, drawing, painting, print, photography, film, installation, and sculpture — thematize a split subject that seeks — usually futilely — wholeness. The fractured subject has been ubiquitous since at least World War I, when global warfare and new weaponry devastated a generation. Industrialization, mass movement from rural to urban areas, and World War II, followed by an ongoing series of massive displacements of peoples and threats to the planet itself, only exacerbate the vexed, multiple, contingent subject. Najarian, Silko, Spiegelman, Chen, Cha, Weems, Ringgold, and Heap of Birds all, in various ways, reimagine the relation between image and text in the service of self-narration. Their visual-verbal interventions are grounded in specific historical, cultural, social, and political contexts. Like online avatars, their autobiographical personae highlight collective subjectivities networked across time and space. Each aims, through image and text, to unsettle inherited forms and the official narratives associated with them, to slow us down in order to engage a multisensory reading process, and to demand that we look anew.

# Notes

## Introduction

1. The enduring interest in self-representation has only ramped up with the latest technology. Opportunities for circulating instantaneous self-expression in text and image are endless: in the blogosphere, on Facebook, and via Twitter, Snapchat, YouTube, Instagram, and other social media. This book, however, is not about digital autobiographical forms.

2. Other metaphors for U.S. society include a mixed salad or a mosaic. Acknowledgment and inclusion of diverse American identities and experiences began to be demanded in literature and art. Curated by the New Museum of Contemporary Art, the Studio Museum in Harlem, and the Museum of Contemporary Hispanic Art, "The Decade Show: Frameworks of Identity in the 1980s" (1990) was one such foundational attempt to address a history of exclusion.

3. Visual studies is distinct from art history in that its focus is not on high art but on the primacy of the visual in everyday life. A segment of it is also devoted to analysis of the power relations embedded in visual regimes and the act of looking.

4. There is a long history of picture narratives, followed by image-text codices, but after the printing press was invented, print became more standardized and less inclusive of images unless they were used to illustrate a point. Even so, books with both images and text have always existed. The *Book of Kells* (c. 800), for example, is an elaborately illustrated codex made by monks. It includes "four Gospels in Latin based on a Vulgate text, written in vellum (prepared calfskin), in a bold and expert version of the script known as 'insular majuscule.'" See Trinity College Dublin website for more information: www.tcd.ie/Library/bookofkells/book-of-kells/.

5. Some of those I discuss identify themselves primarily as writers, others as artists, and several as both. Because all produce texts and images, I use the terms "writer" and "artist" interchangeably throughout.

6. The constricting nature of conventional autobiography has been discussed widely. Some feminist scholars, for example, denounce the conventions of Western life writing as so embedded in patriarchy as to make it an impossibility for a woman to write autobiography. See, e.g., Benstock, *Private Self*; Miller, *Getting Personal*; Brodzki and Schenck, *Life/Lines*; Smith, *Poetics of Women's Autobiography*; Stanton, *Female Autograph*; and Gilmore, *Autobiographics*. See also Smith and Watson, *Women, Autobiography, Theory*, and their comprehensive overview, *Reading Autobiography*.

Similarly, some scholars of Native American literatures conclude that the Western conceptions of self, life, and writing assumed by traditional autobiography studies must be completely redefined to tell an indigenous life story. See Brumble, *American Indian Autobiography*; Krupat, *For Those Who Come After*; and my own *Sending My Heart Back across the Years*. Likewise, many ethnic American, LGBT, and disabled writers, artists, and scholars feel the need to retell American history from marginalized perspectives to create a space in which to be heard. Variously marginalized people search for forms through which to convey their individual and collective experiences, attempting to intervene in the network of power relations necessary to formulate their self-understandings in their own languages, words, and images.

7. For considerations of life narratives focusing on trauma, see Henke, *Shattered Subjects*; Egan, *Mirror Talk*; Fuchs, *Text Is Myself*; Whitlock, *Postcolonial Life Narratives*; and Chute, *Disaster Drawn*.

8. This visual-verbal re-presentation and re-narration resembles what cultural studies theorist Stuart Hall defines as "articulation"—a process by which certain classes or groups appropriate cultural forms and practices for their own purposes as part of a struggle for recognition and coalition building. In Hall, Morley, and

Chen, *Stuart Hall*, Hall explains that, in England, articulation has a double meaning, to speak but also to link together: "An articulation is thus the form of the connection that can make a unity of two different elements" (141).

9. For Eakin's analysis of "narrative identity," see his *Living Autobiographically*.

10. Scholarship in visual studies arises from a variety of traditional departments—art history, English, history, American studies, cognitive science, women's studies—as well as from more recent visual studies programs. Visual studies has been adapted pedagogically for various purposes. For instance, McQuade and McQuade's composition textbooks *Seeing and Writing* (2000) and *Seeing and Writing 2* (2003) emphasize "the interrelationships of the verbal and the visual" (*Seeing and Writing* ix) in a visual age. They are "designed to improve analytical and compositional skills of students by having them see, read, think and write about the verbal and visual dimensions of American culture" (xvi). The theme of the 2011 Modern Language Association (MLA) Annual Conference, under Sidonie Smith's presidency, was "Narrative Lives," with an emphasis on the visual medium of video. The conference not only featured scholarly papers on this topic but afforded conference attendees the opportunity to tell their personal stories on video. Those videos were collected and made available on the MLA website. Similarly, the 2011 International Auto/Biography Association Conference, "Framing Lives," emphasized visual self-narration. Five years after his *Visual Studies*, James Elkins edited a volume of scholarly essays whose purpose was to think about transforming "university education, at least in part, from text-based knowledge to visuality" (*Visual Literacy* vii).

As a backlash to the turn to visuality, scholars are formulating a multisensory matrix, seeking a more balanced integration of all of the human senses. See, e.g., Gingell and Roy, *Listening Up, Writing Down, and Looking Beyond*. Their discussions focus primarily, however, on "the relationship between the oral and written, with some additionally focusing on the visual" (*Listening Up* 29). There is also a burgeoning study of sonics.

11. See Hirsch, *Family Frames*; hooks, *Black Looks*; Lippard, introduction to *Partial Recall*, 13–45; Mirzoeff, *Right to Look*; Mulvey, "Visual Pleasure and Narrative Cinema"; and Sturken and Cartwright, *Practices of Looking*. For a consideration of how the nineteenth-century American photographic archive shaped possibilities for racialized subjects, see Smith, *American Archives*, and her special guest-edited issue of *MELUS*, "Visual Culture and Race."

12. Rugg, *Picturing Ourselves*, and Adams, *Light Writing and Life Writing*, both address photography and autobiography. Rugg argues that photography resulted in "new ways of thinking about and representing selfhood and life histories"; and she distinguishes the literary autobiographical person, the "I," from the photographic autobiographical persona, "a trace of a person's physical presence in space and time" (*Picturing Ourselves* 7). Emphasizing the referential "instability" of both autobiography and photography, Adams explores how "photography may stimulate, inspire, or seem to document autobiography; it may also confound verbal narrative. Conversely, autobiography may meditate on, stimulate, or even take the form of photography. . . . Because both media are located on the border between fact and fiction, they often undercut just as easily as they reinforce each other" (*Light Writing* xxi). Hirsch, *Family Frames*, combines a scholarly consideration of the relationship between photography and autobiography and an exploration of her personal family photographs, focusing on how photographs are used to construct notions of the family.

The study of comics and autobiography has developed dramatically in the past few years and includes Chute and DeKoven, "Graphic Narrative"; Whitlock and Poletti, "Autographics"; Tabachnick, *Teaching the Graphic Novel*; Chute, *Graphic Women* and *Disaster Drawn*; Chute and Jagoda, "Comics and Media"; and Chaney, *Graphic Subjects*.

Punning on filmic projection and psychological projection, Rugg, *Self-Projection*, looks at films that "create a relationship in which a recognized director/author, who is understood by the viewer to be the ultimate source of the vision on-screen, projects an image to the viewer that the viewer in turn identifies with the director—not only with a specific aesthetic association with a director, but with the director as person" (*Self Projection* 1). She argues that "directorial self-projection emerges as a form of intimate address" (2), and she examines "strategies that perform [what she calls] authorial self-projection" (10).

13. See also Amihay and Walsh, *Future of Image and Text*; English and Silvester, *Reading Images and Seeing Words*; and Kostelanetz, *Visual Literature Criticism*.

14. I am thinking here of the imagist poetry movement in particular.

15. There is a well-developed consideration of autobiographical film and digital self-narration in film and media studies. See, e.g., Gaggi, *From Text to Hypertext*; Custen, *Twentieth-Century's Fox*; Davis, Fischer-Hornung, and Kardux, *Aesthetic Practices and Politics in Media, Music, and Art*; Epstein, *Invented Lives, Imagined Communities*; Poletti and Rak, *Identity Technologies*; Rak, *Boom!*; Rugg, "Self Projection and Autobiography in Film"; Zuern, "Online Lives"; and McNeill and Zuern, "Online Lives 2.0."

16. Silko discusses this idea in "As a Child I Loved to Draw and Cut Paper," in *Yellow Woman and a Beauty of Spirit*, as well as in her memoir, *Turquoise Ledge* (258).

17. My readings include work by an African American, an African-Native American, two Native Americans, a Jewish American, a Korean American, a Chinese-Japanese American, and an Armenian American.

## Chapter 1

1. The false letters arise in the 1970s, a time of intense cultural and ethnic reclamation activism designed to assert a presence for heretofore oppressed or unheard peoples.

2. Bedrosian, *Magical Pine Ring*, estimates that one-third of the Armenians in the Ottoman Empire were killed during this time (19). In *Landscape of Memory*, Shirinian claims that the Genocide "destroyed almost half of the Armenian nation between the years 1915 and 1923" (7).

3. The Committee of Union and Progress (CUP) or Ittihad ve Terakki Jemiyeti, known as the Young Turks, was "the political party in power in the Ottoman Empire during World War I." According to the Armenian National Institute, they "forcibly removed [Armenians] from Armenia and Anatolia to Syria." See www.armenian-genocide.org.

4. Both Najarian's mother's first and second husbands, cousins to each other, were thirteen years her senior.

5. His first two books are *Voyages* (1971, republished in 1979), a series of vignettes about growing up in an immigrant community in Union City, New Jersey, and *Wash Me on Home, Mama* (1978), a collection of characterizations of Berkeley residents experimenting with counterculture living arrangements.

6. See, e.g., Eakin, *Fictions in Autobiography*.

7. Najarian conversation, February 9, 2012. In e-mail correspondence (March 23, 2014) Najarian expresses a general dissatisfaction with literary categories. Although he called *Daughters of Memory* a "story" in the subtitle, he finally allowed the publisher to promote it as a novel. He does not consider *Daughters of Memory* a novel, however, but calls it his "own version of narrative in the realm of poesy" since he tends to his "lines in the same way as those who write verse."

8. Najarian explains that when he was about three years old his father had a stroke, leaving him unable to move or speak for the next six to seven years. Archie, Najarian's cousin and an artist, became a surrogate father. In 1953, Najarian accompanied Archie to an art gallery, where he met the abstract expressionist painter Willem de Kooning. He continued visiting museums regularly, absorbing the images of Western art history throughout his childhood. It was Archie who, when Najarian was forty-three years old, inspired Najarian to learn to draw and paint.

9. Exceptions to the drawings of human figures include drawings of a cat (7), a donkey (30, 156), a man riding a donkey (59), and books and apples (157).

10. Here Najarian references the book's epigraph, from a poem written by Edgar Degas when he was going blind: "All this beauty will follow me throughout my life; / If my eyes failed, might my hearing last, / The sound would conjure the gesture she makes."

11. *Odar* is the Armenian term for a non-Armenian.

12. To this day, the Turkish government has not acknowledged the Armenian Genocide.

13. See Eliade, *Myth of Eternal Return*, and Neumann, *Origins and History of Consciousness*. The phrase the "terror of history" is from Eliade.

14. In a conversation on February 9, 2012, Najarian explained that the first two chapters of the first section were originally part of an as-yet-unpublished book entitled *Storytime*. In the first "fictional" story, Harry, a barely veiled representation of Najarian, finds love and happiness in Berkeley. Similarly, the second story is about a woman, a persona for Najarian's "feminine side," who travels throughout India looking for meaning. The two stories are followed by more clearly autobiographical reflections, narrated by an unnamed persona, on the joys of basketball as a youth and dropping acid with Ken Kesey. Interwoven throughout the stories are drawings of people, animals, images from Western art history, death, and female nudes, along with occasional paintings, mostly landscapes.

The third section includes a description of his mother's former vineyard in a village in Adana, a long tribute to the literary figures who have influenced him, his experiences teaching poor students from around the world as a substitute teacher in Oakland, a vignette about his mother, and a final story about his extended family in Pasadena, the younger generation becoming absorbed into America, while his mother's generation dies off. Throughout, Najarian reminisces about the lost innocence of youth, the fall into adulthood, his enduring sense of alienation, his sense of profound failure, and his struggle to accept his lifetime of living below the poverty line in order to devote his life to art and writing.

In "The Big Game," the fourth story in Section One, he shares anecdotes about famous writers: like the time he read the *I Ching* and got high with a just-out-of-prison Ken Kesey and hung out with members of "a new rock group called *The Grateful Dead*" (41); or the time he went to a *Doors* concert, where he experienced a "bad trip" from taking acid; or the Thanksgiving he spent at Kesey's Oregon communal farm with friends and a near-to-death Neal Cassady. He shares stories of his friendship with Richard Brautigan, who "got

famous around the time the flowers were trampled in People's Park" and who committed suicide (cause of death: "the Great American Loneliness") (48). There is a strong hint that, like Brautigan (and Hemingway and Fitzgerald and countless others), what ails the author is also "the Great American Loneliness."

In "Harvest," Najarian returns to focus on his literary friends and provides a history of influences on his writing. He weaves together snippets — learning of Richard Yates's death, visiting William Saroyan, working at Rutgers University Press with Norman Fruchter, taking a class with Paul Fussell, studying with friend Robert Pinsky, reading for hours and hours in the cathedral-like library, and gasping with wonder over a line of Hemingway, a major inspiration.

When Najarian begins to substitute teach in Oakland public schools, he carries his romantic vision with him into traumatized inner-city neighborhoods. In "Window into Eden," Najarian suggests that in the overcrowded, underfunded, often out-of-control classrooms, it is possible to find a new Eden. As he looks at the boys and girls, he selects an especially lovely girl — one resembling the girls and women in his vast repertoire of art and family history images: "She was Juliet's age, the age of Dante's Beatrice and Gauguin's *Nevermore* and Degas' dancers who were the poor girls of the street. She was the age an old mother was a servant in Beirut after orphaned by a genocide, the age when Aunty Manooshag was abducted by a Chechen tribe and when old Khatun who just died in a nursing home was a sexual slave before she escaped, she was the age of all the others from the Italy and Ireland which became Vietnam and Salvador. She was history and everyone was a part of it except the old sub who had felt alien and turned to art for refuge, though it was no refuge at all" (*The Great American Loneliness* 144).

Najarian sees this "beautiful," "unreal," and "eternal" image "everywhere in all the schools in male and female form" (145). This serene image, of course, is a dramatic contrast to all the times the students do not pose like beautiful and enigmatic figures to be captured by the artist's brush, but instead yell obscenities, urinate on classroom doors, strew broken glass through the hallways, "scream like banshees" (174), and punch each other. And yet, he asks, "what art could blossom without *roots in excrement*, what Eden could flower without the rot of a wasteland?" (150)

15. Najarian explained that "the actual Sirpuhi was a younger woman who was much slimmer." He and the graphic designer selected this particular drawing "because of the sitting position" (e-mail correspondence, March 23, 2014).

16. Honoré Daumier (1808–79), French printmaker, painter, and sculptor; Jean-François Millet (1814–75), French painter; and Vincent van Gogh (1853–90), Dutch painter, all produced famous paintings of peasant farmers.

17. In Neumann's now discredited model, failure to individuate fully from the (Great) Mother results in homosexuality.

18. In a conversation with Peter Najarian (February 9, 2010), he pointed to his description on the back cover of *The Artist and His Mother*, explaining that he preferred the term to "autobiography," which he assumed implied an unproblematic identification with the "I" of the writer and the "I" of the autobiographical persona.

19. Najarian reminded me: Gorky was

"important to my story since he was the same age as my mother's older brother who was also an artist but who didn't survive the massacre as Gorky did" (e-mail correspondence, March 23, 2014).

20. Another key photograph that emphasizes the importance of what is not shown is revealed in a staged photograph. A year after her shabby wedding, Zaroohe borrows a wedding dress and takes a respectful, but pseudo–wedding photo that is completely untrue to the historical record, though an important psychological statement for her.

21. Rugg explains that photography "offers an extension and realization of already-imagined things" (2) but that it is also constituted by and constitutive of reality as we view it: "Photography is constructed as it constructs" (9).

22. In a March 23, 2014, e-mail, Najarian explains: "In my last drawing of my mother I forgot to bring my pencil and had only a new ink pen with which I had to be very careful not to make any mistakes that I otherwise could erase and correct, so in order to achieve the correct proportion and perspective I had to draw in dots."

## Chapter 2

1. See Kolodny, *Lay of the Land*.

2. There is also another version of the relation between land and woman that essentializes the "female" into a beneficent and nurturing Mother Earth.

3. Huhndorf, "Contested Images, Contested Lands," is an astute reading of how Silko's *Sacred Water* challenges Western assumptions of space and replaces them with Pueblo concepts.

4. See Basso, *Wisdom Sits in Places*.

5. Here is an example of Silko's imagery: "Sometimes early in the morning when I walk the trail the air is cool and faintly scented with rain. Just before the sun rises over the mountains, incandescence floods over the bright greens of the mesquite leaves and the jade greens of the tall saguaros. A breeze stirs and there is a silence as it might have been five hundred or a thousand years ago. No sound anywhere in the distance from a train, jet, car or even a dog. Here the desert is as it always was" (148). Silko presents a multisensory

scene. Evoking smell, touch, and hearing, she highlights vision.

6. Silko refers explicitly to Native American photographers, but I believe that she is interested in exploring new sets of relations for photographers, generally. She explains that her statement that Pueblo prophecies "foretell the disappearance of all things European" means, not the "death" or "removal" of white people, but the replacement of Western epistemology (which views the world as a dead thing) with an indigenous worldview (which sees everything as alive). Similarly, I do not think that Silko would claim that only indigenous people can practice a reciprocal photography.

7. For a discussion of the long history of photography and Native Americans, see Bernardin et al., *Trading Gazes*; Lidchi and Tsinhnahjinnie, *Visual Currencies*; and Lippard, *Partial Recall*. For a discussion of "visual sovereignty," see Rickard, "Sovereignty."

8. For a discussion of Silko's "apparent homophobia" in *Almanac of the Dead*, see St. Clair, "Cannibal Queers."

9. This process of reassembly of fragments is similar to the process of constructing one's autobiographical narrative, re-membering bits and pieces of memory and shaping them into a story.

10. In the Introduction to *Reckonings*, my coauthors and I describe how "contemporary writings by Native women continue a tradition of verbal art even as they generate new inventions and interventions" (xiv). See also Blaeser, "Like 'Reeds through the Ribs of a Basket.'"

11. Three photographs are attributed to unknown photographers, two to Denny Carr, and one to Virginia L. Hampton.

12. *Storyteller* includes numerous visual and textual references to books and reading and their relationship to storytelling. See Fitz, *Silko*, for an interesting account of how "in Silko's worldview the conflict between the oral and written resolves itself dialectically in a web of cultural syncretism, interweaving the Western and the Indian. This web centripetally gathers towards a syncretic and ancestral figure: the writing storyteller" (8). In *Storyteller*, the writing storyteller appears as Aunt Susie and Grandmother Spider.

13. The photo caption in the back of the book reads: "My father learned photography while he was in the Army during the Second World War. Some of his best work he did with the Speed Graphic. *Photograph: Virginia L. Hampton.*"

14. In *The Turquoise Ledge*, Silko explains that the words describing a photograph can overdetermine or completely change a photograph's meaning. She is "concerned with the way words modify how we may see a photograph. Photographs need only resemble slightly what the words with them described for the viewer to 'see' whatever the words describe" (258).

15. The handmade edition I discuss here is the one with the light blue cover.

16. This comparison is only partially valid. Even though *Sacred Water*'s inexpensive materials and modest production methods are similar to the 1970s "democratic multiple" artists' books, after the early handmade versions of *Sacred Water* were given to friends, the volume was difficult to access and expensive.

17. For a close reading of the "soft ivory"-covered handmade *Sacred Water*, see Coltelli, "Leslie Marmon Silko's *Sacred Water*." The Main (Gardner) Stacks library at the University of California, Berkeley, has a handmade copy of *Sacred Water* with a dusty pink cover. A black-and-white cutout snake, glued to the front cover, slithers from top to bottom along the left side.

18. According to the 2008 *Arizona Republic* report, Jonathan Doody, the seventeen-year-old who was convicted of the murders and in 2008 was thirty-four, is requesting a retrial with the help of high-profile attorney, Alan Dershowitz. Michael Kiefer, "Johnathan Doody Gets 9 Consecutive Life Sentences in 1991 Temple Murders," March 3, 2014, http://www.azcentral.com/story/news/local/surprise/2014/03/14/arizona-doody-temple-murders/6417239/.

19. Silko explained in a letter to Laura Coltelli of July 30, 1993, that after the brutalities of *Almanac of the Dead*, she wanted to give her readers "something generous, yet truthful," something healing. See Coltelli, "Leslie Marmon Silko's *Sacred Water*."

20. Highlighting the ongoing resistance and contemporary survival of Native peoples and cultures, Huhndorf, "Contested Images, Contested Lands," argues that both Louise Erdrich and Silko establish indigenous histories and epistemologies that help to resolve ongoing disputes about land.

21. Water hyacinths have long been considered "a colossal nuisance" because "their rapid growth clogs rivers and streams," but NASA-based research reveals that water hyacinths may offer an inexpensive and "natural water purifier system" ("Success at Stennis" 1). The "water hyacinths thrive on sewage; they absorb and digest wastewater pollutants, converting sewage effluents to relatively clean water" (1). The water hyacinths would need to be "harvested at intervals," but their by-products could be used as fertilizer, "energy in the form of methane gas," and "high-protein animal feed."

## Chapter 3

1. In fact, the Holocaust has served as the focal point for the development of trauma studies as activists collected and published the personal testimonies of survivors, and scholars sought to explain what, why, and how it could happen and, most significantly, if and how it might be possible to recover. Although Holocaust studies is well developed, many scholars object to the term "Holocaust" itself. From the Greek "burnt whole," use of the term "Holocaust" implies a religious or spiritual sacrifice and thus suggests that there was some meaning in the brutal extermination of six million Jews. Here I use Holocaust interchangeably with Shoah, however, because it is the most widely recognizable term and is what Art Spiegelman uses even though he, too, is critical of it.

2. Modern trauma studies has sought to examine not only the enormous collective trauma of Jews during World War II but other sorts of collective trauma, such as genocides, colonizations, wars, and natural disasters. In addition, trauma theory seeks to understand individual cases of trauma such as childhood physical and sexual abuse. The term "post-traumatic stress disorder," or PTSD (in which the original trauma is remembered, as if relived, repeatedly and painfully after the initial trauma), came into being when the American Psychiatric Association included it in the *Diagnostic and Statistical Manual of Mental Disorders*, 3rd ed. (1980). Cathy Caruth explains that what we know now as PTSD "had previously been called *shell shock, combat neurosis,* or *traumatic neurosis,* among other names used at various times in the nineteenth and twentieth centuries" (130n1). PTSD has been most often associated with soldiers returning from war and humanitarian aid workers returning from afflicted areas but is used widely to refer to any posttraumatic dysfunction.

3. This psychoanalytical model of trauma still prevails. According to Traverso and Broderick, "Interrogating Trauma," even as trauma studies has expanded to "the analysis of history, culture, and politics," the "methodological distinction" between trauma's origin in psychology and its sociocultural applications has not been developed (4). Although still arising from psychoanalytical theories, recent work by Mandel and Schwab challenge the claim that trauma is unrepresentable or incurable. See Mandel, *Against the Unspeakable*; and Schwab, *Haunting Legacies*. See also Chute's *Graphic Women*, in which she claims: "The complex visualizing [graphic narrative] undertakes suggests that we need to rethink the dominant tropes of unspeakability, invisibility, and inaudibility that have tended to characterize trauma theory as well as our current censorship-driven culture in general" (3). Nayar introduces the term "radical graphics" to depict "the reinvention of the comic book mode for the purpose of telling . . . monumental stories and histories" of racial and class oppression (147, 165). In addition, see Chute, *Disaster Drawn*, which came out while this book was going into production.

4. Scientists point to a parallel phenomenon in the natural world in which plants and animals that have experienced profound stress (threats to their survival) will pass on to the next generation an adaptive behavior. Some psychologists suggest that trauma victims, especially those who become mothers, may pass on to their children behavioral imprints as a consequence of that trauma. A depressed, and therefore unavailable, mother, for instance, may inadvertently condition her child, whose needs are consistently unmet, to become numb, apathetic, or withdrawn, a pattern of behavior that may very well continue into adulthood and make trust and intimacy difficult. Finally, some neuroimmunological studies suggest that trauma, if prolonged or meeting the criteria of PTSD, can alter hormone production, thereby weakening the immune system and, in turn, literally reshaping brain cells. Medical research, then, offers tangible physical evidence for trauma victims' psychological suffering long after they are nominally safe.

5. Although comics preceded film, film studies has developed a vocabulary that has been used to discuss comics. For a comparison of comics and film, see Christiansen, "Comics and Film"; and Gordon, Jancovich, and McAllister, *Film and Comic Books*. See also McCloud, *Making Comics* and *Understanding Comics*; Eisner, *Graphic Storytelling*; Chute and DeKoven, "Introduction: Graphic Narrative"; and Chute and Jagoda, "Comics and Media."

6. For works focusing on comics and autobiography, see Whitlock and Poletti,

"Autographics," esp. Gardner, "Autography's Biography"; Chute, *Graphic Women*; and Chaney, *Graphic Subjects*. For histories of comics, see Witek, *Comic Books as History*; Sabin, *Comics, Comix, and Graphic Novels*; Spiegelman, "Comic Supplement"; Hatfield, *Alternative Comics*; and Duncan and Smith, *Power of Comics*.

7. See also Duncan and Smith, *Power of Comics*.

8. Mitchell distinguishes "imagetext" from "image/text," in which the slash designates "a problematic gap, cleavage, or rupture in representation," and "image-text," in which the hyphen refers to "*relations* of the visual and verbal" (*Picture Theory* 89).

9. There are radically different histories of comics in different nations. See Magnussen and Christiansen for a discussion of the distinctions "between the Franco-Belgian and the Anglo-American [comics] research traditions" (9). For a brief history of Japanese manga research, see McCloud.

10. For histories of autobiographical comics and comics form, see works cited in note 6, above.

11. Witek urges us to recognize precursors to *Maus*. He insists that "Spiegelman's *Maus* would not exist" without the comic narratives created by Carl Barks, Walt Kelly, Jack Jackson (Jaxon), and Harvey Pekar, as well as the development of "the funny-animal genre in the underground comix of the 1960s and 1970s" (*Comic Books* 10–11). Because of *Maus*'s global recognition, many scholars cite its publication as the moment comics came into its own. Brodzki, for instance, explains that *Maus*'s "genre-bending, metatextual exploration into its own figurative possibilities created a challenging prototype for graphic autobiography" ("Breakdowns" 52). Spiegelman explains: "*Maus* changed the face of the way the medium I work in is perceived" (*MetaMaus* 74).

12. The phrase is from a 1930s newspaper article from Pomerania, Germany, printed as the epigraph to *Maus* II.

13. This scene refers back to the "Prisoner on the Hell Planet" comic-within-a-comic in which Spiegelman tells about his mother's suicide.

14. Spiegelman notes also: "I worked with the metaphor that each panel was analogous to a word, and each row of panels was a sentence, and each page was a paragraph" (*MetaMaus* 175).

15. An open frame is a frame without borders, also called a borderless frame.

16. A bleeding panel is one in which an image from one frame bleeds into another. Spiegelman refers to this explicitly in his subtitle of vol. I: *My Father Bleeds History*. For a comprehensive reading of the many levels of bleeding history in *Maus*, see Levine, "'Necessary Stains.'"

17. Following Marianne Hirsch's lead, by Holocaust photograph I do not mean photographs of the dead and dying at the camps but family photographs of families touched by the Holocaust.

18. See, e.g., Felman and Laub, *Testimony*; and Levine, "'Necessary Stains.'"

19. Countering "the rhetorical performance of evoking the unspeakable . . . that masquerades as ethical practice," Mandel seeks to reclaim and emphasize an embodied speaker as witness to historical trauma. See Mandel, *Against the Unspeakable*.

20. See Anderson and Katz, "Read Only Memory," for a comprehensive discussion of what the CD-ROM (now DVD-R) offers.

## Chapter 4

1. Because artists' books are still a relatively unknown art form to many, I present a brief overview here. Following the lead of Johanna Drucker and others, I speak of artists', not artist's, books.

2. This move was inspired by democratic politics and new (less expensive and more easily accessible) "photographic and printing technologies" (Drucker, *Century of Artists' Books* 69) and linked to conceptual art that emphasized art as a process of intellectual and emotional engagement rather than a rarified and elitist product. There have always, however, been multiple book art practices occurring simultaneously.

3. This is reminiscent of Silko's goal in *Sacred Water*, in which she degrades the photographic image so that neither text nor photograph dominates the page.

4. For a comprehensive look at Chen's artists' books, see Chen, *Reading the Object*.

5. The colophon states: "*Listening* was designed and printed by Julie Chen in an edition of 75

copies. Papers used include Fabriano Ingres Heavyweight and handmade sheets from the St.-Armand paper mill. Typefaces used include Copperplate Gothic and Adobe Garamond."

6. The colophon provides the following information: "*True to Life* was written, illustrated, and designed by Julie Chen. It was letterpress printed using a combination of pressure plates, woodblocks, and photopolymer plates. It was assembled and bound at Flying Fish Press with expert assistance from Macy Chadwick. The image that appears on each page is one section of a long, continuous visual timeline that can never be viewed all at once." One hundred copies were made. Flying Fish Press is Julie Chen's press.

7. This artists' book arises out of an intense dream Chen had after the too-early death of her ex-husband, father of her daughter. Conversation with Chen, April 20, 2012.

8. The colophon states: "*Glimpse* was created and produced by Julie Chen and Barb Tetenbaum. Julie: sleeve text, image and design. Barb: card text, image and design. Julie and Barb: binding design. Printed letterpress from: hand-set type, wire, antique news cuts, dingbats, and photopolymer plates."

## Chapter 5

1. Soon after earning her MFA from the University of California, Berkeley, Cha moved to New York City, where she continued writing and making conceptual art. On November 5, 1982, just days before her experimental book *Dictée* was published, she was murdered. She was thirty-one years old.

2. For early discussions of immigrant autobiography, see Boelhower, "Making of Ethnic Autobiography"; and S. C. Wong, "Immigrant Autobiography." See also Perry, *Cultural Politics of U.S. Immigration.*

3. DeSouza, "Spoken Word," notes also that there are nine grades of titles for Japanese officials' wives, eight titles for the king's concubines with the king as the center and the ninth. In addition, Yu Guan Soon, martyred Korean nationalist, joins with eight schoolmates to resist the Japanese occupation of Korea (*Dictée* 76).

4. Although Wong describes the "Korean phrases etched in stone" as "taken from the wall of a coal mine in Japan" where thousands of Koreans were "pressed into . . . labor by the Japanese" ("Unnaming the Same" 107), Kim reports that Naoki Mizuno of Kyoto University explains that "there is some debate as to who made the inscription, which is carved into the walls of a tunnel leading to a castle being constructed during World War II to provide a safe haven for the Japanese Emperor" (25n9).

5. There are ten Korean vowels but eight Korean vowel graphemes.

6. Ritual is an important feature of Cha's performances. See, for instance, her video *Untitled* (1973), in which she recites poetry in a low chant while ceremonially lighting and later extinguishing the candles.

7. The first letter of the Korean alphabet is ㄱ and is pronounced as "an unaspirated 'k' at the beginning of a word." Conversation with Mia You, 2001.

8. Cha does not provide identifying captions for any of the images in *Dictée.*

9. This is similar to Najarian's never-ending search for the transcendent glow of art. See chapter 1.

10. Lewallen and Rinder have noted French symbolist poet Stéphane Mallarmé's (1842–98) influence on Cha's work. Mallarmé experimented with the arrangement of words and white space on the page, exploring relations between form and content.

11. For a full account of autotopography as a type of self-revelation, see González, "Autotopographies."

12. See, e.g., Kain, *Ideas of Home.*

13. The nine remedies, of course, echo the nine Muses, the Catholic novena, and the nine Chinese aspects of the universe. The tenth remedy and the womblike bowl suggest Sappho and the tenth aspect of the Chinese universe that holds the other nine in concentric circles.

## Chapter 6

1. For recent discussions of visuality and African American female subject formation, see Fleetwood, *Troubling Vision*, in which she claims that "the visual sphere is a performative field where seeing race is not a transparent act," but a form of "doing" (7), and Smith, *Enacting Others*, who considers "racial identity and how it is represented, performed, signified, and embodied in recent American art" (4).

2. The Kamoinge Workshop was founded in 1963 by "Louis Draper, Ray Francis, Herbert Randall, Albert Fennar, with Roy DeCavara serving as its first director. Kamoinge's body of work spans the past forty years and includes numerous images of daily life in black America during the last half of the twentieth century." http://www.kamoinge.com.

3. For the full text of the Moynihan Report, see http://www.the atlantic.com/politics/archive/2015 /09/the-moynihan-report-an annotated-edition /404632.

4. Weems continues her critique of racism in much of her work. In *American Icons*, Weems turns her critical attention to the racist kitsch of the United States. She creates a series of formal photographs of black mammy and cook salt and pepper shakers, an African boy modeled into a ceramic ashtray, a black postal worker mail container, and so on. Not surprisingly, these souvenirs depict black bodies in positions of menial labor or exotic African repose. With their stereotypical representations of black bodies and servant status, Weems allows the objects to speak for themselves.

*Colored People* continues Weems's critique in a more playful and ironic tone. Her photo series displays *Magenta Colored Girl, Burnt Orange Girl, Blue Black Boy, Golden Yella Girl, Violet Colored Girl, Chocolate Colored Man*, and *Honey Colored Boy*. Using color filters, Weems mocks the notion of skin color as a meaningful referent at the same time as she refers to a diverse spectrum of so-called blackness—"golden," "yella," "chocolate."

5. Both interrogation and surgery room lights shed intense light on the subject in order to expose the truth or clarify the vision. Metaphorically, Weems interrogates her subject/s and sheds light on it/them.

6. Hampton Normal and Agricultural Institute became simply Hampton Institute in 1930. I use the shortened name for convenience. In 1984, Hampton Institute became Hampton University.

7. In *Sending My Heart Back across the Years*, I write about Plains Indian men imprisoned at Fort Marion who produced autobiographical artbooks.

8. There has been a proliferation of spatial metaphors to describe the complexity of transcultural contact—frontiers, borderlands, boundary cultures, and contact zones. Here I use Mary Louise Pratt's term.

9. Richard Henry Pratt (founder of Carlisle Indian Industrial School), "The Advantages of Mingling Indians with Whites," an address to an 1892 convention.

10. In some instances, African American students were given books but Native students were not. By design, then, Negro students would read in front of indigenous children as a means to inspire Native children to want to learn to read. See Lindsey, *Indians at Hampton Institute*.

11. For a thoughtful consideration of how nineteenth-century practices of photography reinscribed notions of race, see Smith, *American Archives* and *Photography on the Color Line*.

12. Recall that Hampton's founder was a Williams graduate.

13. These photographs were collected by Lincoln Kirstein and published by the Museum of Modern Art as *The Hampton Album* in 1966.

14. The trilogy includes *Ritual and Revolution, The Jefferson Suites*, and *The Hampton Project*, all produced in 1998–2001.

15. Sevigny, "Twenty Years Later." Sevigny explains that Wojnarowicz photographed a section of a diorama depicting the American West that he found in the National History Museum of Washington, D.C.

16. An anonymous reviewer corrects Zeidler's claim that Firetail was of the "Sioux and Crow Creek" nations: "The Great Sioux Reservation, established under the Fort Laramie Treaty of 1868, originally included Lakota reservations in South Dakota and Nebraska. The inhabitants of the Crow Creek Reservation are primarily descendants of the Mdewakanton Dakota, moved there by the government after the Dakota War of 1862."

## Chapter 7

1. See Fleetwood, *Troubling Vision*, for a discussion of how "the visual sphere is a performative field where seeing race is not a transparent act; it is itself a 'doing'" (7).

2. For a comprehensive discussion about the elevation of fiber into American art as part of a long gendered and racialized history insisting on "the hierarchy of art and craft," in which art is associated with ideas and craft with purpose, see Auther, *String, Felt, Thread*.

3. Ringgold's mother, Willi Posey (Willie Edel Jones) (1907–81), collaborated with Ringgold on many of her early works.

4. In her short story "Everyday Use," Alice Walker thematizes the conflicting functions of African American quilts. For the college-educated older sister, the family quilts become an abstract symbol of African American historical struggle and aesthetic production, while for the younger sister who has remained at home, the quilt is an article of everyday utility and beauty. This scenario parallels the decontextualization of indigenous cultural objects that find a broader (often distorted, generally commodified) meaning and new sets of representations in anthropological museums.

5. In a December 2007 e-mail correspondence, University of California, Berkeley, English graduate student Juliana Chow suggested that in the communal-making traditions of quilt-making stitching links the personal and the collective.

6. Cameron, *Dancing at the Louvre*, 81, 9. From here on, the first number refers to the page of the book *The French Collection*, and the second and subsequent numbers refer to the quilt panel.

7. See Holland, *Raising the Dead*, for a discussion of death and black subjectivity. Referring to Orlando Patterson's *Slavery and Social Death*, and claiming that "black subjects are not just marginal to the culture. Their presence in society is, like the subject of death, almost unspeakable, so black subjects share the space the dead inhabit" (6), she asks: "What if some subjects never achieve, in the eyes of others, the status of the 'living'? What if these subjects merely haunt the periphery of the encountering person's vision, remaining, like the past and the ancestors who inhabit it, at one with the dead?" (15). See also JanMohamed, *Death-Bound Subject*, who argues for the centrality of death to African American subject formation as well as to African American literature. The "death-bound-subject," he writes, is "the subject who is formed, from infancy on, by the imminent and ubiquitous threat of death" (2). What does it mean, he asks, to become a subject continually under the threat of violence and death? Farrington describes how Faith Ringgold and her siblings "experienced race hatred as an unassailable force in their adolescent lives" (*Faith Ringgold* 7).

8. On her website, Ringgold says that "except for the *Change* quilts [quilts that focus on her struggle with body image and weight loss], none of my quilts are autobiographical." See http://www.faithringgold/faq. For an insightful essay about *Change*, see Smith, "Bodies of Evidence."

9. See, e.g., Eakin, *Fictions in Autobiography*; and Zinsser, *Inventing the Truth*.

10. The sizes of the quilts range from 73 inches by 68 inches to 74¾ inches by 94 inches.

11. According to Holton, the "children portrayed are Faith's grandchildren" (*Faith Ringgold* 15).

12. See Rogoff, "Studying Visual Culture."

13. Holton claims that Ringgold "almost single-handedly removed the shackles placed on the possibilities for black people when she sent Willia Marie Simone off to dance at the Louvre" (*Faith Ringgold* 18).

14. Farrington, Holton, and Sheehan note Ringgold's 1970s encounter with tankas—fourteenth- and fifteenth-century Tibetan and Nepali paintings that were framed by "ancient cloth brocade" (Farrington, *Faith Ringgold* 41; Holton, *Faith Ringgold* 44; Sheehan, "Faith Ringgold" 3, 5)—as influential to her work.

15. The artists are: front row, left to right, Pablo Picasso, Moira Roth, Ellie Flomenhaft, Lowery Sims, Judith Lieber, Thalia Gouma-Peterson, Emma Amos, Bernice Steinbaum, Michele Wallace, and Willia Marie Simone; back row, left to right, Ofelia Garcia and Johnetta Cole.

16. Ringgold returns to this point again in the ninth quilt, *Matisse's Model*, in which she presents herself as a nude model: "There is a certain power I keep in the translation of my image from me to canvas" (Cameron et al., *Dancing at the Louvre* 135), Simone insists. Ringgold's epistolary voice desexualizes the beautiful woman lying on the

bed. She is tired, not passively waiting for the
man implied in the male gaze. In this quilt she
challenges that male gaze by offering another
way of seeing the nude woman—sleepy, relaxed,
at home in her body. In the process, she insists
that a woman can be both artist and model, both
producer and product of her own image.

17. The figures are: front row, left to right,
William H. Johnson, Archibald Motley, Willia
Marie Simone, Elizabeth Catlett, Lois Mailous
Jones, Meta Vaux Warrick Fuller, Edmonia
Lewis, and Faith Ringgold; middle row, left
to right, Sargent Johnson, Romare Bearden,
Aaron Douglas, Henry O. Tanner, Paul Gauguin,
Vincent van Gogh, and Augusta Savage; back
row, left to right: Ed Clark, Raymond Saunders,
Jacob Lawrence, Henri de Toulouse-Lautrec, and
Maurice Utrillo.

18. Throughout *The French Collection*, Ringgold
emphasizes the possibilities for African American
expatriate artists. Josephine Baker, famous
expatriate dancer in Paris, serves as a historical
model for the necessity of African American artists
to leave the United States. In the Matisse-inspired
quilt *Jo Baker's Birthday* (1993), Ringgold muses
about Baker's escape from the United States to
France, a move that inspires Simone's.

19. As a former French colony, Morocco evokes
a consideration of the colonial relationships that
inform Ringgold's entire project of attempting to
reform a colonial, racist history.

### Chapter 8

1. Autotopography is a term coined by
Jennifer A. González to explain how a person
can be "read" or mapped by examining his or
her domestic space—how it is ordered, what is
displayed, etc. In this instance, I use the term
to mean simply a self-mapping. See González,
"Autotopographies."

2. See also the work of Luiseño-Mexican
American performance and installation artist
James Luna.

3. For a vibrant collection of perspectives on the
possibilities for contemporary Native American art
in a global context, see *Vision, Space, Desire*. For
a consideration of Heap of Birds in the context of
contemporary global art, see Anthes, *Edgar Heap
of Birds*.

4. For an overview of Plains Indian ledgerbook
art, see Berlo, *Plains Indian Drawings*. For a
discussion of Plains Indian pictography as personal
narrative and its transition from vegetable dye
paintings on animal hides to painted and drawn
images on paper, see my book *Sending My Heart
Back across the Years*, chaps. 2, 3.

5. For an overview of Heap of Birds's art up to
2005, see Rushing, "'In Our Language.'"

6. Admonishing readers to distrust what they
think they know about American Indians, Smith,
associate curator at the National Museum of the
American Indian, advises: "Begin . . . by looking
for the Indian history beneath your own feet"
(*Everything You Know about Indians Is Wrong* 12).

7. At Point State Park, the Allegheny and
Monongahela Rivers join to form the Ohio River.
In the 1700s, France and Britain competed for
control of the important Ohio River valley. It
was controlled by the French until 1758 when,
realizing that they were about to be defeated by
the British, the French fled. The British took over
the abandoned fort. Five years later, the British
were attacked, but not destroyed, during Pontiac's
uprising. Allied with the French who had come for
the fur trade and not the British who had come for
the land grab, the Ottawa leader Pontiac organized
western Native nations from Canada to the Ohio
valley to rise up against the British. Pontiac lost.

8. Warrior describes how Heap of Birds's *Beyond
the Chief* (2009), a sign installation similar to
*Native Hosts* displayed at the University of Illinois,
was vandalized by an angry graduate who did not
appreciate an indigenous interpretation of local
history. Warrior describes "how these panels, in
their memorialization of lives that were ethnically
cleansed from Illinois, present a modern Native
voice critiquing the way the erasure and removal
of those lives has been unmarked, a critique that
some people would rather attack and steal than
appreciate or even just ignore" (45). See Warrior,
"Vandalizing Life Writing at the University of
Illinois."

9. Postcolonialism has never been a useful
frame for Native Americans because colonialism
is ongoing. It is more accurate to say that Native

Americans experience ongoing or internal colonial conditions.

10. For a discussion of the autobiographical dimensions of Plains Indian pictography, see my *Sending My Heart Back across the Years*.

11. See also Rickard, who, commenting on her work at the National Museum of the American Indian, writes about how Native American art can "create an opportunity to call for a shift in the imaginations of non-Native people to recognize our global presence as indigenous people" ("Local and Global" 61–62).

### Coda

1. For a more complete discussion of e-poetry, see Glazier, *Digital Poetics*; Ryan, Emerson, and Robertson, *Johns Hopkins Guide to Digital Media*; Schaefer, "Poetry in Transmedial Perspective"; Funkhouser, *New Directions in Digital Poetry*; and Magearu, "Making Digital Poetry."

# Bibliography

*Unless otherwise indicated, all web addresses are accurate as of October 2017.*

### Archives


Athenaeum Music and Arts Library. Artists' Book Collection. La Jolla, California.

Berkeley Art Museum and Pacific Film Archive. Cha Collection. University of California, Berkeley.

Geisel Library. Mandeville Special Collections. University of California, San Diego.

F. W. Olin Library. The Heller Rare Book Room. Julie Chen Collection in Center for the Book. Mills College, Oakland, California.


### Primary and Secondary Sources


Adams, Timothy Dow. *Light Writing and Life Writing: Photography in Autobiography*. Chapel Hill: University of North Carolina Press, 2000.

Amihay, Ofra, and Lauren Walsh, eds. *The Future of Image and Text: Collected Essays on Literary and Visual Conjunctures*. Newcastle upon Tyne, U.K.: Cambridge Scholars, 2012.

Anderson, John C., and Bradley Katz. "Read Only Memory: *Maus* and Its Marginalia on CD-ROM." In Geis, *Considering "Maus,"* 159–74.

Anthes, Bill. *Edgar Heap of Birds*. Durham, N.C.: Duke University Press, 2015.

*Arizona Republic*. www.azcentral.com.

Armenian National Institute. www.armenian-genocide.org.

*Art Encyclopedia*. www.visual-arts-cork.com.

ARTFL Project. *French-English Dictionary*. https://artfl-project.uchicago.edu/.

Ash-Milby, Kathleen. "*Most Serene Republics*: Remembering and Reconsidering Histories." In Ash-Milby and Lowe, *Edgar Heap of Birds*, 57–83.

Ash-Milby, Kathleen, and Truman T. Lowe, eds. *Edgar Heap of Birds: "Most Serene Republics."* Washington, D.C.: National Museum of the American Indian and Smithsonian Institution, 2009.

Atlanta Contemporary. https://atlantacontemporary.org/.

Auther, Elissa. *String, Felt, Thread: The Hierarchy of Art and Craft in American Art*. Minneapolis: University of Minnesota Press, 2010.

Avrin, Leila. *Scribes, Script and Books.* Chicago: American Library Association, and London: British Library, 1991.

Barker, James, and Leah Ollman. *Brighton Press Art Books, 1985–1993*. [San Marcos, Calif.]: Boehm Gallery, Palomar Community College, 1993.

Basso, Keith. *Wisdom Sits in Places: Landscape and Language among the Western Apache*. Albuquerque: University of New Mexico Press, 1996.

Batuman, Elif. "Into the Eisenshpritz." *London Review of Books*, April 10, 2008, 23–26.

Bedrosian, Margaret. *The Magical Pine Ring: Culture and Imagination in Armenian-American Literature*. Detroit, Mich.: Wayne State University Press, 1991.

Benhabib, Seyla. *The Claims of Culture: Equality and Diversity in the Global Era*. Princeton, N.J.: Princeton University Press, 2002.

Bennett, Steve. "Author Silko Isn't Concerned about Time." *Express News*, 25 July 2010.

Benstock, Shari. *The Private Self*. Chapel Hill: University of North Carolina Press, 1988.

Berger, John. *Ways of Seeing*. London: British Broadcasting Corporation and Penguin Books, 1972.

Berkeley Art Museum and Pacific Film Archive. https://bampfa.org/.

Berlo, Janet Catherine, ed. *Plains Indian Drawings, 1865–1935: Pages from a Visual History*. New York: Harry N. Abrams, in association with American Federation of Arts and Drawing Center, 1996.

Bernardin, Susan, Melody Graulich, Lisa

MacFarlane, and Nicole Tonkovich. *Trading Gazes: Euro-American Women Photographers and Native North Americans, 1880–1940*. New Brunswick, N.J.: Rutgers University Press, 2003.

Bhabha, Homi. *The Location of Culture*. New York: Routledge, 1994.

Blaeser, Kimberly M. "Like 'Reeds through the Ribs of a Basket': Native Women Reading Stories." In *Other Sisterhoods: Literary Theory and U.S. Women of Color*, edited by Sandra Kumamoto Stanley, 265–76. Urbana: University of Illinois Press, 1998.

Boelhower, William Q. "The Making of Ethnic Autobiography in the United States." In *American Autobiography: Retrospect and Prospect*, edited by Paul John Eakin, 123–41. Madison: University of Wisconsin Press, 1991.

*Book of Kells*. Trinity College Library, Dublin. https://www.tcd.ie/library /manuscripts/book-of-kells.php.

Boos, Florence. "An Interview with Leslie Marmon Silko." In *Conversations with Leslie Marmon Silko*, edited by Ellen L. Arnold, 135–45. Jackson: University Press of Mississippi, 2000.

Bosmajian, Hamida. "The Orphaned Voice in Art Spiegelman's *Maus*." In Geis, *Considering "Maus,"* 26–43.

Brighton Press. www.ebrightonarts.com.

Brodzki, Bella. "*Breakdowns* and Breakthroughs: Looking for Art in Young Spiegelman." In Chaney, *Graphic Subjects*, 51–58.

———. *Can These Bones Live? Translation, Survival, and Cultural Memory*. Stanford, Calif.: Stanford University Press, 2007.

Brodzki, Bella, and Celeste Schenck. *Life/Lines: Theorizing Women's Autobiography*. Ithaca, N.Y.: Cornell University Press, 1988.

Brookshier, Frank. *The Burro*. Norman: University of Oklahoma Press, [1974].

Brumble, H. David. *American Indian Autobiography*. Berkeley: University of California Press, 1988.

Butler, Judith. *Bodies That Matter: On the Discursive Limits of "Sex."* New York: Routledge, 1993.

———. *Gender Trouble: Feminism and the Subversion of Identity*. New York: Routledge, 1990.

———. *Giving an Account of Oneself*. New York: Fordham University Press, 2005.

Cameron, Dan, Richard J. Powell, Michele Wallace, Patrick Hill, Thalia Gouma-Peterson, Moira Roth, and Ann Gibson, eds. *Dancing at the Louvre: Faith Ringgold's "French Collection" and Other Story Quilts*. New York: New Museum of Contemporary Art, and Berkeley: University of California Press, 1998.

Caruth, Cathy. *Unclaimed Experience: Trauma, Narrative, and History*. Baltimore: Johns Hopkins University Press, 1996.

Cha, Theresa Hak Kyung. *Audience Distance Relative*. 1977. UC Berkeley Art Museum and Pacific Film Archive.

———. *Dictée*. Berkeley: University of California Press, 2011. Orig. publ. 1982.

———. *Exilée, Temps Morts: Selected Works*. Edited by Constance M. Lewallen. Berkeley: University of California Press, 2009.

———. *Mouth to Mouth*. Film. 1975. UC Berkeley Art Museum and Pacific Film Archive.

———. "Paths." MFA thesis, University of California, Berkeley, 1978. UC Berkeley Art Museum and Pacific Film Archive.

———. "Personal Statement and Outline of Postdoctoral Project." 1978. UC Berkeley Art Museum and Pacific Film Archive.

———. "Statement of Proposed Study— Holland." 1992. UC Berkeley Art Museum and Pacific Film Archive.

Chaney, Michael A., ed. *Graphic Subjects: Critical Essays on Autobiography and Graphic Novels*. Madison: University of Wisconsin Press, 2011.

Chen, Julie. *Bon Bon Mots: A Fine Assortment of Books*. Berkeley, Calif.: Flying Fish Press, 1998.

———. "Books in Balance." MA thesis, Mills College, 1989.

———. Conversation with Hertha D. Sweet Wong. April 20, 2012. Berkeley, Calif.

———. *Life Time*. Berkeley, Calif.: Flying Fish Press, 1996.

———. *Listening*. Berkeley, Calif.: Flying Fish Press, 1992.

———. *Reading the Object: Three Decades of Books by Julie Chen*. Oakland, Calif.: Mills College Center for the Book, and Berkeley, Calif.: Flying Fish Press, 2016.

———. *True to Life*. Berkeley, Calif.: Flying Fish Press, 2004.

———. *View*. Berkeley, Calif.: Flying Fish Press, 2006.

Chen, Julie, and Barbara Tetenbaum. *Glimpse.* Berkeley, Calif.: Flying Fish Press, 2011.

Cheng, Anne Anlin. *The Melancholy of Race: Psychoanalysis, Assimilation, and Hidden Grief.* New York: Oxford University Press, 2000.

Christiansen, Hans-Christian. "Comics and Film: A Narrative Perspective." In Magnussen and Christiansen, *Comics and Culture,* 107–21.

Christiansen, Hans-Christian, and Anne Magnussen. Introduction to Magnussen and Christiansen, *Comics and Culture,* 7–27.

Chute, Hillary L. *Disaster Drawn: Visual Witness, Comics, and Documentary.* Cambridge, Mass.: Harvard University Press, 2016.

———. *Graphic Women: Life Narrative and Contemporary Comics.* New York: Columbia University Press, 2010.

Chute, Hillary L., and Marianne DeKoven. "Introduction: Graphic Narrative." In "Graphic Narrative." Special issue, *Modern Fiction Studies* 52, no. 4 (Winter 2006): 767–82.

Chute, Hillary L., and Patrick Jagoda, eds. "Comics and Media." Special issue, *Critical Inquiry* 40, no. 3 (Spring 2014).

Coltelli, Laura. "Leslie Marmon Silko's *Sacred Water.*" *SAIL* (*Studies in American Indian Literatures*), 2nd ser., 8, no. 4 (Winter 1996): 21–29.

Couser, G. Thomas. *Memoir: An Introduction.* New York: Oxford University Press, 2011.

Custen, George F. *Twentieth-Century's Fox: Darryl L. Zanuck and the Culture of Hollywood.* New York: Basic Books, 1997.

Davis, Rocío G., Dorothea Fischer-Hornung, and Johanna C. Kardux, eds. *Aesthetic Practices and Politics in Media, Music, and Art: Performing Migration.* New York: Routledge, 2011.

deSouza, Allan. "The Spoken Word: Theresa Hak Kyung Cha's *Dictée.*" *Third Text: Third World Perspectives on Contemporary Art and Culture* 24 (Autumn 1993): 73–79.

Drucker, Johanna. *The Century of Artists' Books.* New York: Granary Books, 2004. Orig. publ. 1994.

Duncan, Randy, and Matthew J. Smith, eds. *The Power of Comics: History, Form, and Culture.* New York: Continuum International, 2009.

Eakin, Paul John. *Fictions in Autobiography: Studies in the Art of Self-Invention.* Princeton, N.J.: Princeton University Press, 1985.

———. *How Our Lives Become Stories: Making Selves.* Ithaca, N.Y.: Cornell University Press, 1999.

———. *Living Autobiographically: How We Create Identity in Narrative.* Ithaca, N.Y.: Cornell University Press, 2008.

Egan, Susanna. *Mirror Talk: Genres of Crisis in Contemporary Autobiography.* Chapel Hill: University of North Carolina Press, 1999.

Eisner, Will. *Comics and Sequential Art: Principles and Practice of the World's Most Popular Art Form.* Expanded ed. Tamarac, Fla.: Poorhouse, 1985.

Eliade, Mircea. *The Myth of Eternal Return: Or, Cosmos and History.* Princeton, N.J.: Princeton University Press, 1954.

Elkins, James. *Visual Studies: A Skeptical Introduction.* New York: Routledge, 2003.

———, ed. *Visual Literacy.* New York: Routledge, 2008.

Ellis, Ngarino. "Te Ao Hurihuri O Nga Taonga Tuku Iho: The Evolving Worlds of Our Ancestral Treasures." *Biography* 39, no. 3 (Summer 2016): 438–60.

Ellison, Ralph. Prologue to *Invisible Man.* New York: New American Library, 1947.

English, Alan, and Rosalind Silvester, eds. *Reading Images and Seeing Words.* New York: Rodopi, 2004.

Epstein, William H. *Invented Lives, Imagined Communities: The Biopic and American National Identity.* Albany: SUNY Press, 2017.

Farrington, Lisa E. *Faith Ringgold.* San Francisco: Pomegranate, 2004.

Felman, Shoshana, and Dori Laub. *Testimony: Crises of Witnessing in Literature, Psychoanalysis, and History.* New York: Routledge, 1992.

Fisher, Jean. "Remembering the Future: Tradition and Modernity in the Work of Hock E Aye Vi Edgar Heap of Birds." In Ash-Milby and Lowe, *Edgar Heap of Birds,* 35–55.

Fitz, Brewster E. *Silko: Writing Storyteller and Medicine Woman.* Norman: University of Oklahoma Press, 2004.

Fleetwood, Nicole R. *Troubling Vision: Performance, Visuality, and Blackness.* Chicago: University of Chicago Press, 2011.

Flores, Leonardo. "Digital Poetry." In Ryan et al., *Johns Hopkins Guide to Digital Media,* 155–61.

Flying Fish Press. www.flyingfishpress.com.

Fogg, Katherine, and Denise Ramzy.

"Interview: Carrie Mae Weems." In Patterson, *Carrie Mae Weems*, 78–80.

Fuchs, Miriam. *The Text Is Myself: Women's Life Writing and Catastrophe*. Madison: University of Wisconsin Press, 2004.

Funkhouser, Christopher Townsend. *New Directions in Digital Poetry*. New York: Continuum, 2012.

Gaggi, Silvio. *From Text to Hypertext: Decentering the Subject in Fiction, the Visual Arts, and Electronic Media*. Philadelphia: University of Pennsylvania Press, 1997.

Gardner, Jared. "Autobiography's Biography, 1972–2007." *Biography* 31, no. 1 (Winter 2008): 1–26.

Geis, Deborah R. Introduction to *Considering "Maus": Approaches to Art Spiegelman's "Survivor's Tale" of the Holocaust*, edited by Deborah R. Geis, 1–11. Tuscaloosa: University of Alabama Press, 2011.

———, ed. *Considering "Maus": Approaches to Art Spiegelman's "Survivor's Tale" of the Holocaust*. Tuscaloosa: University of Alabama Press, 2011.

Gibson, Ann. "Faith Ringgold's *Picasso's Studio*." In Cameron et al., *Dancing at the Louvre*, 64–73.

Gilmore, Leigh. *Autobiographics: A Feminist Theory of Women's Self-Representation*. Ithaca, N.Y.: Cornell University Press, 1994.

———. *The Limits of Autobiography: Trauma and Testimony*. Ithaca, N.Y.: Cornell University Press, 2001.

Gingell, Susan, and Wendy Roy, eds. *Listening Up, Writing Down, and Looking Beyond: Interfaces of the Oral, Written, and Visual*. Waterloo, Ont.: Wilfrid Laurier University Press, 2012.

Glazier, Loss Pequeño. *Digital Poetics: The Making of E-Poetries*. Tuscaloosa: University of Alabama Press, 2002.

Glenn, Constance W. "Frances B. Johnston: The Hampton Album." In Patterson, *Carrie Mae Weems*, 62–65.

González, Jennifer A. "Autotopographies." In *Prosthetic Territories: Politics and Hypertechnologies*, edited by Gabriel Brahm Jr. and Mark Driscoll, 133–50. Boulder, Colo.: Westview, 1995.

Gordon, Ian, Mark Jancovich, and Matthew P. McAllister, eds. *Film and Comic Books*. Jackson: University Press of Mississippi, 2007.

Gorky, Arshile. "Letters of Arshile Gorky." *Ararat* 12 (Autumn 1971).

Gover, Kevin. Foreword to Ash-Milby and Lowe, *Edgar Heap of Birds*, 7–9.

Gravett, Paul. *Graphic Novels: Everything You Need to Know*. New York: Collins/Design, 2005.

Grossberg, Lawrence. "On Postmodernism and Articulation: An Interview with Stuart Hall." In Morley and Chen, *Stuart Hall*, 131–50.

Guimond, James. *American Photography and the American Dream*. Chapel Hill: University of North Carolina Press, 1991.

Hadas, Rachel. "Carnal Language." Review of *Daughters of Memory*, by Peter Najarian. *New York Times*, September 21, 1986.

Hall, Stuart. "Subject in History: Making Identity Diasporic." In *The House That Race Built*, edited by Wahneema Lubiano, 289–99. New York: Pantheon Books, 1997.

Hatfield, Charles. *Alternative Comics: An Emerging Literature*. Jackson: University Press of Mississippi, 2005.

Heap of Birds, Edgar. "Born from Sharp Rocks." In *The Myth of Primitivism: Perspectives on Art*, edited by Susan Hiller, 338–44. New York: Routledge, 1991.

———. "Of Circularity and Linearity in the Work of Bear's Heart." In *Plains Indian Drawings, 1865–1935: Pages from a Visual History*, edited by Janet Catherine Berlo, 66–67. New York: Harry N. Abrams, in association with the American Federation of Art and the Drawing Center, 1996.

———. E-mail correspondence. "Re: *Serene Republics* Sign." Received by Hertha D. Sweet Wong, September 9, 2013.

———. *16 Songs: Issues of Personal Assessment and Indigenous Renewal*. VHS. 1995.

Henke, Suzette. *Shattered Subjects: Trauma and Testimony in Women's Life-Writing*. New York: St. Martin's, 1998.

Higgins, Dick. *Horizons: The Poetics and Theory of the Intermedia*. Carbondale: Southern Illinois University Press, 1984.

———. "A Preface." In Lyons, *Artists' Books*, 11–12.

Hirsch, Bernard. "'The Telling Which Continues': Oral Tradition and the Written Word in Leslie Marmon Silko's *Storyteller*." *American Indian Quarterly* 12, no. 1 (1988): 1–26.

Hirsch, Marianne. *Family Frames: Photography, Narrative, and Postmemory*. Cambridge, Mass.: Harvard University Press, 1997.

———. *The Generation of Postmemory: Writing and Visual Culture after the Holocaust*. New York: Columbia University Press, 2012.

Hirsch, Marianne, and Nancy K. Miller, eds. *Rites of Return: Diaspora Poetics and the Politics of Memory*. New York: Columbia University Press, 2011.

Hoffman, Eva. *Complex Histories, Contested Memories: Some Reflections on Remembering Difficult Pasts*. Berkeley: Regents of the University of California and Doreen B. Townsend Center for the Humanities, 2000.

Holland, Sharon Patricia. "'If You Know I Have a History, You Will Respect Me': A Perspective on Afro-Native American Literature." *Callaloo* 17, no. 1 (1994): 334–50.

———. *Raising the Dead: Readings of Death and (Black) Subjectivity*. Durham, N.C.: Duke University Press, 2000.

Holton, Curlee Raven, with Faith Ringgold. *Faith Ringgold: A View from the Studio*. Boston: Bunker Hill in association with Allentown Art Museum, 2004.

hooks, bell. *Black Looks: Race and Representation*. Boston: South End, 1992.

Horn, Maurice. *The World Encyclopedia of Comics*. Philadelphia: Chelsea House, 1999.

Huhndorf, Shari. "Contested Images, Contested Lands: The Politics of Space in Louise Erdrich's *Tracks* and Leslie Marmon Silko's *Sacred Water*." Paper presented at the Institute for the Study of Societal Issues, Joseph A. Meyers Center for Research on Native American Issues, University of California, Berkeley, March 6, 2012.

Janigian, Aris. "An Armenian Man and His Mother." Review of *The Artist and His Mother*, by Peter Najarian. *Ararat*, March 24, 2011. http://www.araratmagazine.org/2011/03/peter-najarian-artist-and-his-mother/.

JanMohamed, Abdul. *The Death-Bound Subject: Richard Wright's Archaeology of Death*. Durham, N.C.: Duke University Press, 2005.

Jaskoski, Helen. "The Stories in *Storyteller*." In *Leslie Marmon Silko: A Study of the Short Fiction*, edited by Helen Jaskoski, 6–88. New York: Simon and Schuster, 1998.

Joyce, Stephen. "The Link and the Chain: The Individual and Communal Self in Theresa Hak Kyung Cha's *Dictée*." *FIAR* (Forum for Inter-American Research) 1, no. 1 (2011). http://www.interamerica.de/volume-1-1/joyce/.

Kain, Geoffrey, ed. *Ideas of Home: Literature of Asian Migration*. East Lansing: Michigan State University Press, 1997.

The Kamoinge Workshop. http://www.kamoinge.com.

Kang, L. Hyun Yi. "The 'Liberatory Voice' of Theresa Hak Kyung Cha's *Dictée*." In *Writing Self/Writing Nation: Essays on Theresa Hak Kyung Cha's "Dictée*," edited by Elaine H. Kim and Norma Alarcón, 73–99. Berkeley, Calif.: Third Woman Press, 1994.

Kaplan, Caren. "Reconfigurations of Geography and Historical Narrative: A Review Essay." *Public Culture* 3, no. 1 (1990): 25–32.

Ketchum, Shanna. "Native American Cosmopolitan Modernism(s): A Re-Articulation of Presence through Time and Space." *Third Text* 19, no. 4 (2005): 357–64.

Kim, Elaine H. "Poised on the In-Between: A Korean American's Reflections on Theresa Hak Kyung Cha's *Dictée*." In *Writing Self/Writing Nation: A Collection of Essays on "Dictée*," edited by Elaine H. Kim and Norma Alarcón, 3–30. Berkeley, Calif.: Third Woman Press, 1994.

Kirsh, Andrea. "Carrie Mae Weems: Issues in Black, White and Color." In *Carrie Mae Weems*. Rev. ed., 9–17. Washington, D.C.: National Museum of Women in the Arts, 1994.

Kirstein, Lincoln. *The Hampton Album*. New York: Museum of Modern Art, 1966.

Klima, Stefan. *Artists' Books: A Critical Survey of the Literature*. New York: Granary Books, 1998.

Kolodny, Annette. *The Lay of the Land: Metaphor as Experience and History in American Life and Letters*. Chapel Hill: University of North Carolina Press, 1975.

Kostelanetz, Richard, ed. *Visual Literature Criticism: A New Collection*. Carbondale: Southern Illinois University Press, 1979

Krumholz, Linda. "Native Designs: Silko's *Storyteller* and the Reader's Initiation." In *Leslie Marmon Silko: A Collection of Critical Essays*, edited by Louise K. Barnett and James L. Thorson, 63–86. Albuquerque: University of New Mexico Press, 1999.

Krupat, Arnold. "The Dialogics of Silko's *Storyteller*." In *Narrative Chance: Postmodern Discourse on Native American Indian Literatures*, edited by Gerald Vizenor, 55–68. Albuquerque: University of New Mexico Press, 1989.

———. *For Those Who Come After: A Study of Native American Autobiography.* Berkeley, Calif.: University of California Press, 1989.

Kunzle, David. *The History of the Comic Strip.* Vol. 1, *The Early Comic Strip: Narrative Strips and Picture Stories in the European Broadsheet from c. 1450 to 1825.* Berkeley, Calif.: University of California Press, 1973.

———. *The History of the Comic Strip.* Vol. 2, *The Nineteenth Century.* Berkeley: University of California Press, 1990.

Lamm, Kimberly. "Getting Close to the Screen of Exile: Visualizing and Resisting the National Mother Tongue in Theresa Hak Kyung Cha's *Dictée.*" In *Transnational, National, and Personal Voices: New Perspectives on Asian American and Asian Diasporic Women Writers,* edited by Begoña Simal and Elisabetta Marino, 43–65. Münster: Lit Verlag, 2004.

Lefebvre, Henri. *The Production of Space.* Translated by Donald Nicholson-Smith. Malden, Mass.: Blackwell, 1991.

Levine, Michael G. "'Necessary Stains': Art Spiegelman's *Maus* and the Bleeding of History." *American Imago* 59, no. 3 (2002): 317–41. Reprinted in Geis, *Considering "Maus,"* 63–104.

Lewallen, Constance M. "Introduction: Theresa Hak Kyung Cha—Her Time and Place." In *The Dream of the Audience: Theresa Hak Kyung Cha (1951–1982),* edited by Constance M. Lewallen, 1–13. Berkeley: University of California Press, 2001.

Lidchi, Henrietta, and Hulleah J. Tsinhnahjinnie, eds. *Visual Currencies: Reflections on Native Photography.* Edinburgh: National Museums Scotland, 2009.

Lim, Shirley Geok-Lin, John Blair Gamber, Stephen Hong Sohn, and Gina Valentino, Introduction to *Transnational Asian American Literature: Sites and Transits,* edited by Shirley Geok-Lin Lim, John Blair Gamber, Stephen Hong Sohn, and Gina Valentino, 1–26. Philadelphia: Temple University Press, 2006.

Lindsey, Donal F. *Indians at Hampton Institute, 1877–1923.* Urbana: University of Illinois Press, 1995.

Lippard, Lucy R. "The Artist's Book Goes Public." In Lyons, *Artists' Books,* 45–48.

———. "Conspicuous Consumption: New Artists' Books." In Lyons, *Artists' Books,* 49–57.

———. Introduction to *Partial Recall: With Essays on Photographs of Native North Americans,* edited by Lucy R. Lippard, 12–45. New York: New Press, 1992.

———. *The Lure of the Local: Senses of Place in a Multicentered Society.* New York: New Press, 1997.

———. "Signs of Unrest: Activist Art by Edgar Heap of Birds." In Ash-Milby and Lowe, *Edgar Heap of Birds,* 17–33.

Lowe, Truman T. "Introduction: On the Horizon." In Ash-Milby and Lowe, *Edgar Heap of Birds,* 11–15.

Lyons, Joan. Introduction to Lyons, *Artists' Book,* 7–9.

———, ed. *Artists' Books: A Critical Anthology and Sourcebook.* Rochester, N.Y.: Visual Studies Workshop, 1985.

Magearu, Mirona. "Making Digital Poetry: Writing with and through the Spaces." *Journal of Literary Theory* 6, no. 2 (2012): 337–57.

Magnussen, Anne, and Hans-Christian Christiansen, eds. *Comics and Culture: Analytical and Theoretical Approaches to Comics.* Copenhagen: Museum Tusculanum, 2000.

Mandel, Naomi. *Against the Unspeakable: Complicity, the Holocaust, and Slavery in America.* Charlottesville: University of Virginia Press, 2006.

Matthews, Lydia. "Fighting Language with Language." *Artweek,* December 6, 1990, 18.

Mazur, Dan, and Alexander Danner. *Comics: A Global History, 1968 to the Present.* London: Thames and Hudson, 2014.

McCloud, Scott. *Making Comics: Storytelling Secrets of Comics, Manga and Graphic Novels.* New York: Harper, 2006.

———. *Understanding Comics: The Invisible Art.* New York: Paradox, 1993.

McInnes, Mary Drach. Introduction to *Telling Histories: Installations by Ellen Rothenberg and Carrie Mae Weems.* Seattle: University of Washington Press, 1999.

McLuhan, Marshall. *Understanding Media: The Extensions of Man.* Cambridge, Mass.: MIT Press, 1994. Orig. publ. 1964.

McMaster, Gerald. "Colonial Alchemy:

Reading the Boarding School Experience." In Lippard, *Partial Recall*, 76–87.

———. "Introduction: New Art/New Contexts." In *Vision, Space, Desire*, 15–29.

McNeill, Laurie. "There is No 'I' in Network: Social Networking Sites and Posthuman Auto/biography." In "(Post)Human Lives," edited by Gillian Whitlock and Thomas Couser. Special issue, *Biography* 35, no. 1 (Winter 2012): 65–82.

McNeill, Laurie, and John Zuern, eds. "Online Lives 2.0." Special issue, *Biography* 38, no. 2 (Spring 2015).

McQuade, Donald, and Christine McQuade, eds. *Seeing and Writing*. 2nd ed. Boston: Bedford/St. Martin's, 2003.

Miller, Nancy K. "Cartoons of the Self: Portrait of the Artist as a Young Murderer—Art Spiegelman's *Maus*." In Geis, *Considering "Maus,"* 44–59.

———. *Getting Personal: Feminist Occasions and Other Autobiographical Acts*. New York: Routledge, 1991.

Mirzoeff, Nicholas. "Introduction: What Is Visual Culture?" In *An Introduction to Visual Culture*, edited by Nicholas Mirzoeff, 1–20. New York: Routledge, 1999.

———. *The Right to Look: A Counterhistory of Visuality*. Durham, N.C.: Duke University Press, 2011.

———, ed. *The Visual Culture Reader*. 2nd ed. New York: Routledge, 2002. Orig. publ. 1998.

Mitchell, W. J. T. *Picture Theory: Essays on Verbal and Visual Representation*. Chicago: University of Chicago Press, 1994.

Momaday, N. Scott. "The Man Made of Words." In *The Remembered Earth: An Anthology of Contemporary Native American Literature*, edited by Geary Hobson, 162–73. Albuquerque: University of New Mexico Press, 1981.

———. *The Names: A Memoir*. New York: Harper Colophon Books, 1976.

Morley, David, and Kuan-Hsing Chen, eds. *Stuart Hall: Critical Dialogues in Cultural Studies*. New York: Routledge, 1996.

Mooradian, Karlen, ed. "The Letters of Arshile Gorky to Vartoosh, Moorad and Karlen Mooradian." In special issue devoted to Arshile Gorky, *Ararat* 12, no. 48 (Autumn 1971): 19–43.

Morrison, Toni. *Beloved*. New York: Vintage Books, 1987.

*The Moynihan Report: An Annotated Edition*. Edited by Daniel Geary. *The Atlantic*, September 14, 2015, http://www.theatlantic.com/politics/archive/2015/09/the_moynihan_report_an_annotated_edition/404632.

Mukherjee, Srimati. "Nation, Immigrant, Text: Theresa Hak Kyung Cha's *Dictée*." In *Transnational Asian American Literatures: Sites and Transits*, edited by Shirley Geok-Lin Lim, John Blair Gamber, Stephen Hong Sohn, and Gina Valentino, 197–215. Philadelphia: Temple University Press, 2006.

Mulvey, Laura. "Visual Pleasure and Narrative Cinema." *Screen* 16, no. 3 (1975): 6–18.

Najarian, Pete(r). *The Artist and His Mother*. Fresno: The Press at California State University, 2010.

Najarian, Peter. E-mail correspondence with the author. March 23, 2014.

———. Conversation with the author. Berkeley, Calif. February 9, 2012.

———. *Daughters of Memory*. Berkeley, Calif.: City Miner Books, 1986.

———. *The Great American Loneliness*. Cambridge, Mass.: Blue Crane Books, 1999.

———. *Voyages*. New York: Ararat Press, 1971.

———. *Wash Me on Home, Mama*. Berkeley, Calif.: Berkeley Poets' Workshop and Press, 1978.

National Aeronautics and Space Administration (NASA). Stennis Space Center. "Success at Stennis: A New Image for the Water Hyacinth." October 6, 2011.

Nayar, Pramod K. "Radical Graphics: Martin Luther King, Jr., B. R. Ambedkar, and Comics Autobiography." *Biography* 39, no. 2 (Spring 2016): 147–65.

Neumann, Erich. *The Origins and History of Consciousness*. Translated by R. F. C. Hull with a foreword by C. G. Jung. Princeton, N.J.: Princeton University Press, 1954. Orig. publ. 1949.

New Advent. www.newadvent.org.

Nisargadatta, Maharaj. *I Am That*. Bombay: Chetana, 1973.

Ollman, Leah. Introduction to *Brighton Press Art Books, 1985–1993*. [San Marcos, Calif.]: Boehm Gallery, Palomar Community College, 1993.

Olney, James. *Memory and Narrative: The Weave of Life-Writing*. Chicago: University of Chicago Press, 1998.

Ortiz, Alfonso. Introduction to *Handbook*

of North American Indians. Vol. 9,
*Southwest*, 1–4. Washington, D.C.:
Smithsonian Institution, 1979.

Park, Ed. "'This Is the Writing You Have Been
Waiting For.'" In Cha, *Exilée, Temps Mort*, 8–15.

Park, Josephine Nock-Hee. *Apparitions of Asia:
Modernist Form and Asian American Poetics.*
New York: Oxford University Press, 2008.

Patterson, Orlando. *Slavery and Social Death:
A Comparative Study.* Cambridge, Mass.:
Harvard University Press, 1982.

Patterson, Vivian. "The Hampton Project."
In Patterson, *Carrie Mae Weems*, 22–37.

Patterson, Vivian, ed. *Carrie Mae Weems:
"The Hampton Project."* Williamstown,
Mass.: Aperture, [2000].

Perry, Leah. *The Cultural Politics of U.S.
Immigration: Gender, Race, and Media.* New
York: New York University Press, 2016.

Phillpot, Clive. "Books by Artists and Books
as Art." In *Artist/Author: Contemporary
Artists' Books*, edited by Cornelia Lauf,
Jane Role, and Glenn O'Brien, 30–64.
New York: Distributed Art Publishers and
American Federation of Arts, 1998.

———. "Some Contemporary Artists and Their
Books." In Lyons, *Artists' Books*, 96–132.

Photo/Graphic/Image/Arts. www
.photo-graphic-image-arts.com.

Piché, Thomas, Jr., and Thelma Golden. *Carrie
Mae Weems: Recent Work, 1992–1998.* New York:
George Braziller in association with Everson
Museum of Art, Syracuse, N.Y., 1998.

Poletti, Anna, and Julie Rak, eds. *Identity
Technologies: Constructing the Self Online.*
Madison: University of Wisconsin Press, 2014.

Pratt, Mary Louise. *Imperial Eyes: Travel Writing
and Transculturation.* London: Routledge, 1992.

Pratt, Richard Henry. *Official Report of the
Nineteenth Annual Conference of Charities
and Correction* (1892), 46–59. Reprinted in
Richard H. Pratt, "The Advantages of Mingling
Indians with Whites." In *Americanizing the
American Indians: Writings by the "Friends
of the Indian," 1880–1900,* edited by Francis
Paul Prucha, 260–71. Cambridge, Mass.:
Harvard University Press, 1973.

Przyblyski, Jeannene M. "American
Visions at the Paris Exposition, 1900:
Another Look at Frances Benjamin
Johnston's Hampton Photographs." *Art
Journal* 57, no. 3 (Fall 1988): 60–68.

Raiford, Leigh. *Imprisoned in a Luminous
Glare: Photography and the African American
Freedom Struggle.* Chapel Hill: University
of North Carolina Press, 2011.

Rak, Julie. *Boom! Manufacturing Memoir
for the Popular Market.* Waterloo, Ont.:
Wilfrid Laurier University Press, 2013.

Rendell, Jane. "Introduction: 'Gender,
Space.'" In *Gender, Space, Architecture: An
Interdisciplinary Introduction,* edited by Ruth
Rendell, Barbara Pennen, and Iain Borden,
101–11. New York: Routledge, 2000.

Rice, Shelley. "Words and Images:
Artists' Books as Visual Literature."
In Lyons, *Artists' Books*, 59–86.

Rickard, Jolene. "The Local and the Global."
In *Vision, Space, Desire*, 59–66.

———. "Sovereignty: A Line in the Sand."
*Aperture* 130 (Summer 1995): 50–59.

Rinder, Lawrence. "The Plurality of Entrances,
the Opening of Networks, the Infinity of
Languages." In *The Dream of the Audience,*
by Constance M. Lewallen, 14–31. Berkeley:
University of California Press, 2001.

Rogoff, Irit. "Studying Visual Culture." In
Mirzoeff, *Visual Culture Reader*, 14–26.

Roth, Moira. "Of Cotton and Sunflower
Fields: The Makings of *The French* and
*The American Collection.*" In Cameron
et al., *Dancing at the Louvre*, 49–63.

Rugg, Linda Haverty. *Picturing Ourselves:
Photography and Autobiography.* Chicago:
University of Chicago Press, 1997.

———. *Self-Projection: The Director's
Image in Art Cinema.* Minneapolis:
University of Minnesota Press, 2014.

———, ed. "Self Projection and
Autobiography in Film." Special issue,
*Biography* 29, no. 1 (Winter 2006).

Rushdie, Salman. *Imaginary Homelands: Essays and
Criticism, 1981–1991.* New York: Viking, 1991.

Rushing, W. Jackson, III. "'In Our Language':
The Art of Hachivi Edgar Heap of Birds."
*Third Text* 19, no. 4 (July 2005): 365–84.

Ryan, Marie-Laure, Lori Emerson, and
Benjamin J. Robertson, eds. *The Johns
Hopkins Guide to Digital Media.* Baltimore:
Johns Hopkins University Press, 2013.

Sabin, Roger. *Comics, Comix, and Graphic Novels: A History of Comic Art*. New York: Phaidon, 1996.

Saltzmann, Lisa, and Eric Rosenberg. Introduction to *Trauma and Visuality in Modernity*, edited by Lisa Saltzmann and Eric Rosenberg. Hanover, N.H.: Dartmouth College Press, 2006.

Sando, Joe S. *Pueblo Nations: Eight Centuries of Pueblo Indian History*. Santa Fe, N.Mex.: Clear Light, 1992.

Schaefer, Heike. "Poetry in Transmedial Perspective: Rethinking Intermedial Literary Studies in the Digital Age." Acta Universitatis Sapiente: *Film and Media Studies* 10, no. 1 (2010): 169–82.

Schwab, Gabriele. *Haunting Legacies: Violent and Transgenerational Trauma*. New York: Columbia University Press, 2010.

Sevigny, John. "Twenty Years Later: David Wojnarowicz's Buffalo Photograph." *Guernica: A Magazine of Art and Politics*, July 25, 2009. https://www.guernicamag .com/john_sevigny_twenty_years_late/.

Sheehan, Tanya. "Faith Ringgold: Forging Freedom and Declaring Independence." In *Declaration of Independence: Fifty Years of Art by Faith Ringgold*, 3–12. Institute for Women and Art. Rutgers: State University of New Jersey, 2009.

Shih, Shu-Mei. "Nationalism and Korean American Women's Writing: Theresa Hak Kyung Cha's *Dictée*." In *Speaking the Other Self: American Women Writing*, edited by Jeanne Campbell Reesman, 144–62. Athens: University of Georgia Press, 1997.

Shirinian, Lorne. *The Landscape of Memory: Perspectives on the Armenian Diaspora*. Kingston, Ont.: Blue Heron Press, 2004.

———. "Peter Najarian's *Voyages*: The Discourse of Negative Space." *Armenian Review* 40, no. 3 (Fall 1987): 17–26.

Shohat, Ella, and Robert Stam. "Narrativizing Visual Culture: Toward a Polycentric Aesthetics." In Mirzoeff, *Visual Culture Reader*, 37–59.

Showalter, Elaine. "Piecing and Writing." In *The Poetics of Gender*, edited by Nancy K. Miller, 222–47. New York: Columbia University Press, 1986.

Silko, Leslie Marmon. *Almanac of the Dead*. New York: Penguin Books, 1991.

———. "As a Child I Loved to Draw and Cut Paper." In *Yellow Woman and a Beauty of the Spirit*, 166–74.

———. "The Indian with a Camera." In *Yellow Woman and a Beauty of the Spirit*, 175–79.

———. Introduction to *Yellow Woman and a Beauty of the Spirit*, 13–24.

———. "Language and Literature from a Pueblo Indian Perspective." In *Yellow Woman and a Beauty of the Spirit*, 48–59.

———. "Notes on *Almanac of the Dead*." In *Yellow Woman and a Beauty of the Spirit*, 135–45.

———. "On Photography." In *Yellow Woman and a Beauty of the Spirit*, 180–86.

———. *Sacred Water: Narratives and Pictures*. Tucson, Ariz.: Flood Plain, 1993.

———. *Storyteller*. New York: Seaver Books, 1981.

———. *The Turquoise Ledge: A Memoir*. New York: Viking Penguin, 2010.

———. *Yellow Woman and a Beauty of the Spirit: Essays on Native American Life Today*. New York: Simon and Schuster, 1996.

Simal, Begoña, and Elisabetta Marino. Introduction to *Transnational, National, and Personal Voices: New Perspectives on Asian American and Asian Diasporic Women Writers*, edited by Begoña Simal and Elisabetta Marino, 11–21. Münster: Lit Verlag, 2004.

Slocum, Elizabeth. "'Insurgent Messages': Hachivi Edgar Heap of Birds and *Building Minnesota*." *Museo* 7 (Spring 2004): 1–7. http://www.columbia.edu/cu/museo/7 /slocum-insurgent.html (site no longer available, hard copy in author's possession).

Smith, Cherise. *Enacting Others: Politics of Identity in Eleanor Antin, Nikki S. Lee, Adrian Piper, and Anna Deveare Smith*. Durham, N.C.: Duke University Press, 2011.

Smith, Keith A. *Structure of the Visual Book*. Rochester, N.Y.: Visual Studies Workshop, 1984.

Smith, Paul Chaat. *Everything You Know about Indians Is Wrong*. Minneapolis: University of Minnesota Press, 2009.

Smith, Shawn Michelle. *American Archives: Gender, Race, and Class in Visual Culture*. Princeton, N.J.: Princeton University Press, 1999.

———. *Photography on the Color Line: W. E. B. DuBois, Race, and Visual Culture*. Durham, N.C.: Duke University Press, 2004.

———, ed. "Visual Culture and Race." Special issue, *MELUS* 39, no. 2 (Summer 2014).

Smith, Sidonie. "Bodies of Evidence: Jenny Saville,

Faith Ringgold, and Janine Antoni Weigh In." In Smith and Watson, *Interfaces* 132–59.

———. *A Poetics of Women's Autobiography: Marginality and the Fictions of Self-Representation.* Bloomington: Indiana University Press, 1987.

Smith, Sidonie, and Julia Watson. "Introduction: Mapping Women's Self-Representation at Visual/Textual Interfaces." In Smith and Watson, *Interfaces*, 1–46.

———. *Reading Autobiography: A Guide for Interpreting Life Narratives.* 2nd ed. Minneapolis: University of Minnesota Press, 2010.

———, eds. *Interfaces: Women/Autobiography/ Image/Performance.* Ann Arbor: University of Michigan Press, 2002.

———. *Women, Autobiography, Theory: A Reader.* Madison: University of Wisconsin Press, 1998.

Snodgrass, Mary Ellen. *Leslie Marmon Silko: Literary Companion.* Jefferson, N.C.: McFarland, 2011.

Somerville, Alice Te Punga, and Daniel Heath Justice. "Introduction: Indigenous Conversations about Biography." *Biography* 39, no. 3 (Summer 2016): 239–47.

Sontag, Susan. *On Photography.* New York: Anchor, Doubleday, 1989.

Sousanis, Nick. *Unflattening.* Cambridge, Mass.: Harvard University Press, 2015.

Spiegelman, Art. "The Comic Supplement." In *In the Shadow of No Towers*, by Art Spiegelman, n.p. New York: Pantheon Books, 2004.

———. *Comix, Essays, Graphics, and Scraps: From Maus to Now to MAUS to Now.* New York: Raw Books, 1999.

———. *The Complete Maus.* CD-ROM.

———. *The Complete Maus: A Survivor's Tale.* Vol. I, *My Father Bleeds History* [1986]. Vol. II, *And Here My Troubles Began* [1991]. New York: Pantheon Books, 1997.

———. "The Sky Is Falling!" In *In The Shadow of No Towers*, by Art Spiegelman, [i–ii]. New York: Pantheon Books, 2004.

Spiegelman, Art, with Hillary Chute. *MetaMaus.* Book and DVD-R. New York: Pantheon Books, 2011.

Stanton, Domna C., ed. *The Female Autograph.* Chicago: University of Chicago Press, 1987.

St. Clair, Janet. "Cannibal Queers: The Problematics of Metaphor in *Almanac of the Dead.*" In *Leslie Marmon Silko: A Collection of Critical Essays*, edited by Louise K. Barnett and James L. Thorson, 207–21. Albuquerque: University of New Mexico Press, 1999.

Sterling, Susan Fisher. "Signifying: Photographs and Texts in the Work of Carrie Mae Weems." In *Carrie Mae Weems.* Rev. ed., 19–36. Washington, D.C.: National Museum of Women in the Arts, 1994.

Sturken, Marita, and Lisa Cartwright, eds. *Practices of Looking: An Introduction to Visual Culture.* New York: Oxford University Press, 2009.

Tabachnick, Ely, ed. *Teaching the Graphic Novel.* New York: Modern Language Association, 2009.

Tousley, Nancy. "Artists' Books." In *Learn to Read Art: Artists' Books*, 4–17. Exh. cat. Hamilton, Ont.: Art Gallery of Hamilton, 1990.

Traverso, Antonio, and Mick Broderick. "Interrogating Trauma: Towards a Critical Trauma Studies." In *Interrogating Trauma: Collective Suffering in Global Arts and Media*, edited by Mick Broderick and Antonio Traverso, 3–15. New York: Routledge, 2011.

Tuan, Yi-Fu. *Space and Place: The Perspective of Experience.* Minneapolis: University of Minnesota Press, 1977.

Twelbeck, Kirsten. "Otherness as Reading Process: Theresa Hak Kyung Cha's *Dictée.*" In *Asian American Literature in the International Context: Readings on Fiction, Poetry, and Performance*, edited by Rocío Davis and Sämi Ludwig, 185–201. Münster: Lit Verlag, 2002.

Vaillant-Gaveau, N., et al. "Removal of Organic Load from Wastewater by Using Datura innoxia Mill." *Current Research, Technology, and Education Topics in Applied Microbiology and Microbial Biotechnology* (2010): 1328–36.

Varnum, Robin, and Christina T. Gibbons, eds. *The Language of Comics: Word and Image.* Jackson: University Press of Mississippi, 2001.

Vico, Giambattista. *The New Science of Giambattista Vico.* Translated by Thomas Goddard Bergin and Max Harold Fisch. Ithaca, N.Y.: Cornell University Press, 1948.

Virilio, Paul. *The Vision Machine.* London: British Film Institute, 1994.

*Vision, Space, Desire: Global Perspectives and Cultural Hybridity.* Washington, D.C.: National Museum of the American Indian, Smithsonian Institution, 2006.

Visual Studies Workshop. www.vsw.org.

Walker, Alice. "Everyday Use." In *In Love and Trouble: Stories of Black Women,* by Alice Walker, 47–59. New York: Houghton, Mifflin, Harcourt, 1973.

Wallace, Michele. "*The French Collection:* Momma Jones, Mommy Fay, and Me." In Cameron et al., *Dancing at the Louvre,* 14–25.

———. *Modernism, Postmodernism and the Problem of the Visual in Afro-American Culture.* New York: New Museum of Contemporary Art, 1990.

Warrior, Robert. "Vandalizing Life Writing at the University of Illinois: Heap of Birds's Signs of Indigenous Life." *Profession* (2011): 44–50.

Weems, Carrie Mae. "Interview: Carrie Mae Weems." With Denise Ramzy and Katherine Fogg. In Patterson, *Carrie Mae Weems,* 78–80.

Wexler, Laura. *Tender Violence: Domestic Visions in an Age of U.S. Imperialism.* Chapel Hill: University of North Carolina Press, 2000.

White, Daniel. "Antidote to Desecration: Leslie Marmon Silko's Nonfiction." In *Leslie Marmon Silko: A Collection of Critical Essays,* edited by Louise K. Barnett and James L. Thorson, 135–48. Albuquerque: University of New Mexico Press, 1999.

Whitlock, Gillian. *Postcolonial Life Narrative: Testimonial Transactions.* New York: Oxford University Press, 2015.

Whitlock, Gillian, and Anna Poletti, eds. "Autographics." Special issue, *Biography* 31, no. 1 (Winter 2008).

Witek, Joseph. *Comic Books as History: The Narrative Art of Jack Jackson, Art Spiegelman, and Harvey Pekar.* Jackson: University Press of Mississippi, 1989.

Wong, Hertha D. Sweet. "Native American Visual Autobiography: Figuring Place, Subjectivity, and History." *Iowa Review* 30, no. 3 (2000): 145–56.

———. *Sending My Heart Back across the Years: Tradition and Innovation in Native American Autobiography.* New York: Oxford University Press, 1992.

Wong, Hertha D. Sweet, Lauren Stuart Muller, and Jana Sequoya Magdaleno. Introduction to *Reckonings: Contemporary Short Fiction by Native American Women,* edited by Hertha D. Sweet Wong, Lauren Stuart Muller, and Jana Sequoya Magdaleno, xiii–xxix. New York: Oxford University Press, 2008.

Wong, Sau-ling Cynthia. "Immigrant Autobiography: Some Questions of Definition and Approach." In *American Autobiography: Retrospect and Prospect,* edited by Paul John Eakin, 142–70. Madison: University of Wisconsin Press, 1991.

Wong, Shelley Sunn. "Unnaming the Same: Theresa Hak Kyung Cha's *Dictée.*" In *Writing Self/Writing Nation: A Collection of Essays on "Dictée,"* edited by Elaine H. Kim and Norma Alarcón, 103–40. Berkeley, Calif.: Third Woman Press, 1994.

Zeidler, Jeanne. "A View from Hampton University." In Patterson, *Carrie Mae Weems,* 76–77.

Zinsser, William, ed. *Inventing the Truth: The Art and Craft of Memoir.* Boston: Houghton Mifflin, 1987.

Zuern, John, ed. "Online Lives." Special issue, *Biography* 26, no. 1 (Winter 2003).

World War II, 232, 241n4
Wright, Richard, 209

Yates, Richard, 236–37n14
*Yellow Woman and a Beauty of Spirit* (Silko), 73
Young Turks (Ittihad ve Terakki Jemiyeti;
    Committee of Union and Progress; CUP), 235n2

*Young Zaroohe with Adult Son in Background*
    (Najarian), 31
YouTube, 7
Yu Guan Soon, 156–57

*Zap #0 and Zap #1* (Crumb), 87
Zeidler, Jeanne, 194

FSC
www.fsc.org
MIX
Paper from
responsible sources
FSC® C013483